PENSION PLANNING
Pensions, Profit Sharing, and Other Deferred Compensation Plans

The Irwin Series in
Insurance and Economic Security

DAVIS W. GREGG   *Consulting Editor*

PENSION PLANNING
Pensions, Profit Sharing, and Other Deferred Compensation Plans

EVERETT T. ALLEN, JR., LL.B.
Vice President
Towers, Perrin, Forster & Crosby, Inc.

JOSEPH J. MELONE, Ph.D., C.L.U.
Vice President
The Prudential Insurance Company of America

JERRY S. ROSENBLOOM, Ph.D., C.L.U., C.P.C.U.
Executive Director
The S. S. Huebner Foundation for Insurance Education
University of Pennsylvania

 Third Edition 1976

RICHARD D. IRWIN, INC. Homewood, Illinois 60430

Irwin-Dorsey Limited Georgetown, Ontario L7G 4B3

Third Edition

First Printing, April 1976
Second Printing, June 1977

ISBN 0-256-01857-X
Library of Congress Catalog Card No. 75–39361
Printed in the United States of America

Preface

The revised edition of this text was published in 1972. Since that time, the enactment of the Employee Retirement Income Security Act of 1974 (ERISA) has caused major revisions in the field of deferred compensation planning. The authors have made every effort to incorporate the requirements of ERISA in this third edition. Needless to say, this law, which is incredibly complex, will undergo continued interpretation during the next few years. Indeed, it is quite likely that remedial legislation of some type will have to be enacted before a complete and consistent body of knowledge about this law is developed. Accordingly, it should be recognized that the material in this edition was prepared in light of ERISA as it was generally understood and interpreted at the close of 1975.

In addition to revising all of the existing text to incorporate ERISA requirements, three new chapters have been added. The first of these extends the rather brief coverage of disclosure requirements that existed under the Welfare and Pension Plans Disclosure Act (formerly included in the chapter on Plan Installation and Administration) to cover the more substantial reporting requirements of ERISA. The second new chapter summarizes the requirements of individual retirement savings programs (IRAs) that were introduced by ERISA. The third new chapter discusses the fiduciary and plan termination provisions of ERISA. In addition, for the benefit of the reader who is experienced in the field of employee benefit planning, this latter chapter also summarizes the requirements of ERISA in terms of changes made in prior law or practice.

Another major change in this third edition is the inclusion of Jerry S. Rosenbloom as a coauthor. Dr. Rosenbloom currently is Executive Director of the S. S. Huebner Foundation of the Wharton School of the University of Pennsylvania. Prior to joining the Wharton School, he was Chairman of the Insurance and Risk Department of Temple University. He has also served as a dean of the American College of Life Underwriters. His experience and writing in the field of employee benefits adds greatly to the value of this text.

We want to express our appreciation, once again, to the individuals who assisted us in the two prior editions of this text. Many of their contributions survive in this third edition.

We are particularly indebted to Mary Flynn, Administrative Assistant, Pension Services, New England Mutual Life Insurance Company. Mrs. Flynn reviewed the manuscript of the prior edition and made innumerable suggestions to improve and update the entire text. Moreover, she reviewed many of the rewritten chapters and offered valuable comments and criticisms.

A number of individuals at Towers, Perrin, Forster & Crosby also reviewed various chapters and made many constructive suggestions. We are grateful to: Preston C. Bassett, F.S.A., Vice President; Mario Leo, Vice President; and Donald E. Sullivan, Vice President. Other TPF&C consultants who assisted us in many ways are John J. Bond, A.S.A., Leo Brown, and Steven W. Kujawski. Special recognition is due to Donald R. Fleischer, F.S.A., who made material contributions to the rewriting and consolidation of the material in this text dealing with funding and actuarial considerations relative to pension plans. Likewise, special recognition is due to Robert Kujawa who made a major contribution to the writing of the chapter dealing with disclosure.

We are also indebted to the following representatives of the Prudential Insurance Company of America: David E. Hurley, Regional Group Pension Managers; Charles H. Patterson, Director of Field Training and Manpower Development; and Peter N. Findley, C.L.U., Senior Research Consultant. To all of these individuals our very special thanks.

Finally, we are most indebted to Jane Beach and Suzanne Revell who labored in the preparation and typing of the manuscript.

March 1976   EVERETT T. ALLEN, JR.
                                               JOSEPH J. MELONE
                                               JERRY S. ROSENBLOOM

Contents

Chapter 20 Tax-Deferred Annuities 368

Statutory Aspects: *Background. The Present Statute.* Requirements of a Tax-Deferred Annuity: *Qualified Employers. Eligible Employees. Annuity Contract Purchased by an Employer. Employee's Rights Nonforfeitable. Exclusion Allowance.* Income Taxation of Benefits: *Income Tax Consequences during Lifetime. Income Tax Consequences after Death.* Estate and Gift Taxes: *Estate Tax. Gift Tax.* Salary Reductions: *Current Salary Reductions. Salary Reduction Agreement. Caveat about Future Salary Reductions.* Arithmetic of the Exclusion Allowance: *Maximum Amount—Negotiated Salary Reduction. Maximum Amounts—Other Tax-Deferred Contributions. Salary Reduction and Other Tax-Deferred Contributions. Employer Pension Contributions Unknown. Part-Time Employees.* Some Further Tax Considerations: *Social Security Taxes and Benefits. Wage Withholding. Measure of Pension Benefits.* Considerations of Local Law: *Employees of Public School Systems. State Income Taxes. State Premium Taxes.*

√ Chapter 21 Employee Retirement Income Security Act of 1974 388

Plan Provisions: *Definition of Service. Eligibility for Participation. Vesting. Spouse Benefits. Limits on Benefits and Contributions. Termination of Plan. Other Plan Provisions.* Funding: *Minimum Funding Standards. Tax Deductible Limits.* Plan Administration: *Disclosure. Fiduciary Responsibilities. Taxation of Lump-Sum Distributions.* Plan Termination Insurance: *Benefits Insured. Premiums. Employer Liability. Recapture of Payments. Reportable Events.* Individual Retirement Savings. Plans for the Self-Employed.

Index 415

1

Development of Private Pension Plans

Individuals are constantly seeking means by which to enhance their economic security. One cause of economic insecurity is the probable reduction of an individual's earning power at an advanced age. In this country, this risk is met through one or more of the following means: personal savings (including individual insurance and annuities), private pensions, and government-sponsored programs. The dramatic growth of private plans[1] since the 1940s has focused considerable interest on this form of income maintenance.

GROWTH OF PRIVATE PLANS

The beginnings of industrial pension plans in the United States date back to the establishment of the American Express Company plan in 1875.[2] The second formal plan was established in 1880 by the Baltimore and Ohio Railroad Company. During the next half century, approximately 400 plans were established. These early pension plans were generally found in the railroad, banking, and public utility fields. The development of pensions in manufacturing companies was somewhat slower, due largely to the fact that most manufacturing companies were still relatively young and therefore not confronted with the superannuation problems of the railroads and public utilities.

---

[1] Private plans, as used in this text, refers to plans established by private agencies, including commercial, industrial, labor, and service organizations, and nonprofit religious, educational, and charitable institutions. Social Security and public plans for governmental employees are only covered in this text when they affect private plans.

[2] Murray Webb Latimer, *Industrial Pension Systems* (New York: Industrial Relations Counselors, Inc., 1932), p. 21.

1

Insurance companies entered the pension business with the issuance of the first group annuity contract by the Metropolitan Life Insurance Company in 1921.[3] The second contract was issued by the Metropolitan in 1924 to an employer who already had a retirement plan on a "pay-as-you-go" basis.[4] In 1924 the Equitable Life Assurance Society announced its intention of offering a group pension service, thus becoming the second company to enter the field.[5]

Although the beginnings of private pensions date back to the 1800s, the significant growth in these programs has come since the 1940s. As recently as 1940, less than one fifth of all employees in commerce and industry were covered under pension plans. These programs now cover about 33 million persons, representing about 44 percent of all persons employed in commerce and industry. The assets of pension funds currently are about $180 billion and are growing at the average rate of about $14 billion a year. Table 1–1 summarizes the growth of private pension plans in the United States.

ECONOMIC PROBLEMS OF OLD AGE

Longevity is a source of economic insecurity in that individuals may outlive their financial capacities to maintain themselves and their dependents. The extent to which an aged person will have the financial capacity to meet self-maintenance costs and those of dependents depends upon the standard of living desired during retirement years, employment opportunities, and the prior provisions made to meet this contingency.

Standard of Living after Retirement

The assumption usually is made that the financial needs of an individual decrease after retirement. To some extent, this assumption is valid. The retired individual generally has no dependent children, and a home and its furnishings generally have been acquired by retirement age. However, the actual aggregate reduction in the financial needs of a person upon retirement has probably been overstated. Social pressures discourage any drastic change in one's standard of living upon retirement. There is an increasing tendency for retired persons to remain fairly active, particularly in terms of civic, social, travel, and other recreational activities. Furthermore, urbanization and its corollary, apartment living, minimize the prospect of retired parents moving in with their children.

The authors are not suggesting that retired workers require income

---

[3] Kenneth Black, Jr., *Group Annuities* (Philadelphia: University of Pennsylvania Press, 1955), p. 9.

[4] Ibid., p. 11.

[5] Ibid.

TABLE 1-1

Growth of Private Pension Plans in the United States

Year	Employer Contributions (in millions)			Employee Contributions (in millions)			Number of Beneficiaries, End of Year (in thousands)			Amount of Benefit Payments (in millions)			Reserves, Book Value End of Year (in billions)		
	Total	In-sured	Nonin-sured	Total	In-sured	Nonin-sured	Total	In-sured	Nonin-sured	Total*	In-sured	Nonin-sured*	Total	In-sured	Nonin-sured
1950	$ 1,750	$ 720	$ 1,030	$ 330	$200	$ 130	450	150	300	$ 370	$ 80	$ 290	$ 12.1	$ 5.6	$ 6.5
1955	3,280	1,100	2,180	560	280	280	980	290	690	850	180	670	27.4	11.3	16.1
1960	4,710	1,190	3,520	780	300	480	1,780	540	1,240	1,720	390	1,330	51.9	18.8	33.1
1961	4,830	1,180	3,650	780	290	490	1,910	570	1,340	1,970	450	1,520	57.7	20.2	37.5
1962	5,200	1,240	3,960	830	310	520	2,100	630	1,470	2,330	510	1,820	63.5	21.6	41.9
1963	5,560	1,390	4,170	860	300	560	2,280	690	1,590	2,590	570	2,020	69.9	23.3	46.6
1964	6,370	1,520	4,850	910	310	600	2,490	740	1,750	2,990	640	2,350	77.6	25.2	52.4
1965	7,370	1,770	5,600	990	320	670	2,750	790	1,960	3,520	720	2,800	86.5	27.3	59.2
1966	8,210	1,850	6,360	1,040	330	710	3,110	870	2,240	4,190	810	3,380	95.5	29.3	66.2
1967	9,050	2,010	7,040	1,130	340	790	3,410	930	2,480	4,790	910	3,880	106.1	31.9	74.2
1968	9,940	2,240	7,700	1,230	340	890	3,770	1,010	2,760	5,530	1,030	4,500	117.9	34.8	83.1
1969	11,420	2,930	8,490	1,360	350	1,010	4,180	1,070	3,110	6,450	1,160	5,290	127.8	37.2	90.6
1970	12,580	2,860	9,720	1,420	350	1,070	4,720	1,220	3,500	7,360	1,330	6,030	137.1	40.1	97.0
1971	15,160	3,840	11,320	1,490	370	1,120	5,100	1,300	3,800	8,590	1,510	7,080	151.4	45.0	106.4
1972	16,940	4,200	12,740	1,600	400	1,200	5,550	1,350	4,200	10,000	1,700	8,300	167.8	50.3	117.5
1973	19,390	5,020	14,370	1,715	445	1,270	6,130	1,480	4,650	11,220	1,910	9,310	180.2	53.7	126.5

* Includes refunds to employees and their survivors and lump sums paid under deferred profit sharing plans.

Source: *Social Security Bulletin*, May 1975, p. 26. Compiled by the Social Security Administration from data furnished primarily by the Institute of Life Insurance and the Securities and Exchange Commission.

benefits equal to their earnings levels immediately preceding retirement, nor even the level of preretirement take-home pay. Presumably, at least at the higher income levels, these individuals were allocating a portion of their take-home pay to individual savings. However, it is suggested that the reduction in standard of living after retirement is not very great; and, more importantly, the trend in social thinking seems to be in the direction of not expecting retired workers to have to take much of a reduction in standard of living after retirement. Therefore, it is questionable whether one should assume any significant decrease in basic financial needs upon retirement, at least for individuals in the low- and middle-income categories.

Employment Opportunities

The proportion of persons 65 and over with some income from active employment is currently about 20 percent, and this percentage has been declining steadily in recent years. Obviously, many reasons account for the withdrawal of the aged from the labor force. A large number of older workers voluntarily retire from the labor force. If workers have the necessary financial resources, they may wish to withdraw from active employment and live out their remaining years at a more leisurely pace. Others find it necessary for reasons of health to withdraw from the labor force at an advanced age. The aging process takes its toll, and many individuals are physically unable to operate at the level of efficiency attainable at the younger ages. Disabilities at the older ages tend to be more frequent and of longer duration.

Voluntary retirement and the physical inability to continue employment are undoubtedly important reasons for the decrease in the percentage of older persons participating in the labor force. However, these are probably not the most important factors affecting employment opportunities for the aged. The effects of industrialization and the development of the federal Old-Age, Survivors, Disability, and Health Insurance program (OASDHI), private pensions, and other employee benefit programs probably have had a more significant impact on this problem.

The rapid pace and dynamic evolution of industrial employment operate to the disadvantage of older persons. Automation and the mass-production assembly lines put a premium on physical dexterity and mental alertness. Employers generally are of the opinion, justifiable or not, that the younger workers are better suited to the demands of industrial employment. In an agricultural economy the able-bodied older person could continue to work, at least on a part-time basis.

The OASDHI program and private pension plans, although created to alleviate the financial risk associated with excessive longevity, have aggravated the problem in that these programs have tended to institutionalize age 65 as the normal retirement age. Also, some employers may hesitate to hire older workers on the assumption that these employees would increase pension and other employee benefit plan costs. It is difficult to generalize as to the impact of the older worker on employee benefit plan costs. Nevertheless, it must be recognized that an employer's attitude toward the hiring of older workers may be influenced by the assumption, justified or not, that employee benefit costs will be adversely affected.

Self-employed members of the labor force have greater control as to the timing of their retirements from active employment. For example, physicians and lawyers frequently continue in practice, at least on a part-time basis, until advanced ages. Owners of businesses also continue to be active in the firm until relatively old ages. The fact remains, however, that employment opportunities for the majority of older workers are becoming more and more limited.

Individual Savings of Aged

If employment opportunities for the aged are decreasing and financial needs are still substantial at advanced ages, the need for savings becomes quite apparent. Relatively little information is available on the extent of savings among the aged. What little data is available clearly indicates that other than equity in a home, assets of persons age 65 and over are relatively small.

However, the value of home ownership for the economic security of the aged should not be underestimated. Studies indicate that a substantial proportion of the homes owned by the aged are clear of any mortgage. Home ownership reduces the income needs of the aged insofar as normal maintenance costs and taxes are less than the amount of rent required for comparable housing accommodations. It has been estimated that the maintenance costs for an unencumbered home are about one third to 40 percent less than the costs of renting comparable facilities. Furthermore, there is the possibility that the home can be used in part as an income-producing asset.

Also, in any evaluation of the economic status of the aged, resources available in time of need from both the immediate and extended family (i.e., children away from home and relatives) cannot be ignored. However, it does appear reasonable to conclude that the accumulated savings alone of many aged persons are not adequate to provide even a subsistence level of income for their remaining years.

Although personal savings rates have been running at historically high levels in recent years, the long-range trend in net personal savings as a percentage of national income has been fairly constant. However, the distribution of savings by savings media has changed considerably over the years. The change that is most pertinent to this discussion is the relative increase in private pension reserves in relation to purely individual forms of saving. Annual contributions to private pension funds now amount to about $22 billion, with the increase in private pension fund assets averaging about 25 percent of personal savings in recent years. The tremendous increases in disposable income over the last quarter century, therefore, have not resulted in any increase in the proportion of personal savings. There have been many forces at work that have restricted the growth of savings. Advertising, installment credit, and the media of mass communications encourage individuals to set their sights on a constantly increasing standard of living. This competition from consumption goods for current income dollars results in a lower priority being placed on the need for accumulating savings for old age. Also, the high levels of federal income tax rates reduce an income earner's capacity to save. In recent decades, inflation has been an additional deterrent to increased levels of saving. Inflation is a particularly serious threat to the adequacy of savings programs of persons who already are retired. For employed persons, increases in the cost of living may be offset, in part or in whole, by increases in current earnings; that possibility does not exist for most aged persons. Therefore, the aged are faced with the alternatives of accepting a lower standard of living or more rapidly liquidating their accumulated savings.

The proportion of individual (as opposed to group) savings, then, is decreasing at a time when the pattern of living of the aged is becoming increasingly more costly. Under such circumstances, the tremendous importance of pension programs in meeting the economic risk of old age is obvious.

Increasing Longevity

Still another dimension to the overall economic problem of old age is the number of aged in the population. The fact that life expectancy has been increasing is well recognized. However, that this increase in longevity is a recent and quite dramatic development is often not appreciated. Within the last 60 years, the life expectancy at birth has increased from 47 years to approximately 70 years. This result has been achieved in spite of the limited gains in life expectancy in the last decade. The rates of mortality at the earlier ages are now so low that further improvements in mortality at these ages would have little impact on further extensions of the average length of life. If additional improvements in longevity are to be realized, reductions in mortality at the older ages are required. This impediment to further extensions in life expectancy may be overcome if medical advances result from the current concentration of research in the areas of the chronic and degenerative diseases.

One effect of the improvements in longevity in the 20th century has been an absolute and relative increase in the population of persons age 65 and over. In 1900, there were approximately 3 million persons age 65 and over, whereas there were about 18 million such persons in 1965. By 1985, it is estimated that persons age 65 and over will number about 25 million. The proportion of the U.S. population age 65 and over currently is about 9 percent, whereas the proportion of the population in these age brackets in 1900 was about 4 percent.

The problem of old-age economic security, therefore, is of concern to an increasing number and percentage of the U.S. population.

REASONS FOR GROWTH OF PRIVATE PENSIONS

In the above discussion, the point was made that the problem of economic security for the aged is a serious and increasingly important problem. However, the mere existence of the problem does not explain the phenomenal growth of private pensions. In other words, given the existence of the old-age economic problem, why did employers and employees choose to meet the need, at least in part, through the vehicle of private pension programs? In a broad sense, the major reason is the fact that private pensions offer substantial advantages to both employers and employees. Without this foundation of mutual benefit, the private pension movement could not have achieved the prolonged and substantial growth that it has enjoyed. In addition, government officials have recognized the social desirability of pension programs and have acted to encourage the growth of these plans through the tax system and through other means.

The specific factors generally considered as having influenced the growth of private pensions are discussed below. It must be recognized that the reasons that give rise to the establishment of one plan might be quite different in the case of another plan.

Increased Productivity

A systematic method of meeting the problem of superannuated employees can be easily justified on sound management grounds. Practically every employee eventually reaches a point where, due to advanced age, he or she is a liability rather than an asset to the employer. That is to say, at some advanced age, an employee's contribution to the productivity of the firm is less than the compensation he or she is receiving.

The employer has several courses of action when an employee reaches this point. One, the employee can be terminated without any further compensation or any retirement benefits as soon as the value of the employee's services is less than the salary being paid. For obvious reasons, this course of action is seldom followed by employers. Two, the employer can retain the superannuated employee in the employee's current position and at current level of compensation. The difference between the employee's productivity and salary is absorbed by the employer as a cost of doing business. This alternative also is undesirable. Such an approach would undoubtedly prove to be the most costly method of meeting the problem of superannuated employees. Furthermore, the longer range indirect costs that would be incurred from the resultant inefficiencies and poor employee morale among the younger workers would be indeed significant. Three, the employer could retain the superannuated worker, but transfer the employee to a less demanding job at the same or a reduced level of compensation. In the former case, the direct costs would be similar to alternative two, but the indirect costs would be reduced in that a younger and more capable person would now be staffing the more demanding position. If the employee's salary is reduced, the direct costs of superannuation also would be reduced.

Most employers who do not have a pension plan generally handle the problem of the older worker in the latter manner. The effectiveness of this approach to the problem has certain important limitations. First of all, a firm usually has only a limited number of positions to which aged workers can be transferred. For a large or even medium-sized firm, only a fraction of the superannuated employees can be efficiently employed. With automation and the increasingly higher levels of skill required in most jobs, the limitations of this solution are apparent. Furthermore, the superannuated employee is generally still overpaid in the less demanding jobs since, for practical purposes, reductions comparable to the decrease in employee productivity are seldom made. Lastly, this approach does not solve the problem of superannuation; it merely defers it, since a point will be reached where the employee's productivity is considerably below even a minimum level of wage.

The fourth alternative available to the employer in meeting the problem of superannuation is to establish a formal pension plan. A pension plan permits employers to terminate superannuated employees in a humanitarian and nondiscriminatory manner. The inefficiencies associated with retaining employees beyond their productive years are, therefore, eliminated. Employees will know that they are expected to retire by a certain age, and they can make the necessary provisions for their retirement. Furthermore, the sense of security derived from the knowledge that provision is made, at least in part, for their retirement income needs should increase the morale and productivity of employees. Also, systematic retirement of older workers will keep the channels of promotion open, thereby offering opportunity and incentive to the young, ambitious employees—particularly those aspiring to executive positions. Therefore, a pension plan should permit an employer to attract and keep a better caliber of employee.

The problem of superannuation, then, exists in all business firms. Any solution, except the unlikely alternative of arbitrary termination of older workers without any retirement benefit, results in some cost, direct or indirect, to the employer. Unfortunately, some employers assume that the pension plan solution is the only approach that carries a price tag. The hidden costs of the other alternatives must be recognized. The decision, therefore, is which solution is best suited to the needs and financial position of the employer. For a large number of employers, the formal pension plan approach has proved to be the superior solution.

Tax Considerations

The bulk of the growth in private pension plans has occurred since 1940. One reason for the growth of these plans during the World War II and Korean War periods was the fact that normal and excess profits tax rates imposed on corporations during these years were extremely high. Since the employer's contributions to a *qualified* pension plan are deductible for federal income tax purposes, a portion of the plan's liabilities could be funded with very little effective cost to the firm. Furthermore, the investment income earned on pension trust assets is exempt from federal income taxation until distributed.[6]

The tax advantages of qualified pension plans are even more impressive from the standpoint of employees covered under the plan; for example, the employer's contributions to a pension fund do not constitute taxable income to the employee in the year in which contributions are made. The pension benefits derived from employer contributions are taxed when distributed or made available to the employee. However, the employee is expected to be in a lower tax bracket when retirement benefits are received. In addition, under certain circumstances, a portion of a lump-sum distribution from a pension plan may be taxed at capital gain rates and a special averaging provision may be available for the balance, instead of the total distribution's being taxed at ordinary income rates. Also, favorable estate tax treatment is accorded death benefits paid under a qualified plan.

Therefore, qualified pension plans offer significant tax advantages to participants generally, and in particular to employees currently in high income tax brackets. Since the high-salaried senior officers of corporations often make the decision regarding the establishment and design of employee benefit plans, their role as participants under the plan may influence their decisions on these matters. However, in the case of large corporations, cost and other considerations minimize or eliminate the personal tax situations of key employees as factors influencing the establish-

---

[6] For a complete discussion of the tax aspects of qualified pension plans, see Chapters 4 and 5.

ment or design of a pension plan. In the case of a small, closely held corporation, on the other hand, one can readily see how the tax implications for stockholder-employees may be a decisive factor in the establishment and design of a pension plan. Lastly, tax considerations are certainly one reason, although not the most important, why some labor leaders negotiate for establishment and liberalization of employee benefit programs in lieu of further wage increases.

Wage Stabilization

The second wartime development that helped to stimulate the growth of pensions was the creation of a wage stabilization program as part of a general price control scheme. Employers, in competing for labor, could not offer the inducement of higher wages. Under these conditions, union leaders found it difficult to prove to their membership the merits of unionism. Therefore, the War Labor Board attempted to relieve the pressure on management and labor for higher wage rates by permitting the establishment of fringe benefit programs, including pensions. This policy further stimulated the growth of pension plans during the period.

Union Demands

Labor leaders have had mixed emotions over the years regarding the desirability of employer-financed pension plans. In the 1920s, labor generally did not favor such plans for its membership. It held the view that pensions represented an additional form of employer paternalism and were instituted to encourage loyalty to the firm. Labor leaders felt that the need would be best met through the establishment of a government-sponsored universal social security system; in the absence of that solution, unions should establish their own pension plans for their members. The former objective was achieved with the passage of the Social Security Act of 1935. By the 1930s, several unions had established their own plans. However, many of these plans were inadequately financed, a condition which became quite apparent during the depression years. Recognition of the financial burden of a pension program and enactment of wage controls led some labor leaders, in the early 1940s, to favor establishment of employer-supported pension plans.

From 1945 to 1949 the rate of growth of new plans fell off markedly. During this postwar period, employee interest centered upon cash wage increases in an attempt to recover the lost ground suffered during the period of wage stabilization. In the latter part of the 1940s, union leaders once again began expressing an interest in the negotiation of pension programs. The renewal of interest in pensions was probably because of two factors. First, there was increasing antagonism on the part of the public toward what were viewed by many persons as excessive union demands for cash wage increases. The negotiation of fringe benefits was one way of possibly reducing pressures from this quarter. Second, some union leaders argued that social security benefits were inadequate, and a supplement in the form of private pension benefits was considered to be necessary. Also, certain labor officials believed that the negotiation of employer-supported pensions would weaken the resistance of the latter toward liberalizations of social security benefit levels. Thus, pension demands became a central issue in the labor negotiations in the coal, automobile, and steel industries in the late 40s. Although unions had negotiated pension benefits prior to this period, it was not until the late 40s that a major segment of labor made a concerted effort to bargain for private pensions.

Labor's drive for pension benefits was facilitated by a National Labor Relations Board ruling in 1948 that employers had a legal obligation to bargain over the terms of pension plans. Until that time, there was some question whether employee benefit programs fell within the traditional subject areas for collective bargaining; i.e., wages, hours, and other conditions of employment. The issue was resolved when the National Labor Relations Board held that pension benefits constitute wages and the provisions of these plans affect conditions of employment.[7] Upon appeal, the court upheld the NLRB decision, although it questioned the assumption that such benefits are wages.[8] The result of these decisions was that an employer cannot install or terminate or alter the terms of a pension plan covering organized workers without the approval of the authorized bargaining agent for those employees. Furthermore, management has this obligation regardless of whether the plan is contributory or noncontributory, voluntary or compulsory, and regardless of whether the plan was established before or after the certification of the bargaining unit.

Labor was quick to respond to these decisions, and the 1950s were marked by union demands for the establishment of new pension plans, liberalization of existing plans, and the supplanting of employer-sponsored programs with negotiated plans. Undoubtedly, labor's interest in private pensions has been an important factor in the tremendous growth in plans since 1949.

Business Necessity

Employers hire employees in a free, competitive labor market. Therefore, as the number of plans increase, employees come to expect a pension

---

[7] *Inland Steel Company v. United Steelworkers of America,* 77 NLRB 4 (1948).

[8] *Inland Steel Company v. National Labor Relations Board,* 170 F.(2d) 247, 251 (1949).

benefit as part of the employment relationship. Employers who do not have such a plan are at a competitive disadvantage in attracting and holding personnel. Therefore, some employers feel they must install a plan even if they are not convinced that the advantages generally associated with a pension plan outweigh the cost of the benefit. Admittedly, this is a negative reason for instituting a plan. In other words, these employers feel that little evidence exists that pension plans truly result in improved morale and efficiency among their work force; but they feel that there would clearly be an adverse employee reaction if they did not offer a pension. Also, in contrast to situations where a plan is established in response to labor demands, an employer may offer a pension plan as part of an employee relations objective of keeping the union out of the firm.

Reward for Service

There is a tendency to argue that employers never provide any increase in employee benefits unless they can expect an economic return in some form. Although this philosophy must prevail generally in a capitalistic system, the fact remains that many employers have established plans out of a sincere desire to reward employees who have served the firm well over a long period of service. Also, some employers may feel a moral responsibility to make some provision for the economic welfare of retired employees.

Efficiency of Approach

Part of the growth of private pensions must be attributed to the fact that a formal group savings approach has certain inherent advantages. The advantages are not such that they eliminate the need for individual savings; but the merits of private pensions as a supplement to social security benefits and individual savings programs are indeed significant. First of all, the economic risk of old age derives from the fact that a point is reached when an employee is unable or unwilling to continue in active employment. A formal plan as an integral part of compensation arrangements and employment relationships, therefore, is quite logical. There is no additional wage cost to the employer to the extent that pension benefits are provided in lieu of other forms of compensation. If pension benefits are provided in addition to prevailing wage rates, the employer's extra wage costs resulting from the pension plan can generally be passed on to the consuming public in the form of higher prices.

It has been argued that from a broad social point of view, the private pension system is the lowest cost method of providing economic security for the aged. In addition to the administrative efficiency of group saving arrangements, it is argued that the small increase in consumer prices that might be required to provide pension benefits is a relatively painless method of meeting the risk. In other words, the burden of retirement security is spread over a large number of people and over a long period of time. The economic principle of marginal utility would support the conclusion that the disutility of the small increase in prices for all consumers would be less than the burdens that would be borne by those individuals who would have inadequate retirement resources in the absence of pension benefits. Still another aspect to the argument is the assumption that private pensions increase consumption levels among the aged, which in turn helps to maintain a high level of economic activity.

Lastly, private pensions constitute a form of forced savings. This advantage is extremely important in view of the apparent desire of many people to maintain a relatively high standard of living during their active employment years. Although it can be argued that employees would, in the absence of private pension programs, make equivalent provision for old age through increased levels of individual savings, the evidence seems to point to the conclusion that a number of people would not do so.[9] Thus, it is economically more efficient if at least part of the risk is met through a forced saving private pension scheme.

Sales Efforts of Funding Agencies

For all of the above-mentioned reasons, there has been a considerable demand over the years for private pensions. However, in many instances, the advantages of these programs had to be called to the attention of specific employers. This function of creating effective demand for the pension product has been aggressively performed by those parties interested in providing services in this area. Insurance companies, through agents, brokers, and salaried representatives, were undoubtedly instrumental in the growth of pensions, particularly in the decades of the 20s and 30s. The trust departments of banks also are equipped to handle pension funds, and many corporate trustees have been actively soliciting pension business, particularly since the early 1950s.

RATIONALE OF PRIVATE PENSIONS

The growth of private pensions in attributable, as seen above, to a variety of reasons. It is difficult to determine the extent to which each factor contributed. Indeed, it seems reasonable to conclude that the dominant reasons leading to the establishment of specific plans vary depending

---

[9] Indeed, there is evidence that private pension coverage tends to stimulate individual savings. See Philip Cagan, *The Effect of Pension Plans on Aggregate Saving* (New York: National Bureau of Economic Research, 1965).

on the circumstances surrounding each case. In other words, productivity considerations were dominant forces leading to the creation of some plans, while labor pressures, tax considerations, or other factors encouraged establishment of still other plans. With such variety of motivation, it is difficult to characterize private pensions in terms of a single philosophy or rationale. Nevertheless, attempts have been made over the years to explain private pensions in terms of an underlying concept or philosophy.[10]

Early industrial pension plans were viewed as gratuities or rewards to employees for long and loyal service to the employer. Closely related to this view is the concept that private pensions constitute a systematic and socially desirable method of releasing employees who are no longer productive members of the employer's labor force. Regardless of the view taken, the fact remains that these early plans were largely discretionary, and management made it quite clear that employees had no contractual rights to benefits under the plan. Continuation of the pension plan was dependent upon competitive conditions and management policy. Furthermore, management reserved the right to terminate benefit payments to pensioners for misconduct on the part of the beneficiary or for any other reasons justifying such action in the opinion of the employer.

Thus, the growth of early pensions might be best categorized by a single concept: *business expediency.* Business expediency, by the very nature of the concept, implies that the establishment of a plan is a management prerogative and that the primary motivation for the creation of such plans was the economic benefit, direct or indirect, that accrued to the employer. But as the economy became more and more industrialized and pension plans became more prevalent, there was increasing interest in the view that employers had a moral obligation to provide for the economic security of retired workers. This point of view was expressed as early as 1912 by Lee Welling Squier, as follows: "From the standpoint of the whole system of social economy, no employer has a right to engage men in any occupation that exhausts the individual's industrial life in 10, 20 or 40 years; and then leave the remnant floating on society at large as a derelict at sea."[11] This rationale of private pensions has come to be known as the *human depreciation concept.* It was the point of view taken by the United Mine Workers of America in their 1946 drive to establish a welfare fund:

> The United Mine Workers of America has assumed the position over the years that the cost of caring for the human equity in the coal industry is inherently as valid as the cost of the replacement of mining machinery, or the cost of paying taxes, or the cost of paying interest

---

[10] For an excellent discussion of pension philosophies, see Jonas E. Mittelman "The Vesting of Private Pensions" (Ph.D. dissertation, University of Pennsylvania, 1959), Chap. 2.

[11] Lee Welling Squier, *Old Age Dependency in the United States* (New York: Macmillan Co., 1912), p. 272.

indebtedness, or any other factor incident to the production of a ton of coal for consumers' bins. . . . [The agreement establishing the Welfare Fund] recognized in principle the fact that the industry owed an obligation to those employees, and the coal miners could no longer be used up, crippled beyond repair and turned out to live or die subject to the charity of the community or the minimum contributions of the state.[12]

This analogy between human labor and industrial machines was also made in the report of the president's fact-finding board in the 1949 steelworkers' labor dispute in support of its conclusion that management had a responsibility to provide for the security of its workers: "We think that all industry, in the absence of adequate Government programs, owes an obligation to workers to provide for maintenance of the human body in the form of medical and similar benefits and full depreciation in the form of old-age retirement—in the same way as it does now for plant and machinery."[13] The report continues as follows: "What does that mean in terms of steelworkers? It should mean the use of earnings to insure against the full depreciation of the human body—say at age 65—in the form of a pension or retirement allowance."[14]

The validity of the human depreciation concept of private pensions has been challenged by many pension experts.[15] The process of aging is physiological and is not attributable to the employment relationship. Admittedly, the hazards of certain occupations undoubtedly shorten the life span of the employees involved. In those instances the employer can logically be held responsible only for the increase in the rate of aging due to the hazards of the occupation. More importantly, the analogy between humans and machines is inherently unsound. A machine is an asset owned by the employer, and depreciation is merely an accounting technique for allocating the costs of equipment to various accounting periods. Employees, on the other hand, are free agents and sell their services to employees for a specified wage rate. An employee, unlike a machine, is free to move from one employer to another. The differences between humans and machines are so great that one must question the value of the analogy as a basis for a rationale of private pensions. As Dearing notes: "Any economic or moral responsibility that is imposed on the employer for the welfare of workers after termination of the labor

---

[12] United Mine Workers of America Welfare and Retirement Fund, *Pensions for Coal Miners* (Washington, D.C., n.d.), p. 4.

[13] Steel Industry Board, *Report to the President of the United States on the Labor Dispute in the Basic Steel Industry* (Washington, D.C.: U.S. Government Printing Office, September 10, 1949), p. 55.

[14] Ibid., p. 65.

[15] For example, see Dan M. McGill, *Fundamentals of Private Pensions,* rev. ed. (Homewood, Ill.: Richard D. Irwin, Inc., 1964), p. 16. See also Charles L. Dearing *Industrial Pensions* (Washington, D.C.: Brookings Institution, 1954), pp. 62–63 and 241–43; and Mittelman, "Vesting of Private Pensions," pp. 28–34.

contract should be grounded on firmer reasoning than is supplied by the machine-worker analogy."[16]

In recent years a view of private pensions that has achieved broader acceptance is the *deferred wage concept*. This concept views a pension benefit as part of a wage package which is composed of cash wages and other employee fringe benefits. The deferred wage concept has particular appeal with reference to negotiated pension plans. The assumption is made that labor and management negotiators think in terms of total labor costs. Therefore, if labor negotiates a pension benefit, the funds available for increases in cash wages are reduced accordingly. This theory of private pensions was expressed as early as 1913:

> In order to get a full understanding of old-age and service pensions, they should be considered as a part of the real wages of a workman. There is a tendency to speak of these pensions as being paid by the company, or, in cases where the employee contributes a portion, as being paid partly by the employer and partly by the employee. In a certain sense, of course, this may be correct, but it leads to confusion. A pension system considered as part of the real wages of an employee is really paid by the employee, not perhaps in money, but in the forgoing of an increase in wages which he might obtain except for the establishment of a pension system.[17]

The deferred wage concept has also been challenged on several grounds. First, it is noted that some employers who pay the prevailing cash wage rate for the particular industry also provide a pension benefit. Thus, it can be argued that in these cases the pension benefit is offered in addition to, rather than in lieu of, a cash wage increase. Second, the deferred wage concept ignores the possible argument that the employer is willing to accept a lower profit margin to provide a pension plan for employees. Third, it is sometimes argued that if pension benefits are a form of wage, then terminating employees should be entitled to the part of the retirement benefit that has been earned to the date of termination. In practice, one finds that only a small proportion of the plans provide for the full and immediate vesting of all benefits. However, it can be argued that the deferred wage concept does not necessarily require the full and immediate vesting of benefits. Proponents ,of this concept view the pension benefits as a wage the receipt of which is conditioned upon the employee's remaining in the service of the employer for a specified number of years. This view of the pension benefit is similar, conceptually, to the pure endowment, the consideration of the employee being the reduction in cash wages accepted in lieu of the pension benefit.

In spite of the appeal of the deferred wage theory, it is questionable

---

[16] Dearing, *Industrial Pensions,* p. 243.

[17] Albert de Roode, "Pensions as Wages," *American Economic Review,* vol. III, no. 2 (June 1913), p. 287.

whether the private pension movement can be explained solely in terms of this concept. Indeed, there is probably no one rationale or theory that fully explains the "reason for being" of private pensions. This conclusion is not surprising in view of the fact that these plans are *private*, and the demands or reasons that give rise to one plan may be quite different from those leading to the introduction of another plan.

EMPLOYEE RETIREMENT INCOME SECURITY ACT OF 1974 (ERISA)

After many years of discussion and debate concerning reform of the private pension system, the Employee Retirement Income Security Act of 1974 (commonly referred to as ERISA) became law on September 2, 1974. This law has effected some of the most important changes ever enacted in the private pension movement. These changes affect virtually all aspects of corporate and self-employed (so-called Keogh or HR-10) pension plans from a legal, tax, and actuarial viewpoint. In addition, ERISA establishes new reporting and fiduciary requirements as well as plan termination insurance guarantees for certain plans.

Another major feature of ERISA was the establishment of the individual retirement accounts law, effective for taxable years beginning after December 31, 1974, permitting any individual who is not covered under a qualified retirement plan or tax deferred annuity to set aside tax deductible contributions under a retirement plan.

The impact of ERISA will be substantial on all facets of private pension plans, but it will be many years before the full implications of this new law will have emerged.

FUTURE GROWTH OF PRIVATE PLANS

Since plans have been established by most large employers, the future extension of private pension coverage depends largely on the extent to which programs are started by smaller employers. The fact that smaller employers generally do not have pension plans is understandable. The costs of a pension program are fairly substantial; and many small firms are unable, or at least hesitant, to assume a financial obligation of such magnitude perhaps especially since the enactment of ERISA with its minimum funding standards and plan termination liabilities. Also, the employees of small firms often are not represented by a union, and this source of pressure to establish plans is nonexistent. Even if the employees are organized, the high rates of turnover among employees or the economic conditions of the employers or the industry may reduce the prospects for negotiating a retirement benefit. Furthermore, small employers do not seem to have the personnel problem of larger firms; that is, the need to match the employee benefit programs being offered by competing firms. The enactment of ERISA which requires more liberal vesting provisions, more stringent funding requirements, and guarantee arrangements for insuring accrued pension credits may deter further expansion of defined benefit private plans among small employers.

However, small employers must compete with the large firms for qualified employees; and as pensions become more common, it may be increasingly necessary for small firms to provide pension benefits. Also, the problem of establishing pension plans in industries characterized by small employers and high rates of employee turnover has been partially met by the recent growth of multiemployer pension plans. A multiemployer pension plan is a plan that covers the employees of two or more financially unrelated employers.[18] Pension contributions are payable into one common fund, and benefits are payable to all employees from the pooled assets of the fund. Employees are free to transfer from one participating employer to another without loss of earned pension credits. These plans generally require uniform contribution rates and uniform benefit provisions. Although there are a few nonnegotiated multiemployer plans in operation, these plans have been established almost exclusively as a result of collective bargaining. These plans cover more than 7 million employees and have been growing at about double the rate of increase for single employer plan coverage during the last decade. In recent years, there has been increasing interest in the possibilities of pooling arrangements as funding vehicles for nonnegotiated plans of small employers.

Another factor which probably to some extent discouraged the establishment of pension plans by small employers has been the unfavorable federal income tax treatment, prior to 1962, accorded plans established by sole proprietorships and partnerships. A sole proprietorship or a partnership can deduct for federal income tax purposes the contributions to a qualified pension plan made on behalf of employees. But no tax deduction was permitted for contributions under those plans made on behalf of the sole proprietors or partners. The Keogh Act, passed by Congress in 1962, amended the Internal Revenue Code to permit tax deductions for contributions made to pension plans on behalf of sole proprietors and partners. The deduction limits for Keogh plans were substantially improved by ERISA and this fact should encourage their continued growth. However, the individual retirement accounts provisions of ERISA which allow individuals to set up their own form of retirement plan when they are not covered by a qualified plan may have the effect of lowering the growth of private plans among small corporations.

Lastly, the development of "master" and "prototype" plans for both

---

[18] For a detailed discussion of such plans, see Joseph J. Melone, *Collectively Bargained Multi-Employer Pension Plans* (Homewood, Ill.: Richard D. Irwin, Inc., 1963).

self-employed and corporate plans is likely to stimulate the growth of qualified plans among small firms. The master or prototype plan is submitted for approval to the Internal Revenue Service by a sponsoring organization; e.g., an insurance company, mutual fund, bank, or professional or trade association. The use of preapproved master plans cuts out a good deal of the delay and red tape in getting IRS approval by employers in adopting a pension plan.

Although it is difficult to determine to what extent these developments will encourage or discourage the growth of pension plans among smaller employers, it seems reasonable to conclude that the number of new plans established each year will continue to grow for some years to come, but at a slower rate than experienced in the past.

2

Basic Features of a Pension Plan

An employer who is adopting a qualified pension plan must make a number of decisions as to the basic features to be included in the plan. The employer must, for example, determine the class of employees to be covered; when and under what conditions these employees will be eligible for participation; what benefits they will receive upon retirement, death, disability, or severance of employment; how and when these benefits will be paid; and whether or not employees will contribute toward the cost of these benefits.

The employer's objectives as to benefit and cost levels are of paramount importance when making these decisions, although a number of other factors must often be taken into account. For example, the employer's existing employee benefit program should be considered if unnecessary duplication or overlapping of benefits is to be avoided. Demands by a collective bargaining unit will also have an impact on the employer's decisions, as might the benefit patterns established by competing business organizations.

The requirements of ERISA, of course, play a major role in plan design. The requirements of the Internal Revenue Code and appropriate regulations are also of vital importance if the employer wishes to obtain the favorable tax benefits that flow from having a "qualified" plan. While the requirements for qualification are discussed at greater length in Chapter 4, it might be observed at this point that such a plan must not discriminate in any way (i.e., in benefits, contributions, or coverage) in favor of officers, stockholders, or highly compensated employees—often called the *prohibited* group of employees. Thus, the organization, if it is to have a qualified plan, cannot pick and choose the employees to be covered nor can it determine their benefits in a selective manner. Instead, the employer must adopt a plan which treats employees fairly and equitably and which does not produce discrimination in favor of this prohibited group of employees.

The design of a pension plan for a particular employer should reflect a thorough evaluation of the objectives and circumstances of that employer. It is possible, of course, that a given combination of plan benefits and features will work out quite well for a number of different employers. As a practical matter, however, each organization has its own specific objectives as well as its own specific circumstances. Thus, a plan provision that might be quite satisfactory for one employer could be completely inadequate for another. For this reason, it is most important that the plan developed for any employer be designed to accomplish that employer's particular objectives while taking into account its own particular problems. All too often, an employer will abruptly adopt a "package" plan only to find, at a later date, that this plan is deficient in some respect. Unfortunately, the remedy to this type of problem frequently involves considerable expense and effort on the part of all concerned. This point deserves particular emphasis with the growing use of master and prototype plans. These plans, while they offer the distinct advantage of ease of installation, also create a situation where a plan can be designed without sufficient thought and analysis of the options available in structuring all of the plan provisions.

This chapter discusses the various factors which bear on an employer's decisions concerning the design of the more prominent features to be included in a pension plan. While much of this material applies equally well to profit sharing plans, it is oriented specifically toward *qualified pension* plans established by *corporate* employers. This material also applies, except as noted, to qualified pension plans adopted by Subchapter S corporations and by professional associations or corporations that possess sufficient corporate characteristics to qualify as corporations under federal tax law. The features discussed include eligibility requirements, retirement ages and benefits, death and disability benefits, severance-of-employment benefits, and employee contributions. The chapter also touches upon some of the other provisions essential to any pension plan (such as the employer's right to amend or terminate the program) but which are more or less straightforward in nature and do not require any major consideration by the employer.

ELIGIBILITY REQUIREMENTS

In the generally accepted sense, eligibility requirements are those conditions an employee must meet to become a participant in the plan.

In noncontributory plans, an employee who meets the eligibility requirements automatically becomes a participant when first eligible. In contributory plans, the employee usually has the option of participating and must take some affirmative action before becoming a participant. Thus, the employee must usually sign an application for participation under which the employee agrees to make contributions and also designates a beneficiary.

There are two broad types of eligibility requirements—those which defer an employee's participation until some stipulated conditions are met, and those which exclude an employee from participation on a permanent basis (or, at least, until the employee has had some change in employment classification). An example of an eligibility requirement that defers participation would be a requirement that the employee must attain some minimum age before becoming eligible. On the other hand, provisions which exclude hourly employees or which prevent participation if an employee has attained some maximum age are illustrative of requirements that may exclude certain employees from ever participating in the plan.

Those eligibility requirements which defer participation are often included for administrative cost considerations. Inclusion of employees who are still in what might be termed the "high turnover" stage of their employment will involve the creation and maintenance of records and, depending upon the funding instrument involved, could create additional and unnecessary costs for the employer. For example, an employee who terminates employment shortly after becoming a participant under an individual policy plan creates a cost to the employer which is measured in terms of the difference between the premiums paid for the employee's coverage and the cash surrender value (including any dividends) which is available from the insurer under the employee's insurance or annuity contract. However, care must be exercised so that the eligibility requirements are not too stringent. Much of the psychological effect of the plan may be lost if a number of employees find that they are not yet eligible to participate. The selection of appropriate eligibility requirements balances these factors so that within the employer's objectives as many employees as possible are eligible, while financial losses and administrative difficulties are kept to a minimum.

Those eligibility requirements which may permanently exclude employees from participation generally are dictated by the employer's objectives, by bargaining agreements, or by cost considerations. For example, it rarely is desirable for an employer to include part-time or seasonal employees in a pension plan. Similarly, if a bargaining unit is negotiating for a penson plan, coverage is generally confined to employees represented by the bargaining unit. Perhaps the most difficult of the eligibility requirements is the maximum age established for the plan. The employer may have many employees who have accumulated a record of long and faithful service with the employer, and, to the extent possible, these employees should be included in the plan. Unfortunately, however, the inclusion of older employees could present definite and immediate cost problems for the employer.[1]

Requirements of the Internal Revenue Code are an extremely important consideration in the establishment of eligibility provisions. The Code requires that: (1) at least 70 percent of all employees be covered; or (2) in a plan requiring employee contributions at least 80 percent of all eligible employees be covered, provided that 70 percent of all employees are eligible. Employees who have not met the minimum age and service requirements of the plan may be excluded in determining "all employees." Similarly, "all employees" need not include any employees who are represented by a collective bargaining unit if there is evidence that retirement benefits were the subject of good faith bargaining. In lieu of the foregoing, the law also permits eligibility to be determined by special classifications of employees if such classifications do not discriminate in favor of officers, stockholders, or highly compensated employees.

The most common eligibility requirements involve the use of a minimum age or a minimum period of service. In the broad sense, other eligibility requirements also may be considered. These include the use of a maximum age, a minimum earnings requirement, and employment classifications.

One further point to note is that eligibility requirements which defer participation also might affect the employee's benefit and the ultimate cost of the plan, since, for example, they could limit the time during which credited service may be accrued. Many plans, however, and particularly those negotiated by collective bargaining units, give credit for total service or give credit for all service up to some maximum such as 30 years.

In designing eligibility requirements, it often is helpful to prepare a chart which shows the distribution of employees by age and service. This type of chart often indicates the proper choice of eligibility requirements. Table 2–1 shows how such a chart might be prepared.

With the above discussion as general background, it is now appropriate to consider certain specific eligibility requirements in greater detail.

Years of Service and Minimum Age

In most situations, it is possible to demonstrate that an employer's highest rate of turnover occurs among employees who have been with the firm for a relatively short period of time. It is generally desirable that any minimum service and age requirements of the plan be set so

---

[1] ERISA permits the use of a maximum age only under defined benefit plans.

TABLE 2–1

Analysis of Employees by Age and Service

Age	Under 1 Year	1	2	3	4	5-9	10-14	15-19	20 or More	Total
						Years of Service				
Under 20.	1									1
20–24.		1								1
25–29.	1		1							2
30–34.			1	1	1	2				5
35–39.	1					1	3			5
40–44.	2	2		1			1	1		7
45–49.	1			5	1	3	1	2		13
50–54.			1		1		1		1	4
55–59.						1	2		1	4
60–64.			1				1			2
65–69.						1	1			2
70 and over							1			1
Total	6	3	4	7	3	8	11	3	2	47

as to provide that only those persons who have been employed beyond this period will be eligible.

Under ERISA, however, eligibility cannot be delayed beyond the time an employee reaches age 25 and completes one year of service. Thus, the maximum service that may be used is one year, and the highest minimum age that may be used is age 25. Further, the use of entry dates cannot delay the participation of an employee more than six months. Thus, if it is desired to use the most stringent minimum age and service requirements possible, the plan should permit entry at least every six months. The use of an annual entry date will be permissible only when the minimum age and/or service requirements are at least six months less than those permissible under the law (age 24½ or six months of service).

An exception to the one-year service requirement is available if the plan provides full and immediate vesting (an infrequent situation in a defined benefit corporate pension plan). Here, a three-year service requirement, along with a minimum age requirement of 25, will be permissible.

The way in which service is determined also is set forth in ERISA. For the purposes of determining eligibility, credit for one year of service must be given if the employee works at least 1,000 hours in the 12-month period beginning on his or her date of employment. If an employee does not complete 1,000 hours of service during the 12-month period beginning on the date his or her employment commenced, credit need not be given for a year of service. The employer may then require that the employee complete at least 1,000 hours of service during any subsequent 12-month period that begins on an anniversary of the employee's date of employment before becoming eligible. The employer also has the choice of converting the computation period to a plan or calendar year basis (after the first 12 months of employment) provided that the beginning of such new computation period overlaps with the first employment year. In the case of seasonal industries where the customary period of employment is less than 1,000 hours during a calendar year, the term "year of service" will be determined by regulation. In the maritime industry, 125 days of service will be treated as the equivalent of 1,000 hours of service.

Service also includes periods of employment with any corporation or organization that is under common control (i.e., where there is 80 percent control). Service with a predecessor employer also must be taken into account if the employer maintains the plan of the predecessor; if the employer maintains a plan which is not the plan of the predecessor service with the predecessor will have to be considered to the extent prescribed in regulations.

Maximum Age

As previously indicated, the use of a maximum age as an eligibility requirement is of considerable cost significance in the case of defined benefit plans. Thus, an employer who is establishing such a plan must give serious thought to the maximum age provisions of the plan.

The cost of including older employees in the plan might prove to be prohibitive. This is particularly true for fully insured individual policy or group permanent plans since the time in which the necessary funds must be accumulated for an older employee is relatively short. This situation is alleviated somewhat in plans using a different funding instrument or where the normal retirement schedule for older employees is staggered so as to give the maximum period possible for accumulating the necessary funds. Even here, however, cost considerations may dictate that certain older employees be excluded from the plan. The problem is further complicated because these older employees may be the very reason that the employer is considering the adoption of a pension plan.

ERISA will not permit the use of a maximum age in a defined benefit plan (including a target benefit plan) that results in the exclusion of any employee hired more than five years before the plan's normal retirement date. Thus, in a plan that uses age 65 as the normal retirement age, the maximum age for entry cannot be lower than age 60. Also, if a defined benfit plan uses a normal retirement schedule of age 65 or the completion of 10 years of service, whichever is later, a maximum age is not possible. It should be noted that ERISA does not permit the use of a maximum age in any circumstances in the case of a defined contribution program (pension, profit sharing, or thrift and savings plan).

Just what should be done varies from case to case, keeping in mind the desires of the employer, the actual cost problems involved, the actuarial cost method used for the plan, and the funding instrument being employed. For example, a plan could be established with a high maximum age for employees on the effective date of the plan (e.g., age 65) but with a maximum age of 60 for future employees.

Earnings Requirement

Some plans require that an employee, to be eligible to participate in the plan, must be earning in excess of some amount such as the amount subject to social security tax. These plans, as well as those plans which provide a greater benefit for earnings over the social security taxable wage base than is provided for earnings under this amount, may qualify under the Internal Revenue Code. When a plan is limited in this fashion, it is required that the plan benefits must *integrate* with the benefits under the Social Security Act. The specific requirements for integrating plan benefits with social security benefits are discussed in the portion of this chapter which deals with benefit formulas.

It also is possible to use an earnings level other than the social security taxable wage base in determining whether an employee will be eligible to participate in the plan. However, such an earnings level is used infrequently.

Employment Classifications

At one time, it was quite common to establish plans with participation limited to salaried employees only. However, it has become increasingly more difficult to qualify plans with this limitation. As a general rule, if the salaried employees are all earning more than the hourly employees, the plan will not be acceptable to the Internal Revenue Service. The acceptability of such a plan increases, however, when the hourly employees earn substantially the same as some of the salaried employees.

Salaried-only plans also may be acceptable where the employer is already making contributions for the hourly employees as, for example, under a union-negotiated plan. Thus, if the salaried-only plan would not qualify on its own, i.e., it would not meet the requirements discussed above, it may still qualify if the plan covering the hourly employees provides contributions or benefits which are comparable to those being provided for salaried employees.

Under ERISA, a plan may exclude employees covered by a collective bargaining agreement if there is evidence of good faith bargaining on pensions. In many situations, this effectively will permit the establishment of a salaried-only plan, even in the absence of a plan providing comparable benefits or contributions for the noncovered employees.

It is possible for a plan to be established for only those employees who work in a specific plant or at a specific location, or who work in a specific occupation. These classifications are not used too frequently and, when used, must not produce discrimination in favor of the prohibited group of employees.

Aliens employed abroad by a branch of a U.S. employer may be excluded from coverage even through U.S. citizens at the branch are included in the plan.

RETIREMENT AGES

Normal Retirement Age

The normal retirement age in most plans is 65. The choice of this age is influenced not only by the fact that this is the age at which full social security benefits commence but also by the fact that retiring employees before age 65 and with full benefits often produces prohibitive costs. ERISA defines normal retirement age to be the age specified in the plan, but no later than age 65 or the completion of 10 years of participation, whichever is last to occur. Occasionally, an earlier age such as 60 will be chosen as the normal retirement age although, to a great extent, this practice has been confined to public, quasi-public, and charitable institutions. Also, in industries in which an employee's working career is shorter than in most other occupations, some plans provide for a normal retirement age which is lower than 65. It should be noted, however, that there has been a growing interest (both with management and employees) in retiring earlier than age 65—frequently by means of some form of subsidized early retirement benefit.

A few existing plans retire female employees at age 60 and male employees at age 65. However, this has been held to be in violation of Title VII of the Civil Rights Act and such plans are required to eliminate this provision, thus treating male and female employees alike.

In certain situations it is quite common to provide a staggered normal retirement schedule for older employees at the time the plan is established. A typical schedule would state that anyone over age 55 will retire at the end of 10 years of participation in the plan, or, if earlier, at age 70. Thus, an employee 56 years old at entry into the plan would retire at 66, while a person 61 would retire at 70. The use of a staggered normal retirement schedule accomplishes several things. First, the cost of providing a given amount of pension will decrease as the employee's normal retirement age increases. Second, it enables the employer to accumulate the cost of an older employee's pension over a longer period of time. Third, if the plan bases benefits on service or uses a defined contribution (money-purchase) formula, the employee will have an additional period of time in which to accrue benefits. Finally, both the employer and employee are given an adequate period of time in which to plan for the employee's retirement.

Early Retirement Age

Most plans provide that an employee may choose early retirement on a reduced pension, although a few plans limit this feature to cases of total and permanent disability. If an early retirement provision is to be included, it is customary to establish some requirements which an employee must fulfill before being allowed to elect early retirement.

A typical requirement for early retirement would be that the employee must have attained at least age 55 and must have completed at least 10 years of participation in the plan. Requirements such as these limit the option to situations where the employee is actually retiring, as opposed to changing jobs. They also tend to create a situation in which the employee will receive a reasonable benefit.

Employer consent generally is not required for early retirement. If employer consent is required, the Internal Revenue Service requires that the value of the benefit payable at early retirement be not greater than the value of the benefit which the employee would have received under the plan's vesting schedule had employment been terminated on the date of retirement.

The benefit payable at early retirement is reduced for two reasons. First, the full benefit will not have accrued by the employee's early retirement date. Second, the benefit, because it is starting several years earlier than anticipated, will be paid over a longer period of time. Thus, an actuarial reduction factor usually is applied to the value of the employee's accrued benefit to determine the amount of early retirement benefit.

Determining the value of the employee's accrued benefit is relatively simple under an allocated funding instrument. In a fully insured individual policy plan, for example, the value of the accrued benefit generally is the cash surrender value of the employee's insurance or annuity contract at the time of retirement. In this type of plan, the actuarial reduction is accomplished by the use of the settlement option rates contained in the contract. The employee's benefit generally is that amount which may be provided by applying the cash surrender value under the option at the employee's attained age on his or her retirement date.

In plans using an unallocated funding instrument, and where the benefit formula reflects the employee's service, the benefit generally is measured in terms of the employee's accrued service to the date of retirement. If the plan uses another type of formula, however, the determination of the value of the employee's accrued benefit is more difficult. One approach, which is used quite often, is to multiply the value of the employee's projected benefit at normal retirement date by a fraction, the numerator being the years of participation or service the employee has completed at early retirement date and the denominator the years of participation or service the employee would have completed at normal retirement date.

In any event, an employee's accrued benefit at early retirement must meet the accrued benefit requirements of ERISA that apply to vested benefits (discussed later in this chapter).

The reduction factor applied to the value of the employee's accrued benefit might be something as simple as a reduction of one half of 1 percent for each month by which early retirement precedes normal retirement; or, as often is the case, an actuarial reduction factor is determined from a table included in the plan or group contract. Table 2–2 shows

TABLE 2–2
Early Retirement Factors*

Years Prior to Normal Retirement Date†	Percentage	
	Male	Female
1	91.0	92.1
2	83.0	85.1
3	75.9	78.7
4	69.9	72.9
5	64.0	67.7
6	58.9	62.9
7	54.4	58.6
8	50.3	54.6
9	46.6	51.0
10	43.3	47.7

* Based on a normal retirement date of 65.
† Years prior to normal retirement date means years and complete months from early retirement date to normal retirement date. Allowance for such months is made by interpolating in the table.

a typical set of actuarial reduction factors which are based upon the 1951 Group Annuity Table with 4½ percent interest and which apply where the normal form for the payment of benefits is a pure life annuity.

As noted earlier, there has been a growing interest in recent years in the possibility of retiring earlier than age 65. While some plans actually establish a normal retirement age that is earlier than age 65, a greater number encourage early retirement by not applying a full actuarial reduction if certain conditions are met. One approach, for example, is to provide for no actuarial reduction at all if the employee retires after attaining some age (such as 60) and after completing some period of service (such as 30 years). A similar approach would be to apply no reduction factor (or a minimum factor) if early retirement occurs when the employee's age and service total to some number such as 90—e.g., an employee who is age 62 and who has completed 28 years of service would satisfy this requirement. Still another approach would be to apply some simple factor, such as one fourth of 1 percent for each month by which early retirement precedes normal retirement, that is considerably less than the reduction that would otherwise be called for by full actuarial reduction factors. Approaches such as these will, of course, increase the cost of the pension plan; however, employees generally find such a provision to be attractive, and quite frequently the employer finds that its overall interests are best served by a provision that encourages early retirement.

Late Retirement Age

Many plans also include a provision allowing an employee to defer his or her retirement. This feature could also be important to the employer, since it permits a greater degree of flexibility in scheduling the actual retirement of a key employee when there is a problem in obtaining or training a replacement.

The right to elect late retirement usually is subject to the employer's consent. While late retirement may be permitted on an unlimited basis as to point of time, it frequently is limited to some period of time after normal retirement date, such as five years.

The benefit payable at late retirement may be the same as would have been payable at the employee's normal retirement date (with the employer in some fashion receiving a credit toward contributions next due under the plan by reason of the excess values created by this provision), or the benefit may be an increased actuarial equivalent. It is even possible to provide that the employee may accrue additional pension credits for service performed between normal and late retirement dates. However, many pension authorities feel that if a pension plan is to accomplish its real purpose, the election of late retirement should not be made attractive to employees. These authorities feel that it generally is desirable that there be no increase in benefits at late retirement or, at the most, that the benefit at late retirement be no more than an actuarial equivalent of the benefit that would have been payable at normal retirement age; otherwise, there is too much of an incentive for the employee to remain employed.

RETIREMENT BENEFITS

The formula selected for determining an employee's retirement benefit is a vital provision in a pension plan. The employer's financial capacity and general philosophy concerning the desired level of retirement benefits, as well as the employer's specific objectives as to the distribution of benefits among employees all play an important role in selecting such a formula.

Many employers feel that a plan should be designed so as to provide a higher paid career employee with an income after retirement which, together with primary social security benefits, will be about 45 to 50 percent of earnings just before retirement. For lower paid employees, the percentage generally is set at a higher level—perhaps as much as 65 or 70 percent. For employees considered to be less than career employees (usually those employees with less than 25 or 30 years of service with the employer), these percentages would be proportionately smaller. From the employer's viewpoint, the benefit formula selected should in no event result in a plan which produces costs so high as to endanger the continuation of the plan when corporate earnings may be decreased or if current tax advantages may be reduced.

Basically, there are two types of benefit formulas for the employer to consider. The first is called a *defined contribution* or a *money-purchase* formula. Under this type of formula, contribution rates are fixed, and an employee's benefit varies depending upon such factors as the amount of the contributions made, investment earnings on plan assets, and the employee's age, sex, and normal retirement age. The second type is called a *defined benefit* or an *annuity purchase* formula. Here, a definite benefit is established for each employee, and contributions are determined to be whatever is necessary to produce the desired benefit results. Defined benefit formulas may be subdivided into several different classifications.[2]

Determination of Earnings

Since the amount of benefit under most formulas is based on an employee's compensation, it is important, before discussing specific formulas, to have a clear idea of the various considerations involved in selecting the earnings base to which the benefit formula will be applied.

Normally, only basic compensation is considered for benefit purposes. Thus, bonuses and other forms of extraordinary compensation are not included. As a matter of fact, the inclusion of these additional items of compensation might receive special attention from the Internal Revenue Service, since the inclusion of bonus and incentive pay could very easily lead to a plan which discriminates in favor of the prohibited group

---

[2] It has been said that a third type of benefit formula is emerging—one in which the employee's benefit will vary depending upon the performance of the common stock market or upon changes in a cost of living index. Actually, this is not so, since variable benefit plans involve either a defined contribution or a defined benefit formula.

of employees. Under a discretionary bonus formula, for example, employees in the prohibited group may tend to receive proportionately greater bonus payments than other employees. Thus, although the plan benefit formula otherwise appears acceptable when applied to base earnings, it could produce disproportionate benefits for key employees when applied to total earnings. On the other hand, if the plan formula is integrated with social security benefits, the Internal Revenue Service may require that total compensation (including overtime pay) be used unless it can be demonstrated that a more restrictive definition of compensation does not result in prohibited discrimination.

Determining the earnings of employees paid on a commission basis can be a difficult problem because of the variation in their total earnings from year to year. Where the employee is paid a basic salary plus commissions, some plans apply the benefit formula only to basic salary. This approach, however, often produces inequitable results, since the employee's true compensation and worth to the employer are reflected by total earnings, and not by basic salary. Another frequently used solution is to consider as compensation in any year the annual average of the total compensation paid to the employee over the preceding three- or five-year period. In plans where sales personnel constitute a major portion of the total employees covered, this problem often dictates the selection of a defined contribution formula in which the amount contributed each year for each employee is a percentage of what the employee actually earned in that year. In any event, it is customary to exclude any portion of the employee's compensation which is allowed for expenses.

Another aspect of the problem of determining the earnings to be used for the benefit formula is the question of whether plan benefits should be based on the average of the earnings paid over the entire period of the employee's participation in the plan or on an average of the employee's earnings during some shorter period of time which is near the employee's normal retirement age. The latter type of provision, often called a final-pay provision, would base benefits on the employee's earnings averaged, for example, over the last five years of employment or over the five consecutive years in the ten-year period immediately prior to retirement during which the employee's earnings are the highest.

The advantage of a final-pay plan is that it relates benefits to the employee's earnings and standard of living during a period just preceding retirement. As a result, the employee's benefits keep pace with any inflationary or deflationary trends. Moreover, a final-pay plan is more likely to meet employer objectives as to benefit levels than is a career-pay plan. This type of plan, however, is usually more expensive than one which bases benefits on career average earnings. It also can create funding problems under certain funding instruments if additional benefits for an employee must be paid for in the short time before retirement. Many employers feel that it is best to use a career average earnings plan and to make periodic adjustments in the benefit formula when economic trends justify such an action.

While a final-pay plan has the disadvantage of committing an employer to increased costs during an extended inflationary period, it should be remembered that in many situations the employer's capacity to absorb these increases also will be increased, particularly if plan assets have been invested in equities. Moreover, a final-pay plan generally produces more favorable results for key employees than the career average approach.

A final point to be noted concerns the requirement of ERISA that an employee's *normal* retirement benefit can never be less than the highest early retirement benefit that he or she could have received. Thus, any salary reductions that occur after an employee first becomes eligible to retire early cannot have the effect of reducing the employee's *normal* retirement benefit (although they could be reflected in determining the level of subsequent *early* retirement benefits).

Defined Contribution Formulas

As previously noted, a defined contribution formula does not provide a fixed benefit for employees. Instead, the rate of contribution of the employer is fixed, usually as a percentage of the employee's earnings, and this contribution is applied (together with the employee's contribution under a contributory plan) to provide whatever pension benefits can be purchased. Since the cost of a given amount of benefit varies by age, sex, and normal retirement age, the benefits for any employee depends upon these factors, as well as contribution levels and investment income.

Defined contribution plans often are contributory. In this case, the employer's contribution either matches or is a multiple of the employee's contribution. For example, the plan could call for the employer and employee each to contribute 5 percent of the employee's compensation; or the employee's contribution could be set at 3 percent of compensation with the employer contributing 6 percent. In fully insured individual policy plans, these contributions usually are applied as a level premium to purchase the amount of insurance available based on the employee's age, sex, and normal retirement age. If the plan utilizes a group deferred annuity contract, these contributions are applied each year to purchase a unit of paid-up deferred annuity for whatever amount can be provided under the insurer's rates, depending upon these same factors. In plans using other funding instruments, the contributions usually are accumulated and are applied at retirement, together with investment earnings, to provide such benefit as may then be available, depending upon the manner of payout contemplated by the plan.

The defined contribution formula has been employed primarily by nonprofit organizations where there often is a need, because of cost considerations, to be able to predict future plan liabilities with some degree of certainty. It also has been used to some extent in plans adopted by professional associations or corporations and, because of the limitation on deductions that apply to the shareholders of Subchapter S corporations, it is expected that the defined contribution formula will become more widely used in plans adopted by such organizations.[3] The requirements of ERISA that apply to defined benefit plans (e.g., minimum funding, liabilities on plan termination) also suggest that the defined contribution plan will become more popular for regular corporate plans. However, it should be recognized that this formula has several inherent limitations. The first of these is that an employee who joins the plan at an older age will have only a short period of time in which to accumulate funds, with the result that the employee's benefit often will be inadequate. Since the owners of a business often are advanced in years when a plan is being established, and since a defined benefit formula generally produces more favorable results for them, it is not hard to see why they frequently find little appeal in a defined contribution formula. It is possible, of course, to include a past service benefit at the time the plan is established; on balance, however, most firms still find a defined benefit formula to be more desirable from this point of view.[4] Table 2–3 indicates the results which could flow under a defined contribution formula and the disparity in benefits that often is produced in such a plan. This table assumes that the compensation shown for each employee will continue until normal retirement; that the contribution made by the employer each year is 10 percent of the employee's compensation; that this contribution will accumulate at 5 percent compound interest until retirement; and that the fund accumulated at retirement will be applied under representative annuity purchase rates to provide a monthly retirement benefit.

---

[3] ERISA limits the annual *deduction* for the contribution made on behalf of an employee who owns more than 5 percent of the stock of a Subchapter S corporation to the lesser of: (*a*) $7,500, and (*b*) 15 percent of the employee's compensation for the year up to $100,000. A similar limitation does not apply to the shareholders of a professional corporation; however, the annual contribution on behalf of such individuals is limited to 25 percent of compensation or $25,000 (or such higher amount as is permitted by Treasury regulation to adjust for cost-of-living increases), whichever is less. The deduction limit for stockholders of a Subchapter S corporation may also be set within the limits applicable to defined benefit plans for self-employed individuals.

[4] The so-called target plan (which is basically a variable benefit plan) has appeal in this type of situation. Under such a plan, a defined benefit is established for each employee. Depending upon the funding instrument and actuarial cost method employed, a contribution to provide this benefit is determined. This contribution (along with future contributions) is invested in a variable account and, depending upon the investment results of the account, can provide more (or less) than the original target benefit.

TABLE 2–3
Illustration of Defined Contribution Formula

Age at Entry	Sex	Normal Retire- ment Age	Compen- sation	Contribu- tion	Fund at Retirement	Monthly Benefit	Benefit as a Percent of Compen- sation
25	F	65	$ 8,000	$ 800	$101,472	$659	98.9%
30	M	65	12,000	1,200	113,804	835	83.5
40	M	65	14,000	1,400	70,187	515	44.2
45	M	65	9,500	950	32,983	242	30.6
45	F	65	9,500	950	32,983	214	27.1
53	M	65	30,000	3,000	50,139	368	14.7
55	M	65	12,000	1,200	15,848	116	11.6

As Table 2–3 shows, younger employees have a much longer time to accumulate funds and will receive a proportionately larger benefit. Moreover, the defined contribution plan has an additional weakness since, because of the effect of compound interest, greater weight is given to the employee's lower compensation at the younger age than will be given to the higher compensation the employee is likely to receive when he or she is older.

This table also indicates the difference in results due to the sex of the employee. The two employees shown in the table who are age 45 have identical compensation and thus have accumulated identically the same amount by retirement. However, the female employee will receive a smaller monthly benefit because she is expected to live longer under the annuity table employed to determine benefits. While it is true that the benefits are equivalent in value, it is questionable, from a pension planning viewpoint, that there should be a difference in benefits due to the sex of the employee. It would seem reasonable that benefit levels should be the same regardless of sex, and that cost differences due to this factor should be absorbed by the employer.

Another observation that should be made about the deficiencies of a defined contribution formula is that with many types of funding instruments and actuarial cost methods, the employee's benefit under this formula can only be estimated. This lack of certainty as to benefits could prove to be an unsatisfactory employee relations feature of such a plan. Finally, the variations in benefit levels for different employees make it difficult, if not impossible, to design a formula that produces benefit levels that are uniformly responsive to employer objectives.

Union-negotiated plans, particularly multiemployer plans, possess characteristics of both defined contribution and defined benefit plans. In many of these situations, an employer's contribution to the plan is fixed, most frequently as a contribution of so many cents for each hour worked by each covered employee or as a percentage of compensation. An actuarial cost method, with appropriate actuarial assumptions, is then employed to make an estimate as to the benefit levels the aggregate employer contributions will provide. The plan is then established with a defined benefit formula, even though funds are received on a defined contribution basis. Only rarely will it turn out that the contribution level will precisely support the benefit level so determined, with the result that future contributions or benefits, or both, are adjusted periodically to conform with the actual experience of the plan.

Defined Benefit Formulas

Broadly speaking, there are four basic defined benefit formulas. These include: (1) a flat amount formula, which provides a flat benefit unrelated to an employee's earnings or service; (2) a flat percentage of earnings formula, which provides a benefit related to the employee's earnings but which does not reflect service; (3) a flat amount per year of service formula, which reflects an employee's service but not earnings; and (4) a percentage of earnings per year of service formula, which reflects both an employee's earnings and service. Defined benefit formulas also may be integrated with social security benefits; however, since the requirements for integrated formulas are detailed and specific, they are discussed separately in this chapter.

Flat Amount Formula. As indicated above, this type of formula provides for a flat benefit which treats all employees alike, regardless of their service, age, or earnings. For example, the benefit might be $75 or $100 a month. The flat amount formula, since it is considered to produce inequitable results, seldom is used by itself, although it is still found in some negotiated plans, particularly in the case of multiemployer plans. The likelihood of fairly comparable wage rates for all employees in the bargaining unit minimizes the potential problem of inequities produced by a flat amount formula. On occasion, this formula is used in conjunction with some other type of formula; for example, a plan may provide a flat benefit of $75 a month for a covered employee, plus a percentage of his or her earnings in excess of the current social security taxable wage base.

While the employee's length of service is not reflected directly in this type of formula, service is in effect recognized since most plans require that an employee, upon attaining the normal retirement age specified by the plan, must have been employed for some period of time, such as 25 years. Plans which include such a requirement provide for a proportionately reduced benefit if the employee has accumulated less than the required number of years, thus creating, in effect, a formula which is weighted for service.

Flat Percentage of Earnings Formula. This type of formula is used frequently today, particularly in plans which cover salaried or clerical employees. Some percentage of earnings, usually ranging from 20 to 40 percent, is selected as the measure of the pension benefit. It may be used with either career average or final average earnings, although it is used most frequently in final pay plans.

This type of formula does not take an employee's service into account, except in those plans which require that the employee must have completed a minimum period of service by normal retirement date and which provide for a proportionately reduced benefit if his or her service is less than the required number of years.

An administrative device that can be used with many formulas, but which frequently is employed with the flat percentage of earnings formula, is the "earnings bracket" schedule. Instead of using actual earnings under the benefit formula, the benefit is determined by an earnings bracket approach and is expressed as a dollar amount per bracket of earnings. Table 2–4 shows a typical earnings bracket schedule. Actually,

TABLE 2–4
Illustrative Earnings Bracket Schedule

Earnings	*Monthly Pension*
$350–$383.	$110
384– 416.	120
417– 449.	130
450– 483.	140
484– 516.	150

a 30 percent of earnings formula has been applied to the midpoint of each earnings bracket.

Flat Amount per Year of Service Formula. This type of formula is often found in negotiated plans. It provides a flat dollar amount for each year of service accumulated by the employee. The dollar amount varies from plan to plan, but a benefit of $8 or $10 or even as much as $12 or $14 a month for each year of service is not uncommon. Thus, in a plan which provides for a benefit of $10 a month for each year of service, an employee with 27 years of employment would receive a monthly pension of $270.

This type of formula frequently requires that an employee must have worked for a minimum number of hours during a plan year in order to receive a full benefit credit for such year. Minimums often used for this purpose are 1,600 and 1,800 hours. An employee who works less than the required number of hours in a given year, usually receives some proportionate credit for the actual hours worked. ERISA requires that a proportionate credit be given if the employee works at least 1,000 hours in the 12-month computation period used by the plan.

Some plans limit benefits to service performed after the plan was made effective, although in most cases credit is given for service prior to the inception of the plan. When this is done, credit may or may not be given for service needed to meet any eligibility requirements of the plan. Also, it is not uncommon to include a provision which limits the total service which may be credited for benefit purposes to a period such as 30 years.

Percentage of Earnings per Year of Service Formula. A formula which gives specific recognition for service as well as earnings is considered by many pension practitioners to produce the most equitable results in terms of a benefit formula that provides benefits for employees in relation to their value or contributions to the firm. A formula producing this result often is called a "unit credit" or "past and future service" formula. Under such a formula, an employee receives a benefit credit equal to a percentage of earnings for each year that he or she is a participant under the plan. This benefit credit is called the employee's future service or current service benefit. The percentage of earnings credited varies from plan to plan, but a typical percentage would be 1 percent or 1¼ percent. It may be used with either career average or final earnings, and works particularly well with career average plans.

Many plans also include a "past service" benefit for employees who enter the plan on its effective date. In a plan which bases future service benefits on career average earnings, the past service benefit usually is expressed as a fixed percentage of the employee's earnings on the effective date of the plan multiplied by the employee's years of past service. In determining past service benefits, however, it is customary to exclude service that would have been required in order to join the plan had it always been in effect. It is also possible to limit the total years of past service credited. For example, past service could be limited to a given number of years (such as 10), to service completed after a certain calendar year (such as the year in which the firm was acquired by the current ownership interests), to service completed after attaining a certain age (such as 25), or to a combination of these factors. The percentage applied to earnings to determine past service benefits usually is a lower rate than is applied for future service benefits. The reason for this is that the earnings of an employee on the effective date of the plan generally are higher than the average of the employee's earnings over the period of his or her past service. Rather than determine the employee's actual average earnings during his or her past service, which often is difficult or even impossible because of the lack of records, a rough approximation is made by reducing the percentage applicable to the employee's higher earnings at the time the plan is established.

If the plan bases benefits on final earnings, a distinction is not usually made between past and future service benefits. Here, the employee's total service (subject to any limitations such as excluding service needed to meet eligibility requirements or such as a maximum service credit provision) is applied to the percentage of final earnings to determine his or her total retirement benefit.

To illustrate the operation of a past and future service formula in a career average earnings plan, assume that the benefit formula of a plan provides a monthly pension of one half of 1 percent of a participant's earnings on the effective date of the plan multiplied by the employee's years of past service, and a future service benefit of 1 percent of earnings during each year that the employee is a participant. The plan has an eligibility requirement of one year of service, and service needed to meet this requirement is excluded when determining the employee's total past service. Normal retirement under the plan will occur at 65. Table 2–5 shows how the monthly pension benefit would be calcu-

TABLE 2–5
Past and Future Service Formula

(1) Years of Total Past Service	(2) Years of Credited Past Service	(3) Monthly Earnings	(4) Past Service Benefit (2) × (3) × ½%	(5) Years of Future Service	(6) Future Service Benefit (3) × (5) × 1%	(7) Total Benefit (4) + (6)
20	19	$1,000	$95	25	$250	$345

lated for a 40-year-old employee who had 20 years of service when he joined the plan at its inception date. This table assumes, for illustrative purposes, that the employee's monthly earnings are $1,000 and remain constant at this level during the period of future service.

A formula that weights both earnings and service is used in a great many plans today. However, if a firm is considering the adoption of a plan shortly after incorporation, and if the former proprietor or the former partners are advanced in years, this formula might produce inadequate results, since the service of such an employee may be measured only from the date of incorporation. In this situation, a flat percentage of earnings formula is often adopted if it would produce more substantial benefits for the stockholder employees.

Variable Benefit Formulas. Variable benefit plans are a relatively recent development in the pension field. These plans are designed to protect against the effects of inflation on a retired employee's pension benefit.

They take either of two general forms: (*a*) the benefit varies to reflect changes in the value of a specific portfolio of common stocks and similar investments, or (*b*) the benefit varies to reflect changes in a recognized cost of living index such as that published by the Bureau of Labor Statistics. In either case, the plan attempts to adjust benefits to keep an employee's purchasing power on a relatively level basis. These plans are discussed in greater detail in Chapter 9.

Integrated Formulas

For most individuals, retirement income will be derived from both social security benefits and private pension plans. Since the employer bears part of the cost of social security benefits, it is only logical for the employer to recognize these benefits in the benefit formula of the plan. Thus, it is not uncommon for an employer to establish a retirement plan on a basis which excludes employees whose earnings are less than the social security taxable wage base. An alternative and more prevalent approach is to provide a higher level of benefits for earnings above this taxable wage base than is provided for earnings below this amount. While at first glance such a plan would appear to discriminate in favor of highly paid employees, federal tax law expressly permits this type of plan provided the benefit formula *integrates* with social security benefits. The basic concept of integration is that the benefits of the employer's plan must be dovetailed with social security benefits in such a manner that employees earning over the taxable wage base will not receive combined benefits under the two programs which are proportionately greater than the benefits for employees earning less than this amount. Therefore, although the benefit formula under the private plan may favor the higher paid employees, the combined social security and private plan benefits must produce a total retirement income that is a relatively equal percentage of compensation for all employees. Thus, the integration requirements are designed to prevent discrimination in favor of the prohibited group of employees.

These requirements take the form of establishing the maximum benefits which may be provided for employees under various circumstances. In arriving at these maximums, a value is placed on the employee's total social security benefits. Essentially, these benefits are valued at 162 percent of the employee's maximum primary benefit. This amount, in turn, is 70 percent of the average monthly wage on which the employee's social security benefit is computed. However, the integration rules reflect the fact that employees also pay a social security tax. Since the tax rate is divided equally between employers and employees, the 70 percent figure is reduced by 50 percent, to a resulting figure of 35 percent. In recognition of possible future increases in social security benefits, the 35 percent figure was raised to 37.5 percent. Thus, for integration purposes, social security benefits currently are considered to be worth 37.5 percent of the average monthly wage on which social security benefits are computed. This percentage, however, applies only to a pure life annuity plan without integrated death or disability benefits. If the plan includes such benefits, this percentage is reduced.

It is important to note that an employee's *average monthly wage* for social security purposes is not the same as his or her current social security *taxable wage base*. This, of course, is due to the fact that when computing an employee's average monthly wage, only earnings which have been subject to social security tax are taken into account. Since the taxable wage bases in prior years were lower than the current taxable wage base, it is impossible, under current social security laws, to develop an average monthly wage equal to the current taxable wage base until the 21st century. For this reason, the provisions of federal tax law relating to integration set forth a schedule showing the maximum average wage for each year of retirement. Thus, the year in which an employee reaches age 65 determines the earnings level for testing integration. This schedule refers to the maximum average wage as *covered compensation* and sets forth covered compensation levels ranging from $7,356 for the year 1976 up to $15,300 for the year 2011. Alternatively, the tax rulings also permit the use of a simpler covered compensation schedule that establishes fewer separate integration periods and applicable covered compensation levels. This simpler schedule is set forth in Table 2–6.[5]

The following is by no means an exhaustive discussion of the integration requirements of federal tax law. It does, however, point out the major requirements for typical integrated formulas. It also assumes that normal retirement under the plan will not occur before age 65 and that employees will not make contributions.[6]

Flat Percentage–Excess.   In plans of this type, benefits are provided only with respect to final average pay in excess of the appropriate covered compensation level or some stated dollar amount that is uniformly applied to all employees. In a plan that provides no integrated death or disability benefits, the maximum percentage that can be provided for final average pay in excess of the appropriate covered compensation level is 37.5 percent. (The appropriate covered compensation level for a particular plan will be determined by the first year in which it is possible

---

[5] In 1975, the Internal Revenue Service had not updated its covered compensation schedules to reflect increases in social security benefits. The levels described in this chapter (including Table 2–6) are unofficial modifications of the published levels.

[6] A decrease in the allowable benefit is required when normal retirement may occur before 65 or when retirement at ages below 65 is permitted on a basis which provides benefits that are higher than the actuarial equivalent of an employee's accrued benefit. An increase in the allowable benefit is permitted when employees contribute.

TABLE 2–6
Schedule of Integration Periods and Applicable
Covered Compensation Levels

Period Employee Reaches Age 65	*Covered Compensation*
1976	$ 7,200
1977	7,800
1978–1979	8,400
1980–1981	9,000
1982–1983	9,600
1984–1987	10,200
1988–1991	10,800
1992–1994	11,400
1995–1996	12,000
1997–1998	12,600
1999–2000	13,200
2001–2003	13,800
2004–2006	14,400
2007–2010	15,000
2011 or later	15,300

for an employee or future employee to retire at age 65 under the plan provisions.) If the plan provides benefits for final average pay in excess of some amount that is higher than the appropriate covered compensation level, the maximum percentage must be reduced. This is done by multiplying 37.5 percent by a fraction, the numerator of which is the appropriate covered compensation level for the plan and the denominator of which is the level actually set in the plan. Thus, for example, if the appropriate covered compensation level for a plan is $7,200 and the plan provides benefits only for final average pay in excess of $10,000 the maximum percentage for the plan would be 72 percent of 37.5 percent, or 27 percent.

Several important requirements must be observed if a flat percentage–excess plan is to completely meet the integration requirements of federal tax law:

1. The plan benefit must be based on *average* pay that is determined over a period of at least five *consecutive* years.[7]
2. This employee must have completed at least 15 years of service with the employer (not necessarily as a participant in the plan) in order to qualify for the maximum percentage. For an employee with less than 15 years of service, a proportionate reduction in benefits must be made.

---

[7] It is permissible to use four or three consecutive years in the averaging period; however, the maximum percentage will be reduced by 5 or 10 percent, respectively, if this is done.

3. Benefits payable in the event of early retirement or termination of employment cannot exceed the actuarial equivalent of the maximum normal retirement benefits multiplied by a fraction the numerator of which is the actual number of years of service completed by the employee at early retirement or termination, and the denominator of which is the total number of years of service the employee would have completed at normal retirement.

Flat Percentage–Stepped Up.   Under a plan of this type, all earnings are taken into account in applying the plan formula; however, the formula contains two percentages—a lower percentage for earnings up to some stipulated level and a higher percentage for earnings in excess of this amount. For integration purposes, the lower percentage is considered a base plan, applicable to all earnings, and only the excess portion must meet the requirements previously discussed. To illustrate, if a plan provides for a monthly benefit of 10 percent of the first $600 of final average pay plus 40 percent of such pay in excess of $600, the plan, for the purpose of meeting integration requirements, would be considered as a flat percentage–excess plan of 30 percent of final average pay in excess of $600. This portion, then, would have to meet the requirements set forth above.

Unit Credit–Excess.   A unit credit–excess plan provides a pension benefit of some percentage of average pay in excess of a stipulated amount for each year of credited service. An important factor in determining the maximum percentage applicable to such a plan is whether the plan bases benefits on career average or final average pay. For a career pay plan, the maximum percentage applicable to each year of future service is 1.4 percent of the employee's earnings in excess of the current social security taxable wage base. There is no limit as to the number of years of service that may receive benefit credit. This maximum percentage is applicable only in a plan without integrated death or disability benefits.

For a final average pay plan with no integrated death or disability benefits, the maximum percentage to be applied to excess earnings is 1 percent, with no limit on the number of years of service that may be credited for benefit purposes. However, unlike the unit credit career pay plan, this percentage can apply only to compensation in excess of the appropriate covered compensation level; and, if a higher level is used, the percentage must be reduced in the same manner applicable to a flat percentage–excess plan; i.e., the 1 percent is multiplied by a fraction the numerator of which is the appropriate covered compensation level and the denominator of which is the actual level being used by the plan.

It should be noted that a unit credit final average pay excess plan may still be acceptable, even though it does not meet the foregoing rules, if it satisfies the requirements for a flat percentage–excess plan. This could be the case where there is a limit on the number of years of service that will be credited for benefit purposes. In this event, the appropriate maximum percentage for the flat percentage–excess plan is divided by the maximum number of years of credited service under the plan. To illustrate, a unit credit final pay excess plan with an applicable covered compensation level of $7,200 that provides a monthly benefit of three fourths of 1 percent of monthly final average pay in excess of $833 for each year of service up to 30 years would meet the integration requirements (assuming that no integrated death or disability benefits are included in the plan). Such a formula would not meet the normal test applicable to such a plan—i.e., the maximum allowable percentage would be only 72 percent of one percent (the ratio of the covered compensation of $7200 to the actual compensation breakpoint of $10,000). However, it does satisfy the requirements of a flat percentage–excess plan, since 72 percent of 37.5 percent is 27 percent, and 27 percent divided by 30 (the maximum years of credited service) results in an allowable maximum percentage of nine tenths of 1 percent—a percentage in excess of that set forth in the plan formula. When a unit credit–excess plan in integrated under the requirements relating to a flat percentage–excess plan, it is necessary that the benefits payable in the event of early retirement or termination of employment be limited to the actuarial equivalent of the maximum projected normal retirement benefits multiplied by a fraction the numerator of which is the actual number of years of service completed by the employee at early retirement or termination and the denominator of which is the total number of years of service the employee would have completed at normal retirement. This restriction does not apply to other unit credit–excess plans, where the benefit payable in the event of early retirement or termination of employment may be based upon the benefit accrued by the employee under the plan formula up to the time of retirement or termination of employment.

Just as with a flat percentage–excess plan, a unit credit final average pay excess plan must base benefits on an average pay that is determined over a period of at least five consecutive years.[8]

Unit Credit–Stepped Up. As is the case with a flat percentage–stepped up formula, a unit credit–stepped up plan bases benefits on all earnings but applies two percentages—a lower percentage with respect to earnings up to some stipulated amount and a higher percentage for earnings in excess of this level. Again, for integration purposes, the lower percentage is considered a base plan applicable to all earnings, and only the excess

---

[8] If the otherwise allowable limit is reduced by 5 or 10 percent, respectively, an averaging period of four or three consecutive years may be used.

portion must meet the requirements previously described for a unit credit–excess plan.

Social Security Offset. Many plans provide a retirement benefit inclusive of benefits payable under the Social Security Act. This type of formula deducts a percentage of the employee's primary social security benefit from the pension benefit which would otherwise be payable under the plan. In other words, any of the earlier described formulas can be used, with social security benefits being deducted from the amount of benefit the formula would otherwise provide. Only the employee's primary insurance amount (i.e., exclusive of dependent's benefits) is taken into account for this purpose. The integration limit in these plans applies not to the percentage of compensation being credited, but to the percentage of the permissible social security offset. For a plan without integrated death or disability benefits, the maximum offset is 83⅓ percent of the employee's primary insurance amount if the offset is based on the benefits payable under the social security laws in effect when the employee retires. If the offset is based on the benefits payable under the 1967 social security amendments, the maximum offset is 105 percent of the employee's primary insurance amount; if based on the 1969 social security amendments, the maximum offset is 92 percent of the primary insurance amount.

It should be noted that the integration rules as such do not require an offset plan to base benefits on a final average pay determined over any specific period of time. Also, the 15 years of service requirement for full benefits does not apply to this type of formula.

Defined Contribution Formulas. It also is possible to integrate defined contribution formulas with social security benefits. If no contribution is being made for earnings up to the current social security taxable wage base, the maximum percentage which may be contributed for earnings in excess of this amount is 7 percent. If a contribution is being made for earnings below the social security taxable wage base, the percentage applicable to earnings above this amount may be increased by the amount of this base contribution.

Death Benefits. If a pension plan provides for the payment of employer-provided integrated death benefits (other than a return of employee contributions with interest) either before or after retirement, the maximum percentages otherwise determined must be reduced, depending upon the level and type of death benefit provided. This reduction is accomplished by multiplying the otherwise allowable percentage by an appropriate factor. In the case of a preretirement spouse benefit in the form of a life income equal to a percentage of the employee's accrued pension, a formula is employed to determine the factor. This formula is $7 \div (7 + 2k)$, where k is the percentage of accrued pension payable to the spouse. Thus, in the case of a 50 percent continuation, the factor is 87.5 percent $(7 \div [7 + 2 \times \frac{1}{2}] = 7 \div 8 = 87.5\%)$. Factors for other forms of death benefits are set forth in Table 2–7. It should be noted that if a plan provides for both a pre- and postretirement death benefit, both reduction factors must be employed.

TABLE 2–7
Reduction Factors for the Inclusion of Death Benefits in
Integrated Plans

Type of Death Benefit	*Reduction Factor*
Preretirement:	
Amount not exceeding reserve	89%
Amount equal to 100 multiplied by expected monthly pension	80
Amount equal to greater of reserve or 100 multiplied by expected monthly pension	78
Postretirement:	
Life annuity with 5 years certain	97
Life annuity with 10 years certain	90
Life annuity with 15 years certain	80
Life annuity with 20 years certain	70
Life annuity with installment refund.	90
Life annuity with cash refund.	85
Life annuity with 50% continued to surviving spouse	80

If any part of the death benefit consists of pure life insurance, the cost of which was includable in the employee's taxable income, no reduction is required with respect to this portion of the death benefit. Also, it is not necessary to apply reduction factors if the only form of postretirement death benefit is that which might be created under an optional form of payment on an actuarially equivalent basis. Finally, it is not necessary to adjust the maximum permissible contribution under an integrated defined contribution formula if any form of death benefit is included. The reason, essentially, is that since the contribution is fixed, these features automatically affect the amount of the employee's retirement benefit.

Disability Benefits. If a pension plan contains an integrated benefit payable before age 65 in the event of disability, the maximum percentage otherwise applicable for normal retirement benefits must be reduced by 10 percent—i.e., the maximum percentage is multiplied by 90 percent. The integrated disability benefit itself also must satisfy integration requirements. The preretirement disability benefit under an excess plan cannot be greater than the employee's accrued benefit (without actuarial reduction) or a percentage of the employee's projected pension. This percentage is the greater of 70 percent or the percentage derived by dividing the employee's actual service by his or her projected service.

If the preretirement disability benefit offsets social security benefits, the maximum offset permitted before age 65 is 64 percent of the employee's primary social security benefit; a 75 percent offset is permitted after age 65.

It should be noted that these rules apply only when plan disability benefits are payable for a disability that also qualifies the employee for social security disability benefits. If disability benefits may be payable to employees who do not satisfy the eligibility requirements for social security disability benefits, then for integration purposes they are treated as early retirement benefits.

Variable Benefit Plans. If the base investment rate under a variable annuity plan is at least 5.5 percent, the maximum integration percentages are the same as for a regular defined benefit plan.[9] At lower base investment rates, the maximum integration percentages must be reduced by one fifteenth for each one half of 1 percent that the base investment rate is less than 5.5 percent.

Minimum Benefits

Closely related to the choice of an adequate benefit formula is the question of whether or not provision for a minimum pension should be included in the plan.

A minimum pension provision generally is a desirable feature of any pension plan. It often is possible for a benefit formula to produce a very small pension benefit as applied to certain employees. The use of a minimum pension can result in the payment of at least a minimum amount to these employees, while at the same time avoiding the embarrassment and ill will that might otherwise be generated in these situations. Apart from these considerations, if the plan is insured, the insurer may insist on the inclusion of a minimum pension provision as a part of its general underwriting requirements—particularly in the case of a plan funded with individual policies. The minimum most frequently used is $20 a month.

Limits on Benefits and Contributions

ERISA imposed limits on the benefits and contributions that can be provided under qualified plans. For a defined benefit plan, the annual employer-provided benefit for an employee cannot exceed $75,000 (adjusted for future increases in the Consumer Price Index) or, if lesser, 100 percent of the employee's average annual pay for the three consecu-

---

[9] The base investment rate for a variable annuity is the assumed rate with which actual investment yields are compared to determine future changes in benefits.

tive years of highest pay.[10] These limits do not apply to employee-provided benefits and need not be adjusted for preretirement ancillary benefits such as death or disability benefits. If early retirement cannot occur before age 55, no adjustment need be made even for subsidized early retirement benefits; however, if retirement can occur prior to age 55, the $75,000 limit must be actuarially reduced. The limits are reduced proportionately if the employee completes less than 10 years of service before retirement. The limits also must be reduced for the value of any pension-related, postretirement death benefits; however, a reduction will not be required if payments are made on a joint and survivor basis (even if the percentage continued is 100 percent) and the joint annuitant is the employee's spouse.

In the case of a defined contribution plan (including a target benefit plan), the limitation is expressed in terms of the maximum annual addition that may be made to the employee's account. This maximum annual addition is limited to the lesser of 25 percent of annual pay or $25,000 (adjusted for future increases in the Consumer Price Index). The annual addition is defined to include employer contributions and (in the case of profit sharing and thrift and savings plans) reallocated forfeitures. In some situations, part of the employee's own contributions will be considered as part of the annual addition. If the employee's contributions do not exceed 6 percent of pay, no part of such contributions will be taken into account; if they exceed 6 percent of pay, the lesser of the employee's contributions that exceed 6 percent of pay or 50 percent of the total employee contributions will be considered as part of the annual addition.

If the employer maintains both a defined benefit and a defined contribution plan, there will be a combined limit of 140 percent of the limits considered individually. The combined limit is applied on a cumulative basis that reflects the maximum allowable amounts for years of prior service. The application of this combined limit might best be illustrated by the following example which, for the sake of simplicity, ignores the cumulative aspects of the limit. Under the employer's profit sharing plan, a highly paid employee will receive a contribution of 12½ percent of annual pay. This contribution equals 50 percent of the limit otherwise allowable for a defined contribution plan (12½% ÷ 25%). The allowable limit for the defined benefit plan for this employee will be 90 percent of the otherwise allowable limit (140% − 50%). Thus, if the employee would otherwise have been entitled to an annual pension of $75,000,

---

[10] If an employee has never been covered by a defined contribution plan, an annual pension of up to $10,000 can be paid even if it exceeds 100 percent of pay. Also, a special maximum provision applies to plans in existence on October 2, 1973. Under such a plan, an annual pension can be paid to an employee in excess of these limits (but not in excess of the employee's pay on October 2, 1973) if it is calculated in accordance with the plan provisions and the employee's pay ignoring any changes in either that occurred after October 2, 1973.

this will be reduced to $67,500 (90 percent of $75,000). Actually, the plans can be structured to apply the combined limit to either of the two plans.

Where the combined limit is applicable, the employer may establish an excess benefit plan to restore the benefits or contributions lost by reason of the application of the limit. Such a plan is not subject to the provisions of ERISA, but may not be qualified or prefunded on a tax deductible basis.

If an employee is participating in the plans of another incorporated or unincorporated business under common control (only a 50 percent interest is necessary for this purpose), the plans of all such businesses must be aggregated for purposes of applying the limitations on benefits and contributions.

DEATH BENEFITS

An employer-provided death benefit is an optional benefit under a pension plan; however, a great many plans include such a benefit. Broadly speaking, such a death benefit may take either of two forms—the first consists of life insurance which is provided under some form of individual policy or group life insurance contract issued by an insurer, and the second consists of cash distributions from plan assets. Death benefits also may be classified as being payable in the event of death either before or after retirement.

Death benefits provided under individual policy plans and death benefits which are provided from plan assets are considered to be a part of the plan and, as such, are subject to the requirement of the Internal Revenue Service that the death benefit must be "incidental." In a defined benefit plan using life insurance, the incidental test is satisfied if the benefit does not exceed 100 times the expected monthly pension benefit or, if greater, the reserve for the pension benefit. In a defined contribution plan which includes life insurance benefits, this test is satisfied if: (1) the aggregate of the premiums paid for a participant's life insurance is *less than* one half of the contributions allocated to him at any particular time; and (2) the plan requires the trustee to convert the entire value of the life insurance contract at or before retirement into cash or to provide periodic income so that no portion of such value may be used to continue life insurance protection beyond retirement or to distribute the contract to the participant. If a surviving spouse benefit is provided, the incidental test is set forth in terms of the maximum percentage of the employee's accrued or projected pension that may be paid to his spouse. Those percentages are set forth in Chapter 4.

While it is possible to have a group term life insurance contract issued to the trustee of a pension trust and thereby make it a part of the plan, the customary procedure is to issue the contract directly to the employer. When this is done, the death benefit under the group term life insurance contract is not considered to be a part of the plan for federal tax purposes, even though the benefit might have been initiated concurrently with the pension plan and even though the amount of the benefit is provided only for participants in the plan or is in some way related to the amount of their pension benefits.

Death Benefits before Retirement.   In fully insured individual policy plans (i.e., plans which employ retirement income or annuity contracts), the death benefit under the plan generally is expressed in terms of the contract benefits. The standard death benefit under a retirement income contract is an amount equal to 100 times the expected pension it will provide or the reserve for the latter benefit, if greater. If the employee is insurable only on an extra-premium basis, the plan may provide for the employee to receive the full benefit and for the employer to pay any additional premium involved. The most common practice, however, is to give the employee the option of paying the additional premium if he or she wants the full benefit; the employee's benefit otherwise is provided by a retirement annuity contract or, if available from the insurer, by a graded or graduated death benefit contract under which the life insurance benefit is reduced to reflect the degree of the employee's impairment.

If retirement annuity contracts are employed, either for the plan as a whole or for individuals who are uninsurable or insurable only on an extra-premium basis, the death benefit is equal to the premiums paid for the coverage or the cash value of the contract, whichever is greater.

In individual policy combination plans (i.e., plans which employ some form of whole life insurance and a conversion fund), the death benefit usually is the same as would be applicable in an individual policy fully insured plan—100 times the employee's expected monthly pension. However, it is possible to develop a schedule of death benefits under such a plan which is related to the earnings of an employee (similar to the schedules frequently employed in group term life insurance contracts), provided the requirements of the "incidental" test of the Internal Revenue Service are met.

Plans funded with group permanent coverages generally provide the same level of death benefits as is provided in comparable individual policy plans.

In plans funded with group pension contracts or in trust fund plans, the death benefit is frequently provided by means of a group term life insurance contract issued to the employer. Subject to any limitations imposed by state law as to group term life insurance, the schedule of death benefits under such a contract can be anything the employer wishes (and the insurer is willing to underwrite), although the schedules most frequently employed relate the death benefit to the employee's current earnings. Typically, the benefit will be equal to the employee's annual earnings (often rounded to the nearest $500) or it might be an amount such as one and one-half or two times the employee's annual earnings.

Group pension and trust fund plans also provide for a return of an employee's contributions, usually accrued at some rate of interest, in the event of his death prior to retirement. On occasion, there also is provision for paying some cash death benefit out of employer contributions. However, such a benefit, when it is provided, is usually limited in amount. If a cash death benefit is provided from employer contributions, it should be correlated with the severance-of-employment benefits of the plan so as to provide consistency in the form and amount of the two benefits.

ERISA requires that an employee who has been married for at least one year must have the option of electing a preretirement spouse benefit. (Presumably, this benefit could be in lieu of any other form of preretirement death benefit the plan would otherwise provide.) This option must be given to an employee who is eligible for early retirement (but need not be made available, in any event, until the employee is within ten years of normal retirement). The benefit payable to a surviving spouse under this option must be at least 50 percent of the actuarially reduced amount the employee would be entitled to receive upon early retirement. The plan may require a preelection period of up to two years but if the employee dies as a result of accidental means after having elected the option and within the preelection period required by the plan, the benefit will become effective. The cost of the benefit may be charged to the employee by reducing the amount of pension payable to the employee after retirement (or to the surviving spouse if the employee dies before retirement).

Death Benefits after Retirement.   The question of postretirement death benefits has been complicated by the requirements of ERISA, which requires that if an employee has been married for at least one year, his or her retirement benefits must be paid on a 50 percent joint and survivor annuity basis—i.e., 50 percent of the amount of the retirement benefit being paid to the employee must be continued to his or her surviving spouse for the lifetime of such survivor. This requirement also applies to disability income payments made under a pension plan—at least to the extent payable after the employee attains an age which is within 10 years of his or her normal retirement date. Major considerations relating to this spouse benefit are as follows:

1. The employee must be given the right to elect another form of annuity and must be given reasonable notice concerning the terms and conditions of the joint and survivor annuity and the effect of an election not to receive benefits under this form of payment.

2. The plan may require that any revocation of the benefit will become effective only after a time period set by the plan (not to exceed two years); if the employee dies as a result of an accident after retiring and within the revocation period set by the plan, the revocation will be rescinded and the surviving spouse will be entitled to receive benefits.
3. The employee may be charged for the cost of this benefit—typically by reducing the amount of benefit payable.

The last item mentioned is significant. Although payment under the joint and survivor form is mandated for a married employee, it is expected that most plans will require that the employee assume the cost of the protection provided. Such plans will continue to use some other basis as the normal form for the payment of plan benefits to any employee who does not have a spouse. This other payment basis also will be the normal form for an employee with a spouse—at least for the purpose of calculating the basic amount (and cost) of the employee's pension. If payments actually are made on the joint and survivor basis—whether because of the requirements of ERISA or because of employee election—the employee's pension will be reduced from what would have been payable under the plan's normal form.

For plans funded with individual policies or with group permanent coverage, the plan normal form typically will provide for monthly payments for the life of the employee with a guaranteed certain period of five or ten years, or with no guaranteed period at all. Most group pension and trust fund plans will establish a pure life annuity as the plan's normal form unless employees make contributions. In this latter event, the normal form typically will be a modified cash refund annuity under which a death benefit is provided if the employee dies before having received total payments which equal his or her own contributions (usually with interest at some rate credited up to the time of retirement). The death benefit is the amount by which the employee's contributions (with interest) exceed the total retirement payments that have been made.

It is, of course, possible for a plan to incorporate the ERISA-required postretirement spouse benefit as an employer-provided benefit. Indeed, some plans provided such a benefit prior to the requirements of ERISA. However, it is expected that this provision will not be found very often—largely because of the relatively high cost associated with providing such a benefit.

Apart from the death benefit included in the normal form, it is also possible to provide some amount of death benefit under various optional forms of payment which generally are made available to a retired employee. If the employee creates or increases a death benefit by making such an election, it will, of course, reduce the employee's retirement benefit. The reason is that in total, the value of the retirement and death benefits under the optional form of payment should be equal to the value of these benefits under the normal form.

DISABILITY BENEFITS

While most employers recognize the possibility of short-term disabilities and usually provide a reasonable level of benefits for this contingency through their wage continuation plans, such is not generally the case in the area of total and permanent disabilities. With the increased availability of insured long-term disability programs, however, more employers are seeking to provide benefits in the event of total and permanent disability via this device, and on a basis which is completely apart from any benefits available under the employer's pension plan.

In the pension area, disability benefits, even in insured plans, generally have been provided on a self-insured basis—i.e., the benefits are paid in some form directly from plan assets, and the employer's experience in this regard is immediately reflected in the cost level of the plan.

A number of pension plans, particularly those funded with individual policies, provide for full vesting if an employee becomes totally and permanently disabled. Other plans treat such a disability as an early retirement if the employee has completed some minimum period of service or participation in the plan and has attained some minimum age. Unfortunately, the disability benefits provided under such provisions either are nonexistent or inadequate for disabilities occurring at younger ages.

Some group pension and trust fund plans, however, and particularly those which have been union-negotiated, provide for a separate and distinct benefit in the event of total and permanent disability. The benefit provided under such plans is sometimes a specified dollar amount, a specified percentage of earnings, or an amount equal to the employee's accrued or projected pension credits (with or without actuarial reduction). Often, the disability benefit under the plan is integrated with benefits available under government plans such as workmen's compensation or social security benefits. Frequently, the plan provides that the disability benefit will terminate when the employee reaches normal retirement age, at which time the accrued normal pension benefit will be payable.

Even in these plans, however, it is common to require that the employee must have attained some minimum age (such as 50) or must have completed some minimum period of service or participation (such as ten years) in order to qualify for the plan disability benefit. For this reason, most pension plans, including those which provide a separate disability benefit, fail to provide adequate benefits for employees becoming disabled at younger ages; yet, a total and permanent disability at a young age could be far more disastrous from a financial point of view than one occurring at a later age when family financial burdens may have somewhat lessened.

SEVERANCE OF EMPLOYMENT BENEFITS

The right of an employee to the benefits attributable to employer contributions under a pension plan in the event of termination of employment prior to retirement has been the subject of considerable discussion for many years. A major accomplishment of ERISA was to require that an employee achieve such rights, or a vested interest, after some reasonable period of service.

Vesting Schedules. ERISA requires that the employee's rights to that portion of his or her accrued benefit that is attributable to his or her own contributions must be fully vested at all times. This does not require a minimum benefit that is equal to the amount the employee has contributed. In a defined contribution plan, for example, there may have been investment losses that result in the value of the employee's contribution being less than the amount actually contributed by the employee. In such a situation, the plan would not have to return to the employee an amount that is greater than the value of the employee's contributions after taking investment losses into account.

Accrued benefits attributable to employer contributions must vest when the employee reaches normal retirement age. Upon termination of employment, accrued benefits attributable to employer contributions must be vested in accordance with one of the three following rules:

1. *The Ten-Year Rule.* The employee must be 100 percent vested after ten years of service.
2. *The 5 to 15 Rule.* Graduated vesting is provided, beginning with 25 percent after 5 years of service, increasing 5 percent a year for the next 5 years, and 10 percent for the next 5 years, thus producing a 50 percent vested interest after 10 years of service, and a 100 percent vested interest after 15 years of service.
3. *The Rule of 45.* The employee achieves a 50 percent interest after the earlier of ten years of service or when the combination of service (minimum of five years) and the employee's age total 45; thereafter, the employee's vested interest increases 10 percent per year for the next five years.

The Internal Revenue Service is given the authority to impose more stringent vesting requirements if such action is necessary, in the opinion of the Service, to prevent discrimination.[11] The Congressional Committee Report, however, directs the Internal Revenue Service not to require

---

[11] The Internal Revenue Service might possibly exercise this discretion in conjunction with profit sharing and thrift and savings plans, or in the case of a pension plan for a small, closely held corporation.

a vesting schedule more stringent than 40 percent vesting after four years of service with 5 percent additional vesting for each of the next two years, and 10 percent vesting for each of the following five years. Of course, more liberal vesting schedules than required by ERISA or the Service will be acceptable.

Definition of Service. ERISA is also quite explicit in defining what constitutes service for the purpose of establishing an employee's vested interest. Generally speaking, a plan must give an employee credit for a year of service for any 12-month computation period during which the employee works 1,000 hours. (The 12-month computation period may be established as a plan year, calendar year, or an employment year.) With the exceptions noted below, service must be taken into account to the extent that it occurs after age 22, even though rendered while the employee is not a participant in the plan. Also, service must include periods of employment with any corporation that is a member of a controlled group of corporations (i.e., where there is 80 percent control). Similar principles apply for service in an unincorporated business under common control. Service with a predecessor employer also must be taken into account if the employer maintains the plan of the predecessor; if the employer maintains a plan which is not the plan of the predecessor, service with the predecessor will have to be considered to the extent prescribed in regulations.

The following periods of service may be disregarded:

1. Service prior to age 22 (unless the plan's vesting provisions are based upon the rule of 45, in which event, service prior to age 22 must be taken into account if it is rendered while the employee is a participant in the plan).
2. Any period during which the employee did not elect to contribute under a plan requiring employee contributions.
3. Service prior to the establishment of the plan (or predecessor plan).
4. Employment prior to January 1, 1971 but only if the employee has not had three years of service after December 31, 1970.

In the case of seasonal industries where the customary period of employment is less than 1,000 hours during a calendar year, the term "year of service" will be determined by regulation. In the maritime industry, 125 days of service will be treated as the equivalent of 1,000 hours of service.

ERISA also contains requirements for periods of broken service. Prior to ERISA, it was relatively unusual for a plan to aggregate separate periods of employment. Under ERISA, however, such broken service must be aggregated under certain conditions. A "break in service" is defined to be any 12-month computation period (the computation period used to measure service for vesting) during which the employee has worked 500 hours or less. If an employee returns to work for at least one year after a break in service, prior service will have to be taken into account if: (1) the employee was vested (even though only partially) when the break in service occurred; or (2) the period of absence was less than the employee's years of pre-break service. In recognition of the practical problems of reconstructing prior employment records, the break-in-service rule of ERISA applies on a prospective basis only; current plan provisions will be permitted to apply to periods of broken service prior to the time the plan must comply with the terms of ERISA. In the case of a defined contribution plan or in the case of a fully insured pension plan, it is not required that years of service after a break in service be taken into account for the purpose of determining the employee's vested interest for employer contributions made prior to the break in service.

Regulations promulgated under ERISA also define what constitutes an "hour" of service. Generally, the minimum required is that an employee be given credit for any hour for which he or she is entitled to compensation and for which he or she has performed services. In applying the break-in-service rule, however, all hours for which the employee is entitled to compensation must be counted even though no services were performed (e.g., sick pay).

Determination of Accrued Benefit.   ERISA stipulates minimum standards that must be followed in determining an employee's accrued benefit for purposes of applying a vesting schedule. A plan will be acceptable if it meets any one of three rules:

1. *The 3 Percent Method.*   The employee's accrued benefit must be at least equal to 3 percent of the projected normal retirement benefit for each year of *participation,* to a maximum of 100 percent after $33\frac{1}{3}$ years of participation.
2. *The $133\frac{1}{3}$ Percent Rule.*   The accrued benefit may be the employee's actual benefit earned to date under the plan, provided that any future rate of benefit accrual is not more than $133\frac{1}{3}$ percent of the current benefit accrual rate.
3. *The Fractional Rule.*   The employee's accrued benefit is not less than the projected normal retirement benefit prorated for years of plan participation.

Most plans are expected to be able to satisfy either or both the $133\frac{1}{3}$ percent rule and the fractional rule. However, any plan that permits the accrual of benefits for more than $33\frac{1}{3}$ years will not be able to satisfy the 3 percent method.

A fully insured plan (under which premiums have been paid to date and where there are no loans outstanding) satisfies the accrued benefit requirements. In the case of a defined contribution plan, the employee's accrued benefit will be his or her current account balance.

If a defined benefit plan requires employee contributions, the accrued benefit attributable to employer contributions is determined by subtracting the life annuity value of the employee's contributions. In making this calculation, the employee's contributions are accumulated with interest compounded annually at the rate of 5 percent per year (from the beginning of the first year that the plan is subject to ERISA), and are multiplied by a factor of 10 percent—e.g., if the employee's contributions with interest amount to $5,000, the annual annuity attributable to the employee's contributions will be $500. This amount will be subtracted from the total accrued benefit to determine the accrued benefit attributable to employer contributions. The Internal Revenue Service has the authority to revise both the factor and the interest rate from time to time.

An employee's accrued benefit is established on a pure life annuity basis only, and does not have to include any ancillary benefits such as death or disability benefits.

Other Vesting Requirements.   ERISA also establishes a number of other requirements concerning the vesting and payment of an employee's benefits.

1. If an employee is less than 50 percent vested and withdraws his or her contributions, any benefits attributable to employer contributions may be canceled, but any such employee must be permitted to "buy back" the forfeited benefits upon repayment of the withdrawn contributions plus, if a defined benefit plan, compound interest (currently 5 percent per year). If the employee's vested interest is 50 percent or more, withdrawal of employee contributions cannot result in a cancellation of benefits attributable to employer contributions.
2. Except as provided above, an employee's vested interest cannot be forfeited under any circumstances (other than death), even if termination of employment is due to dishonesty.
3. The automatic cash-out of an employee's entire interest is permitted upon termination of employment where the value of this benefit does not exceed $1,750. Under such circumstances and for purposes of determining the employee's accrued benefit, the plan may disregard service for which the employee has received such a payment. If the amount exceeds $1,750 the same will hold true but only if the employee agreed to the cash payment. In any event, if the plan wishes to disregard such service, a terminating employee who has received a cash-out must be permitted to "buy back" the accrued benefit by repaying the cash payment with compound interest (currently 5

percent per year). (In the case of a defined contribution plan, such a buy back is required only before the employee has incurred a one-year break in service, and interest need not be paid.)

4. Any employee who terminates employment must be given written notification of his or her rights, the amount of his or her accrued benefits, the portion (if any) that is vested, and the applicable payment provisions.

5. A terminated employee's vested benefit cannot be decreased by reason of increases in social security benefits that take place after the date of termination of employment.

6. If the plan allows an active employee to elect early retirement after attaining a stated age and completing a specified period of service, a terminated employee who has completed the service requirement must have the right to receive vested benefits after reaching the early retirement age specified. However, the benefit for the terminated employee can be reduced actuarially even though the active employee might have the advantage of subsidized early retirement benefits.

7. Any plan amendment cannot decrease the vested percentage of an employee's accrued benefit. Also, if the vesting schedule is changed, any participant with at least five years of service must be given the election to remain under the pre-amendment vesting schedule (for both pre- and post-amendment benefit accruals).

EMPLOYEE CONTRIBUTIONS

A major question that the employer must resolve is whether employees will be required to make contributions toward the cost of plan benefits. Sound arguments may be presented for both contributory and noncontributory plans, although the ability of the employer or employees to pay often is the controlling factor. In any event, the trend is clearly in the direction of noncontributory plans.

Arguments advanced in favor of contributory plans include the following:

1. If employees contribute, it will mean a smaller employer contribution to provide the same overall plan benefits.

2. If the employer does not want to use employee contributions to reduce its own contribution, then by making the plan contributory, the overall plan benefits will be larger.

3. Something for nothing is too often taken for granted, and the deductions from current earnings will continually remind employees that the employer is assuming a large share of providing the plan benefits. (It would seem that this argument could be minimized by an effec-

tive method of repeatedly publicizing the plan and its value to employees.)

4. Employees are encouraged to save and, in the process, to solve a portion of their own retirement problems. The contributory plan also provides an employee with additional funds in the event of termination of employment.

The proponents of a noncontributory plan hold that the contributory plan has the following disadvantages:

1. Employer contributions represent dollars which have not been taxed. On the other hand, dollars received by the employee as earnings which are then contributed under the plan are dollars which have been taxed to the employee. Hence, dollar for dollar, employer contributions provide more than those of an employee.
2. Deductions from earnings are a source of constant irritation to employees.
3. The employer might be forced to increase salaries in order to compensate for the additional deductions.
4. The number of participants required for a qualified plan (or required by the insurer under certain funding instruments) might not enroll.
5. Some employees may refuse to participate, in which case the employer will still have a problem when these employees reach retirement age.
6. Additional records must be kept by the employer, thereby increasing administrative work and costs.
7. If employees contribute, the portion of any death benefit attributable to these contributions will be included in the employee's gross estate for federal estate tax purposes.

If the employer decides that employees should make contributions, the next decision will be the amount which employees should contribute. While employee contributions may be related to the cost of benefits, it generally is much more satisfactory to relate these contributions to earnings. In this way, an employee's contributions are geared to the ability to make them. Furthermore, in most plans it is impossible to predict exactly what the cost of an employee's pension will be until actual retirement. Hence, any contributions which are made by the employee and related to cost are necessarily estimated and do not have an exact relationship.

Employee contribution rates of 2, 3, or even 4 percent of earnings commonly are used. If the plan is to qualify, however, the contribution rate should not exceed 6 percent. If the plan employs a formula integrated with social security benefits, the contribution rate should reflect the different levels of benefits as to earnings under and over the compensation break-point used in the plan. For example, if the benefit formula provides a 1 percent future service benefit with respect to earnings under $650 a month and a 2 percent benefit on earnings in excess of this amount, the corresponding employee contributions could be 2 and 4 percent.

Contributory plans usually require that an employee, before becoming a participant, must sign a request for participation agreeing to make the required contributions and authorizing the employer to withhold contributions from earnings. If an employee fails to make such an election when first eligible, it is customary to impose some form of penalty. In plans using a unit credit formula, for example, past service benefits as well as the future service benefits that otherwise would have accrued might be forfeited until such time as the employee joins the plan. If the plan employs a flat percentage of earnings formula, the benefits might be reduced by multiplying the benefit the late entrant would otherwise have received by a fraction, the numerator being the years of actual contribution and the denominator the number of years the employee could have contributed. A few plans are even more severe and provide that if an employee does not join when first eligible, the right to participate will be forfeited for all time. Another approach used by some employers is to give employees the option of participating if they are employed when the plan becomes effective, but to require participation as a condition of employment for all future employees.

Another provision to be considered in contributory plans is the right of an employee to suspend or discontinue contributions. Many plans do not give an employee either of these privileges. Others will permit a temporary suspension (for a year or so) without affecting benefits, and some will permit a complete discontinuance at any time. Still others permit only a complete discontinuance. If discontinuance of contributions is permitted, there are further questions, such as whether the employee will be permitted to rejoin the plan and, if so, what benefits the employee will then be entitled to receive.

Regardless of whether or not the plan requires employees to make contributions, it may permit an employee to make voluntary contributions (or additional contributions under a contributory plan) to supplement benefits. Generally, such a provision will be acceptable to the Internal Revenue Service provided that the voluntary additional contributions do not exceed 10 percent of earnings. The advantage of such a provision is that the employee will not be required to include the investment income on accumulated contributions as income subject to tax until this income is distributed or made available. Even then, the favorable tax treatment accorded to distributions from a qualified plan will apply to the earnings on these additional contributions. When employees are permitted to make additional contributions, the plan also should contain provisions concerning the amounts which employees may contribute on this basis, how often (if at all) the rate of contribution may be changed by the employee, the conditions under which these contributions may be withdrawn, whether or not employees may suspend or discontinue these additional contributions, and if so, the effect of a suspension or discontinuance, and so on.

GENERAL PLAN PROVISIONS

The preceding portion of this chapter has dealt with the major plan provisions that an employer must consider when establishing a pension plan. There are, of course, a number of other provisions that are a part of any plan and that relate generally to the rights and duties of the interested parties and to the administrative aspects of the program. The following discusses, very briefly, the most significant of these general provisions.

Employer's Right to Amend or Terminate the Plan

While a pension plan is established on an indefinite and presumably permanent basis, an essential plan provision is one which gives the employer the unilateral right to amend or terminate the program at any time. As will be seen, however, the rights reserved to the employer under such a clause are limited to some extent by federal law.

The right-to-amend clause usually is straightforward and reserves the right to the employer to make plan amendments without the consent of employees or their beneficiaries. However, if a plan is to maintain its qualified status, an amendment may not reduce benefits related to contributions made prior to the amendment, deprive any employee of the employee's then accrued vested interest, nor permit the employer to recover any funds previously contributed to the plan. Thus, the amendment clause normally restricts the employer's rights to this extent unless the amendment itself is required to make the plan conform to federal or state laws. Also, as previously noted, if an amendment changes the plan's vesting schedule, any participant with at least five years of service must be given the election to remain under the pre-amendment vesting schedule.

The typical right-to-terminate clause gives the employer the unilateral right to terminate the plan (or to discontinue contributions) for any reason and at any time. However, for a plan to achieve a qualified status under federal tax law, it must be permanent and, while the Internal Revenue Service will approve a plan with such a termination provision, restrictions are imposed on the employer's right to terminate the program. Thus, if an employer terminates the plan for reasons other than "business necessity" within a few years from its inception, the plan may lose its qualified status for all prior open tax years, since this action will be considered by the Service as evidence that the plan, from its inception, was not a bona fide program for the exclusive benefit of employees in general. If business necessity exists, the employer may terminate the plan without adverse tax consequences. Valid reasons for a plan termination include financial incapacity, bankruptcy, insolvency, change of ownership, and so on.

The termination-of-plan clause must make provision for the distribution of plan assets if the plan is terminated or contributions are discontinued. Since federal tax law prohibits the return of any funds to the employer on plan termination (other than excess amounts remaining due to "actuarial error" after satisfaction of all plan liabilities), the plan assets must be applied for the benefit of the employees or their beneficiaries in the following order of priorities:

1. Voluntary employee contributions.
2. Mandatory employee contributions.
3. Benefits for employees who have been retired for at least three years or who were eligible to retire at least three years before the plan termination date (but based upon the provisions of the plan in effect five years prior to the plan termination date).
4. All other benefits which are guaranteed by the Pension Benefit Guaranty Corporation.
5. All other vested benefits.
6. All other accrued benefits.

If assets are insufficient to accommodate the benefits in any one of the first four and the sixth classes, the assets will be prorated within that class. For the fifth class, assets also are to be allocated on a pro rata basis in the event they are insufficient to provide full benefits, but the allocation will recognize any plan amendments made during the preceding five years. Thus, the allocation will be made as of the most recent amendment which permits a full allocation (if at all), and the prorating will apply only to any excess assets on the basis of the next following amendment, and so forth.

In the past, the Internal Revenue Service has required the inclusion of a provision which limits the benefits payable to certain highly paid employees in the event of plan termination. In view of the rights of the Pension Benefit Guaranty Corporation to recapture payments in excess of $10,000 to any participant during each of the three years preceding plan termination, it is uncertain, at this time, that the service will continue requiring the inclusion of such a provision. If the service continues to make such a requirement and follows prior practice, the provision will have to limit benefits payable to the 25 highest paid employees of the employer at the inception of the plan whose individual annual retirement benefit from employer contributions will exceed $1,500. An employee could be within this group even though not a participant when the plan was established. This limitation on benefits applies if the plan is terminated within ten years after its effective date. (It will also apply to any benefits that become payable with respect to this group during the first ten plan years even though the plan has not been terminated if, when the distribution is made, the "full current costs" of the plan have not been met. If, at the end of the ten-year period, full current costs have not been met, the ten-year period is extended until such time as full current costs have been met for the ten-year period.) Essentially, the limitation is that the benefits payable to any such employee or the beneficiary of such an employee cannot exceed those purchasable by the greater of: (*a*) $20,000 or (*b*) 20 percent of the employee's annual compensation up to $50,000 multiplied by the number of years since the effective date of the plan. This limitation may have to be adjusted if the plan is ever changed to improve benefits.

Exculpatory Provisions

To the extent permitted by ERISA (if at all), the trustee, if a trust is involved, and the insurer, in an insured plan, will want to have provisions which protect them in their relationships with the employer, the employees and their beneficiaries, and with each other. These provisions set forth the rights of the insurer and trustee as well as the limits of their responsibilities and liabilities.

Miscellaneous Provisions

The plan also must contain a number of provisions relating to the broad administration of the program, many of these provisions being dictated by the funding instrument employed to provide benefits. The following, while by no means all-inclusive, indicates some of the provisions which must be considered.

Beneficiary Provisions. If the plan contains a death benefit, there must be a provision for the employee's right to name and change beneficiaries. The provision also should cover such matters as the form which any such designation or change should take; when and under what conditions it will become effective; the rights and duties of the interested parties if payment has been made (or has commenced) before a change has been properly recorded; and the distribution of the proceeds in the event the employee dies without having made a beneficiary designation.

Facility of Payment. A related provision is one which permits the trustee or insurer to distribute proceeds to certain individuals if the employee or beneficiary is in any way incompetent to receive the proceeds.

Trustee Provisions. If a trust is involved, several points concerning the trustee should be covered; for example, there should be a provision covering the details of the resignation or removal of the trustee and the manner in which a successor trustee will be appointed. There should also be a provision authorizing payment of the trustee's expenses and, if applicable, payment of the trustee's fee. The powers and duties of the trustee for the plan should be covered, with special emphasis on investment authority. If more than one trustee is involved, there should be a provision indicating whether the trustees are required to act unanimously or whether majority action will suffice. If the trustees are to have the right to delegate authority to one or more of their number to sign documents and perform ministerial duties, a provision to this effect should be included.

Mergers and Consolidations. A plan must provide that the value of an employee's accrued benefit cannot be diminished in any way by any merger or consolidation with, or transfer of assets or liabilities to, any other plan.

Payment of Benefits. Benefit payments must commence, unless otherwise elected by the employee, no later than the 60th day after the *latest* of the close of the plan year in which the participant attains age 65 (or the normal retirement age specified in the plan), completes ten years of participation, or terminates employment.

Small Benefits. Many plans include a provision which permits payment of the employee's retirement benefit in a lump sum if its value is less than $1,750. Obviously, the payment of small amounts on a periodic basis is of little value to the retired employee, and the administrative problems involved in maintaining the necessary records and making the small payments could be significant. Thus, payment of the benefit in a lump sum is generally desirable for all concerned.

Leaves of Absence. A well-designed plan should have a provision dealing with the possibility of an employee's going on leave of absence and the effect this might have on plan benefits. A typical provision would protect an employee's rights while on military leave (normally for the period of time employment rights are protected by law) or while on any other authorized leave for a period not exceeding one or two years. The plan should indicate whether or not time spent on such a leave will be considered as credited service for retirement benefits. If such time is to be considered as credited service, however, and if the employee fails to return to work within the time allowed, he or she usually is considered as having terminated employment when the leave began, subject, of course, to ERISA's requirements concerning the determination of service for vesting purposes. Also, if such credit is given and if the plan is contributory, there is need for a further provision for any employee contributions that might otherwise have been due during the leave of absence. If, under the funding instrument involved, the employer advances the employee's contribution during the leave, there is usually a feature which allows the employer to recover this amount if the employee fails to return to work within the time allowed.

Governing Law. Most plans include a provision stating that the plan and its provisions will be construed in accordance with the laws of a specific state to the extent not preempted by ERISA.

Spendthrift Provision. ERISA requires that the plan prohibit the assignment or alienation of benefits; however, an employee may be permitted to assign up to 10 percent of any benefit payment. Also, an employee may use his or her vested interest as collateral for a loan from the plan (if such loan is not a prohibited transaction).

Limitation of Employee's Rights. A desirable provision in any plan is one which stipulates that the existence of the plan and the employee's participation do not give the employee any right to be retained in the employ of the employer, nor any legal or equitable rights against the employer, except as provided by ERISA.

ERISA-Required Provisions. In addition to some of the provisions already mentioned, ERISA requires that several other items be covered in the plan. For example, the plan must provide for named fiduciaries as well as a procedure for establishing and carrying out the plan's funding policy. The plan should also clearly describe any procedure for the allocation of administrative duties and responsibilities, and should stipulate the basis on which payments will be made to and from the plan.

3

Funding and Cost Considerations

A pension plan, in its simplest form, is a promise by the employer to pay a periodic benefit (usually for life) to employees who meet the requirements set forth in the plan. For a given pension benefit, the amount of annual benefit payments under the plan depends upon the number of retired workers. The number of retired workers, in turn, depends upon the rate at which already retired workers die and the rate at which new employees are added to the retirement rolls. Since the average life expectancy for a 65-year-old male is about 15 years, it is obvious that for some time after the plan is established, more new members are added to the retired employee group than are removed from the group as a result of death. Therefore, under a typical plan, the aggregate annual benefit payout should increase for a substantial number of years after the inception of the plan. The annual benefit payout continues to increase until a point is reached at which the size of the retired employee group tends to stabilize; that is, the point at which the number of retired workers dying is about equal to the number of new additions to the retired group.

Based on the above analysis, the amount of annual *benefit payments* under a plan might resemble the pattern shown in Chart 3–1. However, when the employer funds the plan, the pattern of the annual contributions under the plan will differ from the benefit payout pattern indicated in Chart 3–1 because as indicated earlier, the benefit payout pattern for a given level of pension benefit is dependent on the number of retired workers eligible for benefits during each year and will be the same regardless of the manner in which contributions are made.

CHART 3–1
Annual Benefit Payout Pattern under a Typical Pension Plan

Amount of Annual Benefits Paid

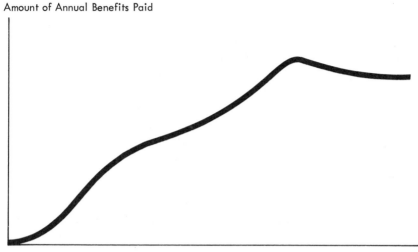

Years of Existence of Plan

The objective of this chapter is to consider some of the important implications of funding and to acquaint the reader with the factors affecting the *ultimate cost* of a pension plan, apart from specific plan provisions and benefits. Particular reference is made to the various actuarial assumptions and cost methods that can be used in determining the incidence and amount of pension costs. The discussion later in this chapter assumes a fixed set of plan specifications and also assumes, for the purpose of simplicity, that the plan is noncontributory.

FINANCING A PENSION PLAN

Two approaches have been used to finance pension plans in the past, but which essentially are no longer permitted under ERISA: the current disbursement approach and the terminal funding approach. Though basically no longer permitted by ERISA, knowledge of these two approaches should provide a better basis for understanding advance funding required by ERISA which follows later in this chapter.

Current Disbursement Approach

Under the current disbursement approach, the employer pays each retired worker's monthly pension as each payment becomes due. There is no accumulation of pension funds in an irrevocable trust or through a contract with an insurance company.

An illustration of the current disbursement approach would be a plan under which the employer promises all employees with at least 25 years of service a lifetime pension of $100 a month beginning at age 65. If no employees are eligible for benefits during the first two years after the plan is established, the employer would not make any pension plan payments during that period. The employer's pension outlay of $100 a month begins with the retirement of the first eligible employee; the outlay increases by that amount as each new retired worker is added to the pension roles and decreases by $100 a month as each retired worker dies. These monthly pension outlays are provided out of current operating income and, in effect, are treated as a part of wage costs.

Terminal Funding

Under the terminal funding approach, the employer sets aside for each employee, on the date that the latter retires, a single-premium sum sufficient to provide the monthly pension benefit promised under the plan. The single-premium sum needed to provide the promised benefit is a function of the amount of benefit, the expected benefit period, and the rate of interest expected to be earned on the investment of this principal sum. For example, based on the 1951 Group Annuity Table (for males, projected on a static basis to 1970 in accordance with Scale C) and 5 percent interest, the sum needed to provide $100 a month for life to a male, age 65, is $12,191.[1] If the mortality and interest assumptions prove to be accurate, the principal plus interest earnings will be sufficient, on the average, to provide the $100-a-month benefit.

The employer, therefore, sets aside the appropriate single-premium sum as each employee retires. Like the current disbursement approach, terminal funding does not require the employer to make any contributions on behalf of the employees who are still actively at work.

The benefits can be funded through the purchase of single-premium annuities from insurance companies, or the employer can transfer the estimated single-premium sums to a trust fund.

The reader should not confuse the concept of terminal funding with the practice of split funding that is prevalent in the pension field. The term split funding, as it is commonly used in pension planning, refers to the use of two different funding agencies in administering the assets of a pension plan. For example, a plan may provide that contributions

---

[1] An expense assumption is ignored in the above calculation since the authors are interested solely in illustrating the concept of terminal funding. In practice, the expenses of administering the benefit would be taken into account in the single-premium rate charged by an insurance company or in determining the amount to be set aside in a trust fund under noninsured plans, if expenses associated with the plan are paid from the trust fund. Normally, the expenses under trust fund plans are paid directly by the employer, and, therefore, no expense allowance is required.

on behalf of active employees are to be administered by a corporate trustee. When an employee retires, the trust agreement may require the corporate trustee to withdraw from the trust fund and transfer to an insurance company the single-premium sum needed to purchase a life annuity equal to the monthly pension earned by the employee under the terms of the pension plan. This type of plan is considered to be an advance funded plan unless the employer is paying to the corporate trustee an annual sum exactly equal to the amount of single premiums needed to provide the benefits for workers retiring each year—a highly unlikely situation.

Advance Funding

Under advance funding, the employer (and the employee, under contributory plans) sets aside funds on some systematic basis prior to the employee's retirement date. Thus, periodic contributions are made on behalf of the group of active employees during their working years. This does not mean that each dollar of contributions is necessarily earmarked for specific employees. As will be noted in subsequent chapters, contributions are not allocated to specific employees under certain funding instruments; for example, trust fund and group deposit administration plans. Thus, it is true that in some plans using unallocated funding instruments, contributions in the early years may only be sufficient to provide lifetime benefits to the first group of employees retiring under the plan. However, if contributions are continued on an advance funding basis, the accumulated assets in the pension fund will soon exceed the aggregate single-premium sums needed to provide benefits to those workers who are already retired. This excess of pension assets, then, represents the advance funding of benefits that have been accrued or credited to the active (non-retired) employees.

Pension plans operating on an advance funded basis are invariably qualified with the Internal Revenue Service. An employer is generally not willing to make advance contributions to an irrevocable trust fund unless it receives the tax advantages of a qualified plan.

From the standpoint of the employer, an important reason for the advance funding of pension benefits is the fact that it requires the smallest outlay of pension contributions for each employee. This point can be best illustrated by the example cited earlier, i.e., a lifetime pension of $100 a month for a male age 65. Let us assume further that the person for whom this pension is to be provided is now age 30. If the pension benefit is to be funded by annual contributions for the next 35 years, the annual outlay required (assuming 5 percent interest and no mortality discount) would be $129. The aggregate outlays made during this period would be $4,515 ($129 a year for 35 years). The aggregate outlay of

$4,515 required under advance funding is clearly lower than the outlays of $12,191 and $18,540 which could have been required under terminal funding and current disbursement financing, respectively.

The relatively even distribution of annual pension outlays under advance funding produces a more equitable charge against the firm's profits over the years. The pension is being provided to employees for the years of service rendered to the firm. Thus, it would seem that the financial statements of the employer should reflect, as a charge against operations, pension contributions in an amount approximately equal to the present value of benefits accruing under the plan. It is true that credit for past service, offered at the inception of the plan, creates a problem. Since the plan was not in existence during those past service years, it is difficult to justify pension charges against operating income for that period of time. The next best solution seems to be to charge off past service costs in the first 20 or 25 years after the inception of the plan. ERISA requires that for new plans, past service costs must be amortized over no more than 30 years.

The accumulation of assets in a pension fund resulting from the advance funding of benefits serves as a buffer during periods of financial stress. During a period of low earnings or operating losses, an employer may find it advisable to reduce or eliminate pension contributions for a year or even a longer period. This can be done in those cases where the pension fund is of sufficient size that a temporary reduction of contributions does not violate the minimum funding requirements imposed by ERISA. It should be noted that this financing flexibility does not necessitate any reduction or termination in pension benefits.

ESTIMATED COST VERSUS ULTIMATE COST

An employer who adopts a pension plan must have some idea of the cost of the program to determine the amount of periodic contribution payments necessary to fund the plan. If one were to choose the most complex and least understood aspect of pension planning from the viewpoint of the employer, a logical candidate would be the area of cost projections.

The point that pension cost projections are *estimates* and not *actual cost* figures cannot be overstressed. A moment's reflection regarding the nature of a pension plan should make this point quite clear. Assume, for example, that a pension plan provides employees with a retirement benefit only after attainment of age 65 and completion of a minimum of ten years of continuous service with the employer. It is obvious that not all current employees of the firm will be entitled to a benefit under the plan. Some employees may die and others may quit, be laid off, or become disabled prior to age 65. Other employees may defer their retirement beyond age 65 (if permitted under the plan); and, also, the number of years that retired workers will live cannot be predicted with certainty. Furthermore, in the case of funded plans, the rate of investment income to be earned in the future on accumulated assets in the pension fund can only be estimated.

The point is sometimes made in pension sales presentations that all of these cost uncertainties facing the employer can be eliminated by using a fully insured individual policy approach to funding the plan. The reader should recognize the weakness in this argument. It is true that individual policies offer very important guarantees as to mortality, inter-est, expense, and annuity options. However, this is not the same as argu-ing that the employer's ultimate outlay or cost under the plan is known with certainty. The guarantees under individual policy plans pertain only to contracts that already have been purchased. Future premium commit-ments will be reduced by dividends and other employer credits. On the other hand, future premium commitments will be increased by the addi-tion of newly covered employees and benefit increases to which currently covered employees may become entitled. Even under individual policy plans, then, projections of employer costs are estimates rather than firm, long-run cost commitments. The conclusion, therefore, is that the ulti-mate cost of a pension plan cannot be determined until the last retired worker dies and all benefit payments under the plan are thereby terminated.

However, no business firm would ever establish a pension plan if the cost of the plan were completely uncertain until the plan is terminated at some date in the distant future. The obvious solution lies in the fact that although the specific ultimate cost is unknown, actuaries are able to estimate the ultimate cost of the plan with reasonable accuracy and thus arrive at a level of estimated plan contributions. To do this, assump-tions must be made regarding the factors that affect the plan's ultimate cost. In subsequent years, adjustments in the estimated amounts of contri-butions required may have to be made, based on comparisons between the actual experience under the plan and the assumed experience. Experi-ence more favorable than expected permits a reduction in future contri-butions. Conversely, adverse experience under the plan requires an in-crease in future contributions.

CHOICE OF ASSUMPTIONS

Two important points should be made regarding the choice of assump-tions for the calculation of estimated pension costs.

First, the flexibility available in choosing a particular set of actuarial assumptions depends in large part on the funding instrument involved. The greatest flexibility is available under trust fund plans and under unallocated group pension contracts such as a group deposit administration contract. If the employer has competent advice, the assumptions used will be reasonable for the type of plan and the characteristics of the employee group covered. Fully insured individual policy plans and group permanent and group deferred annuity instruments offer the employer the least choice in cost assumptions, since the insurance company effectively establishes the assumptions to be used by its premium rates.

Second, the choice of a particular set of assumptions does not normally alter the ultimate cost of the plan. Obviously, the ages at which employees retire or the rate at which they die or leave their jobs is not conditioned by the assumptions in these areas made by the pension actuary. The relative magnitude of actuarial gains and losses under the plan will vary, given different original assumptions, but the end result will be an approximately similar ultimate cost picture except to the extent that investment earnings are affected by the incidence of contributions produced by the funding assumptions chosen. This conclusion does not apply fully in the case of plans funded with individual policies. In the case of individual contracts, there is a certain degree of pooling of experience among the whole class of business. For example, the mortality or expense experience under a particular plan is not reflected directly in the insurance company's dividends paid to that group, since the dividend scale for individual policies is determined by the experience for that class of business as a whole. There also is an element of pooling in some group plans.

COST ASSUMPTIONS

One method of approach in considering the factors affecting the cost of a pension plan is to relate these factors to the formula for determining the ultimate cost of the plan; i.e., benefits paid plus administrative expenses less investment earnings.

Benefits Paid

Number of Employees Retiring. The amount of benefits paid under a plan depends upon several factors. The first factor is the number of workers who ultimately will be entitled to receive benefits under the plan. The number of employees who will be eligible for benefits will depend on four factors: (1) mortality rates among active employees, (2) rates and duration of disabilities among active employees under a plan that offers a disability benefit, (3) layoffs and voluntary terminations of employment, and (4) rate of retirement at different ages. Let us now turn to a consideration of each of these cost factors.

Mortality. The higher the rate of mortality among active employees, the lower will be the cost of retirement benefits under the plan. However, if a participant is entitled to a preretirement death benefit, this will increase the cost of the plan, as additional benefits are being provided.

Mortality among active employees can be an important cost-reducing factor in those plans providing little or no death benefit. This is particularly true for small plans, where a few deaths can have a significant impact on the cost of the plan.

Actuaries generally use the same mortality table in projecting mortality among both active and retired employees.[2] Several mortality tables are available for pension cost calculations. Until recently, the most popular table has been the 1951 Group Annuity Table.[3] Several projections have also been developed to reflect the probable continuing improvements in mortality. Thus, as improvements in mortality occur, or are expected to occur, the actuary can use either the 1951 table or the 1971 table with the projection that he or she believes to be appropriate for the given case. Mortality gains or losses will develop from year to year, and the actuary can keep abreast of the experience through subsequent modifications of the mortality assumption. Table 3–1 shows the probability

TABLE 3–1

Probability of Surviving to Age 65—Males

Age	1937 Std. Annuity	1951 GAT	1971 GAT
20.	.698	.776	.809
25.	.703	.779	.812
30.	.709	.782	.814
35.	.718	.787	.818
40.	.730	.793	.824
45.	.749	.803	.832
50.	.778	.822	.848
55.	.821	.856	.876
60.	.890	.910	.922

of surviving to 65 under the 1937 Standard Annuity Table, the 1951 Group Annuity Table, and the 1971 Group Annuity Mortality Table. Obviously, the results are considerably different, which indicates the im-

---

[2] One exception is individual policy combination plans. Here, an annuity table is used for mortality after retirement and, often, a Commissioners Standard Ordinary (CSO) mortality table for mortality prior to retirement. CSO tables are based on the mortality experience of purchasers of life insurance and generally indicate higher rates of mortality at all ages than the rates indicated in annuity tables. Conservatism in the construction of mortality tables suggests the use of higher-than-expected mortality rates for insurance tables and lower-than-expected mortality for annuity tables.

[3] Many actuarial firms now use an annuity table developed by Harold R. Greenlee, Jr., and Alfonso D. Keh, which they call the 1971 Group Annuity Mortality Table.

pact on estimated costs caused by the mortality assumption chosen by the actuary.

The question often is raised whether a mortality assumption should be used in calculating the amount of contributions that should be paid into a conversion fund under combination plans—particularly those plans covering a small group of employees. Pension practitioners seem to be divided in their opinions on this point. Some planners prefer to use a mortality assumption in these cases, while others believe that the size of the covered group generally involved in plans of this type is too small to permit the law of averages to work. If the expected mortality among a small group of employees does not materialize, the employer will be faced with the need for additional contributions in future years. Those favoring the use of a mortality assumption in these situations argue that its use results in a lower initial contribution requirement, which might be best suited to the current financial needs of some employers, and that any actuarial losses due to the use of such an assumption will be offset by actuarial gains due to severence of employment. Furthermore, it is argued that if the expected mortality is realized, the use of a mortality assumption produces a more realistic projection of future costs. Although there is merit in the latter position, the pension planner should clearly point out to the employer the full implications of using a mortality assumption with relatively small groups.

Rate and Duration of Disability.   If a pension plan offers a disability benefit, cost projections for that plan should include a disability assumption. The plan actuary must establish two sets of probabilities in evaluating the cost of providing a disability benefit. First, a rate of occurrence (frequency) of disabilities of the nature entitling the disabled employee to a benefit under the plan must be estimated. The rates of disability will vary with the plan's definition of disability, the age and sex composition of the covered employee group, the nature of the employment, and the general level of economic activity. In the beginning, the disability experience projected for a particular plan may be based on insurance company data, or on the actual experience of the employer, or on the experience of a large company in the same, or a comparable, industry. Ultimately, the plan's own experience may be used as a yardstick.

Having determined the probable incidence of disability, the actuary must then project the duration of the disability. The duration of the disability will be affected by reemployment opportunities, which in turn are related to the nature of the employment and general economic conditions. The duration of the benefit period will also be affected by the mortality rates among disabled workers.

It can be seen, then, that the ability to project future disability rates is a difficult task. The actuary must keep a careful check on the actual disability experience evolving under the plan.

Turnover. Employees who voluntarily quit or who are laid off represent a cost-reducing factor to a pension fund, assuming the absence of full vesting. Also, as indicated above, in plans that do not provide death or disability benefits, terminations of employment due to these causes also represent cost-reducing factors. In the latter case, separate assumptions may be made regarding mortality, disability, and turnover; or, as is quite common, the plan actuary may use one set of termination rates covering all causes of termination of employment among nonretired workers.

Table 3–2 shows the effect on costs using three different turnover

TABLE 3–2
Present Value of $1 of Monthly Benefit Beginning at Age 65

Male Age	(1) No Turnover	(2) Scale A	(3) Scale B	Ratio (2) ÷ (1)	Ratio (3) ÷ (1)
25	$14.98	$ 8.29	$ 4.50	55%	30%
35	24.59	20.22	16.56	82	67
45	40.70	39.79	38.90	98	96

Source: Based on 1951 GAT, Projection Scale C to 1970, 5% interest and 5% loading.

assumptions. The yearly withdrawal rates under Scale A and Scale B are as follows:

Male Age	Scale A	Scale B
25	5.00%	10.00%
35	2.50	5.00
45	0.75	1.50
50	0	0

As indicated in these examples, most turnover tables assume a greater withdrawal rate at the younger ages than at the older ages, which normally would be the case.

The problems of developing accurate termination rates for a specific plan are obvious. Future withdrawal rates vary among employers and industries and with changing economic conditions. The age composition of the covered group has a significant impact on turnover rates. It generally is recognized that termination rates for younger workers are very high. Turnover rates also vary depending on the length of service of employees. Furthermore, working conditions and the personnel policies and benefit programs of a particular employer may affect turnover rates in that firm. Lastly, economic recessions or periods of prosperity may significantly alter termination rates. During periods of recession, employees will be less likely to quit, while the rate of layoffs probably will increase. The opposite situation generally prevails during periods of economic prosperity.

The concept of turnover is broader for multiemployer plans than it is for single-employer pension funds. In the former, the employee's coverage is terminated only if he or she fails to be reemployed by a participating employer within a specified time period, usually one or two years. In the skilled trades, withdrawal from the industry is less likely than separation from an individual employer. One of the basic assumptions justifying the existence of a multiemployer pension arrangement is the high degree of job mobility of the covered employees. But it also is assumed that there is a tendency for employees to be reemployed within the scope of coverage of the plan.

It is not surprising, therefore, that two actuaries may recommend considerably different withdrawal rates for the same plan. The choice of turnover assumption must rest, in the final analysis, on the sound judgment of the actuary. This judgment is based on the characteristics of the employee group, the factors discussed above, and the actuary's overall experience in pension cost projections. Some turnover tables have been developed to guide pension consultants.[4] These tables are of assistance for initial cost calculations, and adjustments in assumed turnover rates can be made as the actual experience under the plan evolves.

The question arises whether a turnover assumption should be used in calculating the level of annual contributions to be made under a plan using an unallocated funding instrument (including the conversion fund under a combination plan) when the plan covers a relatively small number of employees. The arguments for and against the use of a turnover assumption in these cases are somewhat similar to the arguments set forth earlier regarding the advisability of a mortality assumption under these plans. There is one more argument against use of a turnover assumption, and that is the fact that turnover is even less predictable than mortality for relatively small groups of employees. However, those pension planners who take the opposite stand say that there will obviously be some turnover in a plan (where there may be no mortality) and to ignore it is not to be realistic.

Rate of Retirement. In estimating the cost of pension benefits, one must make an assumption regarding the ages at which individuals will retire under the plan.

For those plans that allow retirement at ages other than the normal retirement age, it would be appropriate to make an assumption about

---

[4] See, for example, T. F. Crocker, H. M. Sarason, and B. W. Straight, *Actuaries Handbook* (Los Angeles: Pension Publications).

the percentage of people retiring at each age (just as the turnover assumption varied by age). However, for practical reasons most actuaries assume that all employees retire at one age.

Obviously, the higher the retirement age, the lower will be the cost of a given amount of retirement benefit. For example, if a plan has a retirement age of 65 rather than 62, there is an additional three-year period during which an employee may die, with the resulting possibility that the employee will never receive retirement benefits. More importantly, the requirement of retiring at 65 will reduce the length of the benefit period. In most plans, offsetting these two factors is the fact that the individual will continue to accrue benefits to age 65 and hence will be entitled to a larger basic pension.

One generally should not use a retirement age assumption lower than the normal retirement age specified in the plan, unless the plan provides some form of subsidized early retirement benefit (i.e., an early retirement benefit that is greater than the actuarial equivalent of the normal retirement benefit).

Unless the plan requires that employees retire no later than at normal retirement age, it is not unusual to find that some employees defer retirement beyond the normal retirement age. Thus, it may be logical to assume in cost estimates that the actual average retirement age is higher than the normal retirement age. Although not typical, some plans provide actuarially equivalent (larger) benefits to persons deferring retirement beyond normal retirement age. In these plans, no discount should be reflected in the cost calculations for postponed retirements.

Length of Benefit Period.   In addition to the number of employees retiring, the amount of benefit paid under the plan is affected by the length of time that retired workers receive their pension benefits (or the length of time payments will be continued under the normal form to a beneficiary of the retired worker after his death). The length of the benefit period depends on the longevity of retired workers and the normal annuity form. Therefore, an assumption must be made regarding mortality among retired lives. As indicated earlier, the mortality table used for retired lives generally is identical to the table used for active lives, except in the case of individual policy plans.

Benefit Formula.   The last factor affecting the total amount paid under the plan is the amount of pension paid to each retired worker. It goes without saying that the higher the benefit level, the greater will be the cost of the plan.

However, projecting benefit levels is more difficult under some benefit formulas than under others. The least difficult formula is one that provides a flat benefit for all retired workers, for example, a $100-a-month benefit. On the other hand, if the benefit formula calls for a pension benefit related to compensation, cost projections may include an assumption regarding expected future increases in the salaries of covered employees. For example, if a plan provides a pension benefit of 1 percent of salary per year of covered service, future increases in salary will increase benefit levels and, therefore, the cost of the plan.

The decision whether to use a salary progression assumption is an extremely important one, because of its dramatic impact on the level of projected costs. The use of a salary progression assumption substantially increases cost estimates; but the absence of such an assumption significantly understates future plan costs. The substantial impact on a cost estimate that results from use of a salary progression can be illustrated as follows: if a salary progression in the future is at the rate of 5 percent a year, the employee hired at age 20, for $6,000 a year would be receiving about $54,000 a year at age 65.

Prior to 1975, social security benefits and the maximum taxable wage base only changed by action of Congress, but commencing in 1975 social security benefits are automatically adjusted for changes in the cost of living while the maximum taxable wage base is adjusted to reflect changes in average wages in the country. Therefore, in the case of plans that are integrated with social security benefits, it is appropriate to project future levels of social security benefits or maximum taxable wage bases.

Also, in the case of negotiated plans providing a flat benefit per year of service, there generally is no advance provision for future increases in the unit benefit amount. It generally is recognized that benefit levels will be increased periodically due to inflationary pressures, but recognition is not given to this fact in cost projections until increases are actually negotiated.

Expenses

The expenses of administering the pension plan must be added to the benefits paid in arriving at the ultimate cost of the plan. The expense assumption used depends on the type of administration and the funding instrument involved. Under individual policy plans and some group pension contracts, the insurance company includes a loading for expenses in the gross premiums charged for purchased benefits. The expense loading is largest under individual policy plans and decreases considerably under group pension contracts. Additionally, some administrative fees necessitated by ERISA may be charged for separately from the gross insurance premium.

In the case of trust fund plans, the employer may pay the actuarial, legal, administrative, and investment expenses associated with the plan separately from the contribution payments to the plan. Nevertheless, these expenses must be added to the amount of benefit payment in arriving at the ultimate cost of the plan, even though they are not included in the actual cost estimates.

Possible differences in the handling of expenses, then, must be recognized in comparisons of cost projections involving different funding instruments.

Interest

The investment income earned on the accumulated assets of a funded pension plan reduces the ultimate cost of the plan. Thus, the higher the interest rate assumption, other things being equal, the lower will be the projected cost of the plan. For example, under one mortality table and assuming a 5 percent loading factor, the single-premium sum required for a 45-year-old male to purchase a pure life annuity of $1 a month beginning at age 65 is $46.47 using a 4.5 percent interest assumption, as compared with a single premium of $40.70 using a 5 percent interest assumption. Thus, in this example, an increase of one half of 1 percent in the interest rate assumption results in a reduction of about 12 percent in the estimated cost of the plan. For a given plan, the impact of a change in the interest assumption on the estimated cost of the plan depends on the age distribution of participants and their relative benefit credits.

The interest assumption used should take into account the size of the fund, the anticipated investment policy of the plan trustees, current and projected long-term rates of return, and any other factors that might affect the future pattern of investment earnings of the fund. The choice of an appropriate rate of interest is particularly difficult if a sizable portion of the assets is invested in common stocks, since these investments are subject to significant fluctuations in value. Also, investments in equities raise the rather difficult issue of how to handle unrealized capital gains. The substantial increase in common stock prices that occurred in the 1960s and the substantial decreases in common stock prices in the early 1970s, generated sizable unrealized capital gains and losses in the investment portfolios of many trust fund plans and group pension plans utilizing separate account facilities. A question arose whether these unrealized gains and losses should be recognized in actuarial valuations of plan assets and liabilities and contribution requirements; and if so, how much of these gains should be recognized and how should they be reflected in valuation procedures.

For a number of reasons, current market values of securities have seldom been used in actuarial valuations. Two of the most important reasons are: (1) market values generally will be relatively high in periods of high corporate earnings, thereby reducing the apparent need for contributions (and also the tax deductible limits) at times when the employer may be best able to make large contributions toward the pension fund (in periods of low corporate earnings the reverse will often be true, with required contributions and tax deductible limits increased at a time when the employer's capacity to contribute is at a minimum) ; and (2) because of market value fluctuations, to measure a plan's unfunded liabilities on any given date by the current market values of the fund's equities could produce a very irregular funding pattern—the antithesis of the orderly procedure which is an essential characteristic of a satisfactory pension funding program.[5]

In spite of the above objections, current market values are used in some situations. In fact, ERISA requires that the value of a defined benefit plan's assets shall be determined by any reasonable actuarial valuation method that takes into account fair market value. Generally, a fair market value alone would be an acceptable method. Cost or book value alone is not an acceptable method unless changes in fair market value are considered. Market values also are often used in valuing the conversion fund under a combination plan. In addition, the position taken by the Accounting Principles Board in *Opinion No. 8* to the effect that unrealized capital gains and losses must be recognized in accounting for pension plan costs combined with ERISA's requirement that pension plan experience gains or losses funded or amortized by level annual payments over no more than 15 years should keep this issue in the forefront.[6]

A number of approaches have been developed to overcome the drawbacks noted above to the use of current market value. For example, to minimize the effects of short-term market fluctuations, a moving average (e.g., a five-year average) of market values may be used; or only a portion (e.g., 75 percent) of the market value may be recognized. Another method used to minimize such fluctuations is to recognize appreciation annually, based on an expected long-range growth rate (e.g., 3 percent) applied to the cost (adjusted for appreciation previously so recognized) of common stocks. When this method is used, the total cost and recognized appreciation usually are not permitted to exceed a specified percentage (e.g., 75 percent) of the market value. Unrealized depreciation is recognized in full or on a basis similar to that used for unrealized appreciation.

Once it is determined how much of unrealized gains and losses is to be recognized, the next question concerns the timing of their recognition in providing for pension cost. In practice, three methods are in use: immediate recognition, spreading, and averaging.[7] Under the imme-

---

[5] William F. Marples, *Actuarial Aspects of Pension Security* (Homewood, Ill.: Richard D. Irwin, Inc., 1965), p. 107.

[6] American Institute of Certified Public Accountants, *Accounting Principles Board Opinion No. 8,* "Accounting for the Cost of Pension Plans," November 1966, p. 79.

[7] Ibid., p. 78.

diate recognition method (not ordinarily used at present for net losses), net gains are applied to reduce pension cost in the year of occurrence or the following year. Under the spreading method, net gains or losses are applied to current and future cost, either through the normal cost or through the past service (supplemental) cost. Under the averaging method, an average of annual net gains and losses, developed from those that occurred in the past with consideration of those expected to occur in the future, is applied to the normal cost.

Summary

The choice of actuarial assumptions, then, has a significant impact on the *estimated* costs of a pension plan. It must be repeated, however, that the choice of a particular set of assumptions generally has little effect on the *ultimate* cost of the plan. As with the choice of an actuarial cost method discussed later in this chapter, the choice of assumptions can have an impact on the incidence of plan costs. As gains or losses arise in the future the annual contribution account will be affected even though the ultimate cost of the plan is unchanged. Table 3–3 illustrates the impact of varying sets of assumptions on the cost estimates for an

TABLE 3–3

Effect of Varying Sets of Actuarial Assumptions on Estimated Cost of a Pension Plan

Assumptions			*Estimated Annual Cost*	
1.	(a)	4½% interest	1. Normal cost. . . . . ⋮ . . .	$18,600
	(b)	No turnover	Initial Supplemental	
	(c)	1951 GAT, projection	Liability ($239,940).	14,095
		Scale C to 1970	Total cost.	$32,695
	(d)	Average normal retirement age: 65		
2.	(a)	5% interest	2. Normal cost.	$16,050
	(b)	No turnover	ISL ($213,580).	13,230
	(c)	1951 GAT, 1970	Total cost.	$29,280
	(d)	ANRA: 65		
3.	(a)	5% interest	3. Normal cost.	$12,135
	(b)	Heavy turnover	ISL ($219,420).	13,595
	(c)	1951 GAT, 1970	Total cost.	$25,730
	(d)	ANRA: 65		
4.	(a)	5% interest	4. Normal cost.	$10,335
	(b)	Heavy turnover	ISL ($186,555).	11,560
	(c)	1951 GAT, 1970	Total cost.	$21,895
	(d)	ANRA: 67		
5.	(a)	5% interest	5. Normal cost.	$ 9,140
	(b)	Heavy turnover	ISL ($165,335).	10,245
	(c)	1951 GAT, no projection	Total cost.	$19,385
	(d)	ANRA: 67		

actual plan. The plan provides a benefit of 1 percent of compensation per year of service, with a normal retirement age of 65. The individual level cost method with a supplemental liability was used to project the cost of the plan. It is assumed that the supplemental liability will be funded over a 30-year period. The nature of the various actuarial cost methods is discussed in detail in the remainder of this chapter.

Unfortunately, an employer is sometimes unduly influenced by these cost estimates in the choice of a funding instrument. In the case illustrated in Table 3–3, proposal 5 may be misinterpreted as the lowest cost arrangement available to the employer. It may well turn out that one of the other cost projections is in fact closer to the cost that is eventually experienced under the plan. The important factors that an employer should consider in the choice of a funding instrument are examined at length in Chapter 10.

BUDGETING PENSION COSTS

The above discussion sets forth the various factors that will affect the ultimate cost of a pension plan. What is still needed, however, is some actuarial technique to determine how these estimated costs of the plan are to be spread over future years. These techniques are referred to as actuarial cost methods. More specifically, an *actuarial cost method* is a particular technique for establishing the amounts and incidence of the normal costs and supplemental costs pertaining to the benefits (or benefits and expenses) of a pension plan.[8]

The plan actuary, then, uses a set of assumptions and an actuarial cost method in estimating the annual cost of a plan. Annual contribution payments usually are based on these estimated annual costs. However, it should be noted that actual annual contribution payments need not be identical to the estimated annual costs generated by a given actuarial cost method. As will be noted in later chapters, the employer has some flexibility in the timing of contribution payments under unallocated funding instruments (for example, deposit administration and trust fund plans) as long as the minimum funding requirements established by ERISA are met. However, under certain insured funding instruments (for example, individual contracts), the actuarial cost method does effectively determine the annual premiums due under the plan.

There are several different actuarial cost methods, each producing different patterns of annual costs under the plan. Having different actu-

---

[8] The terminology pertaining to the actuarial aspects of pension planning reflects, wherever possible, the thinking of the Committee on Pension and Profit Sharing Terminology, sponsored jointly by the American Risk and Insurance Association and the Pension Research Council, University of Pennsylvania.

arial cost methods to calculate annual pension costs is analogous to having different methods for determining the annual amount of depreciation of plant and equipment to charge against operations. The depreciation methods that can be used may produce different annual charges, but the total value of the building and equipment to be depreciated is constant regardless of the depreciation formula used. Similarly, the various actuarial cost methods will produce different levels of annual cost, but the choice of a particular actuarial cost method will not affect the ultimate cost of the plan. One important exception to the latter conclusion is the fact that if an actuarial cost method is chosen that produces higher initial contributions than other methods, then the asset accumulation will be greater in the early years of the plan, thereby producing greater investment income. An increase in investment income will decrease the ultimate cost of the plan.[9]

If the choice of actuarial cost method usually has little effect on the ultimate cost of a pension plan (after taking into consideration interest, and so on), what factors determine which method will be used in calculating the amount and incidence of pension contributions? The answer to this question will become more apparent after the following discussion of the specific cost methods. However, the reader may find it helpful to keep in mind that the choice of a specific actuarial cost method is influenced to a great degree by the degree of flexibility in annual contribution payments desired by the employer and available under the particular funding instrument used.

ACTUARIAL COST METHODS

Actuarial cost methods can be broadly classified into (1) accrued benefit, and (2) projected benefit cost methods.[10] As further explained below, the class into which a particular cost method falls depends upon whether, for cost determination purposes, an employee's benefits under the pension plan are deemed to "accrue" in direct relation to years of service or are viewed as a single "projected" total.

Most actuarial cost methods break down the total actuarial cost into the normal cost and supplemental cost of the plan. The normal cost of the plan is the amount of annual cost, determined in accordance with a particular actuarial cost method, attributable to the given year of the plan's operation.

---

[9] More precisely, the timing of contribution payments has additional cost implications if federal income tax rates change; or if alternative uses of capital vary over time; or if investment return rates vary over the life of the plan.

[10] Parts of the material in this section were drawn from Joseph J. Melone, "Actuarial Cost Methods—New Pension Terminology," *Journal of Insurance,* vol. 30, no. 3 (September 1963).

Most plans provide credit for service rendered prior to the inception date of the plan. If the normal cost under the particular cost method is calculated on the assumption that annual costs have been paid or accrued from the earliest date of credited service (when in fact they have not), the plan starts out with a supplemental liability. At the inception of the plan, the supplemental liability, often called the actuarial or past service liability, arises from the fact that credit for past service is granted or part of the total benefit is imputed to years prior to the inception of this plan. The annual contribution normally will be equal to the normal cost of the plan plus at least enough of a contribution to amortize the supplemental liability over a 30-year period. If the employer wishes to fund this supplemental liability in a more rapid manner (ten years is the minimum period over which it can be funded) larger annual contributions will be required. The portion of the annual cost that is applied toward the reduction of the supplemental liability is referred to as the plan's supplemental cost. As the plan continues in operation, the size of the supplemental liability will normally change. In addition to normal increases in the supplemental liability that may occur as a result of the actuarial method being used, these changes in the size of the supplemental liability result from possible changes in benefit formulas, deviations of actual from expected experience, and changes in the actuarial assumptions or in the actuarial cost method used in subsequent normal cost calculations. A supplemental liability arises, then, whenever the present value of future normal costs is less than the present value of total projected benefits under the plan. The unfunded supplemental liability is the difference between the supplemental liability and any assets which may have accumulated under the plan as a result of prior contributions.

Accrued Benefit Cost Method

An accrued benefit cost method is one under which the actuarial costs are based directly upon benefits accrued to the date of cost determination, such benefits being determined either by the terms of the plan or by some assumed allocation of total prospective benefits to years of service. To determine the actuarial cost of the plan for a given year, the method assumes that a precisely determinable unit of benefit is associated with that year of a participant's credited service.

This method of calculating the actuarial costs of pension plans is sometimes referred to as the single-premium, unit credit, unit cost, or step-rate method.

The accrued benefit method is best adapted to those plans that provide a unit benefit type of formula based on career average compensation (for example, a percentage of each year's compensation), or a specified dollar amount for each year of credited service. Under these benefit formulas, a precisely determinable unit of benefit is associated with each year of a participant's credited service. Although best adapted to those plans that use a unit benefit type of formula, the accrued benefit cost method also can be used when the plan provides a composite benefit based on the participant's total period of credited service. For example, the plan may provide a $100 monthly pension benefit at age 65 after 25 years service, or the plan may use a benefit formula based on final average compensation. In these instances, the accrued benefit method requires that a portion of the prospective benefit be imputed to each year of credited service. This requires some arbitrary basis of allocating total prospective benefits to particular years of service. Thus, it generally is deemed advisable to use one of the projected benefit cost methods for plans of this type.

The first step in the calculation of the normal cost under the accrued benefit cost method is to determine the present value of each participant's benefit credited during the year for which costs are being calculated. The cost per dollar of benefit is a function of the participant's age and sex and of the mortality, interest, and other assumptions used. Thus, the normal cost per dollar of benefit under the accrued benefit cost method increases with the age of the participant, assuming that all other assumptions are held constant. For example, using one mortality table, a 5 percent interest assumption and a 5 percent loading, the normal cost per $1 of monthly benefit beginning at age 65 for a male employee at various ages would be as follows:

Age	Normal Cost
25	$14.98
30	19.18
35	24.59
40	31.58
45	40.70
50	52.91
55	69.69
60	93.40

If the benefit formula is related to salary, increases in compensation also would increase the normal cost for a given participant.

The normal cost for the plan as a whole is simply the sum of the separate normal costs for the benefits credited for each participant during that particular year. Although the normal cost for a given participant increases over time under the accrued benefit cost method, the normal cost for the plan as a whole generally does not increase as rapidly, or may even remain fairly constant or decrease. The reason for this is that some older employees will die or terminate, and they probably will be replaced by much younger workers. If the distribution of current service benefit credits by age and sex remains constant, the total normal cost of the plan will remain constant.

At the inception of the plan, the supplemental liability under the accrued benefit cost method arises either from the fact that past service credits have been granted or from the fact that a part of the benefits of the plan is imputed to past service. An exact relationship between the supplemental liability and the liability for benefits imputed to past service exists under the accrued benefit cost method, if the plan specifically provides benefits on account of past service. After the inception of the plan, this precise relationship between the supplemental liability and the liability for benefits imputed to past service may no longer exist, since the supplemental liability is affected, as indicated earlier, by factors other than credited past service. Therefore, the supplemental liability at the inception of the plan under the accrued benefit cost method is simply the present value of the accrued past service benefits credited as of that date. Using the single-premium rates indicated above, the supplemental liability for a male employee, age 40, as of the inception date of the plan, would be $31.58 per $1 a month of past service benefit payable beginning at age 65. If the benefit formula provides a $4-a-month benefit per year of service and the employee has ten years of credited past service, the supplemental liability for that individual would be $1263.20 ($31.58 × $40 past service benefit). The supplemental liability for the plan as a whole at the inception would be the sum of the supplemental liabilities for each of the covered employees.

It should now be clear why the accrued benefit method is readily adaptable to unit benefit formula plans. Also, this method generally is used under group deferred annuity plans, since a unit of benefit usually is purchased for each year of credited future service under these contracts. The employer has some flexibility in funding the supplemental liability. However, if the plan is funded through a group annuity contract, insurers usually require that the past service benefit of each employee be purchased by retirement date. The requirement that the past service benefits of employees be fully funded by their retirement dates imposes a substantial financial burden on the employer having a larger number of older workers at the inception of the plan.

Projected Benefit Cost Methods

Rather than costing the benefits credited during a specific period, one can project the total benefits that will be credited by retirement date and spread these costs evenly over some future period. These costing techniques are referred to as projected benefit cost methods. More specifically, a *projected benefit cost method* is one under which the actuarial costs are based upon total prospective benefits, whether or not they are attributed to any specific periods of service. The actuarial cost determination assumes regular future accruals of normal cost, generally a level amount or percentage of earnings, whose actuarial present value is equal to the present value of prospective benefits less the value of plan assets and unfunded supplemental liabilities.

From the above definition one can see that projected benefit cost methods differ from accrued benefit cost methods in two important respects. First, the normal cost accrual under a projected benefit cost method is related to the total prospective benefit rather than the benefit for a particular year. The projected benefit methods are almost always used when the plan provides a composite benefit based upon the participant's total period of credited service, such as $100 per month or 30 percent of average earnings for the last five years of service. These latter formulas do not allocate benefits to any particular year. However, it may be necessary, in the case of early retirement or termination of service with vested rights, to allocate the total potential benefit to actual years of service or to define the accrued benefit in terms of the amount purchasable by the accrued level annual cost. A projected benefit cost method can be, and is, used with benefit formulas that do allocate units of benefit to particular years of service. When so used, the normal cost accruals are still calculated on the basis of total projected benefits rather than annual units of benefit. For example, if a plan provides a retirement benefit of $6 a month per year of service, the normal cost computation is based on a projected monthly retirement benefit by $6 times the expected number of years of credited service as of normal retirement age. If the employee is age 35 upon entry into the plan and the normal retirement age is 65, then the total projected benefit is $180 a month.

A second distinguishing characteristic of projected benefit cost methods is that these techniques generally are applied with the objective of generating a normal cost which is a level amount or percentage of earnings for either the individual participants or to the participants as a group. Therefore, these methods can be characterized as level cost methods. A cost method is characterized as level if it is based on an actuarial formula designed to produce a constant year-to-year accrual of normal cost (either in amount or as a percentage of payroll or other index) if (*a*) the experience conforms with the actuarial assumptions, (*b*) there are no changes in the plan, and (*c*) certain characteristics of the employee group remain unchanged.

However, the actual experience of the plan seldom conforms precisely with the actuarial assumptions used, and it is likely that there will be changes in the composition of the group for which cost accruals are assumed. Nevertheless, these methods are characterized as level cost methods, since the theoretical objective of most of these methods is to produce a level normal cost. By contrast, the accrued benefit cost method theoretically should produce increasing annual costs until the plan matures. However, as noted earlier, changes in the composition of the group may, in practice, result in fairly level normal costs under the accrued benefit cost method.

Projected benefit cost methods may be subdivided into (1) individual level cost methods and (2) aggregate level cost methods.

Individual Level Cost Methods.   The individual subcategory of projected benefit cost methods is characterized by the assumed allocation of the actuarial cost for each individual employee, generally as a level amount or percentage of earnings, over all or a part of the employee's period of service or period of coverage under the plan, or some other appropriate period uniformly applied. Under individual cost methods, the total actuarial cost generally is separable as to the various participants; i.e., costs are calculated individually for each employee or are calculated by group methods in such a way as to produce essentially the same total result as though individually calculated.[11] The individual level cost methods may be further subdivided as to whether or not a supplemental liability is created.

Without Supplemental Liability.   As indicated above, projected benefit cost methods have as their objective the spreading of the costs of total projected benefits evenly over some future period. One logical period over which costs can be spread is the period from the attained age of the employee at the time he or she entered the plan to normal retirement age under the plan.

The normal cost accruals are determined by distributing the present value of an individual's total projected benefits as a level amount or percentage of earnings over his or her assumed future period of coverage under the plan. Total projected benefits include past service benefits, if any, as well as future service benefits to be credited by retirement age. Thus, no unfunded supplemental liability is created under this cost method at the inception of the plan, since the present value of future benefits is exactly equal to the present value of future normal cost accruals. Thereafter, there is still no supplemental liability if contribution payments have been made equal to the normal costs that have accrued in prior years.

---

[11] It should be noted, however, that this does not mean that it is possible, at any given time, to identify a participant's "share" in the plan assets. For example, a turnover assumption reduces the normal cost attributable to each participant. However, this normal cost figure is too low for the participant who does not terminate and eventually retires under the plan. Likewise, this normal cost figure is excessive for those participants who subsequently terminate with no vested benefits. For the plan as a whole, however, this normal cost figure may be entirely appropriate. This point should be kept clearly in mind, particularly in those sections of the chapter illustrating the calculations of normal costs under the various actuarial cost methods in terms of an individual participant. The authors recognize the weakness of this approach, but feel that the basic nature of each method is illustrated more clearly through use of individual participant examples.

It must be reemphasized that a supplemental liability may be created for other reasons. The point to be made here is that this actuarial cost method, other things being equal, does not of itself generate a supplemental liability.

This actuarial cost method requires, then, a projection of total benefits distributed by age at inception of coverage, and calculation of the normal cost based on a set of level premium deferred annuity rates.[12] The latter may be determined by dividing the present value of an annuity at normal retirement age by the present value of a temporary annuity running to normal retirement age. For example, assume that the total projected benefit for a participant aged 35 at the inception date of the plan is $200 a month beginning at age 65. The normal cost for this participant's benefit would be equal to the present value at age 35 of an annuity of $200 a month beginning at age 65, divided by the present value of a temporary annuity due of $1 for 30 years.

If there is no change in the projected benefits of any employee and the covered group remains constant, the normal cost under the plan will remain constant (subject to adjustment to the extent that actual experience deviates from the assumptions employed). Obviously, this will not prove to be the case in most plans. For example, if the benefit formula is related to compensation, employees will be entitled to larger projected benefits as they receive salary increases. Where salary scales have not been used in the original cost calculations, the increase in projected benefits due to salary increases is spread evenly over the period from the year in which compensation is increased to the year in which the employee reaches normal retirement age. This, of course, results in an increase in annual contributions for the plan as a whole. Also, new employees will become eligible for participation in the plan, and some currently covered workers will terminate their participation under the plan. Since the age and sex distribution and the benefit levels of new employees are not likely to be identical to those of terminated participants, there are bound to be variations in the annual contributions for the plan as a whole.

The reader will recognize that the individual level cost method without supplemental liability is, in effect, the actuarial cost method used under fully insured individual policy and group permanent plans. Indeed, this

---

[12] Regardless of which actuarial cost method is used, there is the question of whether to include in the cost calculations employees who have not yet met the plan participation requirements. One view is that a certain percentage of the currently noneligible employees will eventually qualify for participation in the plan and, therefore, the cost calculations should recognize this fact. Some actuaries, however, project costs only for those employees who are actually eligible for participation in the plan. The latter approach generally produces lower cost estimates. Either approach can be justified, but the reader should recognize that differences in cost projections may be due, at least in part, to the approach used.

cost method is analogous to the level premium concept used in individual life insurance premium calculations. For this reason, this actuarial cost method is sometimes referred to as the individual level premium method or the attained age level contribution method.

With Supplemental Liability. This cost method is similar to the previous method except that the assumption is made for the initial group of participants, that the period over which costs are spread begins with the first year they could have joined the plan had it always been in effect. For an employee who enters after the inception date of the plan, the normal cost under this method is the same as would be generated by the previous method.[13] This follows since that employee's entry year coincides with the year in which participation began. In the case of the initial group of participants, a supplemental liability automatically is created because of the assumption that normal cost payments have been made prior to the inception date of the plan.

Using the example cited above, assume that an employee is entitled to a total projected benefit at age 65 of $200 a month. The employee is age 35 at the inception of the plan but would have been eligible at age 30 had the plan been in effect. Under the individual level cost method with supplemental liability, the normal cost for this participant's benefit would be equal to the present value at age 30 (rather than age 35, as is the case under the previous cost method) of an annuity of $200 a month beginning at age 65, divided by the present value of a temporary annuity due of $1 for 35 years (rather than 30 years). In the above example, the numerator is smaller and the denominator is larger than the corresponding values calculated under the individual cost method without a supplemental liability. The result, of course, is that the normal costs are lower under the individual cost method with a supplemental liability. However, since the normal costs have not been paid for the prior years, there is a supplemental liability on behalf of this employee. Unlike the accrued benefit cost method, the initial supplemental liability under the individual cost method does not bear a precise relationship to past service benefits.

The difference between the two individual level cost methods can be made clear by reference to a situation in the individual life insurance field. Let us assume that an individual, age 25, purchased a ten-year convertible term life insurance contract. At age 30, the insured decides to convert the policy to an ordinary life insurance policy. If the conversion is made as of issue age (25), the ordinary life premium for age 25 can be viewed conceptually as the annual normal cost under the individual level cost method with supplemental liability. The sum of

---

[13] This statement assumes that the normal cost is calculated in a consistent manner for both the original group and subsequent entrants.

the annual premiums from issue date (age 25) to conversion date (age 30), improved at the assumed rate of interest and adjusted to reflect the insurance cost, would be analogous to the supplemental liability under this method. If the conversion was made as of attained age, the annual premium for age 30, adjusted to reflect the insurance cost, would be analogous to the annual cost required under the individual cost method without supplemental liability.

In valuations after the first year of the plan, the normal cost and supplemental liability would be calculated in the same manner as at the plan's inception. However, the annual contribution would be a payment of the normal cost and some payment toward the unfunded supplemental liability (the supplemental liability less any amounts that have accumulated). The normal cost calculation would be affected by any changes in assumptions or plan provisions, while the calculation of the unfunded supplemental liability would be affected not only by changes in assumptions or plan provisions, but also by any actuarial gains or losses since the plan actually started.

The individual level cost method, with supplemental liability, cannot be used under a fully insured individual policy or group permanent plan. However, this method can be used under a combination plan and under most forms of group pension contracts and trust fund plans.

The individual level cost method with a supplemental liability also is referred to as the entry age normal method.

Aggregate Level Cost Methods. The distinguishing characteristic of aggregate level cost methods is that the normal cost accruals are calculated for the plan as a whole without identifying any part of such cost accruals with the projected benefits of specific individuals. The cost accruals are expressed as a percentage of compensation or as a specified dollar amount.

The normal cost accrual rate under an aggregate method can be determined by dividing the present value of future benefits for all participants by the present value of the estimated future compensation for the group of participants. This accrual rate is then multiplied by the total annual earnings to determine the initial normal cost of the plan. If the normal cost accrual rate is to be expressed in terms of a dollar amount, then the present value of $1 per employee for each year of future service must be computed. Since there is no assumption that any normal costs have been accrued prior to the inception date of the plan, the above method does not create a supplemental liability.

In the determination of cost accruals after the inception of the plan under the above method, recognition must be given to the plan assets that presumably have been accumulated to offset prior normal cost accruals. Thus, for those years subsequent to the establishment of the plan, the accrual rate is determined by dividing the present value of aggregate future benefits, less any plan assets, by the present value of future compensation.

The normal cost accrual can be calculated under an aggregate method so as to produce a supplemental liability. This can be done in many ways, but the most clearly understood approach to creating a supplemental liability under the aggregate method is to exclude past service benefits in the projection of aggregate future benefits. This decreases the numerator of the fraction, thereby producing a smaller normal cost accrual rate. Or the actuary may simply use a supplemental liability that is generated by one of the individual cost methods. However the supplemental liability is calculated, the unfunded supplemental liability must be subtracted (along with plan assets) from the present value of aggregate future benefits in the calculation of subsequent accrual rates.

The aggregate level cost method without supplemental liability also is referred to as the percentage of payroll, the aggregate, or the remaining cost method. When there is a supplemental liability in connection with this method, it is sometimes referred to as the attained age normal or entry age normal method with initial supplemental liability.

Amortization of Supplemental Liability

The actuarial cost methods that create a supplemental liability offer the employer greater flexibility in annual contribution payments than is available under the cost methods without supplemental liability. Under the former cost methods, the employer has the alternative of funding the initial supplemental liability at a pace consistent with its financial objectives and, of course, applicable law in addition to the annual normal costs under the plan. In most cases, the employer makes some contribution toward the amortization of the supplemental liability. The length of the period over which the supplemental liability should be funded varies with the circumstances surrounding each plan. However, amortization periods of 20, 25, or 30 years often are used. Under ERISA, the initial supplemental liability must be amortized by sufficient contributions over no more than 30 plan years (the supplemental liability may be amortized over 40 years for plans in existence on January 1, 1974.) Under federal tax law, the minimum period over which the initial supplemental liability can be funded (and tax deductions allowed) is ten years.

DEFINED CONTRIBUTION PLANS

The discussion thus far in this chapter has been concerned primarily with the role of actuarial assumptions and actuarial cost methods in calculating the annual cost of a plan. The question arises as to the degree to which this discussion is pertinent in the case of defined contribution (money-purchase) plans. In these plans, the employer's contribution commitment is fixed and usually is expressed as a specified percentage of the compensation of covered employees. Thus, it would seem that there is little need for actuarial assumptions and cost methods to determine annual costs under these plans. To allow the employer to estimate future costs or benefits under the plan, projections are required on the choice of appropriate actuarial assumptions and a specific actuarial cost method. In estimating ultimate costs under a defined contribution plan, the actuary could use either the accrued benefit method or a projected benefit cost method, depending on how benefits are defined. Also, under traditional defined contribution plans, the annual contribution on behalf of each employee is viewed as a single-premium payment for a unit of deferred annuity to begin upon attainment of normal retirement age. Indeed, many of the defined contribution plans are funded through group deferred annuity contracts. Thus, the sex of the employee and mortality and interest assumptions determine the amount of benefit being credited each year. The amount of benefit credited each year for a given employee will vary with the size of the contribution payment and the number of years to retirement age.

A variation of the traditional defined contribution plan is found in some negotiated plans that have both a fixed contribution and a fixed benefit. Negotiated multiemployer plans are established on this basis. The union negotiates a fixed pension contribution rate with all participating employers, and the rate usually is expressed in terms of cents per hour worked or as a percentage of the compensation of covered employees. The contributions are paid into a single trust fund, and a uniform benefit schedule applicable to all covered employees is established. Actuarial assumptions and an actuarial cost method are needed to determine the level of benefits that can be supported by the fixed contribution commitment. In these plans, an additional assumption must be made in actuarial computations which was not mentioned earlier in the chapter; i.e., the expected level of future contributions. Since the contribution commitment usually is related to compensation or hours worked, changes in levels of economic activity affect the contribution income of the plan. The actuary, therefore, must project the future flow of contribution income to determine an appropriate benefit formula for the plan.

The cost method normally used in actuarial computations for fixed contribution–fixed benefit plans is the projected benefit cost method with a supplemental liability. This method is used for several reasons. One, this method tends to produce annual normal costs that may be expected to remain fairly stable as a percentage of payroll or in terms of cents per hour, if the actuarial assumptions are in fact realized; and this is consistent with the contribution commitment under these plans, which is normally expressed as a percentage of payroll or in cents per hour of work. Two, the existence of a supplemental liability permits some flexibility in annual contribution income. As indicated above, changes in levels of employment will result in fluctuations in the annual aggregate contribution income of the plan, which may not match fluctuations in the amount of benefits credited. During periods of prosperity, the excess of actual over expected contribution income can be applied toward amortizing the supplemental liability at a rate faster than anticipated; likewise, periods of recession result in extensions of the period over which the supplemental liability is to be amortized. Of course, in both cases, the amortization periods must be in line with the minimums and maximums permitted under federal law. Lastly, other things being equal, the projected benefit method with supplemental liability usually will generate the highest benefit level for a given rate of contribution.

MINIMUM FUNDING STANDARDS

The basic change in the minimum funding standard required by ERISA is that a pension plan having supplemental liabilities must amortize such liabilities over a specified period of time in addition to the funding of normal cost.

The requirement for amortizing supplemental liability applies only to defined benefit plans, since a defined contribution plan cannot technically have a supplemental liability. For defined contribution plans, the minimum contribution is the amount indicated by the plan formula.

In meeting the minimum funding standards, the liabilities of a pension plan must be calculated on the basis of actuarial assumptions and actuarial cost methods which are reasonable and which offer the actuary's best estimate of anticipated experience under the plan.

The amortization periods for unfunded supplemental liabilities differ for single-employer plans and multiemployer plans. For single-employer plans in existence on January 1, 1974, the maximum amortization period is 40 years; for single-employer plans established after January 1, 1974, the maximum amortization period is 30 years. Moreover, experience gains and losses for single-employer plans must be amortized over a shorter period of time; that is, 15 years. The shorter amortization period for gains and losses was designed to stimulate the use of realistic actuarial assumptions.

The amortization periods for multiemployer plans generally are longer than for single-employer plans. The special treatment accorded multiemployer plans has been attributed to some extent to the political pressure of organized labor which felt that too strict a set of funding standards for multiemployer pension plans would limit future plan benefit increases. Supplemental liabilities under multiemployer pension plans can be amortized over 40 years for both plans in existence on January 1, 1974 and also for plans established thereafter. Another advantage is granted these plans since experience gains and losses must be spread over 20 years, not 15 as for single-employer plans. For supplemental liabilities associated with changes in actuarial assumptions, they must be amortized over a period not longer than 30 years, the same as for single-employer plans.

Under ERISA, the secretary of labor may extend for a period of up to ten years the amortization period for supplemental liabilities and experience losses for both single-employer and multiemployer plans. The purpose of such potential extensions are for those cases where a substantial risk exists that unless such an extension were granted, a pension plan would be terminated or greatly reduced employee benefit levels or reduced employee compensation would result.

The Treasury Department also can allow some flexibility in employers meeting the minimum funding standards of ERISA for both single- and multiemployer plans. In those circumstances where an employer would incur substantial business hardship and if strict enforcement of the minimum funding standards would adversely affect plan participants, the secretary of the treasury may waive for a particular year payment of all or a part of a plan's normal cost and the additional liabilities to be funded during that year. No more than five waivers may be granted a plan within a consecutive 15-year period. The amount waived plus interest, must be amortized not less rapidly than ratably over 15 years.

There are certain exemptions from the mandated minimum funding standards. Generally, the minimum funding standards apply to pension plans of private employers in interstate commerce, plans of employee organizations with members in interstate commerce and plans that seek a qualified status under the tax laws. Exempt plans include government plans and church plans unless they elect to comply with the requirements of ERISA. Fully insured pension plans (funded exclusively through individual or group permanent insurance contracts) are exempt from the minimum funding rules as long as all premiums are paid when due and no policy loans are allowed. Additionally, plans that also are exempt are arrangements designed to provide deferred compensation to highly compensated employees, plans that provide supplemental benefits on an unfunded, nonqualified basis, and those plans to which the employer does not contribute.

Funding Standard Account

All pension plans subject to the minimum funding requirements must establish a "funding standard account" that provides a comparison between actual contributions and those required under the minimum funding requirements. The basic purpose of the funding standard account is to provide some flexibility in funding through allowing contributions greater than the required minimum, accumulated with interest, to reduce the minimum contributions required in future years.

Operation of the Account. For each plan year, the funding standard account is charged for the normal cost for the year and with the minimum amortization payment required for initial supplemental liabilities, increases in plan liabilities, experience losses, and waived contributions for each year. The account is credited in each plan year for employer contributions made for that year, with amortized portions of plan cost decreases resulting from plan amendments (presumably decreases in plan benefits) and experience gains, and with amounts of any waived contributions. If the contributions to the plan, adjusted as indicated above, meet the minimum funding standards, the funding standard account will show a zero balance. If the funding standard account has a positive balance at the end of the year, such balance will be credited with interest (at the rate used to determine plan costs). Therefore, the need for future contributions to meet the minimum funding standards will be reduced to the extent of the positive balance plus the interest credited. If, however, the funding standard account shows a deficit balance called the accumulated funding deficiency (minimum contributions in essence have not been made), the account will be charged with interest at the rate used to determine plan costs. Moreover, the plan will be subject to an excise tax of 5 percent of the accumulated funding deficiency (100 percent if not corrected or paid off within 90 days after notice of a deficiency by the secretary of the treasury). In addition to the excise tax, the employer may be subject to civil action in the courts for failure to meet the minimum funding standards.

To illustrate how the funding account works, consider the following example:

In 1979, the Marvele Manufacturing Corporation establishes a pension trust to provide retirement benefits for its employees. In the year it is established the plan has a supplemental liability of $1 million because of employee service prior to the adoption of the pension plan. Normal cost is $82,000. The interest rate used in determining plan cost is 6 percent. In the first plan year, Marvele Corporation contributions amount to $150,536. The funding standard account for 1979 is as follows:

Credits:

Marvele Corporation pension contributions $150,536

Charges:

Normal cost of the plan (current service)   82,000
Amortization of $1,000,000 initial past service
liability plus 6 percent interest over 30 years   68,536

Total $150,536
Net Balance   0

In the above example, the mimimum funding standards would have been met precisely. On the other hand, if Marvele Corporation had contributed $175,000, the funding standard account would show a positive balance of $24,464 plus 6 percent interest amounting to $1,468 (the same rate used in determining plan cost) for a net balance of $25,932 which would be a credit for a future plan year or years.

Conversely, if Marvele Corporation contributed $120,000 for the plan year it would not meet the minimum funding standard of $150,536 and an accumulated funding deficiency is present. The total funding deficiency for this plan year would be $30,536 ($150,636 − $120,000) plus 6 percent interest of $1,832 (the same rate used in determining plan cost) or a total deficiency of $32,368 and subject to the penalties outlined above.

Alternative Minimum Funding Standard

A pension plan using a funding method that requires contributions in all years not less than those required under the "entry age normal funding method" can elect compliance under the alternative minimum funding standard. Under this standard, the minimum annual contribution to the pension plan would be the lesser of the normal cost determined for the plan or the normal cost determined under the accrued benefit cost method plus the excess if any of the actuarial value of the accrued benefits over the fair market value of the assets. All assets, under this standard, are valued at their actual market value on the date of valuation without benefit of averaging or amortization, and the plan liabilities would be valued on the same basis that the Pension Benefit Guaranty Corporation would have used had the plan terminated. Adherence to this standard would assure that the pension plan would have assets, valued at market, at least equal to the actuarial value of all accrued benefits, whether vested or not. The rationale for this alternative approach is that there appears to be little justification to hold assets in excess of those needed to meet accrued benefits.

A pension plan using this approach must set up an alternative minimum funding standard account. Such an account is charged each year with the lesser of the normal cost of the plan or the normal cost determined under the accrued benefit cost method plus the excess of the actuarial value of accrued benefits over plan assets (not less than zero) and will be credited with contributions. There is no carry-over of contributions over the required minimum from one year to the next, since any excess contributions simply become a part of the plan assets for the following year's comparison of assets and liabilities. Conversely, as with the regular funding standard account, any deficiency of contributions is carried over from year to year, with interest, and the excise tax described earlier is payable on the cumulative funding deficiency.

A pension plan electing the alternative funding standard must maintain both an alternate funding standard account and the basic funding standard account. The basic funding standard account is charged and credited under the normal rules, but an excise tax will not be levied on any deficiency in that account if there is no deficiency in the alternate account. A pension plan making this choice is required to maintain both accounts since the minimum required contribution in a particular plan year is the lesser of the contributions called for by the basic and alternate standards. If a plan switches from the alternate standard back to the basic standard, the excess of the deficiency in the standard account over the deficiency in the alternate standard account must be amortized over five years.

Full Funding Limitation

Other than the rules regarding tax deductibility of pension plan contributions discussed in detail in Chapter 4, a general rule that overrides all others is that the tax deduction for any particular year cannot exceed the amount needed to bring the pension plan to a fully funded status. Therefore, no income tax deductions can be taken for contributions that would raise plan assets above the actuarial value of plan liabilities, computed in accordance with the actuarial cost method in regular use by the plan.

ACCOUNTING FOR PENSION COSTS

As can be seen from the above discussion, a variety of acceptable actuarial cost methods exists, permitting employers considerable flexibility in determining the amounts of annual contributions and the rate at which past service liabilities are to be funded. For purposes of financial statement accounting, most employers have treated actual contributions or annuity premium payments made during the year as the firm's pension cost for that period—a cash accounting approach. With the flexibility available in calculating contributions, it is not surprising that the accounting for the cost of pension plans has varied widely among companies and has sometimes resulted in wide year-to-year fluctuations in the provisions for pension costs of a single company.

This wide variation in accounting practice has been of concern to the accounting profession for several years, particularly in view of the increasing magnitude of pension costs relative to a firm's financial position and operating results. After many years of research and study, the Accounting Principles Board of the American Institute of Certified Public

Accountants issued, in November 1966, *Opinion No. 8* to clarify the principles regarding accounting for the cost of pension plans.[14]

Opinion No. 8 specifies that accounting for pension costs should not be discretionary, and that provision for pension costs should be made annually on a consistent and systematic basis, whether or not contributions were actually made during the particular accounting period. Thus, pension costs are to be recognized on an accrual basis rather than a cash accounting basis. Of course, ERISA calls for reports on the status of contributions and funding of pension plans.

Provision for annual pension costs should be based on an accounting method that uses an acceptable actuarial cost method, subject to the minimum and maximum funding standards permitted by ERISA. The minimum annual provision for pension cost should not be less than the total of (1) normal cost, and (2) an amount necessary to fund past service liability over a 30-year period. The maximum annual provision for pension cost should not be greater than the total of (1) normal cost, and (2) an amount that allows for the funding of the initial past service liability over a ten-year period, and (3) an adjustment for interest on the difference between pension expense charges in prior years and the amounts actually funded.

Actuarial gains and losses, including realized investment gains and losses, should be recognized in the provision for pension cost in a consistent manner that reflects the long-range nature of pension cost. Accordingly, actuarial gains and losses should be spread over the current year and future years or applied on the basis of an averaging technique.[15] Actuarial gains and losses should be recognized immediately if they arise from a single occurrence not directly related to the operation of the pension plan and not in the ordinary course of the employer's business. An example of such occurrences is a plant closing, in which case the actuarial gain or loss should be treated as an adjustment of the net gain or loss from that occurrence and not as an adjustment of pension cost for the year. Unrealized appreciation and depreciation of equity securities should be recognized in the determination of the provision for pension cost on a rational and systematic basis that avoids giving undue weight to short-term market fluctuations. Ordinarily, appreciation and depreciation need not be recognized for debt securities expected to be held to maturity and redeemed at face value.

If an employer's actual plan contributions exceed the amount that

---

[14] A further interpretation of *Opinion No. 8,* based on the Employee Retirement Income Security Act is stated in the *Journal of Accountancy,* March 1975, pp. 71–72.

[15] Under ERISA, there is a 15-year maximum in the case of single-employer plans and 20 years for multiemployer plans. Actuarial gains and losses arising out of changes in actuarial assumptions must be amortized over 30 years regardless of the type of plan involved.

has been charged to income, the difference should be shown on the balance sheet as a prepaid pension cost. Likewise, pension charges in excess of actual contributions should be shown as an accrued liability.

Opinion No. 8 does not alter in any way an employer's legal obligation to covered employees as specified in the plan agreement and by ERISA. Nor does this recommended accounting procedure alter IRS rules regarding deductibility of pension contributions, which continue to be based on actual contribution payments.

4

Plan Qualification and Deductibility of Employer Contributions

The tax advantages provided under the Internal Revenue Code for qualified pension and profit sharing plans are most significant—both to an employer and to its employees. The principal tax advantages of such a plan are:

1. Contributions made by the employer, within the limitations prescribed, are deductible as a business expense.
2. Investment income on these contributions normally is not subject to federal income tax until paid in the form of benefits.
3. An employee is not considered to be in receipt of taxable income until benefits are distributed or made available.
4. Death benefits paid on behalf of an employee are not considered as part of the employee's gross estate for federal estate tax purposes to the extent attributable to employer contributions and to the extent paid to a named personal beneficiary.
5. A lump-sum distribution to an employee on account of severance of employment or after the employee attains age 59½ will be taxed on a favorable basis.

To obtain these tax benefits, the plan must achieve a qualified status by meeting the requirements of the Internal Revenue Code and appropriate regulations and rulings issued by the Commissioner of Internal Revenue. This chapter, while not intended as an exhaustive treatise on the tax aspects of qualified plans, should serve as a general guide to the major requirements of federal tax law which a plan must meet if this qualified status is to be obtained. This chapter also includes a summary of the procedures involved in submitting a plan to the Internal Revenue Service for the purpose of obtaining an advance determination letter, as well as a brief discussion of the provisions of federal tax law relating to trust investments for a qualified plan and the deductibility of employer contributions.

QUALIFICATION REQUIREMENTS

Coverage Requirements

One of the most important requirements of a qualified plan is that it must be for the exclusive benefit of employees or their beneficiaries. Officers of a corporation and stockholders may participate in the plan if they are bona fide employees. However, a plan cannot be structured so that it discriminates in any fashion in favor of officers, stockholders, or highly compensated employees, commonly referred to as the *prohibited group* of employees.[1]

It is possible for an attorney or other professional person to be a bona fide employee and, as such, to participate in a qualified plan. The mere fact that a professional employee has income other than from the employer is immaterial. If such an individual is an employee for all purposes, including coverage for social security benefits, and income from the employer is subject to withholding for income tax purposes, he or she may be considered as an employee under the plan.

The Code requires that a plan, if it is to qualify, must meet *either* of the two following requirements:

1.   It must cover 70 percent or more of all employees or, if the plan requires employee contributions and if 70 percent or more of all employees are eligible to participate in the plan, at least 80 percent of those eligible must elect to participate. Under this latter provision, if only 70 percent of the employees are eligible only 56 percent of the total employees have to be covered (80% × 70%). In applying this requirement, those employees who have not satisfied the minimum age and service requirements of the plan need not be taken into consideration.

2.   It will benefit such employees as qualify under a classification set up by the employer and found by the Internal Revenue Service not

---

[1] Before enactment of the Self-Employed Individuals Tax Retirement Act, better known as H.R. 10, sole proprietors and partners could not participate in a qualified plan, although they could establish such a plan for their employees. H.R. 10 gave these individuals the status of "employees" for the purpose of participating in a qualified plan, but under certain restrictions and limitations. The requirements for H.R. 10 plans are considerably different from those of a regular qualified plan and are beyond the scope of this chapter. They are, however, discussed in Chapter 17.

to be discriminatory in favor of officers, stockholders, or highly compensated employees.

In applying these two requirements, it will be permissible to exclude from consideration any employees who are covered by a collective bargaining agreement if there is evidence that retirement benefits were the subject of good faith bargaining. It is also possible to exclude nonresident aliens who receive no income from the employer from sources within the United States.

In actual practice, the second of these two requirements is the one most frequently used. Under this provision, it is possible to establish a plan solely for hourly or salaried employees or for those employees who work in certain designated departments or in other classifications, so long as it does not discriminate in favor of the prohibited group of employees. The Code itself states that a classification shall not be considered discriminatory merely because it excludes employees who earn no more than wages taxable under the Social Security Act or merely because it is limited to salaried or clerical employees. It should be noted, however, that this Code provision does not mean that a "salaried-only" plan automatically will be acceptable. Such a plan must still meet the overriding requirement that there cannot be discrimination in favor of the prohibited group of employees.

The question of whether a plan may qualify if limited to only salaried employees has been of considerable significance in recent years. At one time, advance determination letters were readily granted for such plans by the Internal Revenue Service if all other factors were acceptable. It has, however, become increasingly difficult to qualify plans with this type of eligibility requirement, and the attitude of the Service appears to be that for a salaried-only plan to qualify, it must cover a fair cross section of employees. Thus, for example, if the salaried employees of an employer are all earning more than the hourly employees, it is quite likely that the Service will find the plan objectionable. On the other hand, if the earnings of covered salaried employees, as compared to the earnings of all the employees, reflect both the lowest pay ranges and a satisfactory portion of the intermediate pay levels, it is quite possible that the plan will qualify if all other factors are acceptable.

The coverage requirements of federal tax law also limit the employer's choice of eligibility requirements (for example, minimum service, minimum and maximum ages, minimum compensation) to the extent that the requirements chosen must meet the requirements imposed by ERISA and, in addition, must not produce discrimination in favor of the prohibited group of employees. Here, as in other areas, the question of whether a particular plan provision is discriminatory will depend upon the facts of the particular case and the judgment of the local reviewer of the Internal Revenue Service.

The coverage requirements are also significant in the area of employee contributions. For example, while a plan may require employees to contribute, the employee contribution rate cannot be so high as to make the plan unattractive except to highly compensated employees. As a general rule, an employee contribution rate of 6 percent or less will not be considered burdensome.

The coverage requirements need be met on only one day in each quarter of the plan's taxable year.

Contribution and Benefit Requirements

Another major requirement of a qualified plan is that the contributions or benefits provided cannot discriminate in favor of officers, stockholders, or highly compensated employees—i.e., the prohibited group of employees.

A plan will not be discriminatory merely because it excludes individuals who earn less than the maximum taxable wage for social security purposes, nor does the law prohibit the use of a benefit formula which provides a larger percentage of benefit for earnings in excess of the social security taxable wage base than it does for earnings under this amount. However, if the benefit formula is in any way integrated with social security benefits, certain requirements are imposed to prevent discrimination in favor of the prohibited group of employees. The basic concept of these requirements is that the benefits from the employer's plan must be dovetailed with social security benefits in such a manner that employees earning over the taxable base will not receive combined benefits under the two programs which are proportionately greater than the combined benefits for employees earning under this amount.

These integration requirements take into account the type of benefit formula employed, whether a death benefit is included prior to retirement, and whether there is any death benefit (and the form thereof) after retirement. Other factors such as the normal retirement age specified in the plan, disability benefits, early retirement benefits, the manner of determining earnings, and the presence or absence of employee contributions are also considered. These integration requirements, as they apply to specific formulas and plan provisions, are discussed in Chapter 2.

Other Requirements

Must Be in Writing. A qualified plan must be in writing and must set forth all the provisions necessary for qualification. This is normally accomplished by means of a trust agreement, a plan instrument, or both.

In group pension programs, the plan provisions are sometimes contained in the group contract and, in this event, neither a trust agreement nor a separate plan instrument is necessary.

A trust agreement generally is required for trust fund plans and for plans using individual insurance or, annuity contracts.[2] This allows the employer to make irrevocable contributions on a basis which will permit the employee to defer including these contributions as taxable income until the time they are distributed or made available. If a group pension contract is employed, an intervening trust usually is not necessary, since the same results can be achieved through the group contract itself—i.e., the contract can be written so that employer contributions are irrevocably made without the employees being considered in receipt of these contributions until they are distributed or made available.

Communication to Employees.   The plan also must be communicated to employees. An announcement letter or booklet frequently is used for this purpose. If employees are not given a copy of the actual plan, they should be told that a copy is available for inspection at convenient locations.

Nondiversion of Contributions.   The trust must specifically provide that it is impossible for the employer to divert or recapture contributions before the satisfaction of all plan liabilities—with certain exceptions, funds contributed must be used for the exclusive benefit of employees or their beneficiaries. One exception to this rule may occur at termination of a pension plan, if any funds then remain because of "actuarial error" and all fixed and contingent obligations of the plan have been satisfied. In this event, such excess funds may be returned to the employer. A second exception makes it possible to establish or amend a plan on a conditional basis so that employer contributions are returnable within one year from the denial of qualification if the plan is not approved by the Internal Revenue Service. It is also possible for an employer to make a contribution on the basis that it will be allowed as a deduction; if this is done, the contribution, to the extent it is disallowed, may be returned within one year from the disallowance. Further, contributions made on the basis of a mistake in fact can be returned to the employer within one year from the time they were made.

Definitely Determinable Benefits.   A qualified pension plan must provide definitely determinable benefits. A defined contribution pension plan meets this requirement, since the employer's contribution formula is definite and, for this reason, benefits are considered as being actuarially determinable. Also, variable annuity plans or plans under which the benefit varies with a cost of living index will be acceptable.

---

[2] A trust agreement is not necessary for some fully insured individual policy plans that employ nontransferable contracts. However, a plan instrument of some type would still be required so that the plan provisions can be set forth in writing.

Because of the definitely determinable benefit requirement, any amounts forfeited by terminating employees may not be used to increase benefits for the remaining participants under a pension plan—instead, these forfeitures must be used to reduce employer contributions next due. Under this requirement, the question often arises as to whether dividends under insurance or annuity contracts must be used to reduce employer contributions or whether they may be applied to provide additional benefits. If the benefit formula specifically calls for the use of these dividends to increase benefits and discrimination in favor of the prohibited group of employees does not result, use of dividends in this manner will be permissible under plans funded with individual insurance or annuity contracts.[3] However, if the plan is funded with a group pension contract, dividends generally must be used to reduce employer contributions.

The definitely determinable benefit requirement does not apply to qualified profit sharing plans. Here, there is a requirement that the plan must provide for participation in the profits of the employer by the employees or their beneficiaries. While it is not required that there be a definite formula for determining the amount to be contributed to the profit sharing plan, it is required that there be a definite predetermined formula for allocating contributions among participants and for distributing funds after a fixed number of years, the attainment of a stated age, or upon the happening of some event such as layoff, illness, disability, retirement, death, or severance of employment.

Permanency.   The plan must be a permanent one. While the employer may reserve the right to amend or terminate the plan at any time, it is expected that the plan will be established on a permanent basis. Thus, if a plan is terminated for any reason other than business necessity within a few years after it has been in force, this will be considered as evidence that the plan, from its inception, was not a bona fide one for the benefit of employees. This, of course, could result in adverse tax consequences.

In the profit sharing area, as previously noted, it is not necessary that the employer make contributions in accordance with a definite predetermined formula. However, merely making a single or an occasional contribution out of profits will not be sufficient to create a permanent and continuing plan. The regulations require that "substantial and recurring" contributions must be made out of profits.

Inclusion of Death Benefits.   Death benefits may be included in a qualified plan, but only to the extent that these benefits are "incidental."

In a qualified pension plan (other than one using a defined contribution formula) using life insurance, the incidental test is satisfied if the life insurance benefit does not exceed 100 times the expected monthly retirement benefit or, if greater, the reserve for this benefit. For profit

---

[3] However, additional benefits that result from applying dividends in this manner must be taken into account if the plan is integrated with social security benefits.

sharing plans and pension plans using a defined contribution (money-purchase) formula, the incidental test for the use of life insurance is satisfied if: (1) the aggregate of the premiums paid for a participant's life insurance is less than one half of the contributions allocated to the participant at any particular time; and (2) the plan requires the trustee to convert the entire value of the life insurance contract at or before retirement into cash, or to provide periodic income so that no portion of such value may be used to continue life insurance protection beyond retirement, or to distribute the contract to the participant. The incidental test is not violated if the death benefit does not exceed the sum of the reserve of the life insurance policy and the amount held for the employee in the conversion fund. Also, as long as less than 50 percent of the employer's contributions for an employee have been used to purchase life insurance, the face amount of the life insurance plus the employee's share of the conversion fund may be paid as the death benefit under a defined benefit plan without violating the incidental death benefit rules.

If a plan provides for a surviving spouse benefit in the form of a life annuity, the incidental test is set forth in terms of the maximum percentage of the employee's accrued or projected pension that may be paid to the employee's spouse. Table 4–1 shows the maximum percent-

TABLE 4–1
Maximum Percentages Considered an Incidental
Spouse Benefit

Eligible Age	*Maximum Percentage*	
	Accrued	*Projected*
20 or less	75	45
25	75	50
30	80	55
35	80	60
40	85	$66\frac{2}{3}$
45	90	75
50	100	90
55 and over	100	100

ages of an employee's benefits that may be considered an incidental spouse benefit, depending upon the earliest age at which an employee becomes eligible for the spouse benefit.

Vesting. A plan will not qualify unless it provides for full vesting when an employee attains normal retirement age (or a stated age or some other event in the case of a profit sharing plan) and unless it provides for fully vested rights in all participants upon termination of the plan or permanent discontinuance of plan contributions. Further, the plan must incorporate all of the vesting requirements imposed by ERISA.[4]

U.S. Trust.   If a trust is used, it must be one which is organized or created in the United States and maintained at all times as a domestic trust. The earnings of a trust created outside of the United States will be taxable, although if the trust would otherwise qualify, the employer will be allowed to take appropriate deductions for its contributions and the beneficiaries of the trust will be allowed the same tax treatment for distributions as if the trust had been qualified.[5]

ERISA Requirements.   The Code was amended by ERISA to require that qualified plans include a number of different provisions. Several of these provisions already have been noted in this chapter. The remaining requirements are discussed in greater detail in Chapter 2, and are only summarized below.

1. *Service.*   The determination of service for purposes of eligibility and vesting must be made in accordance with detailed specifications.
2. *Spouse Benefits.*   A plan must provide for an optional preretirement and a mandatory postretirement spouse benefit if the employee and his or her spouse have been married for at least one year.
3. *Maximum Benefits and Contributions.*   The benefit payable to a participant under a defined benefit plan and the annual addition made on behalf of a participant under a defined contribution plan must be limited; further, a combined limit is imposed in any situation where both a defined benefit and a defined contribution plan are in effect.
4. *Plan Termination.*   The manner in which plan assets must be allocated in the event of plan termination is established by ERISA.
5. *Assignments.*   The plan must prohibit assignments (except to the extent of 10 percent of benefit payments and except to the extent of utilizing a vested interest as collateral for a loan made from the plan).
6. *Mergers and Consolidations.*   A provision must be included to protect an employee's benefits in the event of a merger or consolidation of plans.
7. *Payment of Benefits.*   Unless otherwise requested by the employee, benefit payments must commence within 60 days after the later of the plan year in which the employee terminates employment, completes 10 years of participation, or attains age 65 or the normal retirement date specified in the plan.

---

[4] These requirements are discussed in Chapter 2.

[5] Special rules exist with regard to the taxation of distributions to nonresident aliens.

8. *Increases in Social Security.* Any increase in social security benefits that takes place after retirement or after termination of employment cannot operate to reduce an employee's benefits.

Also, for general purposes of qualification, for the application of minimum participation and vesting standards, and for the application of the maximum limitation on benefits and contributions, all organizations under common control (that is, where there is 80 percent control) will be considered as a single employer. (For purposes of applying the limitation on benefits and contributions, only 50 percent control is needed.)

OBTAINING AN ADVANCE DETERMINATION LETTER

The federal tax law does not require submission of a plan to the Internal Revenue Service for an advance determination that the plan meets the requirements of the Code and has achieved a qualified status. As a convenience to the taxpayer, however, the Internal Revenue Service will issue advance determination letters (often called "approval" letters) as to the qualified status of a plan. Most taxpayers take advantage of this and obtain such a ruling.

One reason for taking advantage of this procedure is the possibility that the Service will find some feature or features of the plan to be unacceptable. The Code permits a retroactive change in the plan (to its effective date) if the change is made by the time the employer's tax return for the year is due, including extensions. If changes are necessary, the employer may make the appropriate amendments to the plan within this period and thus preserve the deductions to be claimed for the taxable year involved.

In contrast, if the employer does not file for an advance determination letter, the qualified status of the plan will be examined by the Service at the time the employer's tax return is audited. Any changes then required by the Service will, in all probability, be at a time which is beyond the period allowed for making a retroactive change. Thus, there would be the possibility of the employer losing at least one year's deduction.

The Internal Revenue Service has issued rulings that prescribe the information to be submitted in requesting an advance determination letter. The information required includes the following:

1. The name of the plan and the name and address of the employer (and trustee, if applicable), and the plan administrator if other than the employer.
2. Verified copies of any trust agreement involved.
3. Verified copies of any plan instrument involved.
4. Verified copies of any group pension contract involved.

5. Specimen copies of any individual life insurance or annuity contracts involved.
6. Specimen copies of the formal announcement and detailed description made available to employees.
7. Verified or specimen copies of any amendments to any of the above items.
8. A detailed description of the plan (effective dates, eligibility requirements, employer and employee contribution levels, retirement dates and provisions, vesting and death benefit provisions, rights of the employer to amend or terminate and employee benefits upon termination, funding instrument, method of distributing benefits, and so on).
9. A summary concerning the salaries, benefits, contributions, and other information relating to the 25 highest paid participants of each employer participating in the plan.[6]
10. A schedule concerning the total nondeferred compensation paid or accrued to employees and the total amount allocated by the employer under the plan.
11. A classification of all employees, with reasons indicated as to why certain employees are not eligible to participate.
12. A detailed description of all methods, factors, and assumptions used in determining and adjusting costs.
13. A statement of applicable limitations on deductions.
14. Evidence that all interested parties (e.g., employees) have been properly notified of the application for the advance determination letter.

The application for an advance determination letter is filed with the district director for the district in which the employer's principal place of business is located (or where the parent company's principal place of business is located in the case of a plan covering a parent company and some or all of its subsidiaries). The advance determination letter, however, will be issued by a "key" district office (19 district offices have been so designated). As indicated above, employees must be given written advance notice of the request. This notice must advise the employees that any employee (or class of employees) may comment to the district director on the application within 45 days. Moreover, the Pension Benefit Guaranty Corporation, or the secretary of labor (if requested by 10 percent of the employees or by ten employees, whichever is less) also may comment upon the application. If the district director proposes to issue an adverse letter, this may be appealed to the Office of the Assistant

---

[6] While in most cases the employees affected are the same, this listing of the 25 highest paid participants should not be confused with the 25 highest paid employees on the effective date of the plan who are or who may become participants and whose benefits would be restricted in the event of early termination of the plan.

Regional Commissioner and, if the assistant regional commissioner upholds the proposed adverse determination, the National Office may be requested to consider the application. The basis for requesting National Office consideration must be one or more of the following:

1. The position of the Regional Office is contrary to the law or regulations on the points at issue.
2. The position of the Regional Office is contrary to a published precedent of the Service currently in effect.
3. The position of the Regional Office is contrary to a court decision that is followed by the Service.
4. The contemplated Regional Office action is in conflict with a determination made in a similar case in the same or another region.
5. The issues arise because of unique or novel facts which have not previously been passed upon in any published precedent.

It is customary to arrange for a conference at each appropriate level within the Internal Revenue Service before an adverse letter is proposed for issuance. Also, in addition to the appeal procedure described above, the district director may be requested to refer specific issues to the National Office for technical advice. Technical advice can be requested only for the reasons mentioned above and, if the National Office issues such technical advice on any issue, it may not be the basis for a subsequent appeal.

If the employer has exhausted all remedies within the Internal Revenue Service (including all of the appeal procedures previously described), and if an adverse determination letter is issued, the employer may seek a declaratory judgment in the United States Tax Court as to the qualified status of the plan. An employee who has filed comment with the district director and the Department of Labor also may seek a declaratory judgment with respect to the qualified status of the plan after all administrative remedies have been exhausted.

TRUST INVESTMENTS

As previously noted, a qualified plan must be for the exclusive benefit of employees or their beneficiaries, and this primary purpose must be maintained with respect to the investment of trust funds as well as in other activities of the trust. Generally, the trustee may purchase any investments permitted by the trust agreement to the extent permitted by ERISA and by general law. The fiduciary provisions of ERISA also require that the fiduciaries of the plan use the care, skill, prudence, and diligence in making investments that a prudent man who is familiar with such matters would use under the circumstances then prevailing. A fiduciary is also responsible for diversifying investments so as to minimize the risk of large losses unless it is clearly prudent not to diversify, and must invest only in assets subject to the jurisdiction of the U.S. courts.

Prohibited Transactions

The Internal Revenue Code, as amended by ERISA, prohibits certain transactions between the plan and parties in interest. A party in interest is broadly defined and includes, for example, any fiduciary, a person providing services to the plan, any employer or employee organization whose employees or members are covered by the plan, a direct or indirect owner of 50 percent or more of the business interest, a relative of any of the above, and an employee, officer, director, or a person having 10 percent or more of the ownership interest in any of the above.

The following are prohibited transactions between the plan and a party in interest:

1. The sale, exchange, or leasing of property.
2. Lending money or extending credit (including the funding of the plan by the contribution of debt securities).
3. Furnishing goods, services, or facilities.
4. Transfer to or the use of plan assets.
5. Acquisition of qualifying employer securities and real property in excess of allowable limits.

Additionally, a party in interest is prohibited from dealing with plan assets in his or her own interest or for his or her own account.

Prior to ERISA, it was possible for a party in interest to deal with the plan provided that the transaction was at arm's length and the plan was adequately protected. Under ERISA, any transactions between a party in interest and the plan (with limited exceptions) are prohibited. To provide for a reasonable transition to the new requirements, any investments on July 1, 1974 which were not then in violation of the law will continue to be permissible until June 30, 1984 if the situation continues to be at least as favorable as an arm's length transaction with an unrelated party. The effective date of the prohibited services portion of ERISA also was delayed until June 30, 1977 for services which were ordinarily and customarily offered on June 30, 1974.

If a party in interest engages in a prohibited transaction, an excise tax of 5 percent of the amount involved in the transaction may be levied upon the party in interest. If the situation is not corrected within the time allowed (90 days unless extended by the Internal Revenue Service), a further excise tax of 100 percent of the amount involved will be levied. Prior to ERISA, a plan lost its qualified status if it engaged in a prohibited transaction; this penalty no longer applies.

A significant aspect of the prohibited transaction rules concerns the investment of plan assets in qualifying employer securities and real property. Qualifying employer securities include stock. Marketable obligations also are considered to be qualifying employer securities if certain requirements are met. The first of these requirements relates to the purchase price of the obligation and is satisfied if any one of the following three tests is met:

1. The obligation is acquired on the market either at the price of the obligation prevailing on a national securities exchange which is registered with the Securities and Exchange Commission, or at a price not less favorable to the trust than the offering price as established by current bid and asked prices quoted by persons independent of the issuer.

2. The obligation is acquired from an underwriter at a price not in excess of the public offering price for the obligation as set forth in a prospectus or offering circular filed with the Securities and Exchange Commission if a substantial portion of the same issue is acquired by persons independent of the issuer at the same price.

3. The obligation is acquired directly from the issuer at a price not less favorable to the trust than the price paid currently for a substantial portion of the same issue by persons independent of the issuer.

The second requirement which must be satisfied is that immediately following the acquisition of the obligation, not more than 25 percent of the aggregate amount of obligations issued in such issue and outstanding at the time of acquisition is held by the trust and that at least 50 percent of such amount is held by persons independent of the issuer. A third requirement provides that immediately following such acquisition, not more than 25 percent of the assets of the trust is invested in obligations of the employer or related or controlled interests.

Qualifying employer real property is real property which is dispersed geographically, is suitable for more than one use, and has been leased to the employer.

Generally speaking, a pension plan may not acquire (by any means) employer securities and real property if the immediate effect of this would cause more than 10 percent of the fair market value of plan assets to be so held. If a plan held more than 10 percent of its assets in employer securities and real property on January 1, 1975, it will have until December 31, 1984 to conform to the 10 percent rule; however, 50 percent compliance must be achieved by December 31, 1979.

Profit sharing, stock bonus, and thrift and savings plans that specifically so provide may invest without limit in qualifying employer securities or real property. If such a plan does not specifically provide for the amount of employer securities or real property to be held, the 10 percent limit will apply. A defined contribution pension plan that so provided on September 2, 1974, also may invest without limit in qualifying employer securities or real property; otherwise, however, defined contribution pension plans are subject to the 10 percent limit.

It should be observed that even though investment in qualifying employer securities and real property is permitted under the prohibited transaction rules (and under the requirements for diversity), investments of this type must still satisfy the overriding requirement that they be for the exclusive benefit of employees. Moreover, it also is necessary that any investment in employer securities and real property satisfy the requirements of prudency.

A number of exemptions to the prohibited transaction rules are specifically provided for in ERISA, and there also is a provision for applying for additional exemptions. Among the specific exemptions granted are the furnishing of office space and services for reasonable compensation, the providing of ancillary banking services where this is done without interference with the interests of the plan and the plan participants and, in the case of banks and insurance companies, the utilization of their own facilities to fund their own plans.

UNRELATED BUSINESS INCOME

Generally, the income of a qualified trust is exempt under Section 501(a) of the Code. However, even though such a trust does not lose its qualified status, all or a part of its income may be subject to tax if such income is considered to be unrelated business income.

Unrelated business income is the gross income derived from any unrelated trade or business regularly carried on by the trust, less allowable deductions which are directly connected with the carrying on of such trade or business. An unrelated trade or business means any trade or business the conduct of which is not substantially related to the exempt purpose of the trust.

It should be noted that only income resulting from the direct operation of the business is subject to tax. Thus, if the trust owns all of the stock of a corporation and the corporation directly operates the business, the dividend income received by the trust will not be subject to tax.

The following income is not considered as unrelated business income: dividends, interest, annuities, royalties, rents from real property (including personal property leased with the real property where the rents for such property are incidental) to the extent that such property is not debt-financed, and gains from the sale or exchange of capital assets.[7]

---

[7] Note, however, that income from the rental of personal property not leased with real property is considered as unrelated business income. Also, the rents from real property that is leased with personal property will be taxed if 50 percent or more of the rent is attributable to the personal property. Both the rent from the real and the personal property will be taxable if rentals are based on a percentage of this net income from the property.

If the rent from a business lease is to be taxed to a trust, the unrelated business income is that part of the rent which bears the same relationship to the total rent as the indebtedness at the end of the taxable year bears to the adjusted basis of the property at that time. The same proportion of interest, depreciation, taxes, and so on, will be allowed as a deduction to the trust.

When a trust has unrelated business income, this must be reported by the trustee on Form 990-T. This return must be filed on or before the 15th day of the fourth month following the close of the trust's taxable year. Generally speaking, most qualified trusts will be taxed at personal income tax rates, although a specific deduction of $1,000 is allowed.

DEDUCTIBILITY OF EMPLOYER CONTRIBUTIONS

Apart from the specific provisions of the Internal Revenue Code dealing with the deductibility of employer contributions to a qualified plan, it is first required that if such a contribution is to be deductible, it must otherwise be deductible as an ordinary and necessary business expense under Code Sections 162 (relating to trade or business expenses) or 212 (relating to expenses for the production of income). Also, a deduction will not be allowed for any portion of the contribution for any employee which, together with other deductions allowed for compensation for such employee, exceeds a reasonable allowance for services the employee actually has rendered.

The employer's contributions to a qualified plan generally are deductible under Section 404 of the Internal Revenue Code. Expenses such as actuary's and trustee's fees which are not provided for by contributions under the plan are deductible under Sections 162 or 212 to the extent they are ordinary and necessary expenses.

Employer contributions generally are deductible only in the year in which paid. However, an employer will be deemed to have made a contribution during a taxable year if it is in fact paid by the time prescribed for filing the employer's return for such taxable year (including extensions) and if the employer claims the contribution as a deduction for such year.

It is most important that the liability to make contributions be established by the close of the employer's taxable year in which the plan is made effective. In the case of a plan which involves a trust, there must be a valid existing trust, complete in all respects and recognized as such under the applicable local law, in effect by the close of such taxable year. There need be no trust corpus prior to the close of such taxable year; however, the corpus must be furnished no later than the due date of the employer's tax return for such taxable year (including extensions).

In a group pension program without a trust, the plan will be considered to be in effect if, by the close of the taxable year, the contract has been applied for by the employer and accepted by the insurance company, a contract or abstract has been prepared in sufficient detail outlining all of the terms of the plan, a part payment of premiums has been irrevocably made, the plan has been communicated to employees, and an appropriate resolution of the board of directors has been passed setting forth and authorizing a definite plan for the purchase of annuities and under which a liability is created to provide the benefits. If these steps are taken by the close of the taxable year in question, the actual contract need not be executed and issued until the due date of the employer's tax return for such taxable year (including extensions).

Basically, two provisions determine the maximum amount that an employer can contribute and take as a deduction to a qualified pension plan in any one taxable year.[8] The first of these rules permits a deduction for a contribution which will provide, for all employees who are participating in the plan, the unfunded cost of their past and current service credits distributed as a level amount or as a level percentage over the remaining future service of each such employee. If this rule is followed, and if the remaining unfunded cost for any three individuals is more than 50 percent of the total unfunded cost, the unfunded cost attributable to such individuals must be distributed over a period of at least five taxable years. It might be mentioned that contributions under most individual policy pension plans are claimed under this rule.

The second rule, while occasionally used with individual policy plans, primarily is used in group pension and trust fund plans. This rule permits the employer to deduct the normal cost of the plan plus, if past service or other supplementary pension or annuity credits are provided, an amount to fund completely or purchase such credits over a ten-year period.

In any event, the maximum tax deductible limit will be whatever amount is necessary to satisfy ERISA's minimum funding standards. By the same token, the maximum tax deductible limit cannot exceed the amount needed to bring the plan to a fully funded status.

If amounts contributed in any taxable year are in excess of the amounts allowed as a deduction for that year, the excess may be carried forward and deducted in succeeding taxable years, in order of time, to the extent the amount carried forward to any such succeeding taxable year plus the amount contributed during such succeeding taxable year does not exceed the deductible limit for such succeeding taxable year.

---

[8] The following discussion relates to deductions by regular corporate employers. It also applies to a Subchapter S corporation, with the exception that the annual deduction for the contribution made on behalf of an employee who owns more than 5 percent of the stock of the corporation is limited to the lesser of: (*a*) $7,500; and (*b*) 15 percent of the employee's compensation for the year up to $100,000.

For profit sharing plans, the maximum deductible contribution is equal to 15 percent of the compensation paid or otherwise accrued during the employer's taxable year to all covered employees. If the contribution to the profit sharing plan is less than this amount, the difference between the amount actually paid in and the 15 percent limit (called a "credit carry-over") can be contributed and deducted in succeeding years. However, the credit carry-over contribution in any later year cannot exceed 15 percent of the compensation paid or otherwise accrued during such later year. Also, there is an overall annual limitation when a credit carry-over is involved. This overall limit is 25 percent of current covered payroll.

Carry-over provisions also apply in profit sharing plans when the contribution in one taxable year is greater than the deductible limit for such taxable year. This type of carry-over is called a "contribution carry-over." Thus, if a contribution is made in a given year which is in excess of the allowable deduction for such year, the employer will be allowed to take a deduction for such excess payment in a succeeding taxable year, if it does not bring the deduction of the succeeding year to over 15 percent of the participating payroll for such succeeding year.

If both a pension plan and a profit sharing plan exist, with overlapping payrolls, the total amount deductible in any taxable year under both plans cannot exceed 25 percent of the compensation paid or accrued to covered employees for that year.[9] When excess payments are made in any taxable year, the excess may be carried forward to succeeding taxable years, subject to the limitation that the total amount deducted for such succeeding taxable year (including the deduction for the current contribution) cannot exceed 25 percent of the compensation paid or accrued for such subsequent year.

The 25 percent limitation does not eliminate the requirements that a currently deductible profit sharing contribution must not exceed 15 percent of the payroll of the participating employees and that a currently deductible pension contribution must not exceed the amount which would have been the limit had only a pension plan been in effect.

---

[9] This 25 percent limit will be increased to the extent larger contributions are required by ERISA's minimum funding standards.

5

Taxation of Distributions

Unquestionably, a major advantage of a qualified pension or profit sharing plan is that an employer's contributions, although currently deductible, will not be considered as taxable income to an employee until they are distributed or made available. Moreover, when a distribution does represent taxable income to the employee or a beneficiary, it generally is received under favorable tax circumstances.

Broadly speaking, distributions from a qualified plan are taxable in accordance with the annuity rules of Section 72 of the Internal Revenue Code. If a lump-sum distribution is made on account of the employee's severance of employment or after the employee has attained age $59\frac{1}{2}$, however, a portion may be treated as a long-term capital gain and a special income-averaging device will apply to the balance if certain conditions are met. Although these general principles apply regardless of the contingency which gives rise to the distribution, this chapter discusses the tax aspects of a distribution in terms of the contingency which has brought it about. Thus, this chapter briefly explores the tax situation of an employee during employment, as well as the tax situation when distributions are made because of the employee's retirement, death, severance of employment, or disability, or after the employee has attained age $59\frac{1}{2}$, or because of termination of the plan.

With a view toward achieving some degree of simplicity, the discussion has been confined to the federal taxation of typical forms of distribution under corporate plans which have a qualified status when the distributions are made.

TAXATION DURING EMPLOYMENT

Even though employer contributions may be fully vested in an employee under a qualified plan, the employee will not have to report these contributions as taxable income until such time as they are distributed or made available. Thus, employer contributions made on behalf of an employee generally will not be considered as taxable income to the employee during the period of employment.

If the plan includes a life insurance benefit for employees, however, the employee is considered to have received a distribution each year equal to the portion of the employer's contribution (or the portion of the trust earnings) which has been applied during such year to provide the pure insurance in force on the employee's life.[1] The pure insurance is considered to be the excess, if any, of the face amount of the employee's life insurance contract over its cash value. The amount which the employee must include as taxable income for each year is the one-year term insurance rate for the employee's attained age multiplied by the amount of pure insurance involved. This insurance cost often is called the PS 58 cost because the original Treasury Department ruling on the subject was so numbered.

Since the term insurance rate increases each year with the employee's increasing age, this factor tends to increase the amount which the employee has to include as taxable income each year. An offsetting factor, however, is the increasing cash value of the contract, which reduces the amount of pure insurance in effect each year. For plans which employ some form of whole life insurance or its equivalent, the insurance cost will tend to rise each year, the reduction in the amount of pure insurance being insufficient to offset the increase in the term insurance rate caused by the employee's advancing age. If the plan is funded with retirement income contracts, the yearly increase in cash value is more substantial and, ultimately, the cash value will exceed the face amount of the contract. Under this type of contract, the insurance cost (after the first few years) will tend to decrease and ultimately will disappear.

Normally, the term insurance rates employed to determine the cost of the employee's insurance coverage are the rates contained in PS 58 (reissued as Rev. Rul. 55–747, as amplified by Rev. Rul. 66–110). However, the insurer's own rates may be used if they are lower than the rates set forth in these rulings. If an employee is insurable only on an extra-premium basis and the employer contributes the extra premium

---

[1] Note that the amount applied during any year to provide life insurance often covers a period extending into the following year. The employee, however, will not be permitted to apportion this insurance cost between the two years and will be required to include this amount as taxable income in the year in which it is applied, even though the period of protection extends into the subsequent year.

necessary to obtain full coverage (and follows the same practice for all employees in similar circumstances), the employee's insurance cost will be determined on the basis of the standard rates, and the extra premium paid due to the rating need not be taken into account.[2]

If employees are making contributions, the plan may provide that an employee's contribution will first be applied toward the cost of insurance coverage. This provision makes it possible to reduce or completely eliminate having any portion of the employer's contribution considered as taxable income to the employee during employment.

If the death benefit is being provided outside of the qualified plan by a group term life insurance contract issued to the employer rather than to the trustee of the pension trust, the employee is not required to consider any part of the premium paid by the employer as taxable income, except to the extent that the employee's coverage exceeds $50,000 (or the applicable state maximum for group life insurance, if less than $50,000). However, if the trustee of a qualified trust purchases the group term life insurance instead of the employer, the value of the insurance attributable to employer contributions will be considered as taxable income to the covered employees, regardless of the amounts of coverage involved.

DETERMINATION OF COST BASIS

Before discussing the taxation of benefits, it is important to have a clear idea of the elements that constitute an employee's cost basis (or "investment in the contract"), if any, since the employee's cost basis is an important factor in the taxation of distributions under the plan.

Briefly, Section 72 of the Internal Revenue Code provides that an employee's cost basis includes:

1. The aggregate of any amounts the employee contributed while employed.

2. The aggregate of the prior insurance costs the employee has reported as taxable income. (If the employee has made contributions and the plan provides that employee contributions will first be used to pay any cost of insurance, the employee's reportable income for any year is the excess, if any, of the insurance cost of protection over the amount of the employee's contribution for the year and not the full cost of insurance protection.)

3. Other contributions made by the employer which already have been taxed to the employee. An example of this could be where the employer has maintained a nonqualified plan that was later qualified.

[2] If the contract is issued on a graded or graduated death benefit basis, i.e., a standard premium is paid but there is a reduction in the amount of insurance due to the extra mortality risk involved, the employee's insurance cost will be lower since he is receiving less insurance protection.

There also is provision for the inclusion of other items in an employee's cost basis, such as contributions made by the employer after 1950 but before 1963 while the employee was a resident of a foreign country. For the most part, however, the items listed above will constitute an employee's cost basis in the typical situation.

TAXATION OF RETIREMENT BENEFITS

Lump-Sum Distributions

If an employee's benefit is paid from a qualified plan in the form of a lump-sum benefit at retirement, the employee's cost basis will be recovered free of income tax. The excess of the distribution over the employee's cost basis will qualify for favorable tax treatment if the following conditions are met:

1. The distribution is on account of the employee's separation from the employer's service (which includes the employee's actual retirement), or is made after the employee attains age 59½.
2. The distribution represents the full amount then credited to the employee's account and the entire distribution is received within one of the employee's taxable years.

If these conditions are met, the taxable distribution may qualify for favorable tax treatment.

An employee who did not participate in the plan prior to 1974 and who has been a participant for at least five years may elect to treat such a lump-sum distribution under a ten-year averaging rule. Under this rule, the tax is determined by taking one tenth of the distribution and calculating the ordinary income tax on this portion using single taxpayer rates and assuming no other income, exemptions or deductions. The actual tax is then determined by multiplying this amount by 10. There is a minimum distribution allowance equal to the lesser of $10,000 or 50 percent of the total taxable amount, reduced by 20 percent of the amount by which the total taxable amount exceeds $20,000. If available, the minimum distribution allowance is subtracted from the total taxable distribution before calculating the tax.

If the employee participated prior to 1974, a portion of the lump-sum distribution will be treated as a long-term capital gain. Essentially, this will be determined by dividing the employee's total years of participation into the employee's years of participation prior to 1974, and applying the resulting percentage to the total lump-sum distribution. (Participation is measured in terms of months; however, any fractional year prior to 1974 will be considered a full year.) The result so obtained will be the portion of the distribution that qualifies for long-term capital gains treatment. The balance of the distribution will be treated as ordinary income under the ten-year averaging rule. To determine the amount of tax under the ten-year averaging rule for such balance of the distribution, it first will be necessary to calculate the tax that would be applicable to the total distribution as if the entire amount were being taxed under that rule. The actual amount of the tax on the balance will be determined by dividing the employee's total years of participation into the employee's years of participation after 1973 and applying the resulting percentage to the tax first determined as though the total distribution were being taxed under the ten-year rule.

For purposes of the above, all trusts under a single type of plan (e.g., defined benefit or defined contribution) and all plans within a given category (pension, profit sharing, or stock bonus) are aggregated and treated as a single plan. Also, the election to take advantage of the ten-year averaging rule is available only once after the individual has attained age 59½.

Except in the case of a distribution after age 59½, the requirement that there be an actual separation from the employer's service is most important. If the employee continues to work for the same employer in the same or in a different capacity, the distribution will not qualify for the favorable tax treatment just described. While the question of whether an employee relationship continues generally is determined under rules applicable to federal employment taxes, the fact that the individual no longer receives compensation does not necessarily mean there has been a severance of employment. If, in fact, the individual continues to act in some capacity as an employee, even though without compensation, the favorable tax treatment may be denied to any distribution received under the employer's plan. However, if an employee agrees to remain available as a consultant after retirement, this may, depending upon all the facts and the actual services performed, constitute a severance of employment that will qualify a lump-sum distribution for favorable tax treatment.

A special five-year look back rule will be applied to aggregate distributions and to calculate the marginal tax rate when the recipient has received more than one lump-sum distribution in the six years ending with the year in which the current lump-sum distribution is being made. Also, the value of any annuity contract distributed (including contracts distributed during the preceding five years), even though this amount is not taxable currently, must be taken into account in determining the marginal tax rate on the amount of the distribution that is being taxed under the ten-year averaging rule.

If any part of the distribution consists of employer securities, any unrealized appreciation of these securities will not be taxable currently at the time of distribution. Such unrealized appreciation will be taxed only at such time as the securities are sold.

Distributions in the Form of Periodic Payments

If a retiring employee receives the distribution in the form of periodic payments, these payments will be taxed to the employee as ordinary income in accordance with the annuity rules of Section 72 of the Internal Revenue Code. The retirement income tax credit provided by Section 37 of the Internal Revenue Code will apply to these payments. However, the impact of this credit generally is not significant, since the maximum credit is reduced by social security benefits and by earned income of the type which would, in itself, reduce the employee's social security benefits.

Thus, in a plan where the employee has no cost basis, periodic payments will be subject to tax as ordinary income when received. If the employee has a cost basis, tax treatment will depend upon the length of time it takes the employee to recover an amount equal to such cost basis.

If the employee will receive, within three years of the first payment, total payments which equal or exceed such cost basis, then all payments will be excluded from taxable income until the payments received equal the employee's cost basis. Thereafter, the payments will be taxed as ordinary income when received. To illustrate, take the case of an employee who has contributed $5,400 under the employer's retirement plan and who will receive an annual payment, for life, of $2,400. Since retirement payments for the first three years ($7,200) exceed the employee's cost basis, the employee will not have to report any part of the payments as taxable income for the first two years. At the end of the second year, the employee will have recovered $4,800 of the cost basis and will still have $600 of this amount left to recover. Thus, during the third year of retirement, the employee will exclude $600 of payments from taxable income and will report only $1,800 as income subject to tax. Thereafter, the full $2,400 will be subject to tax each year as ordinary income.

If it will take longer than three years to recover the employee's cost basis, the regular annuity rules of Section 72 apply. First, an exclusion ratio is determined for the employee. The exclusion ratio is the ratio of the employee's cost basis (investment in the contract) to the employee's "expected return." The resulting percentage represents the portion of each income payment which is excluded from taxable income.

For example, assume that a male employee retiring at age 65 is entitled to an annual income of $2,400 for life (with no death benefit payable in the event of his death after retirement) and that the employee has a cost basis of $9,000. The first step would be to determine the employee's expected return. This would be done by obtaining his life expectancy under the tables included in the regulations and multiplying this figure by the amount of the annual payment. In this example, the employee's life expectancy under these tables would be 15. Multiplying 15 by the annual payment of $2,400 produces an expected return of $36,000. The next step would be to divide the employee's cost basis ($9,000) by his expected return ($36,000), which yields an exclusion ratio of 25 percent. Consequently, $600 of each year's payment (25 percent of $2,400) would be excluded from the employee's taxable income, and the balance of $1,800 would be subject to tax as ordinary income.

The exclusion ratio, once established, will apply to all future payments, regardless of the length of time the employee actually lives and receives payments. If the employee lives longer than the average life expectancy assumed in the tables included in the regulations, a portion of each payment will continue to be received free of income tax, even though by that time the employee's cost basis will have been recovered.

If payments are made to the employee for a period certain or with a refund feature, the cost basis will be adjusted, when determining the employee's exclusion ratio, to reflect the value of the refund or period-certain feature. In the example described above, if the retirement benefit of $2,400 were payable for life with a guarantee that payments would be made for at least ten years, it would be necessary to reduce the employee's cost basis of $9,000. Under the tables included in the regulations, the value of the ten-year guarantee for a male, age 65, is 15 percent. Consequently, the $9,000 would be reduced by 15 percent ($1,350) and the employee's adjusted cost basis would be $7,650. His exclusion ratio would then be determined in the regular fashion.

If retirement payments are being made under some form of joint and survivor annuity, the expected return, rather than the cost basis, would be adjusted to reflect the value of the survivorship feature.

TAXATION OF DEATH BENEFITS

Lump-Sum Distributions

A lump-sum distribution to the employee's beneficiary from a qualified plan made on account of the employee's death (either before or after severance of employment), will entitle the beneficiary to the favorable tax treatment previously described if the distribution represents the full amount then credited to the employee's account and if it is received within one taxable year of the beneficiary.

In determining the net amount of gain subject to tax, the beneficiary's cost basis will be the same as the employee's (i.e., the aggregate of the employee's contributions and any amounts, such as insurance costs, on which the employee has previously been taxed) plus, unless otherwise used, the employee death benefit exclusion provided by Section 101(b) of the Internal Revenue Code up to a maximum of $5,000. It should be noted that in the case of a lump-sum distribution that otherwise qualifies for the favorable tax treatment, this exclusion under Section 101(b) applies regardless of whether the employee's rights were forfeitable or nonforfeitable.[3]

If any portion of the distribution consists of life insurance proceeds and the employee either paid the insurance cost or reported this cost as taxable income, the pure insurance, i.e., the difference between the face amount of the contract and its cash value, will pass to the beneficiary free of income tax under Section 101(a) of the Internal Revenue Code. The beneficiary only will have to treat the cash value of the contract, plus any other cash distributions from the plan, as income subject to tax.

The following example illustrates how the death benefit under a typical retirement income contract would be taxed if the employee died before retirement and the face amount of the contract were paid to the beneficiary in a lump sum.

Face amount of contract	$25,000
Cash value of contract	11,000
Amount of pure insurance excludable under Section 101(a)	$14,000
Cash value of contract	$11,000
Amount excludable under Section 101(b) (assuming not otherwise utilized)	5,000
Balance subject to income tax	$ 6,000
Beneficiary's cost basis (aggregate of prior insurance costs which employee reported as taxable income)	940
Balance taxable to beneficiary	$ 5,060

The beneficiary would, therefore, receive $19,940 of the total distribution free of income tax, and only $5,060 would be considered as being taxable. The portion of the $5,060 attributable to post-1973 participation would qualify for the ten-year averaging provision if the employee had participated in the plan for at least five years; any balance would qualify for treatment as a long-term capital gain.

It is important to note that the regulations provide that if the employee did not pay the insurance cost of his or her contract or did not report the cost of insurance as taxable income, the portion of the insurance proceeds consisting of pure insurance will be considered as taxable income to the beneficiary.

When an employee dies after retirement and after having received

---

[3] Briefly, Section 101(b) permits a beneficiary to exclude from gross income any payments made by the employer of a deceased employee up to a maximum of $5,000. Except as noted, this exclusion is available only to the extent the employee's rights to the amounts were forfeitable immediately prior to death.

periodic payments, a lump-sum death payment to the employee's beneficiary, if it meets the requirements previously noted, will qualify for the favorable tax treatment described. The beneficiary's cost basis, however, will be reduced by any amount which the employee had recovered free from income tax.

Distributions in the Form of Periodic Payments

Death before Retirement. If death occurs before retirement and the plan provides for the distribution of the employee's death benefit over a period of years (including payments based upon the life expectancy of the beneficiary), these payments will be taxed in accordance with the annuity rules of Section 72 of the Internal Revenue Code.

The beneficiary's cost basis will consist of the amount which would have been the employee's cost basis had the employee lived and received the payments, plus, if applicable, the exclusion allowed under Section 101(b) of the Internal Revenue Code up to the maximum of $5,000. While the question of whether the employee's rights were forfeitable is immaterial for the application of Section 101(b) to a lump-sum distribution from a qualified plan on death, the same is not so when the distribution is in the form of periodic payments. Here, the exclusion under Section 101(b) is applicable only to amounts to which the employee's rights were forfeitable immediately prior to death.

If any part of the periodic payments arises from pure life insurance, the proceeds are divided into two parts:

1. The cash value of the contract immediately before death.
2. The pure insurance (the excess of the face amount of the contract over its cash value).

That portion of each periodic payment which is attributable to the cash value of the contract will be taxed to the beneficiary under the annuity rules. The balance of each payment which is attributable to the pure insurance will be treated as insurance proceeds under Section 101(d) of the Internal Revenue Code.

To illustrate, if the face amount of the employee's contract was $25,000 and the proceeds were paid to the beneficiary in ten annual payments of $3,000 each, the following would be the manner in which the payments would be taxed to the beneficiary, assuming that the contract had a cash value at death of $11,000, that the employee had forfeitable interest to the extent of $5,000, and that the aggregate of the insurance costs which the employee previously reported as taxable income was $940.

The portion of each annual payment of $3,000 which is attributable to the cash value is $1,320 ($^{11}/_{25}$ of $3,000). The beneficiary's cost basis for this portion would be $5,940 (the $5,000 exclusion under Section 101(b) plus the aggregate insurance costs of $940). The expected return under this portion would be $13,200 (the annual payment of $1,320 multiplied by the ten years of payments). Since the beneficiary's cost basis would not be recovered within the first three years, the three-year rule would not apply. Therefore, an exclusion ratio would be determined by dividing the cost basis ($5,940) by the expected return ($13,200). This produces an exclusion ratio of 45 percent, which would be applied to the portion of each annual payment attributable to the cash value of the contract. As a result, $594 (45 percent of $1,320) would be excluded from income each year, and the balance of $726 would be taxed to the beneficiary as ordinary income.

The portion of each annual payment of $3,000 attributable to the pure insurance is $1,680 ($^{14}/_{25}$ of $3,000). Of this amount, $1,400 ($^{1}/_{10}$ of $14,000) is excludable from gross income as Section 101 proceeds, and only the balance of $280 would be taxable as ordinary income to the beneficiary. Moreover, the $1,000 interest exclusion would be applicable if the beneficiary were the surviving spouse of the employee. The interest exclusion, of course, would not be applicable to any portion of the annual payment attributable to the cash value of the contract.

If the beneficiary in this example were the spouse of the employee, only $726 of each annual payment would be considered as ordinary income. The balance of $2,274 would be received free of income tax. A beneficiary other than the spouse of the employee would include $1,006 ($280 plus $726) as ordinary income each year, and $1,994 of each annual payment would be received free of income tax.

Death after Retirement. The taxation of payments to the beneficiary of an employee who dies after retirement and after periodic payments have begun depends upon whether the employee had a cost basis (and if so, whether it had been recovered by the employee), as well as upon the method of payment involved. If the employee had no cost basis or had recovered such cost basis under the three-year rule, each payment would be considered as taxable income to the beneficiary as received. However, where the payments are being continued under a joint and survivor annuity form, the exclusion ratio established when the annuity became effective would apply for the balance of the survivor's lifetime. If payments are being continued under a period-certain life annuity or under a refund annuity and the cost basis had not been recovered by the employee at the time of death, the beneficiary could exclude all payments from gross income until the total of the portion of the cost basis the employee had recovered and the payments the beneficiary has received equal the employee's cost basis. Thereafter, all payments would be taxed as ordinary income to the beneficiary.

Estate Tax

The foregoing discussion has covered only the income tax liability of the beneficiary. There also is the matter of the federal estate tax to be considered.

Briefly, any amounts distributed from a qualified plan to a beneficiary other than the estate of the employee will be excluded from the employee's gross estate for federal estate tax purposes to the extent that the amount distributed is attributable to employer contributions. This includes the proceeds of a life insurance contract.

This exclusion applies to any such payment made pursuant to a qualified plan even though the individual's death occurs subsequent to separation from the employer's service or even if the benefit is in the form of continued payments to a survivor. Suppose, however, that the individual severed employment with the employer and received a distribution of a life insurance contract from the plan under circumstances such that its cash value was then includable in gross income. Here, the distribution would have become a part of the individual's personal assets, and upon subsequent death the proceeds of the contract would be includable in the individual's gross estate for federal estate tax purposes in accordance with the regular rules.

It should be noted that the exclusion does not apply if the benefit is paid to the employee's estate. Also, the exclusion applies only to amounts attributable to employer contributions.[4] If the employee has contributed, the amount excludable from the gross estate would be that percentage of the total benefit which is determined by dividing the employer's contributions on behalf of the employee by the total contributions for the employee's benefit.[5] If the actuarial method used under the plan is such that the employer's contribution cannot be readily ascertained, the value of the benefit at the time of death (or, if death occurs after

---

[4] In *Comm'r.* v. *Est. of Albright,* USCA–2, No. 29594, 2–9–66, the beneficiary received a return of the employee's contributions under two separate group annuity contracts. Under one contract, the amount paid also included interest on the employee's contributions. The tax court held that only a portion of the distributions was includable in the employee's gross estate. The court of appeals, however, held that the entire distributions under both contracts were includable, as such distributions were solely attributable to the employee's own contributions.

[5] Under the income tax regulations, the agrregate of the insurance costs which an employee has included in gross income are considered as "having been contributed by the employee" and thus form a part of the cost basis in determining the net amount of any subsequent distribution which is subject to income tax. For estate tax purposes, however, insurance costs are not considered as having been contributed by the employee; and in a noncontributory plan, the full amount of the death proceeds may be excluded from the employee's gross estate even though the beneficiary may consider the aggregate of the prior insurance costs as a part of the cost basis in determining the portion of the cash value of the contract to be excluded from gross income.

retirement, as of the employee's retirement date) will be considered to be the total contribution. The employee contributions are then subtracted from this amount, and the balance is considered to be the employer's contribution.

If the death benefit consists of the proceeds of a group term life insurance policy which is owned by the trustee of the pension trust (total premiums having been paid by the employer), the full proceeds fall within the estate tax exclusion. However, if the policy is issued directly to the employer, as usually is the case, the proceeds are includable in the employee's gross estate.[6]

Gift Tax

It is appropriate, in a discussion of the tax aspects of the death benefits payable under a qualified plan, to cover the gift tax aspects of an irrevocable designation by an employee of a beneficiary to receive the benefit payable under the plan at the employee's death.

The provisions of the federal gift tax law are similar to those dealing with the federal estate tax. In a noncontributory plan, the employee will not have to pay a gift tax if such an irrevocable designation is made. If, however, the employee has made contributions, the gift tax exclusion will apply only to the part of the beneficiary's interest attributable to employer contributions. The methods followed to determine the portion of the beneficiary's interest attributable to employer contributions are the same as the methods outlined in determining the estate tax exclusion.

TAXATION OF SEVERANCE-OF-EMPLOYMENT BENEFITS

For the most part, the discussion in this chapter on the taxation of distributions at retirement is equally applicable to the taxation of distributions on severance of employment. If the distribution is in the form of periodic payments, the taxation of payments to the employee will be governed by the annuity rules after taking the employee's cost basis, if any, into account. So, also, a lump-sum distribution, provided that the necessary conditions are met, may qualify for the favorable tax treatment described.

If the distribution is in the form of a life insurance contract, its cash value less the employee's cost basis, if any, will be considered as taxable income in the year in which the employee receives the contract, even though the contract is not then surrendered for its cash value. The distribution may qualify for favorable treatment if all necessary conditions

---

[6] It is possible, under the laws of most states and if the group contract permits, for the employee to assign his or her interest in the group life insurance and thus have the proceeds excluded from the gross estate.

are met. On the other hand, the employee may avoid any current tax liability by transferring this amount, within 60 days, to a qualified individual retirement savings plan. The employee may also avoid any current tax liability by making an irrevocable election, within 60 days of the distribution, to convert the contract to a nontransferable annuity which contains no element of life insurance.[7] If the employee would otherwise receive a cash distribution but has the option under the plan of electing, within 60 days, to receive a nontransferable annuity in lieu of the cash payment, he or she may also avoid current tax liability by making a timely exercise of this option.

If current tax liability is avoided by such an election, the employee will not pay any tax until payments are made from the annuity contract. At that time, the payments will be considered as ordinary income under the annuity rules.

If the distribution is in the form of an annuity contract, the tax situation will be governed by the date of issue of the contract. If issued after December 31, 1962, the distribution will be treated exactly the same as the distribution of a life insurance contract unless the annuity is endorsed or rewritten on a nontransferable basis within the 60 days allowed. If issued before January 1, 1963, the employee will not have to include any amount as taxable income until payments are actually received. At that time, payments will be considered as ordinary income under the annuity rules.

TAXATION OF DISABILITY BENEFITS

Many qualified pension plans provide for a monthly benefit if an employee becomes totally and permanently disabled. Typically, the benefit is payable for life (subject to the continuance of the disability) but only for a disability that occurs after the employee has attained some minimum age, such as 50 or 55, or has completed some minimum period of service, such as ten years. The benefit may or may not be related to the employee's accrued or projected pension. Frequently, the amount of the benefit will be adjusted if disability continues until the employee attains the normal retirement age specified in the plan.

Generally speaking, disability benefits of this type will be taxed to the employee in accordance with the annuity rules of Section 72 of the

---

[7] The regulations spell out what is meant by nontransferable, and the language of the regulations has been used as a guide by many insurers in endorsing their contracts. Such an endorsement might read approximately as follows: "This contract is not transferable except to the ABC Insurance Company. It may not be sold, assigned, discounted, or pledged as collateral for a loan or as security for the performance of an obligation or for any other purpose to any person other than this Company; provided, however, that notwithstanding the foregoing, the owner may designate a beneficiary to receive the proceeds payable upon death, and may elect a joint and survivor annuity."

Internal Revenue Code; however, such disability benefits may qualify for the sick pay exclusion provided for in Section 105(d) of the Code.[8]

The sick pay exclusion applies only to the benefits provided by employer contributions. If the plan is contributory, however, the disability benefit will be presumed to have been financed by the employer's contributions unless the plan specifically provides otherwise.

The sick pay exclusion is available only for disability payments made prior to the employee's normal retirement age; thereafter, all payments will be taxed in accordance with the annuity rules.

TAXATION OF BENEFITS UPON TERMINATION OF PLAN

Generally speaking, distributions on account of the termination of a qualified plan are taxed under the annuity rules of Section 72 of the Internal Revenue Code, and the preceding discussion applies to the taxation of these benefits. The most notable difference, however, concerns the treatment of lump-sum distributions (whether in the form of cash, life insurance contracts, or transferable annuity contracts issued after 1962). If such a lump-sum distribution is made on account of termination of the plan, the favorable tax treatment described will not apply to an employee unless such employee has attained age 59½ at the time of distribution.

It is possible, under some forms of corporate mergers or reorganizations, that severance of employment could take place at the same time. In such an event, a lump-sum distribution might qualify for this favorable tax treatment. Whether a particular distribution has been made on account of severance of employment can be a difficult problem to resolve. The question is influenced greatly by the facts in each particular case and by the timing of events. A number of cases and rulings have dealt with this particular point.

It would appear, from a study of the cases and rulings, that the Internal Revenue Service will require something more than a nominal or technical change in employment relationship if there is to be separation from the employer's service so as to qualify lump-sum distributions for favorable tax treatment. It also would appear that if a plan termination is being contemplated, especially in conjunction with a corporate merger or reorganization, extreme care should be taken during the planning stages to assure the most favorable tax treatment for all concerned. Con-

---

[8] Briefly, the Code provides that after an absence from work of 30 days due to sickness or injuries, an employee may exclude from income, up to a rate of $100 per week, payments which are wages or which are in lieu of wages. During the first 30 days the employee can exclude up to $75 per week if the sick pay does not exceed 75 percent of regular wages. If the employee was hospitalized for at least one day, this exclusion starts from the first day of disability; otherwise, there is no exclusion for the first seven days of disability.

sideration might be given to the possibility of distributing assets in the form of nontransferable annuities, not only to defer tax liability until some future time but also to spread its impact over a period of years. For the same reason, consideration might also be given to the use of qualified individual retirement savings plans for those individuals over age 59½ at the time this plan is terminated.

6

Individual Policy Plans

An employer who is establishing a pension plan must make several decisions under the general heading of *funding policy*. These decisions include choosing both a funding agency and a funding instrument. A funding agency is an organization or individual that provides facilities for the accumulation or administration of assets to be used for the payment of benefits under a pension plan. Funding agencies include life insurance companies, corporate fiduciaries, and individuals acting as trustees. These funding agencies have several different contracts or instruments through which pension benefits are funded. Insured pension plans, for example, may be funded through individual policies, group deferred annuities, deposit administration contracts, and the like. These various contracts are referred to as funding instruments. A funding instrument is an agreement or contract governing the conditions under which assets are accumulated or administered by a funding agency for the payment of benefits under a pension plan. Funding instruments include contracts with life insurance companies and trust agreements with corporate fiduciaries or individuals acting as trustees. A trust agreement may be used in conjunction with a fully insured individual policy plan and, on occasion, in a plan where all assets are being accumulated under a group pension contract. However, in these cases, the insurance or annuity contracts are viewed as the principal funding instruments.

Funding instruments also have been classified on the basis of whether contributions are allocated to provide benefits to specific employees or whether contributions are accumulated in an unallocated fund to provide benefits for employees.[1] Allocated funding instruments include individual insurance and annuity contracts, group permanent insurance contracts,

---

[1] Dan M. McGill, *Fundamentals of Private Pensions,* rev. ed. (Homewood, Ill.: Richard D. Irwin, Inc., 1964), pp. 111–12.

134

and group deferred annuity contracts; deposit administration contracts, immediate participation guarantee contracts, and trust fund plans are unallocated funding instruments.

An *insured plan*, then, is a pension plan for which the funding agency is a life insurance company; all contributions are paid directly or indirectly to the insurer, which pays all benefits to individual participants. A *trust fund plan* is a plan for which the funding agency is a corporate fiduciary or individual(s) acting as trustee(s), the responsibilities of the funding agency for investment of funds, and for any other functions, generally being provided for in a trust agreement. A *combination plan* is an arrangement under which two funding instruments are used, with a portion of the contributions placed in a trust fund (or a conversion fund held by an insurer) and the balance paid to an insurance company as contributions under a group annuity contract or as premiums on individual life insurance or annuity contracts. The entire pension for each participant generally is paid by the insurance company, with transfers from the trust fund or conversion fund being made as required.

This chapter is concerned solely with insured plans that are fully funded through the use of individual life insurance or annuity contracts and with combination plans utilizing both individual contracts and a conversion fund.

The individual policy plan has proved to be a very popular funding arrangement for relatively small employers. About 65 percent of all insured corporate plans currently in force use individual contracts, at least in part, to fund benefits. However, the average-sized individual policy plan has only about ten participants per plan. This is not to say that the individual policy arrangement cannot be used for larger firms. However, the group approaches normally offer cost savings and a greater degree of flexibility, and therefore generally are preferred over the individual policy arrangement by large employers.

Since most large employers already have established pension plans for their employees, future expansion in pension coverage must come from the further establishment of such plans among smaller employers. The development of master and prototype plans is likely to add considerable impetus to the growth of pension plans in the small-sized corporation market. However, because of the complications and additional costs of ERISA, smaller employers may decide against establishing pension plans. The future market for individual policy plans, then, is difficult to predict.

FULLY INSURED PLAN

Type of Contract

The major objective of a pension plan is to provide a periodic income to retired workers. In the case of a defined benefit insured plan, the insurance company generally requires that a specified sum of money be on hand as of the date of the employee's retirement to provide the periodic benefit to which he or she is entitled under the plan. Under individual policy plans, the cash value under the contract as of the retirement date of the employee can be used as the single-premium sum needed to provide the annuity benefit. Thus, in theory, any permanent life insurance or any annuity contract can be used to fund a pension benefit. However, under a fully insured plan, the policy cash values at retirement must be sufficient to provide the full benefit, since no other source of funds is contemplated under the plan. In order to generate sufficient cash values under ordinary life policies, the face amount of the policy must be considerably in excess of 100 times the monthly retirement benefit—the maximum permitted under qualified plans. Thus, retirement income or retirement annuity contracts must be used, since they are designed specifically by insurers to provide the proper ratio of insurance to income and to generate the cash values needed to provide a specified monthly income as of a given retirement age.

Table 6–1 sets forth illustrative cash values at quinquennial ages (five-

TABLE 6–1

Cash Values at Quinquennial Ages per $1,000 of Face Value

Age	Ordinary Life	Paid-Up at 65	Endowment at 65	Retirement Income	Retirement Annuity*
30	$ 0	$ 5	$ 9	$ 0	$ 18
35	46	68	95	117	129
40	130	157	214	286	288
45	216	248	339	470	472
50	300	348	475	676	685
55	387	456	626	919	932
60	475	573	797	1,211	1,219
65	560	701	1,000	1,550	1,550

* Retirement annuity contracts are expressed in terms of units of annuity benefit as of a specified age. The cash values indicated above are for a retirement annuity contract that will provide a life income of $10 a month with 120 payments certain.

year intervals) available under various participating individual policies offered by one insurance company for a male, age 30 as of issue date.

The insurance company whose policy values are described in Table 6–1 currently requires a net sum of $1,550 to provide a male, age 65, with a life annuity of $10 a month with annuity payments guaranteed for ten years. It is obvious, therefore, that a retirement income contract is the only insurance contract that provides sufficient cash values at age 65 to provide monthly income at the rate of $10 for each $1,000 of face value.

General Characteristics

The retirement income and retirement annuity contracts used by some insurance companies for pension cases are identical to the contracts issued to nonpension individual policyholders. Other insurance companies have developed a special series of retirement income and retirement annuity contracts to be used solely for pension cases. Although both lines of policies would be essentially similar, the special pension series policies may provide for different commission scales, premium rates, cash values, death benefits, underwriting standards, and dividend scales. In either case, these contracts are essentially standard forms that have been modified to the extent possible to meet the needs of a pension plan. However, the standard forms cannot be tailored perfectly for this purpose and, therefore, certain plan provisions must be designed to conform to the structure of individual contracts—for example, minimum units of benefit and retirement dates expressed as the policy anniversary nearest to normal retirement age.

The retirement annuity contract is an individual deferred annuity contract and is expressed in units of $10-a-month annuity benefit payable beginning at a specified age, usually the normal retirement age under the plan. The retirement income policy is expressed in terms of $1,000 of face value of life insurance for each $10-a-month annuity benefit on some stipulated annuity form.

Individual policy plans require that separate contracts be issued on the life of every covered employee. In many cases, a trust agreement is executed between the employer and the trustee, and the trustee serves as custodian of the individual contracts. The trustee normally applies for the insurance or annuity contracts and pays the premiums due. The insured employee, of course, must sign the application for the contract. Legal ownership of the contracts is vested in the trustee, either through the use of an ownership clause or by attachment of an appropriate rider to each of the contracts. The use of a trustee under individual policy plans is required under the Internal Revenue Code unless nontransferable retirement income or annuity contracts are used. These requirements are imposed to preclude the possibility of the employer recovering funds that must be irrevocably committed to the plan. Also, the use of a trust assures that funds will not be currently distributed to employees except in accordance with the provisions set forth in the plan.

The use of a trustee under individual policy plans has resulted in the use of the term "pension trust" to describe these plans. This terminology is unfortunate, since plans employing funding instruments other than individual policies quite often use a trust agreement. In the case of a noninsured plan, for example, a trust agreement is a necessary condition to qualification of the plan. Thus, the term "pension trust" should not be used unless it is quite clear what type of funding instrument is involved. Indeed, it would probably be best if the term disappeared entirely from pension terminology.

Employees covered under retirement income contracts must furnish the insurance company with evidence of insurability, since these contracts offer a substantial element of life insurance protection. The evidence of insurability required under these contracts is similar to that required under regular individual policies; i.e., filling out an application and taking a physical examination. Retirement annuity contracts, on the other hand, do not require evidence of insurability, since these contracts provide no element of pure life insurance protection as such. Thus, these latter contracts can always be used to fund the benefits of employees who are not insurable.

The question of the insurability of employees, however, is not generally a serious problem in fully insured individual policy plans. First of all, most insurance companies are willing, under specified conditions, to issue retirement income contracts up to given amount without evidence of insurability.[2] Furthermore, insurers generally are willing to issue retirement income contracts at substandard rates for employees who are insurable, but not standard, risks. Also, many insurance companies now offer retirement income contracts with graded or graduated death benefits for substandard risks, or even for uninsurable risks in some cases, the pure life insurance protection being very low at the issue date of the contract and increasing each year that the contract stays in force. Ultimately, the death benefit under a graded death benefit retirement income contract is identical to that available under a standard contract, since the cash values build up at the same rate under both contracts and eventually exceed the face value. Finally, retirement annuity contracts can be used, and the death benefit ultimately will be about the same as under the other contracts. At any rate, the trust agreement should clearly specify the approach that will be used in funding the benefits of impaired lives; i.e., substandard rating, retirement annuity contracts, or graded death benefit contracts.

The use of retirement annuity contracts solely for the uninsurable employees under a plan is becoming less and less prevalent. Whenever possible, the benefits of all employees under the plan should be funded with one type of individual contract; the retirement annuity contract is most desirable in those cases where life insurance coverage is not needed or desired or where the lower premium cost of these policies is a critical factor. This is particularly true in those cases where a number of older workers are to be included in the plan, thereby presenting a sizable life

---

[2] The nature of the requirements generally imposed by insurance companies under guaranteed issue underwriting are discussed in Chapter 11.

insurance benefit cost. The fact remains, however, that in most instances life insurance protection is desired, and the net premium differential is not normally significant enough to be a major issue. Therefore, one finds that retirement income contracts are the most popular type of contract used under fully insured individual policy plans.

Benefit Structure

Retirement Benefits. Under retirement income and retirement annuity contracts, a given level of benefit is funded through level periodic contribution payments made on behalf of each covered employee. Thus, it is desirable, whenever possible, that the level of retirement benefit be capable of projection with a reasonable degree of accuracy. However, firm projections of retirement benefits are difficult except for plans that provide a fixed benefit ($100 a month, for example) or a unit benefit of, say, $10 a month per year of service. Even in the cases of these plans, the benefit formula is likely to be amended in future years.

The most difficult benefit formula to use under an individual policy plan is one that relates retirement benefits to the average of the employee's compensation over the entire period of participation in the plan; i.e., a career average provision. In this case, estimates of the amount of ultimate benefits are quite uncertain in view of the tremendous possible variation in future salary levels. Furthermore, because of minimum-size policy requirements, substantial increases in compensation are required before additional amounts of insurance can be purchased. Thus, this benefit provision is seldom found in fully insured plans.

The benefit formula under most fully insured plans generally specifies that the percentage be applied to the participant's average earnings during some period near normal retirement date, such as the first five of the last ten years of employment before normal retirement age or compensation during the fifth year preceding normal retirement date; in other words, a final-pay provision. Final-pay provisions that base benefits on a participant's average earnings during a period, say five years, immediately preceding retirement are seldom used under individual policy plans. It is obviously too difficult to predict what a participant's earnings will be during this period. Furthermore, most insurance companies will not issue an individual retirement income contract of less than five year's duration. Therefore, if retirement benefit increases were granted for increases in compensation during the last few years of employment, there would not be sufficient time prior to retirement to fund the additional policy amounts that would have to be purchased. This problem has been minimized somewhat by those insurers that permit a degree of postretirement funding of individual contracts. Nevertheless, most individual policy plans do not permit increases in retirement benefits due to increases in compensation during the five-year period immediately preceding retirement.

Salary projections generally are not used in individual policy plans, even though final-pay provisions are quite prevalent in these plans.[3] The approach normally used is to assume that the current level of compensation for each participant will remain in effect until normal retirement age. If amendments of the plan or changes in compensation result in an increase in a participant's level of benefits, then additional policies must be purchased. Likewise, a decrease in salary which results in a decrease in benefits requires that part or all of one or more policies be canceled.

The requirement generally imposed by insurance companies that benefits under individual policy plans be funded over a minimum of five years also has an impact on the setting of a normal retirement age. It is not unusual for an employer to have employees who are approaching age 65 at the inception of the plan. Furthermore, in future years, the employer may hire employees who are over 55 years old. Thus, it is quite common to find in individual policy plans that the normal retirement age is 65 or ten years after entry date for those participants entering the plan after age 55.

It should also be noted, as mentioned earlier, that individual contracts mature on a policy anniversary date which seldom coincides with the date that a participant reaches normal retirement age. Therefore, it is quite common in an individual policy plan to define the normal retirement date as the policy anniversary nearest the participant's 65th birthday. An alternative provision is to set the normal retirement date as the January 1 nearest the participant's 65th birthday. This is an unfortunate feature of individual contracts, in that the actual retirement dates for two participants who are only a few days apart in age may vary by as much as a full year.

As indicated earlier, retirement income contracts are expressed in terms of $10 a month of pension benefit per $1,000 face value of life insurance. After a period of years from the issue date, the cash value exceeds the face of the contract; thereafter, the cash value rather than the face value is the sum that is payable upon the death of the employee. The amount of retirement income coverage that is purchased depends on the level of pension benefit to which the employee is entitled under the benefit formula. For example, if the benefit formula provides a benefit of 40 percent of compensation, an employee currently earning $500 a month would be entitled to a retirement benefit at age 65 of $200 a month. The trustee would purchase a retirement income contract in the amount of $20,000, since this contract provides $10 a month of annuity

---

[3] For a discussion of the implications of salary projections in actuarial cost estimates, see Chapter 3.

benefit at age 65 for each $1,000 face amount of insurance. The cash value under this contract, at age 65, would be $31,000, the amount required by one insurance company to provide $200 a month with 120 payments certain to a male beginning at age 65.[4]

If the participant's salary at some future date is increased to $525 a month, the projected retirement benefit would then be $210 a month. Another retirement income contract in the amount of $1,000 would be purchased as of that date, so that sufficient cash values would be available at age 65 to provide the annuity benefit of $210 a month. There would be no increase in the monthly pension benefit of the employee for compensation increases between $500 and $525 a month, since most insurers generally will not issue a retirement income contract unless the additional monthly benefit is at least $10. The relatively high administrative costs of issuing contracts for less than $10 of monthly benefit is the primary reason for this limitation. Thus, the benefit provision normally provides that increases in compensation will only be recognized when they result in an increase in benefit at least equal to the minimum-sized contract issuable by the insurer. The exact amount of coverage will be issued once the minimum size requirement is met.

The retirement annuity contract is similar to the retirement income contract except that the former provides no pure life insurance protection. The contract is expressed in terms of $10 units of monthly income benefit, although some insurance companies issue units of $5 a month or even as low as $2.50 a month. Where units of benefit of less than $10 a month are available, adjustment in monthly pensions may be required for relatively small increases in compensation. However, the smaller the available units of benefit, the greater will be the number of contracts that the trustee must buy and hold until retirement date. Regardless of the size of the unit of benefit, it is characteristic of individual policy plans that a number of contracts ultimately will be issued for each participant.

Early retirement benefits often are provided under fully insured plans. A typical provision provides such benefits for employees who have attained their 60th birthday and have completed at least ten years of continuous service as a participant under the plan. The amount of the benefit almost always is expressed as the annuity amount that can be purchased with the accrued cash value for the sex and attained age of the participant under the settlement option rates in the contract or contracts.

---

[4] ERISA requires that for an individual married for at least one year the actual retirement benefits be in the form of a joint and one half survivor annuity unless the participant elects in writing to have benefits paid in a different form. Thus, in this example, if the participant were married and did not elect otherwise, the actual monthly benefit would be $162, rather than $200, but 50 percent of this amount would be payable to the participant's spouse after the participant's death.

Defined contribution (money-purchase) formulas also may be used in fully insured individual policy plans. Under these formulas, contributions normally are expressed as a fixed percentage of compensation, with the amount of benefits varying with the age, sex, and retirement date of each covered employee. Defined contribution formulas are particularly popular in H.R. 10 plans.

Death Benefits.   As indicated above, the preretirement death benefit under retirement income contracts is the greater of the face amount or the cash value of the contract as of the date of death of the employee. The face amount of the contract usually is 100 times the monthly pension benefit on the basic contract option (for example, $1,000 face value per $10 a month of pension benefit payable for life with 120 payments certain).[5] The point at which the cash value exceeds the face of the contract depends on the sex of the employee, the age at issue of the contract, the retirement date, and the actuarial assumptions used by the insurance company in calculating the premium rate and cash value scales. In most cases, the cash value will exceed the face of the policy at an age in the mid- to late-50s. It should be noted, however, that the plan can restrict death benefits to the face amount of the contract. In those instances in which the cash value exceeds the face value, the difference would constitute a credit against future plan contributions. As a practical matter, however, fully insured individual policy plans generally pay a death benefit equal to the larger of the face amount or cash value under the contract.

In the case of retirement annuity contracts, no element of pure insurance protection is built into the contract. Thus, upon the death of an employee prior to retirement, the death benefit would equal the larger of the reserve under the contract or the premiums paid to date under the contract without interest. The reserve under the contract will exceed the accumulated premiums under the contract a few years after its issue date. If no death benefit is provided by the plan, the greater of the reserve or accumulated premiums is returned to the trustee of the plan. This is an unlikely situation, however, and in a plan which provides for no preretirement death benefits, individual retirement annuity contracts would be a poor choice of funding instrument.

Some insurance companies offer double indemnity coverages and family income riders for contracts used to fund a pension plan. The availability of these benefits is particularly valuable when additional amounts of life insurance are desired. Since these additional benefits may result in amounts of life insurance in excess of the maximum permitted

---

[5] Note that although the ratio of insurance to monthly income is expressed in this manner under the insurer's contract requirements, the plan must produce a normal annuity form which is a 50 percent joint and survivor annuity when the participant has been married for at least one year.

under qualified plans, double indemnity and family income coverages are generally paid for by the participant. Thus, these benefits, for tax purposes, are considered to be outside the scope of the plan. The availability to participants of these extra coverages is advantageous in that it may prove convenient for employees to be able to obtain a more complete package of insurance protection through the one underwriting process.

Disability Benefits. Most insurance companies offer waiver-of-premium and disability income coverages with retirement income contracts. However, the latter benefit is seldom provided under these plans, primarily because of the additional cost and the more stringent underwriting by insurers of this benefit. Under either provision, determination of whether a participant is disabled is made by the insurance company.

Waiver of premium, although not providing immediate cash income, does permit the buildup of cash values so that the full pension benefit will be available at normal retirement age. If a disability income rider is used, the typical benefit of $10 a month per $1,000 of insurance is paid during the period of disability, with the normal pension commencing as of normal retirement age. In those cases where waiver of premium is provided, the general practice is to have employees pay for these additional benefits.

Some plans provide that the cash value of the contract is fully vested in the employee in cases of total and permanent disability. This provision does offer the employee some immediate cash benefits.

Vested Benefits. Upon separation from employment for reasons other than retirement, death, or disability, the cash values accumulated under contracts issued on behalf of the terminating employee are available for distribution to the employee, or as a credit against future contributions, or both. The disposition of cash values of separating employees depends on the plan provisions which must be at least as generous as the alternative minimum vesting standards set forth under ERISA.

If the plan is contributory, most plans provide for a return of employee contributions (usually at a stated rate of interest) upon withdrawal from the plan.

Whether the participant is entitled to any part or all of the cash values in excess of his or her own contributions depends on the type of vested benefit under the plan. If the employee terminates employment before becoming entitled to a vested benefit, any excess of the cash value over the employee's contributions is credited to the trustee and serves to reduce future employer contributions. If the plan offers full and immediate vesting, the employee is entitled to the full amount of the cash values under the contracts. A more typical vesting provision entitles the employee to a specified portion (for example, 10 percent per year of covered service) of such excess cash value.

Assuming that the employee is entitled to part or all of the cash values upon termination, the plan can establish one or more of several different methods of providing this benefit to the employee. If the cash values are fully vested, the trustee can transfer the contract to the terminating participant, and the latter can keep the contract in full force through the payment of the required periodic premiums. If the cash values are only partially vested, the participant may choose paid-up life insurance or a paid-up deferred annuity in an amount that can be purchased with the vested portion of the cash value. Another alternative in the latter case is for the trustee to borrow from the insurance company the amount of the nonvested portion of the cash value (assuming this is not considered to be a prohibited transaction under ERISA) and assign the contract, subject to the loan, to the terminating participant. The employee is then free to pay the full premium under the contract and keep the full amount of insurance in force, subject to the loan outstanding. Of course, the employee can amortize or pay off the loan in full, thereby reducing or eliminating the encumbrance against the contract. Finally, the trustee may surrender the contract and use the cash surrender value to pay the terminating participant his or her vested interest, retaining any excess to be applied to reduce employer contributions next due under the plan.

Under ERISA, a plan may provide for the automatic "cash-out" of the vested portion of an employee's benefit if: (1) the cash-out is only made because of the employee's termination of employment, (2) the cash-out represents the value of the employee's entire plan interest, and (3) the value attributable to employer contributions does not exceed $1,750.

Where the employee fails to exercise any of the options available, the automatic nonforfeiture option generally found in contracts issued to pension cases is reduced paid-up insurance.

In a few plans, the vested cash values are not available until the normal retirement age of terminating employees. The trustee elects paid-up insurance or a paid-up deferred annuity and holds the contract in the trust until the employee's normal retirement date. In these cases, the employee generally is required to leave his or her own contributions, if any, in the plan until the retirement date; failure to leave the contributions in the plan could result in a forfeiture of vested benefits. Remember, however, that under ERISA this could only occur with respect to employees whose benefits are less than 50 percent vested. In such cases, employers may continue to cancel benefits for employees who withdraw their own contributions. Even in this case the plan must contain a provision permitting the individual to buy back forfeited benefits by repaying withdrawn contributions with interest, currently at 5 percent, compounded annually.

Contributions

Premium Rate. The premium rate for retirement income and retirement annuity contracts is based on the participant's sex and issue age. The premium rate is level from date of issue to retirement date. If an employee becomes entitled to an increase in benefits, an additional contract is purchased at a level rate appropriate for the participant's then attained age.

The premium rates for these contracts generally are based on the same mortality, interest, and expense assumptions used in the calculation of rates for regular retirement income and retirement annuity contracts. If the insurance company offers a special series of contracts for pension plans, it often uses a different set of actuarial assumptions in calculating premium rates for these contracts. Different assumptions for pension plan contracts can be justified cn the basis of the special tax credit for investment income earned on pension reserves, differences in acquisition costs and administrative expenses associated with pension business, and possible differences in mortality experience due to guaranteed issue underwriting or due to differences in experience among pension plan annuitants as compared with regular annuitants. Some insurers who offer a special series of pension contracts base their premium rates for these contracts on the same assumptions used in rate calculations for regular individual policies and reflect differences in experience in the computation of dividends on the pension contracts.

The insurance company guarantees the premium rates and annuity option rates on contracts that have been purchased. Thus, the employer is guaranteed a minimum rate of interest and, in addition, capital depreciation or adverse mortality and expense experience under purchased contracts must be borne by the insurance company. Likewise, the annuity rate guarantees protect the employer from additional costs due to possible improvement in longevity. The insurance company does not, of course, guarantee the rates at which individual contracts will be purchased in the future for new employees or for additional benefits earned by currently covered employees. Future contracts will be purchased at the premium and option rates in effect at the time these contracts are purchased.

Annual Contributions. The gross annual premium required under the plan is determined by simply adding up the premiums required to fund the amounts of life insurance to which each participant is entitled in accordance with the plan's benefit formula. For example, Table 6–2 sets forth the gross annual premium required under a hypothetical retirement income policy plan which provides a normal retirement benefit at age 65 of 30 percent of monthly earnings. The employer informs the trustee as to the amount of monthly pension to which each participant is entitled,

TABLE 6–2
Fully Insured Plan: Gross Annual Premium

Participant	Sex, Age	Monthly Earnings	Monthly Benefit	Amount of Contract	Gross Annual Premium
J. A. Wenhold	M 54	$2,000	$600.00	$60,000	$ 8,489.20
R. C. Goshay	M 50	1,800	540.00	54,000	5,340.34
S. W. Cain	M 46	1,000	300.00	30,000	2,228.20
R. M. Crowe	M 43	925	277.50	27,750	1,710.24
A. F. Clark	M 34	650	195.00	19,500	755.29
W. C. Black	M 31	525	157.50	15,750	535.74
F. X. Basile	M 28	450	135.00	13,500	406.90
P. A. Zerby	M 27	400	120.00	12,000	348.76
A. G. Luger	M 25	375	112.50	11,250	303.51
B. E. Savastio	F 25	300	90.00	9,000	262.63
G. M. Sarf	F 25	300	90.00	9,000	262.63
Total gross annual premium for plan					$20,643.44

and the trustee then purchases a retirement income contract equal to 100 times the monthly benefit. The gross premium required for each participant is a function of age, sex, and the face amount of the contract. Thus, the sum of the annual gross premiums for each employee in this example is $20,643.44.

The annual contribution required of the employer is equal to the gross annual premiums for the plan less: (1) employee contributions, if any; (2) dividends under participating contracts; and (3) the nonvested cash values of contracts of terminating employees.

The advantages and disadvantages of requiring employee contributions were discussed at length in Chapter 2.[6] If employee contributions are required, the commitment generally is expressed as a fixed percentage of salary, such as 3 percent of annual earnings. However, where employee contributions are required to finance special benefits (such as family income riders, double indemnity benefits, waiver-of-premium, or disability income benefits), each employee generally pays the required premium for his or her particular set of extra benefits. Lastly, employee contributions usually are applied toward meeting the premium cost of the pure

---

[6] It should be noted that a qualified pension plan could be established on an employee-pay-all basis by means of salary reduction (see Rev. Rul. 66–205 and Rev. Rul. 69–421) until June 27, 1974. This date was established as a cutoff date while such plans are being studied. No final regulations are expected before January 1, 1977. Under such plans, no employer contributions on behalf of participating employees were required and stockholder-employees could participate in the plan. This type of plan had appeal for companies not able to assume the financial commitment of a pension plan, while offering employees a systematic savings plan under which investment earnings on their contributions are not taxed until benefits are actually paid. IRAs do represent a viable alternative to this approach.

life insurance portion of the contract, thereby minimizing or eliminating the employee's PS 58 cost.

If participating contracts are used, then dividends are available, at least after the first or second year, to reduce the amount of annual contribution required under the plan. Dividends are almost always used to reduce the employer's contribution requirement for the following year. This practice generally is followed even in the case of contributory plans. Crediting the employer with the full amount of dividends is reasonable in view of the fact that it generally bears a substantial portion of the cost of the plan. Furthermore, administrative difficulties discourage the alternative procedure of allocating dividends between the employer and covered employees. The use of dividends to purchase additional amounts of benefits is permissible if specified in the terms of the plan and if such procedures do not discriminate in favor of stockholders, executives, or highly compensated participants.

The employer's annual contribution requirement is reduced further whenever a covered employee terminates without full vesting. The employer does not know which employees will terminate employment in the future, and therefore it must purchase the necessary amount of insurance for all currently covered employees. The reduction in cost due to turnover, then, is recognized only when the actual terminations take place. At that time, the nonvested portion of the cash value under the contract is held by the trustee and is used to reduce the amount of the employer's next premium payment. The Internal Revenue Code does not permit the trustee of the plan to reallocate the nonvested cash values among the remaining covered employees. Such a practice would often result in discrimination in favor of the highly compensated employees and also would violate the Internal Revenue Code requirement that benefits be actuarially determinable.

The effect of employee contributions and expected dividends on the employer's annual cost under the hypothetical plan set forth in Table 6–2 can now be illustrated. The following projections are based on employee contributions of 3 percent of salary and an estimate of average annual dividends expected to be paid over the next ten years under the insurer's retirement income contracts.

Gross annual premium		$20,643.44
Less: Employer credits:		
Employee contributions.	$3,141.00	
Average annual dividends	3,439.42	6,580.42
Average annual employer contribution.		$14,063.02

The above illustration does not represent an actuarial projection of the long-range cost of the plan, since the effects of salary increases, new participants, and employee turnover are not reflected in these calculations.

It should now be clear why the statement, sometimes heard, that individual policy plans have a level cost is seldom, if ever, true. The level annual gross premiums for a given set of purchased contracts are not descriptive of the contribution pattern for the plan as a whole. The gross premiums for the plan will change with increases in benefit levels and with additions and terminations among covered employees. Furthermore, annual dividends and termination credits will vary over time, thus producing some variation in the amount of employer contributions required in future years.

Contribution Flexibility. One of the major disadvantages of fully insured individual policy plans is the fact that the employer has little flexibility in determining the timing and amount of contribution payments. Premiums must be paid as they come due. Furthermore, the insurance company chooses the actuarial assumptions used in the calculation of appropriate premium rates. Nor can the employer discount in advance for expected turnover among covered employees. It is true that deviations of actual from expected mortality, investment, and expense experience under these contracts eventually are reflected in the insurance company's dividend scale. Also, employer credits are received for terminations among employees who do not have fully vested benefits. Nevertheless, these cost-reducing factors cannot be discounted by the employer in advance of the date that they are actually realized.

The allocation of contributions to pay the premiums for contracts on specific employees creates inflexibility in meeting the costs of benefits for those employees who are at advanced ages at the inception of the plan. The employer will have only a relatively short period over which to fund the benefits of these older workers. The relatively high premiums for these employees plus the premium payments due for younger employees may produce a substantial contribution commitment in the early years of the plan. This problem is reduced somewhat if the insurance company permits a degree of postretirement funding of the benefits of older participants. Under unallocated funding instruments, plan contributions could be applied to provide the benefits of those at or near retirement age, the benefits of younger workers being provided for by future contributions, as long as the minimum funding standards promulgated by ERISA are observed.

One element of flexibility in employer contributions is available under fully insured individual policy plans.[7] If an employer finds it impossible to pay part or all of the premium due under issued contracts in a given year, the trustee can be directed to borrow on their cash values to meet the premium payments due. If the trustee does borrow to pay premiums, the loan must be charged against all contracts in the trust in a manner

---

[7] The question of whether ERISA considers policy loans from a trust or plan to an employer to be a prohibited transaction has not been definitely settled in 1975.

that precludes discrimination in favor of the highly compensated employees. In other words, the loan would be distributed in the proportion that the premium for each contract bears to the total premium for all contracts. If the trustee borrows on the cash value, it should be recognized that the actuarial cost method employed is in effect changed from an individual level cost method without a supplemental liability. Thus, the Internal Revenue Service requirements pertaining to minimum and maximum limitations on funding must be observed. For example, employer contributions in future periods including amounts applied toward repayment of the loans are deductible only to the extent that the total annual contribution does not exceed the normal cost of the plan plus the amount necessary to fund the past service liability over a minimum of ten years.

An alternative to having the trustee borrow to pay premiums would be for the employer to borrow the needed sums directly from a bank without using plan assets as collateral. The employer could then pay the required premiums to the plan trustee and take the normal tax deduction for annual pension contributions. Also, the interest charged on the loan would be deductible as a necessary and reasonable business expense. Furthermore, since the borrowing takes place outside of the scope of the plan, there would be no resultant change in actuarial cost method. The employer could repay the loan at any rate permitted by the bank without reference to pension plan tax regulations. This approach would be particularly useful if the employer were faced with temporary financial difficulties while at the same time having some older employees who are to be retired in a relatively short period of time. The employer also may wish to borrow the needed premium sums in a period of operating losses to increase the carry-over loss for tax purposes.

The relative inflexibility of the employer's contribution commitment under fully insured individual policy plans may be viewed as an advantage of this funding instrument from the viewpoint of the employee. To the extent that the employer views the periodic premiums due as a fixed commitment, the long-run effect might be a greater degree of funding of benefits than might result if a more flexible funding instrument were used.

COMBINATION PLANS

General Characteristics

The term "combination plan" can be used to describe any funding arrangement that employs two or more different funding instruments. However, the term generally is used in practice to describe those plans that use a combination of individual contracts and an unallocated conversion fund. The conversion fund is sometimes also referred to as the auxiliary fund or the side fund. The objective of the combination plan is to retain, in part, the guarantees and life insurance benefits associated with individual contracts, while at the same time obtaining a degree of the flexibility inherent in unallocated funding instruments.

The mechanics of the plan involve the purchase of a whole life insurance contract (or its equivalent) on the life of each participant, frequently with a face amount equal to 100 times the monthly expected pension benefit. Although paid-up at 65 contracts can be used, the general practice is to purchase ordinary life contracts. Some insurance companies use an endowment-type contract that provides a relatively small fixed cash value as of age 65 regardless of the issue date of the contract: for example, $400 per $1,000 of face value. Standardization of the amount of cash value available at retirement simplifies the calculation of the amounts required in the conversion fund. Ordinary life contracts or endowment contracts generate the lowest scale of cash values of the various whole life and endowment contracts, and therefore a significant portion of the funding may be provided through the conversion fund. Thus, ordinary life contracts are favored, since the flexibility inherent in the conversion fund often is a prime factor in the employer's decision to use a combination plan. On the average, the cash values of the ordinary life contract will equal about 35 percent of the net single-premium sum required at normal retirement age to provide the monthly pension benefit, the remaining 65 percent being provided out of the conversion fund. The exact proportion of the cash value to the principal sum required at retirement will, of course, vary somewhat with the age of issue and the length of time that the contract is in force as of retirement date, unless the endowment-type contracts are used.

The combination plan requires the use of a trustee. If the conversion fund is administered by a corporate trustee, the latter party normally also serves as the trustee to own the ordinary life insurance contracts. The conversion fund often is held and administered by the life insurance company that issues the insurance contracts. In this case, the trustee is generally an individual—often one of the officers of the firm. Only one trust agreement is required, regardless of whether the conversion fund is administered by a corporate trustee or an insurance company.

Evidence of insurability may be required for the insurance contracts issued under a combination plan. However, most insurers are willing to issue these contracts up to some limit on a guaranteed issue basis, subject to certain underwriting restrictions.

Benefit Structure

Retirement Benefits.   Combination plans offer considerable flexibility in the choice of retirement benefit formulas. Practically any type of benefit formula can be used under these plans. Even a final-pay provision that bases benefits on the participant's average earnings during the five-year period immediately preceding retirement can be utilized effectively under a combination plan. As indicated earlier in this chapter, it is difficult to estimate precisely the level of compensation to be earned by an employee during his or her final years of employment, and therefore it is almost impossible to determine the exact face amount of retirement income coverage to be purchased to fund the ultimate retirement benefit. In the case of a combination plan, the problem of estimating the needed amount of ordinary life insurance coverage is not as compelling an issue, since a substantial proportion of the benefit is funded through the unallocated conversion fund. If the employee's final earnings prove to be higher than expected, the additional annuity consideration required can simply be withdrawn from the conversion fund. This cannot be readily done in the case of a fully insured plan, since benefits are funded solely from the cash values under the contracts issued on behalf of that particular employee.

The difficulty of projecting final earnings does present one problem when this formula is used under a combination plan; that is, the problem of determining the amount of ordinary life insurance to purchase for each employee. The approach generally used is not to reflect, for purpose of the ordinary life coverage, the increases in monthly pension benefits resulting from increases in the employee's compensation after age 55 or 60. Of course, any increases in pension benefit after this age could be credited to the employee, but they will be funded exclusively from the conversion fund.

As noted above, the face amount of the ordinary life insurance contract frequently is 100 times the expected monthly pension benefit. Thus, if a pension plan provides a retirement benefit of 40 percent of compensation, an employee earning $700 a month is entitled to a pension of $280 a month. The trustee would purchase an ordinary life contract of $28,000 on the life of that employee. Additional contracts will be purchased for increases in pension benefit equal to at least $10 a month to which the employee will become entitled because of future increases in salary. Likewise, reductions in compensation would result in a termination of ordinary life coverage at the rate of $1,000 for every $10-a-month decrease in pension benefit. If the employee were age 35 as of the issue date of the contract (and assuming no change in compensation), the cash value of a typical ordinary life contract at age 65 would be $15,680. However, the net single-premium sum required for a male, age 65, to provide a ten-year-certain immediate life annuity of $280 a month would be $43,400. The difference between the principal sum of $43,400 and the contract cash value of $15,680 would be withdrawn from the conversion fund. In addition, most insurers impose a conversion charge (such as 2.5 percent) on the difference between the net single premium and the cash value under the contract; in this example, a 2.5 percent charge would be $693. After retirement, the employee would have an annuity benefit of $280 a month, guaranteed for life by the insurance company.

Death Benefits. The preretirement death benefit under combination plans generally is restricted to the face amount of the contract. There usually is no benefit payment from the conversion fund in the event of the death of a participant. Thus, unlike fully insured plans, the death benefit under combination plans remains fixed, usually at 100 times the monthly pension until the date of retirement. Of course, if a lower amount of life insurance is desired, the death benefit can be reduced—for example, to 50 times the monthly pension. In other plans, the death benefit is equal to one year's salary. Lastly, the death benefit under a combination plan can be made comparable to the benefit available under a fully insured plan by providing for an additional payment from the conversion fund upon the death of a participant.[8]

If the participant is uninsurable under the rules of the insurer at standard premium rates, the trustee may be able to purchase a contract at a substandard rate or with a graded or graduated death benefit at the level annual premium applicable on a standard basis, the amount of the death benefit being determined by the rating assigned by the insurer.

Life insurance coverage may be continued beyond the normal retirement age in plans that permit deferred retirement. If an endowment-type contract is used, the insurer may require satisfactory evidence of insurability before extending coverage in this manner. In that case, the premiums necessary to maintain the contract in force on the participant's life on a premium-paying basis are generally obtained by the trustee making appropriate withdrawals from the conversion fund.

Disability Benefits. Waiver-of-premium and disability income riders can be provided under a combination plan. Of course, a waiver-of-premium benefit would apply only to the whole life contracts. Thus, even if the contract were kept in force to normal retirement date as a result of the waiver-of-premium benefit, the cash value would not be adequate to provide the full monthly pension the participant would otherwise have received. Therefore, payments would have to be made from the conversion fund to make up the difference needed for the full benefit. The disability income rider, on the other hand, would provide an immediate cash benefit (generally $10 a month per $1,000 of life insurance), with the usual provision that the contract will mature as an endowment at

---

[8] Again, note should be taken of ERISA's requirements concerning the plan's normal annuity form. If the participant has been married for at least one year, the normal annuity form must be a joint and 50 percent survivorship annuity unless a different option is selected by the participant.

age 65. If a waiver-of-premium or disability income rider is used, the determination of whether a participant is totally and permanently disabled is made by the insurance company in accordance with the terms of the contract provisions.

The typical provision in these plans regarding total and permanent disability, however, is to provide the participant with his or her share of the conversion fund plus all benefits then available under the contract in force on the employee's life. The determination of disability, in these cases, generally is based on a written certification of a licensed physician, usually selected by the participant and approved by the employer and the plan trustee. The trustee, upon receipt from the employer of such written certification, distributes the appropriate conversion fund share and the contract or its values in accordance with the terms of the plan, the wishes of the participant, and the rules of the insurer.

Vested Benefits. It is customary, in combination plans, to provide that the participant has a vested interest in the full surrender value of the contract in force on his or her life. Where a terminating participant has a vested interest in the share of the conversion fund, a graduated vesting schedule often is used. This vesting schedule must be at least as generous as the various alternatives allowed under ERISA. The disposition of the cash values of the contracts of a terminating participant depends on plan provisions and generally follows the analysis set forth earlier in this chapter for vested benefits under fully insured plans.

Contributions

The periodic contributions required under a combination plan are composed of premium payments for the whole life insurance contracts and contributions to the conversion fund. The premium rates for purchased contracts are guaranteed and level in amount, subject to reduction through dividends. Of course, if an employee's benefits are increased, additional amounts of life insurance will have to be purchased at the rates in effect at the time the contract actually is purchased. In addition to the guarantee of premium rates, the issued contracts also carry an insurer guarantee of the annuity rates applicable at the employee's retirement date. The guaranteed annuity rates apply to the sums withdrawn at retirement date from the conversion fund, as well as to the cash values accumulated under the life insurance contract as of that date. The extent of the annuity rate guarantee applicable to the monies from the conversion fund normally is expressed as some multiple of the face amount of insurance; i.e., at the rate of $10 to $30 of monthly income for each $1,000 of face amount. Some insurers impose a conversion charge, usually expressed as a percentage of the difference between the principal sum required at retirement age to provide the pension and the cash value of the policy as of that date. This charge generally is 2 or 2.5 percent although a higher effective percentage may be imposed where the insurance benefit is less than 100 times the monthly benefit. The higher charge is required in the latter cases to offset the reduced amount of loading available to the insurer due to the relatively lower amounts of insurance.

If the conversion fund is held by an insurance company in a fixed dollar account, the insurer guarantees that the fund will be credited with a minimum rate of interest and that there will be no capital depreciation. In addition, most insurers pay interest in excess of the guaranteed rate, as conditions permit. The conversion fund can be administered by a trustee, if the employer desires, in which case there is no guarantee of principal or interest. The significance of the combined annuity rate guarantee and the guarantee of principal and interest for the conversion fund (when administered by an insurance company) oftentimes is not fully appreciated. In these cases, the insurer's guarantees approximate those available under fully insured individual policy plans.

The amount of annual contribution to the conversion fund depends on the actuarial assumptions and the actuarial cost method used. Since the assets in the conversion fund are not allocated to specific employees, the employer can discount in advance for expected mortality and turnover. In practice, a mortality assumption frequently is used, but seldom is there a discount for turnover. Also, the employer has considerable flexibility in its choice of an interest assumption for the conversion fund. Thus, different estimates of the amount of contribution required for the conversion fund can be generated depending upon the choice of assumptions. The effect of mortality and interest assumptions on the required contributions to the conversion fund is illustrated in Table 6–3.

The employer also has considerable flexibility in its choice of an actuarial cost method to be used in calculating its contribution requirements

TABLE 6–3
Annual Contributions Required under Combination Plan

Issue Age	Retirement Age	Annual $1,000 Whole Life Premium (Male)	Annual Contribution to Conversion Fund,* Based on:			
			Annuity Table for 1949†			Interest Only 5%
			4%	4.5%	5%	
20 65		$11.64	$ 6.47	$ 5.60	$ 4.84	$ 5.82
30 65		16.27	11.27	10.12	9.10	10.76
40 65		23.98	21.80	20.25	18.79	21.79
50 65		36.98	52.29	50.09	47.98	53.62

* $10 monthly income per $1,000 of life insurance.
† Rated three years.

under a combination plan. For example, an individual level cost method with supplemental liability can be used. As discussed in Chapter 3, this method generates a low annual normal cost. The employer is free to fund the supplemental liability as it sees fit, subject to the limitations imposed by the Internal Revenue Service. During periods of financial difficulty, the employer may reduce its contributions to the conversion fund, again within the limitations imposed by the Internal Revenue Service. Thus, the combination plan provides considerably greater flexibility as to the timing of contribution payments than is available under a fully insured plan. Furthermore, the employer has a great deal of investment flexibility with reference to the conversion fund. If the fund is administered by a trustee, the assets can be fully invested in common stocks, if such an investment policy is desired. Also, in the past several years, most major life insurance companies have developed equity products in which conversion fund assets can be invested.

However, since contributions to the conversion fund do not constitute premiums as such, responsibility for the adequacy of the fund rests with the employer.[9] If the actuarial assumptions prove to be erroneous, the assets in the conversion fund may not be adequate to provide the promised benefits. Also, it must be remembered, as indicated earlier, that the choice of actuarial cost method has little effect on the ultimate cost of the plan. Lower contributions in the early years must be offset by a higher level of contribution payments in future years. Nevertheless, the flexibility in the timing of contribution payments under combination plans is offered as an important advantage of this funding arrangement over fully insured individual policy plans.

The calculation of the amounts of required periodic contributions for the conversion fund generally is performed by the insurance company, although some companies provide this service only if they hold the conversion fund. If the employer desires, he can retain a consulting actuary to perform this service. In any event, the actuarial valuation must be performed by an enrolled actuary who has the professional, educational, and experience qualifications required by ERISA.

---

[9] An exception to this general statement is the "target pension plan." Under a target pension plan, participants assume the risk of variation between actual and expected investment experience as well as variations in actuarial assumptions. Under Rev. Rul. 185, it is permissible to establish "a pension plan . . . which provides benefits that vary with the increase or decrease in the market value of the assets from which such benefits are payable, or which vary with the fluctuations of a specified and generally recognized cost-of-living index." Contributions to the conversion fund are calculated on the basis of reasonable actuarial assumptions relative to the specified benefit formula, but the actual benefit will vary with the actual investment experience of the fund. The target pension concept, while not restricted to plans utilizing equity funding, is becoming increasingly popular with the advent of mutual funds and variable annuities as funding vehicles.

7

Group Insured Pension Plans

The major development in the group pension field in the last decade is the substantial increase in flexibility made available under these contracts. Insurers are now in a position to pretty much tailor the contract to the specific needs of the employer. Employer demands for greater flexibility in investment policy and in the timing of contribution payments has led to a strong preference for the unallocated type of contract in the group pension market. This demand for greater flexibility has extended to the small employer market, and insurers have accommodated this demand by making unallocated contracts available to relatively small firms. The result has been a dramatic decline in the relative importance of the group deferred annuity contract.

Group pension contracts include group permanent, group deferred annuity, group deposit administration, and immediate participation guarantee contracts. In addition, group single-premium annuity contracts are available to fund the benefits of retired employees under noninsured pension or profit sharing plans or to fund the benefits of employees under plans terminated due to business failure, merger, or corporate takeover. Some insurers have designed contracts that provide an investment facility for pension, profit sharing, and savings plan contributions, and it is not mandatory that annuities ever be purchased under these contracts. In other words, if the client so desires, the insurer can provide investment services only. Lastly, group annuity contracts have been developed to fund corporate profit sharing plans, H.R.10, IRA, and tax deferred annuity programs.

EQUITY FUNDING

Historically, life insurance companies have invested the bulk of their assets in fixed dollar investments. The laws in most states restrict the investments of life insurance companies' general account assets in common stocks to some specified percentage (e.g., 5 percent) of the total assets of the company. This restriction is imposed because of the fixed dollar obligations and contractual guarantees provided in traditional life insurance and annuity contracts and, also, because of the relatively small surplus maintained by life insurance companies.

However, with the advent of separate accounts in 1962, insurers could offer group clients a wide range of investment choices. The assets held in separate accounts are not commingled with the general assets of the insurer and are exempt from state statutory investment restrictions normally applied to life insurance companies.

There is much variety in the manner in which separate accounts are operated by the various insurance companies. Some insurers offer accounts only on a commingled basis; others also offer accounts maintained solely for a single customer. For the most part, separate accounts have been invested primarily in common stocks, but other forms are available and we can expect further major developments in the nature and form of the separate accounts available as the types of underlying investments in these accounts are broadened. For example, some insurers have established separate accounts invested primarily in mortgages, including equity participations; at least one company has established a commingled separate account invested primarily in the ownership of income-producing real property; and other accounts are invested in publicly traded bonds, short term securities, and direct placements.

Separate accounts were developed for two reasons: (1) to compete with trust fund plans in making equity investments available to employers for funding fixed dollar plans, and (2) to fund variable annuity plans. In the first case, many employers believe that the long-term rate of return on equities will be greater than the return on fixed income investments and the increased return will serve to reduce their cost of providing the fixed benefits promised under the plan. In the second case, equity-based variable annuities by definition require that the assets supporting these annuities generally be fully invested in equity securities. Assets held in separate accounts increased from $85 million at the end of 1964 to $8.9 billion at the end of 1974. The great bulk of these assets represent equity funding of fixed benefit plans rather than variable annuities.

More recently separate accounts have been developed in response to the demand from pension funds for further investment diversity and in response to competition from other insurers for the pension investment dollar.

The insurer does not guarantee principal or interest for plan assets held in a separate account. The income and gains or losses, realized or unrealized, on separate account investments are credited to or charged against the separate account without regard to the other income, gains, or losses of the insurance company.

Separate accounts are subject to regulation by the Securities and Exchange Commission. However, exemptions from certain provisions of the acts administered by the SEC have been accorded to qualified retirement plans over the years. First, exemptions under the Securities Act of 1933 and the Investment Company Act of 1940 were provided by Rule 156 and Rule 3(c)3 for noncontributory, qualified plans covering at least 25 lives at the time the contract is issued. Later, Rule 6(e)1 extended the exemption to contributory plans, provided that certain conditions were satisfied regarding employee contributions allocated to separate accounts. Lastly, the Investment Company Amendments Act of 1970 exempts from the 1940 Act separate accounts used exclusively to fund qualified plans, and from the 1933 Act and the Securities Exchange Act of 1934 separate accounts interests issued in connection with qualified plans (except for H.R. 10 and IRA plans). Separate accounts also are subject to state regulatory requirements.

GROUP PERMANENT CONTRACTS

Group permanent insurance contracts are basically quite similar to the individual insurance contracts used to fund pension plans. Since individual policy plans were discussed in some detail in Chapter 6, the treatment of group permanent contracts is restricted primarily to a consideration of the differences between these two funding instruments.

General Characteristics

Group permanent insurance was developed to solve the problem of increasing premium costs under group term life insurance contracts in those instances where employers chose to continue group life insurance protection for their retired workers. The group permanent arrangement, in essence, offered the combined advantages of individual level premium life insurance protection for employees and mass or group underwriting. Thus, group permanent contracts, like individual contracts, were developed in response to a life insurance need rather than a retirement or pension need. However, both contracts provide cash values which can be converted readily into annuity benefits at retirement. Therefore, it was quite logical that some insurance companies would adapt their group permanent contracts to meet the needs of the pension market.

Group permanent contracts can be used as the sole funding instrument for a pension plan or they can be used in combination with a conversion fund. In the case of a fully insured group permanent plan, the nature of the plan is practically identical to an individual policy retirement income plan. If the employer prefers a combination plan, ordinary life or some similar coverage will be issued under the group contract.

The group permanent arrangement, then, has the greatest appeal in those cases where the employer desires a plan with general features characteristic of individual policy plans and where the number of participants is large enough to enjoy the advantages of group underwriting. The major advantage of the group approach is the lower premium rate attributable to the reduced commission scales, other acquisition costs, and general administrative expense levels. In addition, group permanent insurance is issued without evidence of insurability, subject to the underwriting limits imposed by the insurer. The nonmedical maximum normally is based on the size of the group and the distribution of amounts of insurance on the lives of participants. In some instances, this limit may be more liberal under group permanent than the guaranteed issue limit available under individual policies.

Benefit Structure

The benefit structures under group permanent plans are generally similar to those provided under individual policy plans. The normal retirement benefit formula usually is expressed as a flat percentage of compensation. Pure life insurance protection is available if retirement income or whole life forms of group permanent insurance are used. Therefore, the amount of preretirement death benefit depends on the type of coverage employed, as described in the previous chapter. Postretirement death benefits normally are available in the form of annuity options; the greater the death benefit (extent of annuity guarantee), the lower the amount of the monthly annuity benefit, assuming that a constant principal sum is being applied. Disability benefits and early retirement benefits can also be provided on essentially the same bases as these benefits are available under individual policy plans.

Contributions

The contributions required under a fully insured group permanent plan are composed solely of premiums for the insurance coverage, while contributions under a combination plan are divided between premiums for the group permanent coverage and contributions to the conversion fund.

The premium rate for group permanent insurance is a fixed level premium from date of entry of each participant (or date of increase in benefits) to normal retirement date. The premium rate is lower than the rate for a comparable individual contract, reflecting a lower expense loading in the group permanent rate. Because of the fixed level premium, the fully insured group permanent plan possesses the same contribution inflexibility found in fully insured individual policy plans. Likewise, participants near retirement age at the inception of the plan present a significant funding problem under fully insured plans, whether individual policy or group permanent. These problems are minimized in the case of a combination plan.

The premium and annuity rates for all units of group permanent insurance in force are guaranteed. In addition, the contract normally provides that the premium rate guarantee applies to all units of benefit purchased within some period of time, such as three years following the issue date of the master contract. Thereafter, benefits are purchased at whatever rate is in effect at the time of purchase. Thus, the premium rate guarantee is slightly more significant under group permanent contracts than under individual policy plans.

GROUP DEFERRED ANNUITY CONTRACTS

The group annuity contract, unlike individual insurance and group permanent contracts, was devised specifically to meet the funding needs of pension plans, the first such contract being issued in 1921. Group annuity plans grew very rapidly in the following two decades and constituted by far the most prevalent group insured funding instrument prior to the growth of deposit administration plans in the 1950s.

Although the provisions of a group annuity contract can be tailored to meet the needs of a particular employer, certain basic features generally are associated with this funding instrument.

General Characteristics

Group annuity contracts provide for the funding of benefits through the purchase of units of single-premium deferred annuities for each participant. However, some insurance companies offer level premium deferred annuities on a group underwriting basis.

The terms of the pension plan usually are incorporated in the master contract issued to the employer. Thus, as is true in the case of any fully insured group plan, there is no need for a trustee. Certificates outlining the benefits and conditions of coverage under the plan often are issued to employees, but there is no requirement that this be done except in a few states that require issuance of certificates if the plan is contributory.

These certificates do not constitute a contract between the insurance company and plan participants. Nevertheless, some insurers take the precaution of requiring employees to turn in their certificates immediately prior to receiving benefits under the plan. Also, certificates are sometimes recovered at retirement for the purpose of issuing new certificates which specify the amount of monthly income payable.

Unlike group life insurance, group annuity contracts are subject to very little statutory regulation regarding eligible groups or minimum number of covered lives. However, insurance companies do impose, as a matter of underwriting policy, certain requirements for these contracts. Most insurers require that there be a minimum number of eligible employees (ten, for example) for an employer to be eligible for a group annuity contract. If the plan is contributory, at least 75 percent of the eligible employees must participate in the plan, 100 percent participation being required in the case of noncontributory plans. These underwriting requirements are not imposed so much to minimize adverse selection as they are to produce a sufficient-sized case to justify the insurer expenses incurred in setting up the plan. A minimum annual premium per participant or for the plan as a whole also is imposed to assure the above objective. Also, the insurer imposes an administrative charge if the total premium in a contract year is less than a specified amount, the actual charge being determined by the amount of the annual premium. For example, one insurance company imposes an administrative charge in any contract year in which total premiums, exclusive of any administrative charge, are less than $85,000. The amount of the administrative charge in those years is $600 decreased by an amount equal to 1 percent of that part of the total premiums paid in such contract year in excess of $25,000.

Benefit Structure

Retirement Benefits. As indicated earlier, benefits under traditional group annuity contracts usually are funded through the purchase of single-premium deferred annuities. Thus, the inherent nature of this funding instrument suggests the use of a unit benefit formula. Most group annuity plans use a benefit formula of a specified percentage of compensation per year of service. These plans generally provide a different level of benefit for past service as compared with future service. For example, future service benefits may accrue at the rate of $1\frac{1}{4}$ percent of compensation, with past service benefits being calculated on the basis of three-fourths of 1 percent of compensation as of the inception date of the plan per year of past service. Unit benefit formulas that provide a flat dollar benefit per year of service also are ideally suited to the group annuity mechanism.

Under either of the above benefit formulas, a unit of accrued benefit is associated with each year of service. Thus, a single-premium deferred annuity can be purchased for each employee equal to the future service benefit that accrues with each year of service. If the plan provides a benefit of 1 percent of compensation per year of service, an employee earning $10,000 a year would accrue a benefit of $100 a year beginning at normal retirement age.

The past service benefit of a participant is determined by multiplying the participant's compensation as of the inception date of the plan by the past service benefit percentage. Therefore, if the plan provides a past service benefit of one half of 1 percent of compensation per year of service and the above-mentioned employee earned $6,000 a year at the inception of the plan and is credited with five years of past service, his or her past service benefit is $150 a year beginning at age 65. The premium required to purchase these past service benefits would be determined by multiplying $150 by the appropriate single-premium rate for a deferred annuity of $1 a year beginning at age 65, the rate being determined by the participant's age at inception of the plan. For a given retirement age, the single-premium rate increases with the age at which the participant's benefits are actually purchased. However, the employer seldom, for reasons noted later in this chapter, purchases the past service benefits of all participants on the inception date of the plan. The typical procedure is to apply past service premiums on an age priority basis, i.e., funding the past service benefits of older workers first.

By retirement date, the participant will have been credited with a series of paid-up deferred annuities. The employee will receive a single monthly pension check upon retirement representing the sum of the units of annuities purchased on his or her behalf.

Group annuity contracts also can be used without difficulty in the case of defined contribution (money-purchase) plans. It will be recalled that under these plans the employer and the employee (if the plan is contributory) contribute specified percentages of annual compensation. The annual contribution can be applied, under a group annuity contract, as a single premium to purchase a unit of deferred annuity. The amount of annuity purchased would depend on the sex and attained age of the participant at the time of purchase, the annuity form, and the normal retirement age. As the participant grows older, a given sum of annual contributions would buy smaller and smaller units of paid-up deferred annuities.

Early retirement benefits can be accommodated readily under group annuity contracts. The master contract includes a table of percentage reduction factors for retirements prior to normal retirement date. The appropriate percentage is applied to the total amount of a participant's accrued deferred annuity on the normal annuity form commencing at normal retirement date, to obtain the total monthly amount of immediate annuity on the normal annuity form commencing at early retirement date. For a male employee retiring at age 62 under a plan with a normal retirement age of 65, the reduction in benefit is usually about 25 percent. In addition, this employee sacrifices the additional future service benefits that would accrue between ages 62 and 65 if he continued employment until normal retirement date. Application of early retirement provisions under group annuity contracts assumes that all benefits accrued to the date of early retirement, including past service benefits, have actually been purchased. If past service premiums are applied on an age priority basis, this requirement should present little problem, except possibly in the early years of the plan.

Death Benefits. Group annuity contracts are not designed to provide life insurance protection as an integral part of the contract. The contract is designed solely as a vehicle for systematically funding employees' retirement benefits. Therefore, if a participant dies prior to his or her retirement date, the benefits paid under group annuity plans generally are restricted to a return of the employee's contributions, accumulated with interest at the rate specified in the contract. Preretirement death benefits attributable to employer contributions seldom are provided under group annuity contracts, although benefits of this type can be readily provided if the employer so desires. ERISA requires that a pension plan give the participant the option of providing a spouse's benefit at the participant's own expense from the time the participant becomes eligible for early retirement and is within ten years of normal retirement date. The benefit would be equal to 50 percent or more of the amount that would have been payable had the participant retired early and elected the joint and 50 percent survivor benefit. Postretirement death benefits depend on the normal annuity form under the plan and the annuity options available to and elected by, participants. Once again, under ERISA, a postretirement death benefit may be payable since the normal annuity form required for a participant with a spouse is a joint and one half survivor annuity unless the participant elects some other form of payment.

Disability Benefits. Disability benefits are seldom provided under a group annuity plan. If such benefits are desired, they can be provided through a separate group disability income contract issued to the employer.

Vested Benefits. The benefits available to participants who terminate employment for reasons other than death or retirement depend on whether the plan is contributory and the nature of the vesting provisions of the plan which must comply with ERISA. If the plan is contributory, the participant always is entitled to an accrued benefit attributable to his or her contributions. The participant's accumulated contributions can be withdrawn in cash or left with the insurance company to purchase a paid-up annuity on the normal annuity form commencing on the normal retirement date.

Vested benefits usually are stated as the amount of monthly income, payable at the normal retirement date, accrued to the date of termination. Under group deferred annuity plans, these benefits usually are provided through paid-up deferred annuities commencing at the normal retirement date stipulated in the plan.

Often, in contributory plans a provision was found that resulted in the forfeiture of vested benefits if the terminating employee withdrew his or her contributions. However, ERISA allows employees to withdraw their own contributions without a cancellation of vested benefits. An exception to this general rule is where an employee is less than 50 percent vested. In such cases, an employer may cancel vested benefits when an employee terminates employment, if he or she withdraws his or her own contributions. The plan, however, must contain a buy back provision under which the forfeited benefits must be restored if the employee repays the withdrawn contributions with interest, currently at 5 percent compounded annually.

In the case of noncontributory plans, the availability of benefits for terminating participants, of course, depends solely on the vesting provisions of the plan.

Contributions

Guarantees. Group annuity plans, as already noted, are funded through the purchase of units of single-premium deferred annuities. The premium rate scale at which annuities are to be purchased is set forth in the master contract. The premium rate scale is generally guaranteed for annuities purchased during the first five contract years under a group annuity contract. Thereafter, the insurance company has the right to revise all rates and values included in the policy, provided that written notice is given to the policyholder some period (such as 45 days) prior to the effective date of any such revision. Of course, any such revision will not affect the premium rates and annuity values applicable to premiums which have been paid prior to the effective date of the revision.

Other factors in the contract, such as early or late retirement and annuity option factors, also may be guaranteed in the same fashion as the premium rates. Often, however, these factors are guaranteed only for a specified period of time (such as ten years), regardless of when the annuities were purchased. In this latter case, it is customary to have a longer notice period regarding rate changes—for example, three years.

The burden of any rate increase in the case of defined benefit plans generally is borne in full by the employer. Even if the plan is contributory, employee contributions usually are expressed as a fixed percentage of compensation, and these percentages seldom are increased merely to offset the increased cost of an insurer's rate revision. However, in the case of a defined contribution plan, the benefit that can be purchased by both employer and employee contributions is affected directly by insurer rate revisions.

Annual Contributions. The annual premiums due under group annuity contracts may be subdivided into premiums for future service benefits credited during the contract year and premiums to purchase part or all of the unfunded past service benefits. The premium for future service benefits is simply the aggregate of the single premiums required to purchase the units of deferred annuity income credited to all participants for service rendered during the current contract year. The annual premium for future service benefits will tend to increase for several years after the inception of the plan. This rise in future service premiums is because of the increasing ages of participants and the fact that benefit formulas under group annuity plans generally are related to compensation, which normally increases with years of service. However, the employer's pattern of annual contributions also is affected by changing patterns of the group covered as well as by the rate of funding of past service benefits and the availability of employer credits. Thus, employer contributions for the plan as a whole may not show an upward trend. Indeed, some pension consultants claim that in practice the increase in annual future service premiums, if any, tends to be relatively small.

Determination of the premium for past service benefits is somewhat more complex. It will be recalled that past service benefits are credited for service rendered prior to the inception date of the plan. Thus, it is a relatively simple matter to apply the past service benefit formula and determine the exact amount of past service benefit credited to each participant as of the inception date of the plan. The single-premium sum required in the first year of the plan to fully fund all participants' past service benefits would be equal to the sum of the products of each employee's total past service benefit times the appropriate single-premium rates. However, it is not likely that any employer is interested in fully funding all past service benefits in the first year of the plan. The premium expenditure required would be quite sizable. Furthermore, the Internal Revenue Code, especially as changed by ERISA, imposes certain limitations regarding the deductibility, for federal income tax purposes, of contributions applied toward the funding of past service benefits. Under the provisions of the Internal Revenue Code, deductions for past service contributions must be spread over a minimum period of ten years.

Each year that the past service benefits remain unfunded, the single-premium sum required to fund those benefits increases. This point can be best illustrated with reference to an individual participant. The single-premium rate per dollar of deferred annuity income beginning at age 65 increases with the attained age of the participant, since each passing year brings the employee closer to retirement age. Thus, if the past service benefits of this participant are not purchased in the first year of the plan, the single-premium cost of purchasing his or her benefits increases each year. The same analysis applies for the funding of past service benefits for the plan as a whole.

In applying the annual premiums for past service benefits, the employer may decide to purchase a portion of the past service benefits of all employees, or allocate these premiums toward the funding of the past service benefits of those participants near retirement age. The latter approach is used most frequently, since insurance companies usually require a participant's annuity benefit to be fully purchased by retirement date. Some insurance companies offer what is called a "deposit administration rider" to a group annuity contract for purposes of funding past service benefits. Past service contributions are paid into a deposit fund, with appropriate sums being withdrawn at retirement age to purchase the past service benefits of retiring employees. This approach minimizes the possibility of employer dissatisfaction that might otherwise result from loss of rather substantial credits if an older participant dies immediately after a sizable annuity has been purchased on his or her behalf.

The annual contributions under a group deferred annuity contract, then, are composed of premiums for future service and past service benefits. The employer's share of annual contributions can be reduced by requiring employee contributions. Employee contributions are almost always applied toward the purchase of future service benefits; past service costs are borne solely by the employer. The employee contribution rate under a group annuity plan is generally related to the benefit formula. For example, if the plan provides a benefit of 1 percent of compensation per year of service, the employee contribution rate is expressed as some multiple of that benefit, for example, twice the benefit, in this case 2 percent of compensation. If the benefit formula is $10 per month per year of service, the employee contribution rate may be, for example, three times the benefit or $30 a month in this case.

Under defined contribution plans, employee contribution rates are related to the employer's rate of contribution. A typical provision is to require identical rates of contribution for both employer and employees; for example, each contributes 5 percent of the employee's compensation.

The employer's share of annual contributions is reduced further to the extent that employer credits are available on premium due dates. Employer credits under group annuity contracts can arise from employee terminations, late retirements, and dividend or experience rate credits. The availability of employer credits because of employee terminations, in turn, depends on the cause of the termination and the nature of the plan's vesting provision. If termination of employment is the result of the death of a participant, no employer credit is available. Employer contributions are used to purchase pure deferred annuities. A pure deferred annuity does not provide for a refund of the purchase price if the annuitant fails to live to the specified retirement age. Therefore, mortality has been already discounted in the annuity premium rates used to determine employer contributions. For this same reason, the insurance company requires evidence that participants terminating for reasons other than death are in fact in good health.

Units of deferred annuity income are purchased under group annuity contracts on the assumption that participants retire at the normal retirement age. Therefore, an employer credit generally is available whenever a participant defers retirement beyond normal retirement age, assuming that the benefit is not actuarially increased. Most group annuity plans provide that the same retirement benefit will be paid at a late retirement date as would be payable as of the participant's normal retirement date. Thus, the annuity payments due between the normal retirement date and the late retirement date are credited to the employer. If postretirement death benefits are available, the employer credit will be withheld until subsequent annuity payments exceed the minimum death benefit.

Dividends or retroactive premium rate credits are a third source of employer credits under group annuity contracts. The amount of dividend credited to the employer's account reflects, at least in part, actual experience for participants under the plan. The weight or credibility assigned to the experience of participants in the plan depends on the size of the group and the length of time that the contract has been in force. Initially, the administrative charge and the loading in the premium rate are not adequate to meet all acquisition costs and expenses of setting up the plan. Therefore, the remainder of these expenses must be amortized over the first few years of the plan. Furthermore, the long-term nature of guarantees under group annuity contracts does not permit an accurate testing of the reasonableness of the mortality assumption in the premium rate within a few years after establishment of the plan. For example, if mortality among participants in the first few years of the plan is higher than assumed in the rate, one could not conclude that these savings should be immediately credited to the employer. Meaningful comparisons of actual and expected mortality experience can only be made over a relatively long period of time. In contrast, current experience can be reflected immediately in the dividends or rate adjustments under larger group medical expense plans. This is possible in the group health field, since the insurer's liabilities can be estimated fairly accurately on a contract-year basis and the following year's premium can be adjusted when necessary. The true liability of the insurer under annuity contracts, on the other hand, will not emerge until many years after the inception of the plan. For these reasons, it is not uncommon for a number of years to elapse before dividends become payable under a group annuity contract.

New-Money Concept. Virtually all insurance companies now use the so-called new-money method of determining the rate of investment income to be credited to each group annuity contract for dividend purposes. Prior to the development of the new-money method, insurers used the overall net rate of return earned on their portfolios of investments. This rate often is referred to as the average or portfolio rate of return.

In the 1950s, a few insurers began questioning the desirability of using the average rate of return method for allocating investment income among group annuity cases. Interest rates on new investments made during this period rose significantly from the low rates of return that prevailed in the 1940s. However, insurance companies held in their portfolios a substantial amount of relatively long-term investments that were acquired in the 1940s and carried the low rates of return in effect during that decade. Thus, the average rates of investment income for most insurance companies were below the yields being earned on new investments acquired in the 1950s, and insurance companies were somewhat at a disadvantage in competing with banks for new pension business, particularly for the larger cases. In the case of a trust fund plan, all contributions would be invested at the prevailing higher rates of return. In addition to the loss of some new cases, insurers found that some employers discontinued purchases of annuities under existing group annuity contracts, while other employers went one step further and withdrew funds from insurers, where possible, and transferred these sums to bank trustees. Therefore, insurance companies decided to change their basis of allocating investment income for dividend purposes under group annuity contracts to improve their competitive position and to reduce the adverse financial selection they were experiencing under the average rate method. The investment income allocation technique that was devised is generally referred to as the new-money or investment-year method.

Under the new-money approach, an attempt is made to allocate investment income on the basis of the rate of return earned on new investments made in the year in which each block of contributions was received. Since yields on investments acquired each year are seldom identical, the allocation of investment income in dividend calculations for a given year of necessity involves the use of a number of different rates of return. Furthermore, investments made in previous years constantly are maturing and must be reinvested. Therefore, the contributions received, say, five years ago cannot be assumed to be still invested at the yields earned on new investments acquired in that year. Thus, the new-money method requires an assumption as to the rate of turnover of investments, with appropriate adjustments in the interest rates applied toward previous contributions.

Contribution Flexibility. Group annuity contracts offer the employer a greater degree of contribution flexibility than is available under individual policy and group permanent plans. In the latter plans, it will be recalled that an employee's total benefits (including past service as well as future service benefits) are projected and usually funded on a level premium basis. Group annuity contracts, on the other hand, permit a clear separation, for funding purposes, of past and future service benefits. While the employer has flexibility in the funding of past service benefits, subject to the limitations imposed by the Internal Revenue Service and the insurance company, as discussed earlier, the employer has little flexibility in the funding of future service benefits. Group annuity contracts provide for the annual purchase of future service benefits on behalf of each participant, as such benefits accrue. While group annuity contracts permit temporary suspensions of annual purchases of future service annuities, the annuities not purchased during such period of suspension are purchased upon the resumption of premium payments.[1] Thus, although suspension of future service annuity purchases is permitted, the objective of the contract provision is to provide relief during periods of financial stress rather than significant contribution flexibility for the employer. As a result, employers interested in a greater degree of contribution flexibility are prone to favor one of the unallocated funding instruments.

GROUP DEPOSIT ADMINISTRATION CONTRACTS

The deposit administration contract, which first appeared in the 1920s, evolved from the basic group deferred annuity contract. For this reason, it often is referred to as a deposit administration group annuity contract. The deposit administration contract was developed to overcome certain of the inflexibilities associated with the group annuity contract. Although originally developed as a result of interinsurer competition, the growth in popularity of the deposit administration plan began in the early 1950s largely in reponse to the increased competition from the trust fund arrangement, which offers a great deal of flexibility in plan design, timing of employer contributions, and investment alternatives.

General Characteristics

The distinguishing characteristic of deposit administration contracts, as contrasted with group deferred annuity contracts, is the fact that em-

---

[1] It is assumed in this discussion that such suspensions would not be in violation of the minimum funding requirements imposed by the Internal Revenue Service.

ployer contributions are not allocated to specific employees until retirement date. Stated differently, the actual purchase of annuities does not take place until an employee retires.

Contributions are credited to an unallocated fund which, under a conventional deposit administration contract, is variously referred to as the deposit fund, active life fund, deposit account, or purchase payment fund. However, the dramatic growth of separate account funding (which many insurance companies make available under their deposit administration plans) has led to changes in contract terminology. For example, instead of deposit account, some insurers now use the terms "general investment portfolio account" or "fixed dollar account," since contributions credited to the deposit account are invested in the insurer's general investment portfolio, which in turn is composed principally of fixed-income securities. The insurer offering a separate account facility must append some appropriate term to distinguish this account (or accounts, if more than one is established) from its general investment account. A variety of terms have been used to identify the separate account, e.g., equity account, separate account, variable contract account.

The main thrust of the separate accounts development, from the policyholder's point of view, is the broadened choice of investments between fixed dollar and equity securities. Therefore, "fixed dollar account" and "equity account" are the terms that are used when discussing the features of deposit administration contracts from the policyholder's viewpoint. The terms "general investment account" and "separate account" are used when discussing investment alternatives under these plans from the insurer's point of view.

A fixed dollar account is maintained for each policyholder which represents a record of the portion of plan funds held to be invested primarily in fixed-income obligations. An equity account also is maintained for each policyholder, which represents a record of the portion of plan funds held to be invested primarily in common stocks. The policyholder has complete discretion as to the proportion of plan contributions that is to be credited to each of these accounts. If the employer so desires, 100 percent of both employer and employee contributions (assuming state regulatory requirements are met) can be credited to the fixed dollar account or to the equity account, although the usual decision is to allocate some portion to each of the accounts.

The contributions credited to the fixed dollar account become part of the general assets of the insurance company for investment purposes. If the insurer has established a separate account for fixed dollar investments, plan contributions can be allocated to the general investment account or the fixed dollar separate account in accordance with policyholder instructions. The fixed dollar account is credited with the rate of interest guaranteed in the contract. Also, dividends due under the contract are credited to the fixed dollar account. As pensions become payable to retiring employees, annuities may be provided by allocations from either the fixed dollar or the equity account, although generally annuities are provided by allocations from the fixed dollar account. When an annuity is established, a certificate is issued to the retired employee describing his or her benefits.

The contributions credited to the policyholder's equity account are invested in the insurer's separate account. While equity account accounting procedures differ among insurance companies, the following approach is illustrative of the general concepts involved in separate account funding. Each policyholder's share of the separate account is determined on a participation unit (or variable unit) basis. The policyholder's equity account provides a cumulative record of the number of participation units credited to the account and the number of units allocated or withdrawn from the account. The balance of participation units credited to the account multiplied by the current participation unit value equals the amount of equity account assets held on behalf of the policyholder at any given point in time. The participation unit value is adjusted periodically, usually each business day, to reflect investment results under the separate account. The insurer offers no guarantee as to principal or interest on monies credited to the equity account.

The policyholder has considerable flexibility in transferring funds between the fixed dollar account and the equity account. Generally, advance written notice to the insurer (e.g., 15 business days) is required. The advance notice requirement serves to minimize the potential problem of an undue amount of switching activity that might arise from attempts to "play the market." Also, the insurer generally reserves the right to limit the amount permitted to be transferred from the fixed dollar account to the equity account in any one month, e.g., the total of the amounts so transferred in any month may not exceed $1 million. The objective of this provision is to minimize potential financial antiselection and liquidity problems arising from such transfers. Likewise, the insurer has the right—which it might exercise under some conditions, as when the stock markets are unstable—to limit transfers in a given month from the equity account to the fixed dollar account to some specified amount, e.g., $1 million of participation units.

If the policyholder decides to place future contributions with a new funding agency, such as another insurance company or a bank, the policyholder may either:

1. Permit the fixed dollar and equity accounts to be used to purchase annuities until exhausted.
2. Elect a transfer date for the transfer of funds credited to the fixed dollar and equity accounts.

If the policyholder has elected to transfer the funds in his or her accounts, purchase of annuities will cease as of a specified date, e.g., the 15th business day after the insurer receives such request. Monthly transfer payments begin on the transfer date. The minimum amount that can be transferred monthly from the fixed-income account is specified in the contract, e.g., 1 percent of the amount of the account on the date annuity purchases cease, or the balance of the account if less, with insurer permission required to transfer amounts in excess of the minimum monthly amount. Thus, the insurer reserves the right to spread transfer payments over a period of time. In other words, if the contract provides that monthly transfer payments will not be less than 1 percent of the amount of the account on the date purchases cease, the insurer has the right to stretch transfer payments over a 100-month period. In practice, the agreed-upon transfer schedules generally are considerably shorter than the maximum permissible contractual period. With reference to the equity account, the contract generally provides that the sum transferable is the contract fund balance valued on a market value basis. The insurer generally permits a lump-sum transfer, although for very large accounts the insurer may reserve the right to spread payments over a period of time. In the latter case, the maximum period generally is shorter than the period applicable to the fixed dollar account. For example, the contract might provide that monthly transfer payments from the equity account will not be less than (1) the greater of $1 million worth of participation units or 5 percent of the amount of the account on the date annuity purchases cease, or (2) the balance of the account, if less. In this latter case, the maximum period over which insurer transfer payments can be made is 20 months. The difference in treatment of transfers from each account is due to the differences in liquidity and marketability between fixed dollar and equity securities.

In the case of transfers to another funding agency, the insurer usually reserves the right to withhold some amount of the fund (usually up to 5 percent, the specific percentage to be determined by the insurer) to cover expenses not yet recovered and to offset possible financial antiselection (although transfers on a market value basis minimize the latter problem).

Deposit administration contracts originally were only available to larger plans. However, competition and increased insurer experience with this contract have resulted in substantial reductions in minimum size underwriting requirements for these plans. Minimum size requirements generally are expressed in terms of total annual contributions and average annual contributions per life according to the type of policyholder and plan involved. For example, the contribution requirements of one insurance company are as follows:

	Total Annual	Average per Life
Fixed dollar funding and benefits:		
Single private employer	$10,000	$250
Negotiated labor-management trust	$20,000	$100
Public employee retirement system (political		
subdivision)	$50,000	$250
Equity funding or variable annuities included with		
any of the above	$50,000	

Some insurers will issue deposit administration contracts on even smaller plans than those indicated in the above example.

An administration charge normally is levied when annual premiums are less than a specified amount. For example, one insurer imposes an annual administration charge under its fixed dollar contracts equal to $800 less 2 percent of any amount of annual contributions paid in excess of $25,000 but not in excess of $65,000. Thus, there is no charge if the previous year's contributions were at least $65,000. If equity funding is utilized under the contract, the annual charge is somewhat higher, (e.g., $1,100 less 2 percent of the amount by which the previous year's contributions exceeded $25,000 but not $80,000). The charge for the first contract year is based on the appropriate expense formula, but using as a base the contributions anticipated in the first contract year. The contract administration charge generally is allocated from the fixed dollar account.

Benefit Structure

One major advantage of deposit administration contracts is the flexibility available in designing the plan's benefit provisions. Whereas group deferred annuity plans are limited largely to unit benefit formulas, any type of retirement benefit formula can be employed without difficulty under a deposit administration contract. Also, deposit administration contracts may be used without difficulty in plans that base benefits on final average earnings. The fact that benefits cannot be precisely determined until the employee actually retires presents no problem under these contracts, since annuities are not purchased until the date of retirement. Likewise, minimum retirement benefits and the most complex integrated benefit formulas can be handled readily under deposit administration plans. Furthermore, the availability of equity funding permits the use of variable annuity benefits. The absence of annuity purchases until retirement date permits considerable flexibility in the establishment of early and late retirement benefit provisions. For example, early retirement benefits may be provided on a more liberal basis than the actuarial equivalent of normal retirement benefits (subject to Internal Revenue Service limitations), while additional benefits may be permitted for service rendered after the normal retirement date.

Deposit administration plans generally do not provide a preretirement death benefit beyond the accrued benefit attributable to employee contributions. However, as required by ERISA, the plan must give the participant the option of providing a preretirement death benefit at the participant's own expense from the time the participant becomes eligible for early retirement if he or she is within 10 years of normal retirement.

A death benefit can be readily provided as part of the plan under these contracts. In this case, death benefit payments would be withdrawn from one of the unallocated accounts. The actuary would have to project the cost of these benefits in estimating the required contributions under the plan. Adjustments in future contribution requirements would be required if future actuarial valuations discovered variations in actual from expected mortality experience. The availability of postretirement death benefits depends on the normal annuity form under the plan and the annuity options available to participants.

Separate and distinct disability benefits are becoming more prevalent under deposit administration contracts. Disability payments under the plan can be charged directly to the unallocated account, the procedure being quite similar to that outlined in the discussion of preretirement death benefits. If disability benefits are provided, the determination and policing of the existence of disability is generally the responsibility of the employer. Upon receipt of certification of disability, the insurance company begins making disability payments to the participant from the unallocated account. As an alternative to the above procedure, the employer can choose to make the disability payments directly to disabled workers.

Vested benefits, beyond provision for the accrued benefit attributable to employee contributions, also can be provided under deposit administration plans. Where available, these vested benefits generally are treated as an obligation of the plan similar to that of the accrued benefits of participants of the plan—i.e., as deferred annuity credits subject to the requirements that terminated employees be alive and claim the benefit at normal or early retirement age.

It should also be noted that the insurer generally imposes an expense charge for cash payments (for example, for death, disability, or vested benefits) from the unallocated account. Therefore, it is advisable whenever possible for the employer to make these cash payments directly to eligible participants rather than from the unallocated account.

Contributions

Since contributions are not allocated to specific participants until retirement date, contribution payments to one of the unallocated accounts are not premiums in the more commonly accepted sense of the term. Other than the minimum funding requirements of ERISA, the employer, rather than the insurance company, has primary control over deciding the amount and frequency of contributions to be made to the plan each year. Of course, the insurance company determines the premium rates that will be charged for the immediate annuities purchased at retirement age.

Guarantees.   As noted earlier, contributions may be made directly to the fixed dollar account or amounts may be added by transfer from the equity account. For every dollar credited to the fixed dollar account, the insurer guarantees at the time of receipt: (1) the preservation of principal, (2) an interest accumulation rate, and (3) a schedule of annuity purchase rates.

A guaranteed minimum interest rate is credited on all monies paid into the fixed dollar account during the first five contract years. While guaranteed rate levels differ somewhat among insurers, the following rate schedule is illustrative of a typical rate guarantee provision. For contracts issued in 1975, interest guarantees will be:

1975–76	8%
1977–80	7
1981–85	6
1986–95	4
1996 and thereafter	3

Interest rate guarantees can be changed annually for contributions received after the beginning of the sixth contract year. Actual investment income in excess of the guaranteed rate is credited to the policyholder via the dividend formula. Some insurance companies follow the practice of anticipating a portion of the dividend by crediting the fixed dollar account with a rate of interest greater than the minimum rate of interest guaranteed in the contract. For example, if the insurer has guaranteed 7 percent interest and expects to earn 8 percent for the year, the account might be credited with 7.5 percent interest. Of course, the advance interest credit is taken into account in the calculation of the annual dividend for the contract.

The insurer also specifies a set of guaranteed annuity purchase rates in the contract. The guaranteed annuity rates normally apply to contributions received during the first five contract years, with the rates being subject to revision on an annual basis thereafter. The guaranteed annuity rates usually are graduated upward for annuity purchases made in future years. For example, a typical guarantee provision provides that the purchase rate for any calendar year after the year of contract issue is equal to the rate for the preceding calendar year increased by an annual incremental factor.

The above guarantees apply only to the fixed dollar account. In the case of the equity account, contributions may be made directly to the account or amounts may be added by transfer from the fixed dollar account. Each contribution paid into the equity account is applied to credit participation units. The number of participation units credited is determined by dividing the amount contributed or transferred by the dollar value of a participation unit on that date. Unit values are an index of the day-to-day value of each unit in the equity account. Unit values reflect actual investment income; realized and unrealized capital appreciation or depreciation; taxes incurred, if any; brokerage fees; and a margin for expenses. The insurer makes no guarantee as to principal and interest on funds in the equity account.

Insurance company practices differ for annuity rate guarantees for purchases made from the equity account. Some insurers provide no annuity rate guarantee except that transfers made from the equity fund to the fixed dollar fund are entitled to whatever guarantees are applicable to new premium income in the fixed dollar account at the time of transfer. Other insurance companies provide annuity purchase rate guarantees for equity account money used to purchase annuities during a specified period, e.g., within five years or ten years from the issue date of the contract. Still other insurers provide an annuity rate guarantee on the total funds held under the contract on a first-in, first-out basis, without reference to whether the purchase funds are allocated from the fixed dollar or equity accounts.

Annual Contributions.   Under a deposit administration plan, the actuarial calculations can be done by the insurance company or the employer can hire a consulting actuary to perform this function. In the latter case, the reduction in insurer services required under the plan is recognized through lower expense charges or the payment of service fees to consultants. In either case, there is considerable flexibility in the choice of an actuarial cost method. Typically, the actuarial cost method chosen is one that generates a supplemental liability, which in turn offers the employer flexibility in terms of the rate at which the supplemental liability is funded. Of course, the contributions must meet the minimum funding standards established by ERISA. The deposit administration contract also offers flexibility in the choice of actuarial assumptions. Since contributions are not allocated prior to retirement, an interest assumption may be used which approximates the expected rate of return rather than the guaranteed rate, and expected terminations of employment or late retirements may be anticipated thereby permitting lower levels of annual contributions in the early years of the plan. Also, if the benefit formula is related to compensation, projected future increases in the salaries of participants can be reflected in contribution calculations.

The contribution flexibility available under a deposit administration contract is particularly important in the case of collectively bargained plans under which the employer is required to contribute a specified percentage of payroll. Thus, annual contributions to the plan fluctuate with changes in the amount of covered payroll. It would obviously be difficult to use an allocated funding instrument under these circumstances, unless a defined contribution benefit formula were used.

However, it must be recognized that an increase in the degree of contribution and investment flexibility under an insured funding instrument can only be achieved by a reduction in insurer guarantees. For example, the insurance company does not guarantee that the unallocated account amounts will be sufficient to provide the accrued benefits of active employees. Such a guarantee is obviously not possible, since the timing and amount of contribution payments is largely within the control of the employer. Therefore, the adequacy of the unallocated accounts is the responsibility of the employer. The few minimum contribution requirements imposed by insurers under deposit administration contracts are not meant to assure the adequacy of the unallocated account balances. For example, the contract may require that total contributions in any policy year not be less than the minimum sum required by ERISA.[2] Lastly, the insurance company usually requires that the unallocated accounts be sufficient to purchase annuities for participants due to retire.[3] If the amount in the fixed dollar account is inadequate to purchase annuities for a retiring employee, the insurer has the right to allocate funds from the policyholder's equity account. If the amounts in both accounts are inadequate, the contract provides that a contribution is immediately due and payable by the policyholder. Of course, once the annuity is purchased, the annuitant is guaranteed his or her pension payments regardless of plan experience.

Generally, there are no employer credits of the type that result under allocated funding instruments, other than a dividend or rate adjustment. This is logical, since calculations of contributions under deposit administration plans usually discount in advance for expected mortality among participants, terminations of employment, and late retirements. Any sig-

---

[2] The insurance company also may impose a maximum on the annual contributions permitted under a deposit administration plan. This requirement is imposed to minimize adverse financial selection. The maximum permissible annual contribution could be defined, for example, as the maximum permitted by the Internal Revenue Service as a deductible contribution to the plan.

[3] However, during the early years of the plan, the insurer generally permits a degree of postretirement funding to minimize the financial impact of older participants with sizable past service benefits at the inception of the plan.

nificant deviations of actual experience from expected experience under the plan for the above factors can be recognized through adjustments in future levels of required contributions.

Since the insurer guarantees annuity and interest rates on the fixed dollar account under deposit administration contracts, more favorable experience than assumed in the guaranteed rates provides a basis for a rate credit or dividends under these contracts. The procedure for calculating dividends under deposit administration contracts is similar to the procedure for calculating dividends under group deferred annuity contracts. An internal record account is maintained for each deposit administration policyholder. This account is a cumulative record of the cash income and cash outgo under each contract. The account is credited with contributions received from the policyholder during the policy year, along with the actual investment income allocated to this particular contract. The allocation of investment income for fixed dollar account assets and annuities purchased usually are based on new-money rates. The internal record account is then debited with all benefit payments made during the year and all expenses directly incurred or allocated to the particular contract. It should be noted that the account is debited with benefit payments actually made during the year and not with the single-premium annuity sums withdrawn from the unallocated accounts to purchase annuities for participants retiring during the year.

A credit balance in the account represents an excess of cash income over cash outgo for the particular contract. The liabilities of the company under the contract are then compared with the cash balance in the internal record account to determine whether a dividend should be paid. There are two basic approaches in determining the insurer's liability under the contract's unallocated accounts. The first, and probably most prevalent approach, is to value the liability for the unallocated accounts as the amount the insurer would be liable to pay under the liquidation option of the contract. This valuation method is sound if the contract is terminated and the monies transferred to another insurer or a corporate trustee.

A second approach is to recognize that each dollar in the unallocated account carries some specified annuity rate guarantee. Therefore, at the end of each contract year, the insurer can calculate its liabilities under the unallocated accounts on the basis of mortality, interest, and expense assumptions that it deems appropriate at that given time. If the assets in the unallocated accounts exceed the liability calculated on this basis, this would be an additional source of dividend. If the guaranteed annuity rates are currently viewed as being too low, the annuity reserve for active lives may exceed the assets in the unallocated accounts, and therefore may reduce or eliminate the amount of dividend that would otherwise be available from favorable experience under annuities on retired lives.

GROUP IMMEDIATE PARTICIPATION
GUARANTEE CONTRACTS

The deposit administration contract went a long way toward providing employers with the desired degree of flexibility not available under the traditional group annuity contract. In addition, the deposit administration contract offers certain interest and annuity rate guarantees. However, the insurance company is able to provide these guarantees only because it accumulates a contingency reserve and because it has control, through dividend computations, over the rate at which actuarial gains pertaining to guaranteed items are credited to the employer. Some employers object to these features of deposit administration plans. These employers prefer an immediate reflection of the actual experience under their plans and are willing to give up the guarantees of the deposit administration plan to get it. Thus, insurance companies developed the immediate participation guarantee (IPG) contract,[4] the first contract of this type being issued in 1950.

In an IPG plan, the employer's account is credited with the contributions received during the contract period plus its share of actual investment income for the year. There is generally no guarantee of principal or a minimum rate of interest under these contracts. The account is charged with all the expenses associated with the particular contract. As issued by many insurance companies, these contracts provide that all benefits, including annuity payments, are charged directly against the account as they are paid. In other words, annuities are not actually purchased for participants at retirement date, as is the practice under deposit administration plans. Some insurance companies do charge the account with the gross premium for the annuities of retired workers. However, in these latter cases, the annuities generally are canceled at the end of each year, with the unearned portion of the annuity consideration being credited to the employer's account and repurchased on a current rate basis. The result is similar to that achieved by insurers that only charge to the account the annuity payments actually made. There is no charge to the account for an allocation toward building up a contingency reserve. Also, since no dividend as such is paid, all the record keeping pertaining to a particular contract can be maintained in one account. Thus, the employer can be quickly apprised of the experience to date under the plan.

If annuities are not actually purchased at retirement date, the insurer does perform periodic valuations to be certain that the credit balance in the account is at least sufficient to provide the promised annuity payments to retired workers. If the credit balance approaches the amount

---

[4] This type of contract also is referred to as a pension administration contract.

of reserve required to provide the benefits of already retired employees, annuities actually are purchased for the retired workers. The reserve basis used in these valuations is more conservative than the assumptions used in valuing liabilities under deposit administration plans, thereby permitting a margin for contingencies.

The IPG contract also specifies a schedule of guaranteed annuity gross premium rates. However, since annuities are not actually purchased at retirement date, these guaranteed annuity rates are only of significance if the plan is terminated.

All the aspects of flexibility in contribution timing and plan design discussed under deposit administration plans are equally applicable to IPG contracts. The further reduction in insurer guarantees and the immediate reflection of actual experience under the plan bring the IPG contracts one step closer to trust fund arrangements.

Some insurance companies have developed a contract that possesses characteristics of both deposit administration and IPG contracts; it usually is referred to as a modified immediate participation guarantee contract or a direct-rated deposit administration contract. The major characteristic of this latter contract is that the unallocated account is maintained on an immediate participation basis, but single-premium immediate annuities actually are purchased for each participant upon retirement.

Equity funding and variable annuity benefits generally are available under IPG contracts. The features of equity funding are basically similar to those discussed under deposit administration contracts.

MATURITY FUNDING CONTRACTS

Some insurers have developed group single-premium immediate annuity contracts to be used for noninsured pension, profit sharing, and savings plans. Both fixed dollar and variable annuities usually are available under these contracts. When used with a noninsured pension plan, sufficient funds are transferred to the contract at retirement to purchase an annuity equal to the employee's accrued pension. In the case of a profit sharing or savings plan, funds from the employee's account are transferred to the contract at retirement to purchase an annuity for the employee. The insurer issues an annuity certificate to the policyholder for delivery to each person for whom an annuity is effected under the contract. Each such certificate sets forth in substance the benefits to which such person is entitled under the contract.

The annuities issued under this type of contract generally are nonparticipating. The contract includes a schedule of annuity purchase rates, which can be changed by the insurer on at least 90 days' notice to the policyholder; although variable annuity purchase rates usually are not subject to change within the first two years from issue date of the contract, since they are not affected by changes in the rate of return on new fixed dollar investments.

Issuance of the contract generally requires an expectation that an average of $50,000 per year will be applied under the contract to purchase annuities during the first five contract years. The contract can be issued to a bank to provide an annuity option for the various plans administered by the bank. In other words, the contract is available on a multiemployer basis.

The maturity funding contract offers several advantages: (1) it can be an additional option under a profit sharing plan at no cost to the policyholder; (2) it offers employees a more favorable annuity purchase rate than can be obtained through purchase of individual annuities; (3) annuity purchase is optional with the employee; (4) the contract can be implemented without upsetting existing plan and trust arrangements; (5) the contract can be discontinued at any time without penalty; and (6) fixed dollar and variable annuities, or a combination of both (a balanced annuity) generally are available.

INVESTMENT FACILITY CONTRACTS

The competitive demand for funding flexibility has reached such a point that a few insurers offer a group annuity contract under which purchase of annuities is not mandatory and the insurer has no contractual obligation to guarantee benefits even for retired employees. Benefit payments may be made directly by the plan's trustee (if the plan is split-funded) or, if directed by the policyholder, the insurer can make benefit payments to the extent that funds are available. The contract includes a schedule of annuity purchase rates, and annuities can be purchased at the option of the policyholder. However, a policyholder seeking the degree of flexibility available under this contract is not likely to elect annuity purchases. In essence then, this type of contract is designed to permit the employer or trustees of a pension plan to take advantage of the investment facilities of an insurance company with the right but not the obligation to purchase annuities for retiring employees or to utilize any of the other typical services offered by an insurance company.

Contributions can be credited to a fixed dollar account or an equity account. The insurer also may maintain a temporary investment account composed of cash equivalent assets such as commercial paper, bank certificates of deposit, and U.S. Treasury bills. Contributions placed in the temporary investment account generally are transferred to the policyholder's equity account over a period of time, thus permitting an opportunity for dollar cost averaging of equity investments.

Transfers between accounts or to another funding agency are freely permitted, within broad limits, thus providing ample flexibility in achieving, maintaining, or changing the desired investment mix for total plan assets. For example, the contract may guarantee the minimum amount that the insurer can be required to transfer from the fixed dollar or equity accounts; e.g., $2 million a month, with amounts in excess of this figure requiring insurer approval. Transfers or withdrawals from the temporary investment account generally can be effected without limit on the amount that may be transferred in any month. Transfers usually are made on a 100 percent of market value basis.

No guarantees as to principal or interest are made by the insurer. The monies allocated to the fixed dollar account are credited with a specified rate of interest from the day of deposit, subject to a periodic interest adjustment to reflect actual net investment results for the preceding period.

The insurance company may be given authority to provide total management of the pension plan assets, with the right to allocate the plan assets among various investment accounts as it deems desirable. The employer also may provide the insurer with certain investment guidelines to follow in handling plan assets.

A general expense charge is made each year, generally by a reduction from the equity account. The insurer may require a minimum balance (e.g., $50,000) in the equity account to keep the contract in force.

Some insurance companies have developed contracts for special lump-sum arrangements designed to attract pension funds. Under this type of arrangement, the insurer guarantees on a lump-sum payment made to it, a fairly high interest rate such as $8\frac{1}{2}$ to 9 percent and guarantees this rate for eight to ten years. Various liquidation features often are available under these contracts either to meet special needs of the contract-holder or to limit the liability of the insurer.

SINGLE PURCHASE ANNUITY CONTRACTS

Group single-premium annuity contracts have been designed to provide annuities for participants in an uninsured pension or profit sharing plan that has terminated.[5] Frequent causes of the termination of such plans are business failure, merger, or takeover. In recent years, the accelerating pace of corporate mergers and takeovers has led to considerable interest in single purchase group annuity arrangements. Apparently, there sometimes is concern among the officers of the corporation being absorbed that pension assets will be used by the new management for subsequent acquisitions or that the rate of funding will be reduced to a point at which the security of their pension benefits will be impaired though this should not be as much of a problem since the enactment of ERISA.

---

[5] For a detailed discussion of what happens when a pension plan terminates, see Chapter 2.

If annuities are purchased, the funds are unavailable to the new management and the purchased annuity benefits are guaranteed by the insurance company.

Under a single purchase contract, immediate annuities are provided for present pensioners and deferred annuities for those who are below retirement age. This type of contract almost always is nonparticipating. Since single purchase situations invariably involve substantial sums of money, and with relatively high rates of interest prevailing in today's money markets, there is a great deal of competition among insurers for this type of business. These contracts generally are available for single purchases of $50,000 or more.

INDIVIDUAL ACCOUNT CONTRACTS

Several types of plans, by their nature, require an individual account to be maintained for each covered employee. These include H.R. 10 (Keogh) plans for self-employed persons and their employees, IRAs (individual retirement programs), tax-deferred annuity programs for teachers and employees of certain tax-exempt organizations, profit sharing and savings plans, and pension plans of the money-purchase or defined contribution type. For these plans, some insurers have designed group annuity contracts utilizing individual accounts. These contracts permit fixed dollar and equity funding during the accumulation period and offer both fixed dollar and variable annuities at retirement. While conventional group deferred annuity contracts provide for allocated funding (i.e., individual account treatment), they do not offer the flexibility available under the new individual accumulation account contracts.

The participant can elect to apply contributions to the purchase of units of deferred annuities, or can accumulate contributions in a fixed dollar and an equity account in any proportions he or she wishes. An accumulation rate of interest may be guaranteed by the insurer for the first five contract years on contributions to the fixed dollar account, with periodic adjustments made to reflect the current rates of return being earned in the appropriate investment account. Contributions accumulated in the equity account carry no guarantees as to principal or interest, with the changing unit values reflecting the actual net investment experience of the separate account. The purchase of an annuity, if so elected, is in the form of an immediate annuity.

The insurer normally imposes some minimum expected annual contribution requirement (e.g., $25,000) for issuance of this type of contract to a single employer. In the case of a tax-deferred annuity plan, the requirement generally is expressed in terms of a minimum number of employees eligible for solicitation (e.g., 150 employees). Likewise, for association H.R. 10 plans, eligibility might be expressed in terms of the number of eligible employees (e.g., 500 eligible members for state and county associations of doctors, dentists, accountants, and lawyers; 2,500 eligible members for other state and county associations; 5,000 eligible members for national associations). The insurer also may require a minimum annual contribution for each participant (e.g., $200).

A sales charge is levied on each dollar of contribution, e.g., 4 or 5 percent, with the remainder being credited to the participant's account. An annual administration charge also may be made against each participant's account. For example, under a tax-deferred annuity plan, a charge of $22.50 would be made against each participant's account in the first accounting year and $10 in each subsequent accounting year. If both fixed dollar and equity funding are utilized by the participant, a maximum combined administration charge for both accounts is imposed (e.g., $25 and $12.50 for the first and subsequent accounting years, respectively). For H.R. 10 plans and employer pension and profit sharing plans, the administration charge per participant generally is lower than the above figures. A fee for investment management services may be handled in one of two ways: charged directly to each participant's account, or charged to the appropriate investment fund and therefore reflected in the net investment result credited to the participant's account.

Transfer of funds between the fixed dollar and equity accounts is freely permitted. No sales charge is imposed on such transfers; therefore 100 percent of the sums so transferred is credited to the participant's account. Likewise, transfers to a new funding agency are permitted and are made on the basis of 100 percent of the sums so allocated. However, the insurer may reserve the right to spread the transfer payments over a period of time. For example, if contributions are discontinued for all participants, the insurer may limit the amount of monthly transfer payment to the greater of $2 million or 5 percent of the amounts held under the contract.

These contracts generally permit withdrawals by participants, according to the plan document. Participant withdrawal privileges are generally available under profit sharing and savings or thrift plans. The contract normally specifies that participant withdrawals are permitted equal to 100 percent of the lesser of the amount requested and the dollar value of the participant's account as of the day of receipt of such request.

If a participant dies, his or her beneficiary may elect a single sum payment of the amount accumulated in the participant's account or an annuity option.

A newer type of contract emerging particularly for profit sharing and savings plans is an arrangement whereby an insurer guarantees relatively high interest rates for various time periods. For example an insurer may guarantee a 9 percent rate of interest for eight years or 8.5 percent for ten years.

8

Trust Fund Plans

The trust fund arrangement was the first of the existing funding instruments to be used to fund private pension benefits. In addition to being the oldest of the funding instruments, trust fund plans currently account for the bulk of the employees covered and the assets held by private plans. Of the 33 million participants under private plans, about 20 million are covered under trust fund plans, with about 70 percent of all pension fund assets being held by these plans. The trust fund approach is used extensively in the case of multiemployer plans, although the increased flexibility now available under group pension contracts has resulted in greater life insurance company competition for multiemployer plan business.

This chapter is concerned with those plans in which all or a substantial portion of the plan assets are accumulated and invested by the trustee. In other words, the discussion in this chapter does not pertain to plans in which a trustee is used but benefits are funded entirely through insurance company contracts (for example, a fully insured individual policy plan). The discussion in this chapter is pertinent to the trust fund portion of combination plans, including trust fund plans that provide for purchases of annuities at retirement or investment of a part of the trust assets in deposit administration or immediate participation guarantee contracts.

GENERAL CHARACTERISTICS

A trust fund plan is an arrangement under which employer and employee contributions, if any, are deposited with a trustee who is responsible for the administration and investment of these monies and the income earned on accumulated assets of the fund, and who normally is responsible for the direct payment of benefits to eligible participants under the plan. If the trust fund arrangement is used in combination with an insured funding instrument, benefit payments to participants generally are made by the insurance company, with transfers from the trust fund made as required. The trustee usually is a corporate trustee (trust company). Individuals also can serve as trustees of the plan although this practice will undoubtedly become less frequent because of the fiduciary requirements of ERISA.

Trust Agreement

The duties and responsibilities of the trustee are set forth in a trust agreement which is executed by the employer and the trustee. In the case of a negotiated multiemployer plan, the trust agreement is executed by individuals representing the unions and an equal number of individuals representing the employers, and these persons often compose the board of trustees responsible for the administration of the plan. The board of trustees may retain the task of investing plan assets, or it may choose to delegate this duty to a corporate trustee. In the latter case, a trust agreement setting forth the duties and responsibilities of the corporate trustee is executed by the the board of trustees and the corporate trustee.

A typical trust agreement between an employer and a corporate trustee contains provisions, among others, regarding the irrevocability and nondiversion of trust assets; the investment powers of the trustee; the allocation of fiduciary responsibilities; the payment of legal, trustee, and other fees relative to the plan; periodic reports to the employer to be prepared by the trustees; the records and accounts to be maintained by the trustee; the conditions for removal or resignation of the trustee and the appointment of a new trustee; the payment of benefits under the plan; and the rights and duties of the trustee in case of amendment or termination of the plan.

The trust agreement, then, is concerned primarily with the receipt, investment, and disbursement of funds under a pension plan. The plan provisions may be incorporated in the trust agreement or they can be set forth in a separate plan document. The use of two separate documents is quite prevalent in trust fund plans and is almost always the approach used in multiemployer plans. The advantage of a separate plan document is that amendments of the plan can be made without the need to involve the trustee in frequent amendments to the trust agreement.

Administrative Duties of Trustee

The bulk of the record keeping associated with a pension plan is normally performed by the employer under single-employer trust fund plans. If the plan is contributory, the employer generally retains responsibility for maintaining a record of employee contributions. In this case, total contributions are paid to the trustee without reference to any division of employer and employee contributions. The employer normally also assumes responsibility for the maintenance of records of earnings and credited service for each participant. In some cases, the record-keeping function is performed by the consulting actuary for the plan.

Most corporate trustees are able to relieve the employer of the burden of maintaining the necessary records associated with the plans. Corporate trustees sometimes maintain records in the case of profit sharing plans or defined contribution pension plans and, to a more limited extent, in connection with multiemployer plans. If the trustee performs any record-keeping function, a service charge, in addition to the trustee's investment fee, is levied on an account basis, as explained later in this chapter. The advantages of specialization and the economies of size permit corporate trustees who handle a substantial volume of pension business to perform these services for a reasonable fee. The employer must decide whether it is more economical in its case to maintain these records itself or to have this service provided by the trustee or by a consulting actuary or service organization.

In the case of a negotiated multiemployer plan, the board of trustees, rather than the individual employers, generally is responsible for the maintenance of plan records. The record-keeping function usually is performed by a pension fund office created by the board of trustees. If a corporate trustee is retained to manage the assets of the fund, the plan trustees may delegate the task of record keeping to the corporate trustee. In recent years, there has been a significant growth of so-called professional plan administrators, whose market is composed principally of multiemployer plans. The function of a professional administrator is to keep all the specific records of service and earnings for individual members of the plan and to handle all routine administrative transactions.

Regardless of whether the corporate trustee performs the record-keeping function, he or she never makes any benefit distributions from the fund without authorization from the employer or retirement committee. In the case of a single-employer trust fund plan, the employer generally appoints a plan or retirement committee, usually composed of officers of the company. It is the responsibility of this committee to determine a participant's eligibility for benefits under the plan. Under multiemployer plans, authorization of benefit payments is the responsibility of the board of trustees or a committee of its members appointed by the board; but in some cases, this function is delegated to a professional administrator.

Apart from the above-mentioned administrative aspects of trust fund plans, a corporate trustee always is responsible for maintaining accurate and detailed records of all investments, receipts, disbursements, and other transactions involving the trust assets. In addition, the trustee is required to submit an annual statement regarding the above trust transactions to the plan or retirement committee, usually within 90 days of the close of the plan's fiscal year. The trust agreement may require that statements be rendered to the committee more frequently than annually, for example, quarterly or monthly. Also, in some cases, the trustee assumes responsibility for the filing of forms for the trust as required by tax regulations.

Additionally, the trustee must make annual reports under the provisions of ERISA and the basic information must be made available in summary form to all participants and beneficiaries.

Investment Powers of Trustee

The primary function of a trustee is the investment management of trust assets.[1] The trustee invests the trust assets (including contributions and investment income) in accordance with the provisions of the trust agreement, the investment policy desired by the plan or retirement committee, and the fiduciary standards imposed by ERISA, and by general trust laws. The investment power granted to a trustee by the trust agreement varies among plans; it may range from approval by the retirement committee of every action affecting the fund's assets to full discretion in investment affairs. Furthermore, the corporate trustee does maintain personal contact with the employer, and therefore the latter may influence, directly or indirectly, investment decisions. If the trust agreement fails to specify the investment powers of the trustee, the trustee is restricted to investments that are legal for trust funds in the state in which the trust is established and the federal staute governing fiduciary investments.

The trustee, until the enactment of ERISA, could invest all trust assets in the securities of the employer. Essentially, ERISA restricts investment of pension plan assets in an employer's securities to 10 percent of the fund value. Moreover, pension plans must reduce current "excess investments" in employer securities to this maximum 10 percent level by December 31, 1984 (with 50 percent of the excess to be eliminated by

---

[1] However, there is a growing interest, in the case of very large plans, in the utilization of investment advisory services for the management of plan assets, with the corporate trustee serving as custodian.

December 31, 1979). The limit does not apply to profit sharing or thrift plans that explicitly permit larger investments in employer securities. Nor does it apply to stock bonus plans, Employee Stock Ownership Plans (ESOPs) that typically are invested exclusively in employer securities. Loans to the employer made from plan assets, except for ESOPs, have been generally forbidden by ERISA even though there is adequate security for the loan and the rate of return is reasonable. The new law considers as a possible prohibited transaction a loan or extension of credit between the qualified plan and a party-in-interest such as the employer.[2]

The trustee is required to maintain a separate accounting and an actual segregation of the assets of each trust. In other words, the assets of a trust generally cannot be commingled with the assets of other trusts or with the general assets of the trustee. Thus, under these circumstances, there is no pooling of the investment experience of a number of trusts. If the investment experience has been exceptionally favorable for a particular trust, the full benefit of that experience is credited to the trust account. On the other hand, the trust must bear the full impact of adverse investment income and capital loss experience. Therefore, a relatively small trust fund plan would be subject to the danger of inadequate diversification of its investment portfolio. To meet this problem, corporate trustees have established common trust funds. A common trust fund permits the commingling of assets of all participating trusts. Although originally established to meet the needs of smaller trusts, corporate trustees have obtained permission to permit pension trusts of any size to participate in common trusts established specifically for qualified pension plans. A trust participating in a commingled fund for investment purposes buys units, or shares, of the fund.[3] Dividends are paid on each unit, each dividend being a proportionate share of the total income earned by the commingled fund. These units fluctuate in value as the value of the assets of the commingled fund fluctuates.

The principal advantage of a common trust fund is that it permits any trust to enjoy the investment advantages normally available only to the very large funds. These advantages have been described as follows:[4]

> 1. Higher rate of return on fixed income investments. Commingled investment permits purchases in amounts large enough to take advantage of private placements and special offerings of securities, which generally carry higher yields than regular market offerings; and in mortgages, lease-back arrangements or other interests in real property.

---

[2] For a discussion of this aspect of trust investments, see Chapter 4.

[3] "Trusteed Employee Benefit Plans" (New York: Bank of New York, 1966), p. 10.

[4] Ibid., pp. 10–11.

2.   Increased potential through selective stock holding. Commingled investment permits such funds to achieve a degree of selective diversification in equities that would be impossible to attain through individual investment, except in sizable funds.

3.   Maximum liquidity of funds for cash requirements. Commingled investment permits redemption of units at the end of any month, at the current market value of units, so that money required for payouts is made available through use of current cash flow rather than having to sell investments, as might have to be done in a separate fund.

4.   Dollar averaging on investment purchases. Current cash flow from incoming contributions, spaced as they are at intervals throughout a given year, has the effect of dollar averaging on investment purchases, which generally works to the advantage of all participating trusts.

5.   Lower investment brokerage fees. A commingled trust can purchase stocks in round-lots and in amounts that entail lower brokerage commissions.[5]

Most corporate trustees believe that common trusts offer significant advantages to the larger plans as well as the smaller plans. In one large urban bank, approximately 55 percent of all of its pension trust accounts participate in the bank's commingled pension trust. However, there is an element of inflexibility in the use of a common trust fund that should be noted; i.e., the inability to transfer specific fund assets to another funding agency. Units can be liquidated, but during a period of depressed security prices the employer may prefer to transfer trust assets in kind, with the expectation that market prices will be higher at some future date.

Participation in a commingled pension trust is restricted to qualified plans. Participation by a nonqualified trust could result in loss of the qualified tax status of the entire common trust fund.

Some corporate trustees have established several common trust funds, with each fund designed to provide an investment medium having certain principal characteristics and objectives. For example, one fund may emphasize investments in bonds, notes, debentures, and other fixed-income obligations. A second fund may be invested principally in private placements, mortgages, or other interests in real property. A third fund may be invested in a selection of good-quality common stocks with the objective of growth of principal and income over the long term. In addition, a special equity fund may be available for those trusts interested in pursuing a more aggressive investment policy. The multiple common trust funds offer the employer considerable flexibility in the proportion of trust assets to be invested in each of the classes of investments.

---

[5] A small trust fund plan can also obtain the advantages of commingling through investments in mutual fund shares.

Investment flexibility has been an attractive feature of the trust arrangement for many employers. During the past two decades, many employers have expressed a preference for investment of a relatively large proportion of pension assets in common stocks. This preference is evident in the composition of investments of noninsured pension funds set forth in Table 8–1. Insured plans were not able to offer this investment flexibility until the development of separate account funding.

TABLE 8–1
Assets of Private Noninsured Pension Funds
(as of end of 1974; millions of dollars)

	Book Value		Market Value	
	Amount	*Percent*	*Amount*	*Percent**
Cash and deposits................	4,290	3.2	4,400	3.8
U.S. government securities...........	5,530	4.1	5,600	5.0
Corporate and other bonds	35,030	26.2	30,800	27.6
Preferred stock	1,100	0.8	700	0.6
Common stock	79,320	59.3	62,600	56.0
Mortgages	2,370	1.8	2,100	1.8
Other assets	6,100	4.6	5,700	5.1
Total assets	133,740	100.0	111,900	100.0

* Figures may not add to totals due to rounding.
Source: U.S. Securities and Exchange Commission, *Statistical Bulletin*, vol. 34, no. 4, April 1975.

BENEFIT STRUCTURE

Retirement Benefits

The trust fund arrangement offers maximum flexibility in the design of a retirement benefit formula. Since funds are not allocated, even for retired employees, any type of benefit formula can be utilized under a trust fund plan. As is true in the case of deposit administration and immediate participation guarantee plans, retirement benefits based on final earnings can be provided without difficulty under trust fund plans. Likewise, benefit formulas that provide for the integration of social security benefits (including social security offset provisions) can be readily accommodated under the trust fund arrangement.

It is true that the more complex the benefit formula, the more difficult will be the task of the actuary in projecting costs and calculating contribution payments under the plan. The fact remains, however, that the trust fund instrument does not of itself present any obstacles to the use of the most complex of benefit formulas. For example, provision for adjustments of retired employees' benefits in accordance with a designated cost of living index can be provided under this funding instrument. The actuary can include in the cost calculations an assumption regarding future price level changes, which admittedly is not readily predictable with a great degree of accuracy. However, actuarial gains and losses due to variations of actual from expected price levels can be reflected in subsequent valuations and determinations of contribution payments. Trust fund plans also can provide a retirement benefit that varies with the market value of the assets supporting the pension benefits of retired workers (so-called variable annuities). A few trust fund plans do provide for cost of living adjustments and equity or variable annuity benefits.

Defined contribution formulas can be used in trust fund pension plans. A pension plan generally provides a lifetime annuity benefit to retired employees. ERISA requires the plan to provide a joint and one-half survivor annuity for an employee and his or her spouse unless the employee elects in writing not to take the joint and survivor option. Therefore, under a defined contribution pension plan formula, at some point in time the accumulations on behalf of each participant must be expressed in terms of a lifetime monthly benefit (except in cases where lump-sum distributions are made). The monthly benefit may be calculated as each annual contribution is received, or annual contributions may be accumulated to retirement date and the determination of the level of monthly benefits may be made at that time.

In the case of some negotiated plans, particularly multiemployer plans, the employer's financial commitment is expressed as some specified cents per hour worked or as a fixed percentage of compensation. However, these plans generally are not traditional defined contribution plans in that they also provide a defined benefit. The trust fund instrument can accommodate these plans without any difficulty.

Early retirement benefits can be, and frequently are, provided under trust fund plans. The amount of early retirement benefit may be the actuarial equivalent of the participant's accrued normal retirement benefit, or, if the employer desires, a more liberal early retirement benefit may be provided. The additional cost under the latter alternative can be anticipated in computations of contribution payments required under the plan.

Death Benefits

An increasing proportion of the larger trust fund plans provide preretirement death benefits. In the 1975 Bankers Trust Company Study of Industrial Retirement Plans, 63 percent of such plans provided preretirement death benefits during the period 1970–75 compared with 56 percent during the period 1965–70, and 28 percent during the period 1960–65. Preretirement death benefits have seldom been provided under small-sized trust fund plans. ERISA requires that by 1976 all qualified plans must include an option providing at least a 50 percent joint and survivor annuity. A married employee who has completed the plan's early retirement requirements will have the right to choose this option.

The availability of postretirement death benefits depends on the normal annuity form under the plan. A pure life annuity has been the typical normal annuity form under trust fund plans, or a modified refund annuity in the case of contributory plans. Once again, however, ERISA provides that the joint and one-half survivor annuity be the normal annuity form for a participant and his or her spouse unless the participant selects another option. The level of benefits under a joint and one-half survivor annuity can be greater than the actuarial equivalent of the previous normal annuity form. If the cost of this increase in benefit is not passed on to the participants and is assumed by the employer, it can be projected in the actuary's calculations of the periodic contributions required under the plan. These benefits can be provided without difficulty under trust fund plans.

Disability Benefits

A great proportion of trust fund plans provide disability benefits. Responsibility for determining whether a participant is eligible for disability benefits usually rests with a retirement committee appointed by the employer. In the case of a multiemployer plan, this function is assumed by the board of trustees or a committee composed of board members. The trustee begins payment of disability benefits upon receipt of certification by the retirement committee of a participant's eligibility for benefits. The retirement committee also assumes responsibility for reviewing approved disability claims to determine whether continuance of disability exists.

There are several reasons for the prevalence of disability benefits under trust fund plans. First, union leaders strongly favor provision of disability benefits under pension plans, and a substantial proportion of negotiated plans utilize the trust fund approach. Second, disability benefits provide employers with a desirable personnel management tool if control over the determination of disability rests with the employer. A disability pension can be used as a graceful, and often relatively economical, method of retiring unproductive employees. Third, the reluctance of insurance companies (at least until recent years) to insure long-term disability benefits encouraged the self-insuring of these benefits under trust fund plans.[6]

---

[6] It should be noted that under deposit administration and immediate participation guarantee plans, disability benefits, when provided, generally are self-insured by the employer in that these benefits are paid directly by the employer or charged directly to the unallocated account.

However, in recent years the use of insured group long-term disability plans has increased.

Vested Benefits

The rights of trust fund plan participants in the benefits attributable to benefits derived from employer contributions, as is true under other funding instruments, depend upon the vesting provisions of the plan. The vesting provisions in the plan must be at least as generous as those required under ERISA. If the actuarial value of the employee's vested benefit is less than $1,750, the employer may "cash-out" the benefit. This would reduce the administrative expense of keeping records of terminated employees. Additionally, if the terminating employee agrees, a vested benefit in excess of $1,750 may be cashed out. The value of the vested benefit may be transferred to an IRA or, with the consent of the employer, to the pension plan of the employee's next employer and if the new employer consents. Of course, terminating employees are always entitled to the benefit attributable to their own contributions. Under most trust fund plans, the availability of vested benefits is deferred until the terminating employee reaches the normal retirement age. If the plan is contributory, entitlement to the vested benefit generally has been conditioned upon the terminating employee leaving his or her own contributions in the plan; withdrawal of the contributions results, in these cases, in the foreiture of the portion of the vested benefit attributable to employer contributions. ERISA permits employees to withdraw their own contributions without having vested benefits canceled unless an employee is less than 50 percent vested. In those cases, an employer can cancel vested benefits if an employee withdraws his or her own contributions. The plan must contain a payback provision allowing employees to restore their benefits by repaying prior distributions with interest, currently 5 percent compounded annually.

Since contributions to a trust fund are not allocated to specific participants under the plan (with the possible exception of a traditional defined contribution plan), vesting always is expressed in terms of benefits rather than contributions. A terminating employee's vested benefits represent a deferred claim against the assets of the trust fund. This claim is conditioned upon (1) the terminating employee living to retirement age (except for his or her own contributions), (2) the employee making application for the benefit in accordance with plan provisions, and (3) the adequacy of the trust fund to provide the vested benefit and the protection afforded by the Pension Benefit Guaranty Corporation. In case of termination of the plan, the priority, if any, of vested benefits is dependent upon plan provisions subject to the requirements of ERISA.

CONTRIBUTIONS

The annual contribution payments under a trust fund plan are determined by periodic actuarial valuations by the plan actuary who must be an "enrolled" actuary under ERISA. The plan actuary calculates the amount of contributions to be made to the trust fund on the basis of (1) a given set of actuarial assumptions, (2) a particular actuarial cost method, and (3) the census data for the group of employees covered under the plan. It is the task of the actuary, as strongly reinforced by ERISA, to choose a set of actuarial assumptions and techniques which, based on his or her judgment and experience, appear to be reasonable for the particular plan. This obligation is imposed on all "enrolled" actuaries who provide actuarial services for plans covered under ERISA, whether such actuaries are acting in a consulting capacity or working for insurance companies. Generally, the actuary will choose assumptions that are more conservative than the experience actually expected under the plan, to provide a margin for contingencies. It also is the responsibility of the actuary to choose an appropriate actuarial cost method to be used in calculations of contribution payments. Since the choice of an actuarial cost method has a significant impact on the incidence of contribution payments, it is important that the employer have a clear understanding of the factors involved in the final selection of a cost method.

Under trust fund plans, the employer has some input in decisions regarding the choice of actuarial assumptions and the cost method to be used in calculations of contribution payments. Thus, the employer has maximum flexibility under a trust fund plan in directing the timing of contribution payments as long as such contributions meet the minimum funding standards of ERISA.

Of course, this does not mean that the ultimate cost of the plan is necessarily lower under trust fund plans. The actuarial gains from turnover and mortality under allocated funding instruments are eventually recognized in the form of employer credits against premiums due in future years. Also, lower levels of contributions in the initial years of the plan must be offset by higher contribution levels in subsequent years. Actuarial assumptions and cost methods do not affect the ultimate cost of the plan, except to the extent that they influence levels of funding and, therefore, the amount of investment income earned on plan assets. The fact remains that the employer has greater control over the incidence of contribution payments under trust fund plans, due to the way in which actuarial assumptions and methods are established and the unallocated nature of the funding instrument. It will be recalled that this flexibility is also available, to almost the same degree, under most group pension contracts.

Subject to the minimum funding standards of ERISA, contribution payments under trust fund plans are made at the convenience of the employer. In other words, there are no fixed contribution due dates. The employer may make contribution payments on a monthly, quarterly, or annual basis. Of course, Internal Revenue Service requirements regarding the timing of contributions must be observed if deductibility of contribution payments is desired.

In addition to the contribution payments necessary to provide the benefits to participants of the plan, the employer must make some provision for the expenses associated with trust fund plans. The major expenses under trust fund plans are trustee, consulting actuary, and legal fees, as well as record keeping and other administrative expenses. Investment fees of corporate trustees usually are expressed as a percentage of the trust corpus, the percentage being graded downward with the size of the fund.

The trustee imposes additional charges if it maintains plan records, makes pension payments to retired employees, or holds insurance and annuity contracts. Because of the additional reporting and other administrative requirements of ERISA, additional fees for the additional services will probably be necessary. If the employer performs the administrative functions associated with the plan, the cost of performing these duties should be recognized in determining the true cost of a trust fund plan.

With reference to legal and actuarial fees, it is virtually impossible to quote any figures that can be viewed as typical charges under trust fund plans, since fees for these services vary so widely among plans. The legal services required for the plan normally are performed by the attorney who handles all other legal work for the employer, and therefore usually are incorporated into the overall legal retainer paid by the employer. A consulting actuary's fee varies with the type and amount of service rendered. The actuary may perform preliminary cost studies or special projects on a fixed fee basis, but most of his or her services to the plan are billed on an hourly or daily rate basis. The fees for legal and actuarial services can be paid by the trustee out of trust assets or they can be paid directly by the employer. The latter approach is the procedure followed in most cases.

No guarantees are available under trust fund plans. The trustee cannot guarantee a minimum rate of investment income, nor can it guarantee plan assets against capital losses. Likewise, the mortality risk cannot be transferred to the trustee. The absence of guarantees is consistent with the legal nature of trust arrangements. A trustee's obligation is limited to the management of trust assets in a reasonable and prudent manner and in accordance with the duties set forth in the trust agreement and state and federal law. The adequacy of the fund to provide the benefits promised under the plan is the responsibility of the employer. The high degree of responsibility imposed on the employer under a trust fund plan is consistent with the maximum degree of flexibility available to the employer under this funding instrument. Guarantees must be minimized or eliminated if an employer desires maximum contribution flexibility and complete and immediate reflection of plan experience. Therefore, in choosing a funding instrument, the employer should consider the extent to which guarantees and flexibility are desired.

Many large employers have chosen funding instruments that offer a high degree of flexibility and immediate reflection of plan experience. In the case of a trust fund plan, the actual experience of the plan is reflected immediately in the status of the fund. For example, if investment experience has been favorable, the fund receives the full benefit of the favorable experience. Likewise, the full impact of adverse investment experience is borne by the individual trust. However, the investment risk can be spread to some extent through the use of a commingled investment fund. The use of a common trust reduces a plan's investment risk as a result of the greater investment diversification available; but it still does not offer a guarantee of principal or a minimum rate of return. The employer cannot shift the mortality risk under trust fund plans. If the plan covers a large number of employees, the employer may be willing to assume the mortality risk. The mortality risk becomes a more significant consideration as the size of the group covered decreases. Deviations of actual from expected experience for other factors (for example, turnover, disability rates, and actual retirement ages) also are immediately reflected in the status of the trust fund.

Under trust fund plans, actuarial valuations are performed periodically (usually annually, but no less frequently than every three years for regulatory purposes) to determine the adequacy of the fund. If the actual experience evolving under the plan indicates that the current level of funding is inadequate, actuarial assumptions can be revised to produce higher levels of contributions in future years. Since the liabilities under a pension plan evolve over a long period of time, adequate provision for these liabilities can be made if frequent actuarial valuations are performed and if the employer is willing and able to make the necessary contributions.

TERMINATION OF PLAN

In the event of termination of a trust fund plan, the disposition of plan assets is determined in accordance with the provisions of ERISA.

Situations sometimes arise in which an employer desires to switch funding agencies without any intention of terminating the plan. A transfer of assets to another trustee or to an insurance company can be effected without difficulty under trust fund plans. The trust agreement contains no prohibitions against transfers of plans assets (assuming that such transfers are made in accordance with the requirements of the Internal Revenue Service). The trustee may impose a minor charge for the administrative duties associated with a termination of the trust. Of course, losses may be sustained if assets must be liquidated over a relatively short period of time. In some cases, transfers of securities and other assets may be permitted rather than requiring liquidation of investments, unless the assets are held in a commingled trust, in which case transfers of securites generally are not permitted. The freedom to transfer plan assets and the flexibility that it offers in case of mergers or other circumstances is viewed by some employers as an important advantage of trust fund plans.

SPLIT FUNDING

In Chapter 6 it was noted that the trust fund arrangement can be used in conjunction with group permanent contracts or individual insurance and annuity contracts as one approach in funding pension benefits. This approach generally is referred to as a combination plan. Group pension contacts also can be used in combination with the trust fund arrangement. These latter arrangements usually are referred to as split-funded plans (although the term "combination plan" can be applied to describe any plan utilizing two or more funding instruments).

Split-funded plans generally utilize group deposit administration, or immediate participation guarantee or modified immediate participation guarantee contracts. The decision of the employer to split-fund its pension plan usually is motivated by a desire to obtain, at least in part, the advantages of an insurer's guarantees and a possibly favorable investment opportunity. For example, the trust agreement may provide that the trustee administer all assets held on behalf of active employees and that an immediate annuity be purchased as each employee retires. Likewise, an insurer may enjoy relatively high yields on direct placement and mortgage investments, and therefore the employer may decide to invest a portion of plan assets in a deposit administration or an immediate participation guarantee contract.

9

Inflation and Pension Planning

In recent years concern has been growing over the effects of inflation in our economy, particularly concern for its impact on retired persons and others largely dependent upon fixed incomes. The purpose of this chapter is to discuss briefly the nature of inflation as it affects pension planning, and the various approaches that have been utilized in pension plan design to minimize its adverse effects. Considerably greater treatment is given to the topic of variable annuities than to the other approaches because of the complex nature of this product.

INFLATION AND PENSION INCOME

For many decades the traditional concept of retirement security reflected the desire for an adequate income at retirement in relation to salary earned during the working lifetime. A "secure" pension plan meant that the employer was willing and able to provide a fixed level of benefits at retirement and that the plan was adequately funded to provide the benefits promised under the plan. The insurance industry thrived on its unquestioned ability, through strict investment and reserve regulations, to guarantee a specified level of benefit.

With the emergence of inflation as a significant problem in the last two decades, it has become necessary to devote specific attention to that problem in pension plan design decisions. Although the "final earnings" concept has been used for many years in the design of pension plans, the principal objective of this benefit formula in earlier years was to recognize improvements over time in the standard of living rather than to serve as an offset to the adverse effects of inflation.

Thus, it was not until the early 1950s that pension planners recognized that planning in terms of only fixed dollar levels might not be enough. They pointed out that it would be impossible to design a plan directed at retirement security without recognizing the independent element that has thwarted the objectives of countless pension plans, i.e., inflation. Although fixed dollar pensions might be secure in the traditional sense, pensioners were, in fact, faced with economic insecurity due to erosion of the purchasing power of pension dollars. Historical Consumer Price Index statistics demonstrate this erosion, as indicated in Table 9–1.

TABLE 9–1
Trends in Consumer Price Index and
Purchasing Power of the Dollar

Year	CPI	Purchasing Power
1940	48.4	1.00
1945	62.7	0.77
1950	83.8	0.58
1955	92.3	0.52
1960	103.1	0.47
1965	109.9	0.44
1966	113.1	0.43
1967	116.3	0.42
1968	121.2	0.40
1969	127.7	0.38
1970	135.3	0.36
1971	138.6	0.35
1972	142.9	0.34
1973	154.2	0.31
1974	171.8	0.28

While there is growing concern over the high rates of inflation experienced in recent years, underlying factors and pressures for its continuing existence are quite apparent. Methods of government financing, taxation, and subsidization; the implications of defense, poverty, and space programs; and private developments in areas of cost-plus contracts and wage agreements: all suggest that inflation may well continue for the foreseeable future.

The consequent erosion of the purchasing power of fixed pension income and fears of future inflation have:

1. Caused hardship, or at least serious concern, for retired employees living on fixed incomes and employees who are planning for retirement.
2. Prompted Congress to adjust social security income automatically

with changes in the Consumer Price Index to preserve its purchasing power during periods of inflation. (Many foreign systems also provide for such adjustments.)

3. Generated union pressure for "inflation-proof" pension benefits.

The general expectation that inflation will continue and anticipated increases in employee retirement periods (as a result of recent trends toward earlier retirement and continued medical advances which affect life expectancy) make the problem of pension income erosion particularly acute at this time.

A related, but not identical, trend which has given many pensioners the feeling that they are being treated as second-class citizens is the continually rising standard of living of their younger employee counterparts. Changes in an employee's standard of living generally are indicated by the changing ratios of employee earnings to Consumer Price Index figures over any specified duration. Admittedly, this is an imprecise measurement of standard of living changes, since it ignores the increasing impact of federal, state, and local income and personal property taxes, makes no adjustments for the diversity of state and local excise taxes, and includes other shortcomings of the Consumer Price Index as a measurement of cost of living changes. Nevertheless, it is the most commonly used, at least currently, and is regarded as the most satisfactory indicator of standard of living changes presently available.

Naturally, retired employees have received social security benefit increases over the years, and these have offset (to varying degrees, depending on the employee's retirement date and income bracket) the effects of price increases and standard of living changes.

APPROACHES TO "DOLLAR SECURITY" IN PENSIONS

In attempting to combat the erosion of pension dollars, two inflation risks must be recognized. For example, from the point of view of the employee, benefits based on a career-average salary could easily fail to grow as the cost of living grows; on the other hand, the employer who establishes a plan with benefits based on final earnings assumes the risk that increasing salaries might lead to unforeseen levels of pension costs.

Pension adjustment techniques are designed to give employees greater assurance that pensions deemed adequate when credited will continue to prove adequate at or even after an employee's retirement.

It is worth noting that the approaches to combatting the erosion of pension dollars discussed below are examples of techniques that have been employed in pension planning under conditions of relatively moderate inflation. The recent experiences with double digit inflation have produced such significant distortions in all aspects of the economy that it would be difficult to anticipate what types of pension planning techniques would be utilized over prolonged periods of high rates of inflation. The experience of variable annuities might be a good case in support of this observation. The variable annuity product was designed to offset the adverse effects of inflation based on the premise that over the long run prices of common stocks generally moved in the same directions as changes in the Consumer Price Index. But in the past few years persistent high rates of inflation created such distortions in the economy that owners of variable annuity contracts found themselves in the unenviable position of declining annuity values and a dramatically increasing cost of living environment. It is questionable whether there is any effective device for protecting retirees, or active employees for that matter, under conditions of rampant inflation. Adjustment techniques invariably involve direct or indirect relation to one of the following factors:

1. The standard of living for a specific employee, employee group, or even population, with pension adjustments made to reflect changes in employee earnings levels.
2. The cost of living, with pension adjustment made to reflect changes in the costs for goods and services.
3. The value of a pension plan investment portfolio, with pension plan adjustments made to reflect changes in investment earnings rates.

The adjustment technique selected may be applied in either of the following ways:

1. Periodically as determined by the employer, in which case the employer retains flexibility as to the timing of the adjustments and control over the cost of any adjustments but employees have no assurance that adjustments will be made as needed; or
2. By a predetermined automatic adjustment formula, which involves the employer's relinquishment of some or substantially all of its flexibility and control, but gives much greater assurance to employees during their working years that adjustments will be determined automatically by the formula selected.

Several techniques of planning for dollar erosion are discussed in this section. A common characteristic of the methods appearing under "Final-Pay Plans" is the concentration of benefit adjustments in the preretirement period. A compromise solution to the inflation problem is a cost of living annuity, which is considered in the subsequent section. Finally, the variable annuity is defined and analyzed.

Final-Pay Plans

An employee's retirement benefits may be based on either a career earnings or final salary concept. In those plans utilizing a career-average formula, a comparatively simple approach to dollar security consists of updating accrued benefits to reflect changing salary levels and provide more reasonable benefit levels for long-term employees. The rationale is: past service credits, usually based on salary at the inception of a plan, eventually become quite outdated, as do credits earned by an employee during his or her early years of participation under the plan. Unfortunately, this approach has a somewhat arbitrary effect on employees; those retiring shortly after their entry into a plan receive what essentially is a final-pay pension, while those retiring farther and farther from the change find their benefits gradually outdated.

Another simple technique is the combination of a benefit based upon career-average salary with a minimum benefit based on final earnings. Improvements generally are modest, costs are lower than those associated with other devices, and financial difficulties of pensioners are somewhat less than those encountered in a straight career-average plan.

Benefit formulas also can be solely a function of the final active work year's earnings, or, more often, relate to final earnings averaged over the last five to ten years. This plan emphasizes levels of compensation just prior to retirement, which reflect increased productivity, greater employee value, and inflationary activity during the working years.

The final-salary concept is a big step in an effort to keep retirement benefits in line with wage scales, but it presents problems for both the employer and the employee. Living costs for retirees will increase without any commensurate adjustments in benefit levels, and an abrupt inflationary spin could initiate earnings spirals, with attendant adverse impact on employer costs (hopefully to be offset, at least in part, by the investment of fund assets in equities).

Attempts in the area of final-pay plans, final-average minimums, and adjusted accrued service benefits are not fully satisfactory because they offer no assistance to the retiree whose benefit dollars may gradually be eroded by inflation. Thus, many employers, particularly during recent years of heavy inflation, have periodically increased benefits of retired employees.

Cost of Living Plans

An obvious vehicle for providing pension benefits containing secure purchasing power is a plan which stipulates that payments be adjusted according to variations in a specified price index. Under the simplest of these arrangements, benefits of retirees may be adjusted to reflect changes subsequent to retirement; a representative contract would provide for an upward adjustment in a year when the index exceeds a certain percentage (say, 105 percent) of a chosen base period level, and downward when it drops below, say, 90 percent.

A modification of this cost of living plan is applicable where a portion of the pension benefit is credited for each year of service. This consists of adjustments in accrued benefits to reflect variations in the price index following the crediting of each benefit unit. It may involve only a single adjustment, at retirement, but it effectively provides a retirement benefit with yearly accrual components modified for price index patterns following purchase.

The Consumer Price Index is probably the most frequently consulted basis for adjusting annuity values under a cost of living plan. It is computed by the U.S. Department of Labor and published monthly. A CPI cost of living annuity relates its benefit adjustments to fluctuations in that index.

The advantages of a cost of living annuity may include the existence of a more budgetable cost pattern than under other approaches and the lessening of risks to the retiree. Compared to final-pay plans, the increases under this arrangement are more moderate during working years (since they relate only to cost of living changes rather than improvements in the standard of living); but benefits are adjusted continually after retirement in order to maintain purchasing power throughout the retiree's lifetime. The cost of living plan is an acceptable alternative to other methods.

Cost of living plans can be established in many different ways. As mentioned previously, the most popular index used for such plans is the Consumer Price Index. The following are two examples of how a CPI-type plan might work. One approach is to base the monthly benefit of the pension plan on the exact change in the Consumer Price Index; that is, if the CPI went up by 6 percent in a certain period, pension benefits would increase 6 percent. This is a very costly procedure if the CPI continues to rise; for example, it is estimated that an annual compounded increase of 3 percent for retirees will increase the long-run cost of the plan by 25–30 percent. To try and hold the costs of CPI adjustments within reason, variations of the straight linkage with the CPI are used. One technique is that before any increase will be granted the CPI will have had to increase by a certain amount such as 3 percentage points. Under such a plan benefit adjustments would be made, for example, if the CPI increased 4 percent since the last adjustment period (the annual valuation point), the plan's benefits would be increased by 4 percent for the next 12 monthly benefit payments. If the cost of living only increased by 2 percent, no adjustment would be made for that particular valuation period. There usually is also a "cap" such as 5 percent on this type of plan.

In the above example, if the cost of living increased by 8 percent in a given year, the maximum increase would be limited by the "cap" of 5 percent. The idea of the maximum limit is designed to protect the fiscal integrity of a pension plan. Also, cost of living plans generally are not cumulative; that is, if the CPI increased by 8 points in one year and only 3 points the next year, in the second year there would be a maximum increase of 3 percent. Again, this technique is used to attempt to hold down the cost of cost of living benefits.

Furthermore, there is increasing concern among employers of the cost implications of Cost of Living adjustment provisions in private pension plans combined with the cost impact of present automatic adjustment features under Social Security. There may be increased interest in integrating private pensions with Social Security to minimize the adverse cost results of increase in the CPI under both programs, subject, of course, to the requirement under ERISA that any increase in Social Security benefits that take place after retirement cannot be used to offset private pension plan benefits.

A pension plan adjusting benefits according to the changes in a cost of living index is probably more sensitive to swings in purchasing power than the variable annuity described below. However, variable annuities generally contain more investment potential. Furthermore, the cost of living index may be a questionable indicator of spending habits of retirees since the market basket purchased by retirees may be materially different than that of active employees.

Variable Annuities

Variable annuities provide for investment of contributions in a segregated portfolio of equity securities. Here, they are used to establish a fund or account which, with additional deposits and investment growth, is used to purchase a lifetime income at a designated retirement date. Account values under these contracts and the retirement income purchased with the proceeds reflect the performance of the invested funds, rising or falling as the market values of its securities increase or decrease.

The basis underlying the variable annuity concept is the historical long-range relationship between the cost of living and the investment performance of diversified portfolios of common stocks. Although short-term patterns reveal dissimilar, even opposite movements, many feel that the overall long-term trend supports the conclusion that equity investments offer potential answers to the inflation problem. However, the recent experience of high rates of inflation during a period of depressed stock values has led many people to question this basic assumption.

Detailed studies over many historical time periods were conducted by variable annuity pioneers to demonstrate the comparative purchasing power of annuities invested entirely in equities, entirely in fixed dollars, and in a balanced program. The most widely circulated report was prepared by Teachers Insurance and Annuity Association, and was a major influence in the establishment of CREF (College Retirement Equities Fund), the first insured variable annuity company in the United States. The study showed equity investments to be more effective than fixed dollar programs in maintaining purchasing power, but subject to downside risks even in periods of rising prices. It concluded that a balanced program, partially in fixed income and partially in equity investments, offers the best possibility of income that is both free from wild fluctuations and protected from serious erosion by inflation.

Experience over the years has confirmed this opinion (see Table 9-2).

TABLE 9–2
Indicators of Inflation and Investment Returns
(ten-year annualized results)

10 Years Through	Consumer Price Index	S&P High Grade Bond Index	S&P 500 Stock Index*
1929	−0.98%	5.88%	11.15%
1934	−2.48	5.98	3.75
1939	−2.05	6.98	0.01
1944	2.86	5.09	10.03
1949	5.41	3.77	9.44
1954	4.16	3.20	17.12
1959	2.20	0.81	19.38
1964	1.57	1.98	12.84
1969	2.52	0.74	7.82
1974	5.20	0.49	1.24

* Prior to 1926, dividend—exclusive.
Source: *1975 Survey of Investment Performance,* Dreher, Rogers and Associates, Inc., p. 8.

There have been many years of outstanding equity performance, far outstripping increases in the cost of living. And there have been severe market downturns, emphasizing the need for balance in both personal and group pension programs.

It is important to recognize that the scope of the variable annuity has broadened greatly since its pioneers first advanced it as a means of enhancing retirement security. Over the long run, equity prices are expected to rise, reflecting increases in industrial productivity; thus variable annuities provide an opportunity to participate in the growth of the economy.

A number of tax advantages accrue in special situations for variable annuity policyholders. Thus, the concept of the variable annuity as an investment device and tax shelter as well as an inflation hedge has attracted some interest.

Thus, the potential advantages of the variable annuity are (1) protection against long-term inflationary erosion of pension purchasing power, and (2) possible performance surpassing that of an index-linked (e.g., cost of living plan) annuity. The attendant disadvantage is the risk of loss of capital; insurance companies cannot guarantee a floor on cash values or minimum income levels.

From the standpoint of the employer offering a pension plan, the variable annuity presents a potential disadvantage of relative cost. Under fixed benefit plans, excess interest earnings of trust assets serve to reduce employer costs under the plan; while under the variable annuity, investment earnings are passed on to plan participants. Under noncontributory pension plans, therefore, variable annuities shift a portion of the cost of inflation from employees and retirees to employers. Furthermore, there is no way to guarantee that variable annuities will provide benefit levels exactly equivalent to cost of living changes or improvements in the standard of living. Thus, plan experience might produce results quite contrary to the employer's plan objectives.

Variable Annuity Markets

Variable annuities have not achieved the degree of acceptance and growth in the corporate pension market expected by proponents of this concept. Undoubtedly, a major reason for the limited growth of variable annuities in this market is the loss to the employer of the investment gains realized on fund assets, as noted in the previous section. In addition, there has been concern that employee dissatisfaction and adverse reaction might result during periods of declining stock market values, with the attendant reductions in amounts of retirement checks. This concern has been reinforced by recent adverse experience in the stock market accompanied by continued inflation. Still another reason for the limited growth in variable annuities to date is the absence of strong support for these plans from major labor unions. Labor leaders appear to be favoring cost of living indexed formulas in their efforts to counteract the adverse effects of inflation on pension benefits.

There is some interest in the use of a variable annuity option under corporate pension plans. The variable annuity option offers an amelioration of the adverse cost implications of variable annuities to the employer, while still providing retired employees with the benefits of such an arrangement after retirement.

The principal markets for variable annuities appear to be the tax-deferred annuity and H.R. 10 markets and perhaps since ERISA, in the IRA market. Tax-deferred annuities and contribution payments constitute employee money in the sense that such contributions frequently reflect voluntary reductions in compensation. Thus, no employer cost implication is involved in the choice of variable annuities by these individuals.

The same conclusion substantially applies in the case of H.R. 10 plans. Furthermore, most H.R. 10 plans utilize defined contribution or money purchase benefit formulas. Thus, for all intents and purposes, self-employed persons do not reap any investment gain advantages on funds held for the benefit of employees under H.R. 10 plans.

Variable annuities also have good growth potential in the areas of thrift and savings plans and profit sharing plans. Variable annuities can be used both during the accumulation and payout periods under such plans, although the principal appeal of variable annuities is likely to be in the form of an option at retirement.

It should be noted that variable annuity benefits can be provided on both an insured and noninsured basis. The first variable annuity plan was established in 1952 by the Teachers Insurance and Annuity Association and its companion organization, the College Retirement Equities Fund. In the same year, the Long Island Lighting Company and Chemstrand, Inc. established variable annuity plans on a noninsured, trusteed basis. The Prudential Insurance Company of America issued its first group variable annuity contract in 1963, becoming the first major life insurance company to enter this field. Today, most major life insurance companies have entered the individual or group variable annuity business.

Since the bulk of the variable annuity business currently is underwritten by insurance companies, much of the remaining discussion is devoted to characteristics of insured variable annuity plans.

VARIABLE ANNUITY PLAN FEATURES

Benefit Structure

Retirement Benefit Formula. The types of benefit formulas available for use under variable annuity plans are identical to those used in fixed dollar benefit plans. Either a defined contribution or a defined benefit formula may be used.

As a practical matter, most plans that use the variable annuity concept prior to retirement utilize a defined contribution or money-purchase formula. This is probably due to the fact that variable annuities have had their greatest sales growth to date in the H.R. 10 and tax-deferred annuity markets, and defined contribution formulas generally are utilized in these plans whether benefits are on a fixed dollar or variable annuity basis.

However, variable annuity plans also can use a defined benefit formula, with the career-average formula generally being used in such cases. For example, the plan may provide a benefit of 1 percent of compensation per year of service. Under such a plan, an employee earning $1,000 a month would earn a retirement benefit of $10 a month for that year of service. The retirement benefits earned during a year of current service are then converted to units of benefits, which in the above example may be done by dividing the $10 by the current value of an accumulation unit. Thus, the employee under a career-average plan accumulates units of benefits the total value of which vary with the value of an accumulation unit at any given point in time.

Final-average formulas seldom are used under preretirement variable annuity plans (except under so-called target plans, which are discussed in a later section of this chapter). Such a formula would substantially increase pension costs for employers, since they would bear the dual inflationary cost impact of both escalating salaries and loss of investment gains. Also, a final-pay variable annuity plan would be more complicated to communicate to employees and to administer.

Death Benefits. Preretirement death benefits are available under group pension variable annuity plans, if provision is made for such benefits in the plan design. In the case of H.R. 10 and tax-deferred annuity plans, death benefits are always provided. The same will probably be true for IRAs. Upon death prior to commencement of benefits, the value of the employee's account is payable to his or her beneficiary. Additional options may be available to the beneficiary: for example, (1) conversion of the account to inactive status for later payment of a monthly income, (2) conversion of part or all of the account balance to fixed dollar benefits, and (3) immediate inception of variable annuity benefits. Of course, death benefits always are provided under combination plans utilizing life insurance and variable annuity contracts to fund benefits.

Postretirement benefits generally are restricted to the optional annuity forms available under the contract, e.g., life annuity with a ten-year-certain period or a joint and survivor annuity.

Vested Benefits. Vesting provisions under variable annuity plans are similar to those found under fixed dollar plans. H.R. 10, IRA, and tax-deferred variable annuity plans provide for full and immediate vesting of contributions on behalf of covered participants. In general, the withdrawal options relative to vested benefits are similar to those described in the previous section on death benefits. Of course, the tax implications of withdrawals under qualified plans must be recognized.

In the case of corporate variable annuity pension plans (and HR-10 plans not covering owner-employees), deferred vesting is permissible. The nonvested accumulated values of terminating employees are used to reduce future employer contributions.

Target Plans. In recent years, there has been growing interest in so-called target level of benefit plans. Target plans are an effort to obtain the combined advantages of defined benefit and defined contribution plans.

The employer chooses a target level of benefits (e.g., 30 percent of compensation), and a level contribution amount is determined for each participant based on a reasonable interest assumption (and mortality assumption, if no preretirement death benefits are provided). The amount of contribution so determined for an employee is then invested on his or her behalf in a life insurance contract, variable annuity, mutual fund, or other investment media. The actual retirement benefit will vary from the target or expected level of benefit, depending on the actual investment experience under the plan.

The target level of benefit approach permits relatively high benefit amounts for older employees (generally the owners or key employees in a small firm) and results in a large proportion of the employer's contribution being allocated to these individuals. Also, the employer has the advantage of the fixed contribution amount or rate generally associated with defined contribution plans. Annual contributions do not vary except as affected by salary changes. It should be noted that while the basic concept of target plans has not been affected by ERISA, target plans are regarded as money-purchase-type plans for purposes of the "annual additions" limitation. Thus, the maximum annual addition for any participant cannot exceed the lesser of 25 percent of compensation or $25,000. This latter figure will be adjusted for changes in the cost of living. The result is that target plans for older participants may lose some of their appeal since the target benefit at retirement may require a contribution in excess of the allowable limitation.

The contributions allocated to an individual participant can be used to purchase life insurance, fixed annuity contracts, variable annuity contracts, or mutual fund shares. Thus, participants have considerable flexibility in their choice of funding instruments. Death benefits generally include all sums accumulated on behalf of a participant in addition to life insurance proceeds. Forfeitures of nonvested employer contributions are applied against future employer contributions.

Although the target plan approach can be used with fixed dollar investment vehicles, the recent interest in this concept is because of the greater use of variable annuities and mutual fund shares in the funding of pension plans. Several life insurance companies have established prototype target plans and offer their own mutual fund or variable annuity contracts for funding plan benefits. The target plan approach is particularly attractive for small firms, and has had considerable appeal in the professional corporation pension market.

Integration Rules.   An integrated variable annuity plan must meet the same maximum integration requirements as fixed dollar benefit plans. However, variable annuities present a unique problem in that favorable investment experience might produce actual retirement benefits that are greater than the maximum percentage permitted by the integration rules.

This potential result is acceptable to the Internal Revenue Service if under a unit benefit formula based on actual compensation, the assumed investment return used to calculate the initial benefit level is 5.5 percent.

If a lower assumed investment return is used and if investment experience results in variable annuity benefits greater than the maximum permissible integration percentage, the excess interest earnings must be used to reduce employer contributions or, alternatively, the excess interest may be allocated among employees in a way that assumes that the plan is not integrated. This restriction does not apply in the case of variable benefit plans where variations in benefits after retirement are due solely to changes in a cost of living index.

Unit Values

A pension plan may provide variable benefits both during the accumulation period (active service period) and the payout period (retirement period) or it may restrict the variable annuity benefit to the payout period, as is the case under the variable annuity option. If a pension plan provides for variable annuity benefits during both the active service and payout periods, values generally are assigned to accumulation units (sometimes called variable units) different from those assigned to annuity units.

In calculating the accumulation unit, a deduction is made for sales and administrative expenses from the contributions or gross premium payments received. The net payment is invested in the separate account or equity fund, creating a unit value that grows or declines in accordance with the investment performance (dividends and capital gains) of the fund. Variations in accumulation unit values are based on gross investment performance, adjusted for (1) a charge against fund assets for investment management, and (2) a deduction for mortality and expense guarantees.

Each additional net premium payment purchases a number of accumulation units which varies with the current unit value and the amount of the deposit. Each additional purchase adds to the aggregate number of units in the participant's account, the value of the account at any point being equal to the total number of units credited multiplied by the current value of one unit.

At retirement, the account value is applied to a table of annuity purchase rates (i.e., the initial periodic income payment per $1,000 of proceeds) to determine an initial level of annuity benefits. Often referred to as conversion rates, annuity purchase rates employ assumptions of mortality and an assumed investment return to provide an annuity benefit, in a manner similar to the calculation of fixed annuity benefits. The assumed investment return such as 3.5 or 4 percent, is a form of advancement by the insurance company of a portion of the expected investment return; without it, the initial level of benefits would be much lower.

The initial level of annuity benefits is divided by the current value of an annuity unit to determine the guaranteed number of annuity units that will be paid each month thereafter. In practice, the initial annuity benefit is expressed as a number of annuity units. The insurance company guarantees the payment of that quantity of units each month for the lifetime of the annuitant; the amount of each payment is equal to the number of units so guaranteed multiplied by the current value of one annuity unit. Annuity units thus represent participation in the equity fund, varying according to gross investment return as adjusted for management fees, insurer guarantees, and advanced investment earnings.

Guaranteed annuity conversion rate options can be purchased under most individual plans; otherwise the rates in effect at the time of conversion will apply. Most group variable annuity contracts limit the term of guarantees for future deposits to periods of about five years, reserving the right to revise contractual guarantees for new deposits after that point. Accordingly, charges for guarantees under such plans are lower.

Assumed Investment Return

The assumed investment return (AIR) used by the insurer in determining the amount of the initial monthly payment has dual significance:

1. It directly affects the size of the initial payment. For each accumulated dollar (or dollar of proceeds), a high AIR produces a larger initial benefit (by anticipating more of future investment results) than a lower AIR.

2. It indirectly determines the pattern of income payments. Since the AIR is compared to actual net investment return in calculating future changes in annuity unit values, a high AIR produces benefits that rise more slowly or fall faster than a low AIR.

The higher the AIR, the greater will be the initial annuity payment. For example, under the rate schedule of one large insurer, a 5.5 percent AIR produces a 15 to 20 percent larger initial payment than a 3.5 percent AIR. On the other hand, when stock prices are rising, the income resulting from the 3.5 percent AIR will increase at a rate which is about 2 percent per year faster than the increase under a 5.5 percent AIR. Correspondingly, when stock prices are declining, the lower AIR will result in less of a decrease in income.

Regardless of fluctuations in common stock prices, the monthly annuity payment based on the lower AIR will first exceed the monthly payment based on the higher AIR about 8.5 years after retirement if the annuity is purchased for a male at age 65. This crossover point will occur sooner for an older male but later for a female, a younger male, or for a joint and survivor annuity. If the crossover point is 8.5 years, the total payments since retirement based on the lower AIR will first exceed the total payments based on the higher AIR after a period which is normally between 14 years and 17 years but depends on the actual investment results. Thus, the main advantage to the annuitant of a lower AIR is that it produces a greater income later in life than does a higher AIR; and with an increasing cost and standard of living, it may be in later years that a retired employee will have the greatest need for increased income.

In the case of noninsured or group pension variable annuity contracts, the assumed investment return is an element of individual plan design. It is chosen by the employer from a reasonable range of alternatives (e.g., 3.5, 4, 4.5, 5, and 5.5 percent) and reflects a careful determination of his or her objectives, the long-term investment expectations, the cost implications, and the advice of the insurer or consulting actuary. Under a defined benefit plan, a higher AIR reduces the cost of the plan to the employer, since the AIR is a guaranteed rate actually credited against employer costs. If the actual net investment return is less than the AIR, the difference is absorbed by employees in the form of reduced unit values.

Funding Instruments

As indicated earlier, variable annuity benefits may be insured or self-insured through a trust fund arrangement. Insurance companies offer a variety of variable annuity contracts, both on a group and an individual contract basis. Single-premium immediate annuities, single-premium deferred annuities, and periodic payment deferred annuities are available.

Differences between group and individual insured variable annuity funding instruments are much less significant than those found between group and individual fixed dollar contracts. Because of administrative and regulatory requirements, most participants, including employees under group plans, must be handled on an individual basis; exceptions are deferred benefit, employer-financed variable annuity plans providing for unallocated deposits. Hence administrative procedures are quite similar under group and individual plans, as are costs of administration. Guarantees often are identical, although some group contract holders prefer to assume greater mortality or expense risks in exchange for a lower guarantee charge. The sales process also is individualized and strictly controlled for both group and individual plans, so distribution costs are similar, although occasional variations in loadings occur among some insurers. Thus, with the possible exception of some variations in loading levels, there are strong similarities between group and individual variable annuity funding instruments.

10

Selection of a Funding Instrument

An employer who is establishing a funded pension plan must select a funding instrument under which plan assets will be accumulated and through which plan benefits will be provided. Making such a selection is not always easy. To begin with, the employer is faced with a broad choice between the insured and trust fund approaches. Within the concept of insured plans there is a wide variety of individual and group contracts—the employer's choice ranging from the fully insured individual policy plan to a group immediate participation guarantee contract with a separate account facility. As pointed out in previous chapters, each of these funding instruments produces certain advantages and disadvantages—but they are relative to the needs and objectives of the employer. A specific advantage of one funding instrument may be of significant value or importance to one employer; yet this same advantage could be of little or no value to another firm.

From the employer's viewpoint, the selection of the appropriate funding instrument is complicated by the differences of opinion that exist among those individuals who are active in the design and administration of pension programs. Actuarial consulting firms, for example, have been identified primarily with the trust fund approach. On the other hand, insurance agents and group field representatives quite obviously support the insured plan. Even here, however, there frequently is some difference of opinion between these two groups as to whether individual or group contracts are the best funding instrument.

The authors do not wish to imply that the difference of opinion that exists among pension practitioners is wrong or undesirable. On the contrary, such difference of opinion is a direct result of healthy and vigorous competition between financial institutions—a condition which is highly desirable from the viewpoint of the consumer and for the continued growth of private pension plans. In the long run, both employers and employees benefit from such a competitive environment in terms of broader choices, more efficient administration, lower costs, and innovations in plan design.

In the last analysis, no one funding instrument is preferable over all others in all situations. However, it generally is possible to establish that for a given plan, and under a given set of circumstances and objectives, one or a few funding instruments are more suitable to the needs of a particular employer. The purpose of this chapter is to review the factors that bear on the selection of a funding instrument. While an understanding of the specific characteristics of the different funding instruments is most important in the selection of a funding instrument, these characteristics are not discussed at length in this chapter.

PRELIMINARY CONSIDERATIONS

At the outset, it should be made clear that the selection of a funding instrument is not the primary consideration of an employer who is establishing a pension plan. Rather, it is secondary to the more important consideration of the plan provisions. The employer should first determine the class or classes of employees to be covered, the type and amount of benefits they are to receive, and the conditions under which these benefits will be paid. Often, decisions on these matters will influence or even dictate the selection of a funding instrument; in general, the selection of a funding instrument should not dictate the choice of benefits.

One example of the influence of plan provisions and objectives on the selection of a funding instrument would be the case of a small employer who desires to take maximum advantage of the federal estate tax exclusion applicable to qualified plans and who wishes to have the death benefit under the plan as large as permitted under federal tax law. The only feasible way of creating an immediate and substantial death benefit is through the use of life insurance. However, the employer's size might be such that the desired amount could not be made available on a group basis from an underwriting viewpoint or, as sometimes is the case, state law might limit the amount of group insurance that could be issued on any one life. Thus, in this situation (and in the absence of other influencing factors), the use of individual life insurance contracts as the funding instrument would be strongly indicated.

Another example might be the case of an employer who wishes to use a flat percentage of earnings formula and to apply this formula to some type of final earnings. While this does not necessarily dictate or suggest the funding instrument to be used, it does, by the process of elimination, suggest that a group deferred annuity contract not be employed. To carry the example a step further, if the employer wishes to base benefits on the average of an employee's earnings over the final five years of employment, it becomes impractical to adopt a fully insured individual policy or group permanent plan. Other examples could be cited, but the above are sufficient to illustrate the point.

It also should be emphasized that the selection of a funding instrument should not be based solely upon the cost *estimates* furnished to the employer. Estimating the cost of a pension plan can be most complex, and many funding instruments permit a wide choice of actuarial cost methods and assumptions. As was pointed out in Chapter 3, the choice of the actuarial cost method and assumptions will not influence the ultimate cost of the plan (except to the extent that investment income will be affected by the incidence of contributions). Unfortunately, however, many employers seem to be influenced in their choice of funding instrument or funding agency by the various cost estimates they have received when, in fact, these cost estimates should have little or no bearing on the selection.[1] On the other hand, the employer's choice of a funding instrument might well be influenced by the fact that a particular funding instrument permits a wide choice of actuarial methods and assumptions, thus creating a significant degree of desired contribution flexibility.

Finally, it is most important that the employer's own specific circumstances and objectives be carefully analyzed before a decision is made on the funding instrument to be used. The employer's size, for example, is of considerable significance when weighing the cost implications of the various funding instruments. Also of significance is the need or desire for investment and contribution flexibility. The terms of any bargaining agreement in effect could influence this choice and, of course, the employer's tax objectives quite often are an item of considerable importance. These and similar items must all be taken into account.

INSURED VERSUS TRUST FUND PLANS

A most important question for the employer to resolve is whether to employ an insured funding instrument, the trust fund approach, or

---

[1] Table 3–3 shows the varying cost levels that can be produced for the same plan by simply shifting the actuarial assumptions. The ultimate cost of a plan, of course, will be determined by actual plan experience as to benefits paid, expenses, and investment income, which may or may not be close to the lowest estimated cost produced by the most liberal assumptions. An employer should not choose a funding instrument or a funding agency on the basis that the funding instrument with the lowest cost estimate is the cheapest. In fact, this course of action might prove to involve the greatest contribution outlay in the long run, since lower contributions in the early years of the plan could lead to greater contributions in later years, with the likely result that a significant portion of the benefits paid will consist of contributions rather than investment earnings.

a combination of the two. At one time, the employer's choice was a little easier to make—at least, the broad features of the two concepts of funding differed to the extent that the employer could weigh the advantages and disadvantages of each approach and select the one best suited to its needs. Proponents of the insured plan, for example, stressed the guarantees inherent in this approach with reference to both the financial and mortality risks involved. Advocates of the trust fund plan, on the other hand, stressed flexibility and the opportunity to have plan assets invested in equities with the potential of capital gains. In recent years, however, the insurance industry has developed several new products which possess many of the characteristics of the trust fund approach. In particular, group contracts such as deposit administration and immediate participation guarantee contracts, coupled with the new-money method of crediting investment earnings and a separate account facility, offer many of the features normally associated with trust fund plans. As a result, an employer's choice between insured and trust fund plans is not as clear-cut as was formerly the case. Indeed, the choice today is quite often between funding agencies, be they banks or insurance companies, rather than between funding instruments.

It has been suggested that the selection of a funding instrument involves considerations of cost, benefit security, flexibility, and service.[2] The question of insured versus trust fund plans should be reviewed with these considerations in mind.

Cost Considerations

As indicated in Chapter 3, the factors involved in the cost of a pension plan are the benefits paid, the expenses of plan operation, and the investment earnings on plan assets. Each of these factors must be reviewed in terms of their application under trust fund plans and under the various insured funding instruments.

Benefits Paid. In a trust fund plan, this element of cost will be determined by the level of benefits established in the plan, by the actual number of employees who survive until benefits become payable, and by the length of time they receive benefits. Except to the extent that the employer establishes the benefit level and retirement ages, it has no control over this item of cost under a trust fund plan. Thus, this aspect of its cost will be determined by the plan's actual experience. Dividend and experience rating formulas (in the absence of pooling techniques) will ultimately cause the same result to emerge under most group pension contracts.[3] Where, however, the insured funding instrument involves a

---

[2] Dan M. McGill, *Fundamentals of Private Pensions,* rev. ed. (Homewood, Ill.: Richard D. Irwin, Inc., 1964), chap. 9.

[3] This result will emerge on a current basis as experience unfolds in the case of a group immediate participation guarantee contract.

pooling of mortality experience, this element of cost will not be determined by the plan's actual experience; rather, it will be determined by the insurer's rate guarantees and by the experience of all contracts in the pool. (Some insurers use a combination of actual plan experience and the experience of a pool when determining dividends for smaller group pension plans.)

From the foregoing, the general observation might be made that for a larger employer, there will be no difference in cost between an insured and a trust fund plan insofar as the element of "benefits paid" is concerned.[4] For a smaller employer, whose experience under an insured plan will be pooled to some extent, the same observation cannot be made. Here, the employer must decide whether to assume the cost attributable to the actual experience of its own group of employees, be that experience good or bad, or whether to obtain the protection of the insurer's rate guarantees and participate in the insurer's pool, thus obtaining experience results which will be reasonably stable and, as a result, reasonably predictable.

Expenses of Plan Operation.   A comparison of expenses between an insured and a trust fund plan is difficult to make. An insured plan will involve certain expenses not present in a trust fund plan. These expenses include the agent's commissions, state premium taxes (where applicable), and, to a slight extent, federal income tax. On the other hand, certain expenses of a trust fund plan (such as actuarial fees) generally will be at a higher level than would be the case in an insured plan.

It has been suggested that a valid expense analysis involves a comparison of development expenses, premium taxes, insurance company administrative expenses, and employer administrative and legal expenses of the insured plan with actuarial fees and the employer administrative and legal expenses of a trust fund plan.[5] This would include any administrative fees charged by the trustee. There is no doubt that these expenses will be greater for an individual policy plan than for a comparable trust fund plan. When comparing a group pension plan with a trust fund plan, however, the difference is much narrower and, for a given plan which includes a comparison of the expense charges of specific funding agencies, the differential could exist in favor of either type of funding instrument.

In group pension and trust fund plans, the expense differential (in the absence of a substantial annuity premium tax) is relatively small

---

[4] It could be argued that this statement is not correct in the case of an insured plan that is terminated in its early years. However, since the selection of a funding instrument is being made on the assumption that the plan will continue indefinitely, the authors feel that in this context, the general observation is properly made.

[5] McGill, *Fundamentals of Private Pensions,* p. 302.

in terms of the other cost factors.[6] Thus, when comparing these plans, it would appear that expense levels should not be a significant factor. When individual policy funding instruments are being considered, other factors such as rate guarantees and benefit and tax objectives often are more significant than the relatively higher expense levels of these plans.

Investment Earnings. Perhaps the most significant item affecting the cost of a pension plan is the investment earnings on plan assets. As noted in Chapter 3, an increase in investment earnings of one half of 1 percent could produce a reduction in costs in the neighborhood of 12 percent.

Historically, insured plans placed heavy emphasis on financial guarantees. Premiums collected in connection with pension plans became a part of the insurer's general assets and, because of limits imposed by state laws, were invested predominantly in real estate mortgages, government and high-grade corporate bonds, privately placed corporate securities, and the like. Generally, these state laws are such that an insurer is prohibited from having more than a small percentage of its general portfolio invested in common stocks. As a result, the insured plan was characterized by a guarantee of principal and by a guarantee of some stipulated rate of interest to be credited to funds held by the insurer. Moreover, the insurer's actual earnings in excess of the guaranteed rate, based on its total portfolio, were credited to the plan reserves through the insurer's dividend or experience rating formula. While this produced a substantial degree of financial security for the plan and, to a great extent, a higher rate of return than could be obtained on the fixed income investments of a trust fund plan, the employer did not have the choice of having a portion of its plan assets invested in common stocks with the resulting opportunity for capital appreciation. For this reason, the trust fund plan (or a combination of an insured and a trust fund plan) took on greater appeal during the rising common stock market that followed World War II. The insurance industry, however, in an aggressive effort to retain a competitive position in the pension field, was successful in obtaining legislative authority in most states to segregate assets held in connection with qualified pension plans and to invest these assets in common stocks.

In addition to obtaining the authority to invest in common stocks, most insurers active in the group pension field have adopted the new-money method of crediting interest to group pension contracts, thus reflecting the yields obtainable at the time funds are invested. The net effect of these two changes has been to produce insured funding instru-

---

[6] If the plan is located in a state which imposes a substantial premium tax on annuities, the expenses of the insured plan will almost always be greater. However, a large number of states exclude annuity premiums under qualified plans from premium tax. At the time this material was prepared, the following jurisdictions imposed an annuity premium tax in excess of 1 percent on such plans: District of Columbia, Georgia, Illinois, Kentucky, Louisiana, Massachusetts, Mississippi, North Carolina, and North Dakota.

ments which are very similar to the trust fund approach in terms of investment yield.

Thus, in the area of certain group pension contracts, the trust fund plan is no longer automatically in a preferential position in terms of potential investment yield. Advocates of the insured plan maintain that overall, the investment yield should be higher under a group pension contract with a separate account facility than under a trust fund plan. In support of this, they argue that insurance companies, because of factors such as cash flow and investment facilities (including greater opportunities for private placements and advance commitments), have had, and will continue to have, a greater return on fixed-income investments than corporate trustees. Proponents of the trust fund plan, on the other hand, point out that if the corporate trustee maintains a common trust fund, its opportunities in the area of fixed-income investments are similar to those of an insurance company. Moreover, the employer has total control over the investment policy of a trust fund plan and, as a result, can direct the trustee to take a more aggressive investment posture than could be obtained under an insured plan. Advocates of the insured plan make the further observation that in an insured plan, the fixed-income portion of the plan assets could be protected by guarantees as to the integrity of principal and as to a minimum rate of return. In any event, the fiduciary provisions of ERISA might cause some employers to adopt a more conservative investment policy.

It must be remembered that not all insured funding instruments offer the same type of investment flexibility as that just discussed. If a fully insured individual policy plan is under consideration, for example, there will be no opportunity for equity investment unless variable annuity contracts are used. Moreover, the share of the insurer's investment earnings which the plan will receive generally will be based on the average method of crediting interest to contracts of the type involved.[7] Thus, when comparing a typical fully insured individual policy plan with a trust fund plan, it must be recognized that the earnings potential of the trust fund plan will be greater.[8]

In the case of a combination plan, the employer will have the opportunity to have the conversion fund invested in common stocks. Alternately, if the employer does not want to accept the financial risk associ-

---

[7] In the case of a group permanent fully insured plan, the investment earnings credited might be based on the new-money method. Also, some companies have introduced individual flexible annuity contracts which use the new-money method of crediting interest.

[8] As a practical matter, however, if an employer is considering the adoption of a fully insured individual policy plan, the size of the group will generally be such that the financial and mortality guarantees of the insurer are of more importance, considering the risks the employer would have to assume in these areas under a trust fund plan.

ated with investing funds in common stocks, it may request the insurer to hold this conversion fund as part of its general assets. In this event, the insurer will guarantee this fund as to principal and as to a minimum rate of return. Earnings in excess of the guaranteed rate will be credited by the insurer in accordance with its dividend or experience rating formula.[9]

Summary. As the reader has probably observed, comparison and competition between insured and trust fund plans generally are involved only in plans covering large groups of employees. Smaller employers have more frequently adopted insured plans, partly because of benefit and tax objectives and partly because of the financial and mortality protection and stability offered to small groups by the insurer's guarantees and pooling practices. For larger employers, investment earnings are the most significant factor in comparing the costs of group funding instruments and the trust fund plan. The amount of benefits paid will, in the long run, be the same under both funding instruments. The expenses of operation will be very close under both funding instruments—to the point of being insignificant except in the case of a plan in a state which imposes a heavy annuity premium tax on qualified plans.[10] Thus, of the three factors involved in determining the ultimate cost of a pension plan, investment earnings remain as the one item where real cost differences could result. As noted earlier, the choice in this regard quite often is between funding agencies, be they banks or insurance companies, rather than between funding instruments.

Security of Benefits

Ultimately, the benefit security under any pension plan rests with the continued existence and financial strength of the employer, as well as with the continued existence of the plan. Whether a plan is insured or not, there is no guarantee that the employer will remain in business or that the plan will be continued in effect. The plan termination insurance provisions of ERISA, of course, offer meaningful protection for employees in the event of plan termination. However, some plans are not covered by these insurance provisions and, even if a plan is covered, not all of its benefits may be insured.

Prior to the enactment of ERISA, the benefit security for employees depended upon whether an allocated or an unallocated funding instrument was involved. ERISA mandates the order in which assets will be

---

[9] For the most part, this will be at the insurer's average or portfolio rate, although a few insurers have adopted the new-money method of crediting interest for conversion funds held in connection with individual policy combination plans. Also, in the case of a group permanent combination plan, the interest credited might be based on the new-money method.

[10] See footnote 6.

allocated in the event of plan termination, and this order of priorities would seem to override the way in which assets might have been previously allocated under the specific funding instrument involved. Thus, at any given time and regardless of the funding instrument involved, an employee's benefit security depends upon the level of funding achieved and the amount of the plan assets the employee would be entitled to receive under the provisions of ERISA if the plan were then to be terminated.

Flexibility

The flexibility associated with various funding instruments may be considered from the viewpoint of benefit structure, funding policy, investment policy, and the ability to change funding agencies.[11]

Historically, there is no question that in the early development of private pensions, the trust fund plan offered a greater degree of flexibility in all of these areas than did the insured funding instruments. To meet this competitive disadvantage, the insurance industry developed a number of different products, such as group deposit administration and immediate participation guarantee contracts, and, more recently, has made separate account facilities available. As a result, several insured funding instruments now offer, for all practical purposes, almost as much flexibility in these areas as is offered by trust fund plans. However, certain insured funding instruments are still relatively inflexible in this regard.

Benefit Structure. As previously indicated, the determination of plan provisions should precede the selection of a funding instrument. Once the desired plan provisions have been determined, it is necessary that the funding instrument be examined to see if it can be employed to provide the plan benefits.

Individual policy and group permanent fully insured plans are the least flexible of the insured funding instruments. For example, formulas which offset social security benefits or which base benefits on final earnings are difficult to employ in a fully insured plan. Likewise, the insurer's contract requirements (both as to minimum amounts of insurance and minimum duration of the contract) might not be adaptable to plan provisions concerning benefit levels and retirement schedules. Individual policy and group permanent combination plans are somewhat more flexible than fully insured plans in this regard; even here, however, a certain degree of relative inflexibility exists.

Among the group insured funding instruments, the group deferred annuity contract also is relatively inflexible. Generally, this funding instrument works well only for plans that base benefits on career-average

---

[11] McGill, *Fundamentals of Private Pensions,* p. 315.

earnings and where benefits may be associated with a particular year of service. The unallocated group funding instruments, such as deposit administration and immediate participation guarantee contracts, are extremely flexible in this respect and, for all practical purposes, are comparable to the trust fund approach. Advocates of the trust fund plan, however, point out that although this flexibility exists, it is available and may be utilized only with the consent of the insurer, whereas in the trust fund plan, the trustee's consent is not required.

In summary, the trust fund approach offers a great deal of flexibility as to the benefit structure of the plan. Equivalent flexibility is also afforded by the unallocated insured funding instruments. The allocated insured funding instruments, both group and individual policy, are less flexible and, if flexibility is desired or required, the plan requirements in this regard should be compared with the flexibility available to ascertain if the particular funding instrument under consideration may be conveniently employed.

Funding Policy. As is the case with respect to the benefit structure of the plan, the trust fund approach offers considerable flexibility to the employer in terms of the funding policy of the plan. Within limits imposed by ERISA, the actuary has considerable flexibility in selecting the actuarial cost method and assumptions to be used. The employer's contributions to the plan may vary considerably and, subject to ERISA's minimum funding standards, it is not required, for example, that there be sufficient funds on hand to adequately cover expected payments to retired employees.

A similar degree of flexibility as to funding policy exists in the unallocated insured funding instruments; however, there is one notable exception. The insurer generally requires that benefits for retired employees be backed by sufficient reserves; thus, the insurer, when it is guaranteeing benefits to the retired employee, will insist that a sufficient amount of money be in its possession to meet this liability.

Allocated insured funding instruments of necessity are less flexible with regard to the employer's funding policy. To a large extent, employer contributions will be determined from year to year by the insurer's rate structure and, while some degree of flexibility is obtained via "stop-and-go" provisions and policy loan features, this does not compare with the flexibility obtainable in unallocated funding instruments.

Investment Policy. With the exception of insured funding instruments that employ a separate account facility, an employer has no degree of control over the investment policy in an insured plan. All amounts contributed to the insurer become part of its general assets and are invested by the insurer in accordance with its own investment policies and subject to any statutory requirements as to the investment of such funds. If a separate account facility is involved, the employer may establish investment policy to some extent in terms of the portion of the total plan assets that the employer wishes to be invested in equities; however, many insurers, as an underwriting requirement, place a limit on the amount of the plan assets that may be placed in the separate account, and statutory requirements also may result in similar limitations.[12] Moreover, even if amounts are placed in a separate account, most insurers will not permit the employer to exercise any direction or control over the specific stocks that are acquired or disposed of in this account.[13]

In the matter of investment policy, then, the trust fund approach must be considered more flexible than the insured funding instruments.

Change of Funding Agency. It is a relatively simple matter, under a trust fund plan, to change the trustee or to transfer assets to another funding agency, such as an insurance company. This applies to the total assets of the plan, including any amounts held with regard to retired employees.

It will not be possible to transfer the reserves held for retired employees under most insured funding instruments. The insurance company, when it has guaranteed these benefits, will continue to make payments and will continue to hold the reserve for these benefits. Under some forms of group pension contracts, however, the benefits for retired employees will be purchased on a limited basis and the insurer's guarantees to the retired employee will be limited to the annuity actually purchased. Under such a contract, most of the amounts held by the insurer would be available for transfer. As to funds held with regard to active employees, most insured funding instruments permit a change in funding agency without difficulty. Individual policy and group permanent plans are such that coverage may be surrendered and the surrender values may be turned over to the new funding agency. Similarly, the unallocated or active life fund under group deposit administration and immediate participation guarantee contracts may be transferred to the new funding agency. Because of the possibility of financial antiselection, most insurers reserve the right to spread payment of this amount over a period of years.[14]

---

[12] Some state laws authorizing the use of a separate account facility require that employee contributions and reserves for guaranteed annuities purchased be held in the insurer's general portfolio.

[13] If the employer is large enough to have its own separate account (i.e., its plan assets are not in a pooled separate account), it is not unreasonable to expect the insurer to recognize the employer's desires in selecting the stocks which comprise the portfolio of the employer's separate account. As a practical matter, however, the practice of establishing individual separate accounts is still relatively uncommon.

[14] See p. 243. The liquidation option generally associated with a group deposit administration contract allows the insurer to retain a small percentage (usually not more than 5 percent) of the fund being held for active employees. This is sometimes referred to as a termination charge. It must be remembered, however, that in such a plan, most of the insurer's loading for expenses will not be received until annuities are purchased, even though the insurer has incurred expenses with regard to amounts

Alternately, the full amount may be made available for transfer in a lump sum. In this event, the insurer will transfer the market value of the fund, thus reflecting differences in rates of investment return and protecting itself against financial antiselection. Group deferred annuity contracts are the least flexible in terms of transferring funds, since most such contracts do not contain a surrender privilege. Thus, under a group deferred annuity contract, a change in funding agency may generally be made only with respect to future plan contributions.

Summary. The trust fund plan is more flexible than most of the insured funding instruments. In some situations, the need for this greater flexibility will dictate the choice of the trust fund plan as the appropriate funding instrument even though a necessary corollary is that the employer must assume a greater degree of responsibility under the plan.

Service

In insured plans, service normally is provided by the home office of the insurance company and by its agency and group field offices. In trust fund plans, the employer generally handles the administrative work of the plan or this is performed by an actuarial consultant.

It is difficult to measure the quality of the services performed by the various institutions and firms active in the pension field. Obviously, there can be marked differences in this regard which are not inherent in the different funding instruments.

GROUP VERSUS INDIVIDUAL POLICY PLANS

An employer who decides to use the insured approach is faced with a choice between a number of different individual policy and group funding instruments. The employer's choice in this regard may be complicated by the competition that exists within the insurance industry and, on occasion, within the same insurance company.

As might be expected, many life insurance agents have, over the years, favored using the individual policy approach. Group field personnel, on the other hand, have strongly advocated the use of group funding instruments. The situation has been further complicated by the fact that many insurers maintain completely separate and distinct home office pension departments, depending upon the type of coverage involved. Thus, it is possible for the same insurer to issue both individual policy and group

---

in the unallocated fund. Thus, one reason for this charge is to reimburse the insurer for expenses already incurred but not yet recovered. In contrast, expenses associated with a trust fund plan are normally paid for as incurred, with the result that if there is to be a change in funding agency, only current unpaid expenses need be deducted from the fund.

proposals to the same employer and for essentially the same plan benefits. Often, the proposals will be issued through different sources—for example, a full-time agent of the insurer will obtain an individual policy proposal while a competing broker consults with the insurer's group field office and obtains a group proposal. When conditions such as these exist, it is not difficult to understand why an employer may become confused in the selection of the proper funding instrument.

Even though already mentioned several times in this chapter, it is worthy of repetition once again that no one funding instrument is preferable over all others. In some situations, the individual policy approach will be indicated, while in others, some form of group funding instrument will more adequately meet the employer's needs and objectives. The remaining portion of this chapter will discuss some of the more important factors that might affect the choice of a particular insured funding instrument and will review some of the most commonly used individual policy and group funding instruments with an indication of their application to particular situations.

Basic Considerations

Broadly speaking, a comparison of individual policy and group funding instruments involves the same elements that were previously discussed in terms of insured and trust fund plans—i.e., costs, benefit security, flexibility, and service.

Costs.   In the area of costs, it will be recalled, the three elements to be considered are benefits paid, expenses, and investment earnings. As to benefits paid, the individual policy plan offers the employer the protection of the insurer's rate guarantees as well as participation in the insurer's experience pool. For this reason, the employer may expect reasonably stable and predictable costs in an individual policy plan. Depending upon the employer's size, the group funding instrument involved, and the insurer's dividend or experience rating formula, some or all of the experience of the employer's plan might be pooled with the experience of similar groups. Where such pooling exists, there should be little difference between individual policy and group funding instruments in terms of ultimate cost to the employer of benefits paid. To the extent that the group funding instrument takes into account the employer's own actual experience, the employer assumes the risk of this experience, good or bad, and plan costs ultimately will reflect this experience rather than the more stable experience of the larger group of lives participating in the insurer's pool.

As to expenses, the individual policy plan generally will run higher than an equivalent group plan. The agent's compensation is one reason for this; other reasons are the lower acquisition and maintenance costs associated with issuing and administering a master contract rather than a number of individual contracts for each employee.

It is a little more difficult to assess the investment earnings aspects of the different insured funding instruments. In a fully insured individual policy plan, reserves generally will be credited with interest based upon the insurer's average or portfolio rate of interest. In an individual policy combination plan, the same will be true of the portion of the plan assets consisting of insurance contracts. The conversion fund of a combination plan, however, may be invested in equities, thus affording the opportunity of capital appreciation (along with the attendant possibility of capital loss). Most insurers use the new-money method when crediting interest to reserves held for group funding instruments. If large enough to qualify for a separate account facility, a portion of the plan assets also may be invested in equities. Generally, if investment earnings are of paramount importance to the employer, the use of a group funding instrument (or, possibly, an individual policy combination plan) might be preferable. Usually, however, the choice between individual policy and group funding instruments will be influenced by factors other than investment earnings.

It would be well to reiterate, at this point, that a funding instrument should not be selected on the basis of cost estimates. This is particularly true when comparing individual policy and group funding instruments, since not only are there the differences which could result from the use of different funding assumptions, but these cost estimates could reflect differences in true costs due to different plan provisions and benefits frequently suggested by the different funding instruments. For example, most individual policy plans automatically include a substantial preretirement death benefit, which is not always the case when a group funding instrument is involved. Moreover, most individual policy plans are funded on a level premium basis, while most group plans employ a funding method which creates an initial supplemental liability. Since such a supplemental liability may be amortized over a period of time which could extend beyond the normal retirement dates of many of the initial group of participants, a significant difference in the incidence of contributions could be produced, creating the impression that the group funding instrument is considerably less expensive. For these reasons, extreme care should be taken when comparing the cost levels suggested in connection with specific funding instruments.

Benefit Security. There is little difference in benefit security between individual policy and group funding instruments since ERISA. The degree of benefit security will depend upon the level of funding achieved regardless of the funding instrument employed, and the amount of the plan assets that the employee would be entitled to receive under the provisions of ERISA if the plan were to be terminated.

Flexibility. Unallocated group funding instruments offer a greater degree of flexibility, particularly in the area of benefit structure, than do individual policy plans. It is no problem under an unallocated group funding instrument, for example, to have benefits based upon final earnings. Similarly, benefit formulas which offset social security benefits may be accommodated, along with survivor benefits and various forms of disability benefits. Other examples of this greater flexibility include the ability to establish a wider range of normal retirement schedules, as well as varying levels of death benefits.

The individual policy combination plan is much more flexible in this regard than is the fully insured plan; nonetheless, when compared with the unallocated group funding instruments, it must still be considered as relatively inflexible in terms of designing the plan's benefit structure.

The group funding instruments also are more flexible in terms of the funding policy of the plan. Again, the individual policy combination plan is somewhat more flexible in this regard than is the fully insured plan, since contributions to the conversion fund may be determined by several different actuarial methods and with varying actuarial assumptions. Even so, the group funding instruments permit a wider degree of flexibility as to funding policy than does the individual policy combination plan.

For smaller employers, the individual policy combination plan provides greater investment flexibility than the group funding instruments. For larger employers, flexibility as to investment policy probably is greater under the unallocated group funding instruments.

With the exception of the group deferred annuity contract, the insured funding instruments generally permit a change in funding agency for funds held for active employees. The group funding instruments, however, usually reserve to the insurer the right to spread out payment of this fund over a period of years or, alternately, transfer only the market value of the fund, while such restrictions are not found in individual policy plans.

Service.   As far as the home office of the insurer is concerned, there should not be any appreciable difference in the servicing of pension plans funded with either individual or group contracts. There could, of course, be material differences in the case of a given insurer or between different insurers, but this would not be attributable to differences inherent in the particular insured funding instruments.

At the field level, there might be slight differences in service between individual policy and group plans. The servicing of individual policy plans will largely be conducted by the insurer's agency office. In group plans, this servicing will be done, to a great extent, directly by the home office of the insurer or through a group field office. Because the servicing of group plans is done under home office direction by salaried employees, there is a greater probability of consistency and continuity of service.

The quality of service of individual policy plans depends more directly upon the individuals involved at the field level and is more responsive to change if these individuals should retire or terminate their affiliations with the insurer.

Tax Considerations

Before turning to a discussion of the specific insured funding instruments, it is important to recognize that tax considerations often influence the choice between group and individual policy funding instruments.

Most group plans are established so that any death benefit is provided by a group term life insurance contract issued directly to the employer. When death benefits are being provided under a group plan in the above manner, the following tax results occur:

1. The employee does not have to include the cost of insurance as taxable income each year (except to the extent the employer is providing the employee with total group term life insurance in excess of $50,000 or the state limit, if lower).
2. Since the entire proceeds consist of pure insurance, no portion of a lump-sum payment will have to be considered as taxable income by the beneficiary.
3. The proceeds of the insurance will be included in the employee's gross estate for federal estate tax purposes. (If permitted under applicable state law and the group contract, the employee may assign his or her incidents of ownership in group life insurance. Where this is done and all necessary conditions are met, the proceeds will not be included in the employee's gross estate for federal estate tax purposes.)

In contrast, the death proceeds under an individual policy plan will not be includable in the employee's gross estate to the extent provided by employer contributions and if paid to a named personal beneficiary; however, the cash value of the insurance contract, subject to certain deductions, will be taxable as income to the beneficiary, and the employee will be required to include the cost of insurance (offset by his or her own contributions, if any) as taxable income during the employee's lifetime.

This difference in tax treatment leads to the broad observation that lower paid employees (i.e., at least those employees who do not have an estate tax problem) are better off, tax-wise, with a plan funded by group coverages. For such an employee, the fact that the proceeds are includable in his or her estate is not a disadvantage, and the fact that the premium for the life insurance will not be taxable to the employee while alive, coupled with the fact that the proceeds will be received free of income tax by his or her beneficiary, creates a distinct tax advantage.

For an employee who has estate tax problems, however, the individual policy plan could produce distinct tax advantages. The fact that the entire proceeds could pass completely free from federal estate tax may produce tax savings to such an extent that having to include the cost of insurance as taxable income each year would be relatively insignificant. Moreover, the aggregate of these prior insurance costs, along with the $5,000 employee death benefit exclusion provided by Section 101(b) of the Code, could be used upon the death of a participant to reduce the beneficiary's income tax liability. Finally, the beneficiary's tax liability would be softened in that any portion of the cash value that is taxable could receive favorable tax treatment if certain ncecessary conditions are met.

While these tax considerations are significant, it must be remembered that federal tax law may be changed at any time. Thus, in a long-range program such as a pension plan, probable tax consequences should not be given undue consideration—particularly when other factors would indicate a contrary course of action.

The Fully Insured Plan

Whether group or individual policy, the fully insured plan offers an employer the greatest degree of guarantees available from an insurance company. The employer has the security that the cost of the coverage in force cannot exceed the premium level stipulated for this coverage.[15] This is so regardless of the actual experience of the plan and regardless of future economic trends.

This is of great significance to some employers. For many, particularly those with only a few employees, this factor alone is enough to warrant the selection of a fully insured plan as the funding instrument for the plan.

It should also be noted that smaller employers, since the enactment of ERISA, are showing greater interest in the fully insured plan—largely because of administrative and risk considerations.

Along with this advantage, however, certain disadvantages are associated with the fully insured plan. One of the most notable of these is the lack of flexibility in terms of benefit structure, funding policy, and investment policy. The basic structure of the insurance contract is considered by many practitioners to be a further disadvantage. It will be re-

---

[15] The employer does not, of course, have a guarantee as to the cost of additional benefits that accrue in the future for existing participants or for new participants (except, possibly, to a limited extent under group permanent contracts).

called that under a retirement income contract, the cash value increases to the point where it ultimately exceeds the face amount of the coverage. This leads to a situation in which the death benefit increases in the years just prior to retirement—at a time in life when there usually is little justification for an individual to receive (or for an employer to provide) larger death benefits. Moreover, as previously pointed out, the cash value of the contract will be considered as taxable income to the beneficiary when received. In the later years of the contract, this could mean that all or most of the death proceeds will be taxable as income.[16] Finally, since the entire amount accumulated to provide the employee's retirement benefit is paid as a death benefit, there is no recovery to the trust on account of the employee's death.

For these reasons, the fully insured plan is rarely used for larger groups of employees. Although this type of coverage may be written on a group permanent basis, the fact that this approach is used primarily for small groups results in a fully insured group permanent plan being relatively uncommon. While it is difficult to draw the line as to what constitutes a small group, it generally appears that the fully insured plan is used predominantly for groups of fewer than ten covered employees. The fully insured plan also works quite well in defined contribution (money-purchase) plans, where it often is desirable to make a full allocation of contributions among employees and where it is not desirable, for administrative reasons, to maintain a separate fund and to allocate investment earnings among employees.

The Combination Plan

The combination plan is one of the most popular of the insured funding instruments. While it does not offer an employer the complete protection associated with a fully insured plan, significant guarantees are still available to the employer—particularly in terms of the cost of retirement benefits for insurance contracts in force.[17]

The combination plan is much more flexible than the fully insured plan in terms of benefit structure, funding policy, and investment policy.

---

[16] This aspect could be quite significant. For example, it is not uncommon for an executive to qualify for a monthly pension of $1,000. Under a fully insured plan, this would require a retirement income contract with a face amount of $100,000. In the years just prior to retirement, this death benefit could increase to an amount in the vicinity of $150,000. Even though the death benefit could qualify for favorable tax treatment, the beneficiary's tax liability could be quite large if, for all practical purposes, most of the $150,000 would be considered as taxable income.

[17] For an interesting comparison of fully insured and combination plans in which the author concludes in favor of the combination plan, see Samuel J. Savitz, "The Case for the Combination Plan," *Journal of the American Society of Chartered Life Underwriters,* vol. 20, no. 1 (Winter 1966), pp. 66–74.

It is possible, for example, to relate death benefits to earnings or to make the death benefit some multiple (not in excess of 100) of the employee's expected pension. Benefit formulas that offset social security benefits or that base benefits on final earnings also may be employed. The existence of the conversion fund permits greater latitude in the choice of actuarial cost methods and assumptions, and in the actual incidence of contributions. Finally, the conversion fund may be invested in equities or in more conservative investments, as the employer sees fit.

Since not all of the reserve being accumulated for an employee's retirement benefit will be paid as a benefit in the event of death before retirement, it is reasonable to expect that the ultimate cost of a combination plan will be less than under a fully insured plan.[18] Moreover, since the cash value of the insurance contract will be lower than under a retirement income contract, the income tax liability of the employee's beneficiary will not be as great as under a fully insured plan.

The combination plan may be written on either an individual policy or a group permanent basis, although most frequently individual contracts are used. The combination plan generally is used where the group of employees to be covered is between 5 and 50. While occasionally employed for groups of more than 50 employees, this is relatively uncommon because of the cost and flexibility considerations of the group and trust fund approaches.

Group Deferred Annuity Contract

At one time the major form of group funding instrument, the group deferred annuity contract is now used very infrequently. It is relatively inflexible in terms of benefit structure, working well only for defined contribution (money-purchase) plans or in defined benefit plans where the benefit is based on career-average compensation or where benefits may be imputed to various years of service. For all practical purposes, the group deferred annuity contract offers little flexibility in funding policy (except to the extent of the amortization of supplemental liabilities) and, of course, no flexibility in terms of investment policy.

On the other hand, the group deferred annuity contract offers greater guarantees to the employer than do the unallocated group funding instruments. Moreover, since it is an allocated funding instrument, record keeping and plan administration are relatively straight-forward and simple.

Most insurers will not offer this type of coverage to groups of fewer than ten. While there is no upper limit as to the size of the group that

---

[18] As a matter of fact, this aspect often is reflected in cost estimatees which employ a discount for expected mortality insofar as contributions to the conversion fund are concerned.

could be covered, practical considerations tend to limit its use to groups of under 100.[19]

Unallocated Group Funding Instruments

The unallocated group funding instruments include the group deposit administration and immediate participation guarantee contracts; the modified immediate participation guarantee or, as it is sometimes called, the direct rated deposit administration contract; and the so-called investment contracts. Depending upon the size of the group covered, the state involved, and the insurer's underwriting practices, these contracts may also be written with a separate account facility.

As has been previously discussed, the unallocated group funding instruments more nearly approach the trust fund plan in terms of the factors the employer might consider when selecting a funding instrument. They offer a wide degree of flexibility in terms of the benefit structure of the plan and the employer's funding policy. With a separate account facility, the employer also has a degree of flexibility in determining the portion of plan assets to be invested in equities.

The insurer's guarantees, both from a financial and a mortality viewpoint, are considerably more limited as to duration of time than under an individual policy plan. Typically, these guarantees attach to amounts which become part of the insurer's general assets during the first five years of the contract and continue to provide or purchase benefits until the fund so created has been exhausted on a first-in, first-out basis. Thus, the insurer's guarantees attach to the fund rather than to individual employees. For this reason, in a defined contribution (money-purchase) plan, the insurer's guarantees under an unallocated group funding instrument are relatively meaningless except to older employees. Younger employees in such a plan receive little or no protection in terms of the annuity purchase rates that might apply when they retire at some future date.

Most insurers offer unallocated group funding instruments to groups of as few as ten covered lives. As a practical matter, they usually are employed for groups of 25 or more.

---

[19] There are, of course, a number of older plans that are still funded with group deferred annuity contracts where the number of employees covered is far in excess of 100. This statement is intended to cover current attitudes and practices with regard to new plans.

11

Underwriting Aspects of Insured Plans

Apart from the usual underwriting considerations applicable to the individual lives or to the group of lives covered under a pension or a profit sharing plan, an insurer also must decide whether it is willing to underwrite the plan as a whole. A pension or a profit sharing plan is a long-range undertaking, both for the employer and for the insurance company underwriting the plan benefits. For this reason the insurer must recognize, when it accepts the underwriting risks associated with such a plan, that its commitments will extend well into the future.

From the insurer's point of view, a pension or a profit sharing plan involves sales and administrative costs which are greater than the normal expenses incurred by the insurer in the acquisition and maintenance of its other business—particularly in view of the administrative burdens imposed by ERISA. In the sales area, for example, many insurers furnish proposals and cost calculations for pension and profit sharing plans—a service not generally provided for its individual life and health insurance business. In the administrative area, the question of providing special services also is a problem because of the need for periodic actuarial valuations of the plan and because of the information the employer may request or require (such as information to support its claim that plan contributions are deductible for income tax purposes). The expenses associated with services of this type must be taken into account by the insurer when the plan is underwritten.

The purpose of this chapter is to examine some of the factors which bear on the overall underwriting decision of the insurer and to review the broader underwriting aspects of group and individual policy pension coverages. This chapter also discusses the use of the guaranteed issue underwriting technique for individual policy plans.

GENERAL UNDERWRITING CONSIDERATIONS

Early Termination

Before accepting the underwriting risk of the plan as a whole, the insurer must satisfy itself that the plan will be reasonably permanent and that there will not, in all probability, be an early lapse of coverage. The reason, of course, is that the initial cost of acquiring and installing the plan will not be recovered until the plan has been in operation for several years. Thus, one of the insurer's first underwriting considerations is the possibility of early plan termination.

An important factor in this area is the stability of the employer's business and profit history. If the employer has been in business for only a short period of time or if its profits have fluctuated widely in recent years, the insurer would be rightly concerned over the possibility that the cost of the plan may prove to be too burdensome, with the attendant possibility of early plan termination. If a profit sharing plan is involved, these factors do not have the same significance so far as the future of the plan is concerned—as a matter of fact, these factors may very well be the reason a profit sharing plan is being considered instead of a pension plan. From the insurer's viewpoint, however, the fact that a profit sharing plan need not be terminated if the employer is unable to make a contribution is of little solace if coverage is lapsed due to the lack of funds needed to pay premiums due on insurance contracts that might have been purchased through the plan.

Closely related to this problem is the question of whether or not the cost of the plan is too high in relation to the employer's financial capacity. Even though the employer has been in business for a substantial length of time, and even though profits have been stable, the cost of the plan may still be too high to undertake on any comfortable basis. Unless the employer has a sufficient profit margin, the future of the plan could be in jeopardy as a result of even a slight shift in business conditions.

Another factor which bears on the consideration of early plan termination is the question of whether the plan will achieve a qualified status under federal tax law.[1] Most insurers are unwilling to underwrite a plan which, in all likelihood, will not be approved by the Internal Revenue Service. However, it is important to distinguish between plan provisions which are grossly unacceptable and those which are marginal. If the plan provisions are marginal and if there is a general understanding

---

[1] This aspect is also important to the insurer in connection with its premium rates and its dividend or experience rating treatment of the plan. See p. 239 and 244.

between the insurer and the employer that the plan will be changed to conform to any requirements imposed by the Internal Revenue Service, the insurer will probably be willing to underwrite the plan if the potential cost of any contract changes needed to meet the requirements of the Service is not too high.

The insurer also will show some degree of interest in the funding instrument chosen, particularly if circumstances indicate that within a short time this funding instrument might be discarded in favor of one better suited to the employer's needs. While there is a considerable difference of opinion as to where the line is drawn, there is general agreement that at some point the use of individual contracts to fund pension benefits becomes questionable. For this reason, the insurer must make an underwriting decision if it is being asked to use individual contracts in a plan where, in the judgment of the insurer, some other funding instrument should be employed. By the same token, the insurer also will be concerned with the choice between a fully insured individual policy plan and an individual policy combination plan and with the choice between the different group funding instruments available.

Administrative Aspects

Another major underwriting consideration for the insurer concerns the administrative requirements and complexities of the plan.

The plan, for example, may include requirements which conflict with the insurer's contract forms, regulations, or procedures. Each plan provision must be checked against the insurer's requirements and any conflict should be resolved before the plan is underwritten. The following list is by no means all-inclusive, but does give some indication of areas where difficulties could arise:

1.   Discrepancies between the normal retirement dates specified by the plan and the maturity dates available under the insurer's contracts. For example, the typical retirement income contract used for a fully insured individual policy plan will mature on the contract anniversary nearest the insured's 65th birthday. The plan, however, may call for normal retirement to occur on the first of the month coincident with or next following the employee's 65th birthday, with the result that, unless some adjustments are made, the contract will have either too little or too much cash value on the employee's normal retirement date.

2.   Plan provisions which require that coverage be issued at ages when the coverage would not be available from the insurer.

3.   Plan provisions which require that coverage be issued for amounts below the insurer's minimums. This is especially significant as it applies to small increases in coverage which accrue after the employee has become a participant in the plan.

4. Plan provisions dealing with late retirement which require the continuation of coverage or the accumulation of funds after normal retirement in a manner which the insurer will not or cannot permit. Many insurers, for example, have developed a special type of contract for individual policy combination plans which matures for a stipulated cash value on the employee's normal retirement date. The plan may require continued life insurance coverage between normal and late retirement, but the insurer may not be willing to continue this coverage after the contract maturity date unless satisfactory evidence of insurability is submitted.

5. Plan provisions which require that certain options be available to a retiring employee. The insurer, however, may not be willing or able to make these options available—or may be able to make them available but only under conditions not included in the plan. The plan, for example, may permit an employee who retires before age 65 to elect to have higher payments before 65 and lower payments thereafter, so as to produce an approximately level income when full social security benefits commence at age 65. While this form of payment is readily available under most group pension contracts, it generally is not available for individual policy plans. Another example of the problems in this area would be a plan which permits the election of a certain optional form of payment immediately prior to retirement whereas the insurer, under the funding instrument involved, would require some preelection period before that particular option could become effective.

6. Conflicts between the billing practices of the insurer and plan provisions which could affect the dates and frequency of premium payments. A plan, for example, could permit participation to begin on the day on which the employee meets all eligibility requirements (which could be any day of any month), and could require that coverage be made effective on that date. This would result in a number of contracts being issued under the plan with different premium due dates. For billing purposes, however, the insurer might want to have all contracts issued with a common premium due date.

7. Plan provisions which require ownership or beneficiary designations which conflict with the insurer's contract provisions and practices. Some insurers, for example, prefer to write contracts under a pension or a profit sharing plan with the trustee as the owner and beneficiary (with the employee's personal beneficiary designations being filed with the trustee). However, the plan may stipulate that the employee's personal beneficiaries be named in the contract, or may require that the ownership provisions of the contract be split between the trustee and employee, so that the employee has the absolute right, under the contract, to name and change the beneficiary without the trustee's consent or approval.

8. Procedures spelled out in the plan in the event of death, disability, retirement, or termination of employment which require the insurer to do (or not to do) certain things which are in conflict with the insurer's contract provisions or practices. An example of this type of problem would be a plan requirement that the contract be owned by the employee after retirement, along with an additional requirement that any dividends after maturity should be paid to the trustee. This provision could present complications if the insurer's contract stipulates that any dividends after maturity must be paid to the owner of the contract.

Conflicts of the type enumerated are found most frequently in individual policy plans rather than in group plans. Also, many are of the type that may readily be solved by a simple adjustment to the plan, by the insurer waiving its normal requirements, or by the insurer finding an acceptable alternate solution. Finally, it should also be pointed out that any particular item, while a matter of concern to one insurer, may be of little or no significance to another. In any event, the insurer will examine each plan with points such as these in mind to ascertain if the plan may be underwritten on a satisfactory basis.

Closely related to the question of potential conflict between plan provisions and the insurer's administrative requirements is the further question of whether the insurer will be required to perform any special services and, if so, the relative cost of these services. For example, does the employer expect the insurer to prepare employee announcement material? Is the insurer expected to supply financial information each year for the covered employees, such as insurance (PS 58) costs, a statement of accrued benefits, and so on? Is it expected that the insurer will furnish yearly assistance in the preparation of the employer's tax return? Will the insurer be required to maintain records relative to the participation of employees, such as a record of their accumulated contributions? If some or all of these services are required, along with the additional administrative burden imposed by ERISA, the insurer must evaluate the potential cost involved in determining the acceptability of the case.

Depending upon the coverage involved, many of these services are made available to all employers on a regular basis. Others are readily available as a by-product of the insurer's administrative system at very little additional cost. In any event, the insurer must take these factors into account as a part of its underwriting judgment of the desirability of the plan as a whole.

Exculpatory Provisions

ERISA states that any provision in an agreement or instrument which purports to relieve a fiduciary from responsibility or liability for any responsibility, obligation, or duty under ERISA will be void. Nevertheless, it is expected that most insurers and other fiduciaries will continue to require the use of exculpatory provisions with the indication that they will apply except where prohibited by law. Thus, if the plan involves a trust, most insurers will continue to require, as a part of their general underwriting process, that the trust contain provisions which protect the insurer in its relationships with the trustee, the employer, the employees, and their beneficiaries. Similar provisions are usually included in group pension contracts.

UNDERWRITING CONSIDERATIONS OF GROUP PENSION PLANS

Apart from the general underwriting considerations already noted, there are several broad concepts specifically related to the underwriting of group pension plans.

The first of these is that group pension coverages (other than group permanent) do not involve immediate life insurance benefits and that the annuity risk assumed by the insurer is relatively long range in nature. For this reason, any mortality antiselection will usually occur at some time subsequent to the effective date of the plan, rather than at its inception. Also, unlike individual annuity contracts, where any mortality antiselection is exercised primarily by the annuitant, mortality antiselection under a group pension contract may be exercised both by the employer and by the covered employees.

Another broad aspect of group pension underwriting is the fact that the contract involves the accumulation of substantial reserves over a long period of time and, therefore, insurers are quite concerned about the possibilities of financial antiselection. Thus, the insurer will be particularly concerned with the financial aspects of its group pension contract. The financial implications of group pension contracts have taken on greater significance in recent years with the development of newer contracts that provide relatively little in the way of mortality and expense guarantees.

As previously noted, acceptability of the plan to the Internal Revenue Service is a major underwriting consideration. Insurance companies receive federal tax relief for investment income earned on assets attributable to reserves under qualified plans, and it is customary for most insurers to reflect this anticipated tax relief in the form of lower premium rates (or higher interest guarantees) for their group pension contracts. For this reason, the acceptability of the plan to the Internal Revenue Service takes on additional significance to the insurer, since the contract rates could very well be inadequate if the plan does not attain a qualified status and the annuities purchased remain in force.

Finally, because of the nature of group pension contracts and their tailor-made aspects, and because of dividend or experience rating techniques which permit the insurer to charge each case with its own expenses, the insurer is in a position to offer broad administrative services to the employer and to do this on a basis which is equitable to all of its group pension policyholders. Thus, special services to be rendered are not as significant an underwriting consideration in group pension plans as they are in individual policy plans.

Minimum Requirements

Most insurers have established certain minimum requirements which must be met before a group pension contract will be offered. These minimums vary considerably from insurer to insurer and also will vary according to the type of funding instrument involved. In some insurance companies, the minimum requirements for the same funding instrument may be different depending upon whether or not the plan requires employee contributions.

A typical minimum requirement for a group deposit administration contract or a group deferred annuity contract is that the plan must cover at least ten lives and must generate an annual premium of at least $5,000 (possibly $10,000 if the plan is contributory). If employees are to contribute, the insurer may require that 75 percent of the eligible employees participate. It should be noted that these requirements are not imposed by statute but are usually established by the companies as underwriting minimums.[2] Other group pension coverages, such as immediate participation guarantee or separate account contracts, usually have higher minimum requirements.

Mortality Aspects

The insurer generally will require that the contract be established on a basis which does not permit the employer to individually select the persons to be covered or the amount of a participant's annuity. The purpose, of course, is to prevent mortality antiselection.

Just as an insurer is concerned about the maximum amount of group term life insurance it has in force on any one individual, it will also be concerned about the maximum amount of annuity it has in force on any one life. As a practical matter, however, cost considerations, the

---

[2] Group permanent coverage is generally subject to the various state group insurance statutes, with the result that eligibility provisions, schedules of insurance, the minimum number of covered lives, the minimum percentage of participation, etc., must also conform to the requirements of these laws. However, any limitation in the state law as to the maximum amount of group life insurance usually applies only to group term life insurance and not to group permanent coverage.

maximum benefit provisions of ERISA, and the requirements of the Internal Revenue Service tend to limit this underwriting problem.

Individual mortality antiselection may occur in the choice of options at retirement—for example, if the basic form of payment under the plan is a pure life annuity with no death benefit and the employee has the right to elect a reduced benefit with a guarantee that a minimum number of payments will be made. Obviously, an employee in poor health could elect this optional form of payment and thus create a form of death benefit unless some restriction is placed upon his or her right to make this election. Thus, most insurers require that if an optional form of payment is to be elected, evidence of the employee's good heath will be required unless the election is made prior to some specified period before retirement. The preelection period varies from insurer to insurer, but a requirement of two or three years prior to retirement is common. If an election has been made and if the employee is within this preelection period, the employee will not be allowed to change or revoke the option without submitting satisfactory evidence of good health. Evidence of the good health of the employee's joint annuitant might be required to revoke the election of a joint and survivor option. Under ERISA, however, an employee must be allowed to revoke or change a prior revocation of the post-retirement joint and survivor spouse benefit up until his retirement date.

By the same token, the insurer's consent will be required if an employee wants to change the retirement date after having elected an optional form of payment (assuming the plan otherwise permits the employee to change the retirement date). For example, the joint and survivor option might have been elected and it is learned that the employee may not live until the scheduled retirement date. It would be to the employee's advantage to elect an early retirement date so as to assure a benefit for the joint annuitant. On the other hand, if the employee finds the joint annuitant to be in poor health, the employee could, if not so restricted, elect a late retirement date. If the employee did this and if the joint annuitant died prior to the late retirement date elected, this would have the effect of automatically revoking the optional form of payment, thus restoring the higher benefits the employee would receive under the basic form for the payment of benefits. To prevent the possible antiselection in this latter example, the insurer's consent to the request for late retirement would generally be conditioned upon receiving satisfactory evidence of the good health of the employee's joint annuitant.

Group pension underwriting also is concerned with the mortality aspects of the cancellation of annuities purchased under a group deferred annuity contract. The problem usually arises under a contract written on a deferred pure life annuity or modified cash refund basis (i.e., where no death benefit is payable before retirement other than a return of any employee contributions) and when an employee terminates employment under such conditions that he or she is not fully vested. The question, of course, is whether a credit will be made available to the employer with respect to the premiums paid for the nonvested portion of the annuity being canceled. Since the premium rates have been discounted for expected mortality, the insurer will generally be unwilling to make any such credit available unless satisfactory evidence of the terminating employee's good health (at the date of termination) is received within a specified period of time—usually six months from the date of termination of employment.

The good-health requirement under any of the situations previously described will vary depending upon the amount of risk involved for the insurer with respect to the particular employee. The evidence may range from a simple employer's statement as to the employee's good health up to a full medical examination of the type normally associated with the issue of new individual life insurance. A factor which also bears on this aspect is the "experience status" the contract has reached under the insurer's dividend or experience rating formula. If the experience of the case is such that dividends are being paid, adverse mortality experience will be borne to a great extent by the employer, since such experience will directly affect the amount of these dividends.

Financial Aspects

As previously indicated, a group pension contract involves the contribution of substantial amounts of money each year which must be held, invested, and reinvested by the insurer over a long period of time. Because of this, the financial aspects of the contract are underwritten carefully.

Most insurers limit their financial guarantees to amounts deposited during the first five years of the contract and reserve the right to change the terms of these guarantees for amounts received after the fifth contract year. The guarantees that attach to the fund or reserve created during the first five years generally will continue in effect as to such amounts until they have been applied or distributed under the contract on a first-in, first-out basis. For this reason, the initial guarantee may extend for a long period of time, and it is not uncommon to find that by the terms of the contract, the features of the initial guarantee will scale down with the passage of time.

The insurer also will be faced with the question of whether to extend these guarantees for existing plans when the initial five-year period has expired. Factors the insurer will take into account at that time are the guarantees it is then offering to new policyholders and the experience status the contract has achieved under the insurer's dividend or experience rating formula.

Because of these guarantees and the possibility of an adverse change in the investment market, the insurer also may limit the amount which the employer may contribute in any one contract year. Thus, the employer would be prevented from making excessive contributions in a particular year to take advantage of the insurer's guarantees at a time when adverse investment conditions prevail.

Another aspect of investment antiselection is involved in those unallocated funding instruments that contain a liquidation provision which allows the employer to transfer the unallocated or active life fund to another insurer or funding agency. The insurer, while generally granting the employer this privilege, usually will reserve the right to spread out payment of the fund over a period of time so as to be able to soften the impact of having to liquidate part of its assets under adverse investment conditions. Alternatively, the insurer may permit a lump-sum transfer of the market value of this amount—i.e., the amount otherwise available for transfer adjusted to reflect the differences between the investment conditions that existed when the insurer received premiums under the funding instrument and those prevailing when the lump-sum transfer is being made.

UNDERWRITING CONSIDERATIONS OF INDIVIDUAL POLICY PLANS

Individual policy pension and profit sharing plans present an insurer with several underwriting problems that are considerably different from those associated with group programs.

One of the most important distinctions is that practically all individual policy plans include immediate life insurance coverage as well as a deferred annuity benefit. The insurer is, therefore, faced with all the underwriting considerations associated with individual life insurance. Most insurers will underwrite contracts issued in conjunction with a pension or a profit sharing plan in exactly the same fashion as they underwrite regular individual life insurance contracts—with the exception of utilizing guaranteed issue underwriting if the case meets with the insurer's requirements for the use of this underwriting technique. Some insurers refer to the guaranteed issue process as "simplified issue" or "automatic issue."

A second major distinction concerns the administrative aspects of individual policy plans. While the insurer may classify this entire line of business as a separate class for dividend purposes there is no effective way, within its premium structure, of charging each plan for its own unusual expenses. Moreover, the insurer, for a number of internal administrative reasons, must make an effort to adopt and maintain uniform rules and practices for the administration of this type of business. As a result, the insurer generally is limited by cost and by administrative and equity considerations in the extent to which services can be tailored to meet the needs of a particular individual policy plan.

In the past, most insurers utilized their standard contracts for individual policy plans, making only those adjustments absolutely necessary to permit their use in this fashion. However, a number of insurers now have designed a special line of contracts for these plans—thus enabling the development of special contract provisions, the greater use of guaranteed issue underwriting, and the use of special systems and procedures. Special contracts also permit the insurer to classify this business separately for premium rate and dividend purposes.

While most insurers have reflected their federal tax relief directly in rates or guarantees for group pension contracts, this practice generally is not followed for individual policy plans. Here, as the insurer's guarantees usually are for a longer term, this tax relief is passed on either in the form of a special lump-sum payment each year or in the form of increased dividends. Because of these added payments or dividends, the insurer, from an underwriting viewpoint, is vitally interested in the acceptability of the plan to the Internal Revenue Service.

The underwriting considerations of investment antiselection under individual policy plans, while of interest to an insurer, do not have the same significance as under group pension plans. The employer is more or less limited by the provisions of the contracts as to how much money may be deposited with the insurer each year, as well as to how much money may be withdrawn. For these reasons, the insurer is not quite as concerned about problems of investment antiselection under individual policy plans as under group programs.

Minimum Requirements

Most insurers do not have any minimum requirements as to the number of lives that must be covered under an individual policy plan. As a result, most insurers will underwrite such a plan even if it involves only one employee.

However, there is some concern over the minimum size of the contracts issued, as well as the average contract size at the time the plan is established. The majority of insurers will require that their standard minimum contract size requirement be met with regard to the first layer of coverage an employee receives under such a plan. This requirement usually is relaxed, however, as to the coverage an employee becomes entitled to receive at a later time due to increases in salary. Here, most insurers will write a contract with a face amount as low as $1,000, even though this might not meet their normal minimum contract requirements. Because this exposes the insurer to writing a large number of small contracts, it often will require that the total amount of initial insurance generated at the outset of the plan produce an average contract size which is considerably higher than its normal minimum contract requirements.

Eligibility Requirements

Adequate eligibility requirements are of particular importance to the insurer of an individual policy plan, since the lack of them would permit temporary or short-term employees to be included in the plan. This could result in a loss to both the employer and the insurer in the event of an early lapse of contracts due to termination of employment. Most insurers will insist that the plan be designed with the most stringent service and age requirements permitted by ERISA.

Mortality Aspects

An individual policy plan affords the insurer a certain degree of protection as to mortality antiselection, since many of the features which permit individual selection in the purchase of life insurance are absent. The insured, for example, cannot select the time that the insurance will become effective. The employee cannot modify the plan's eligibility requirements and the amount of insurance is not subject to individual determination—rather, it is determined by the benefit formula of the plan. Also the group covered is actively at work. Thus, to a great extent, many of the safeguards of group underwriting are present.

Nevertheless, a certain amount of mortality antiselection may exist. The largest individual amounts of insurance will be on key executives of the firm, who may have a voice in establishing the eligibility requirements and benefit formula of the plan. Also, in most instances, the group covered will be small, thus preventing the effective application of true group underwriting principles. Therefore, most insurers will insist, to some extent, that normal medical and underwriting requirements be met before insurance will be issued. The insurer will also look closely at the nature of the employer's business and the occupations of the covered employees, in order to determine whether an undue underwriting hazard exists.

Guaranteed Issue Underwriting

If the group is large and there is a satisfactory distribution of risk by amount and age, most insurers will consider issuing some or all of the coverage on a guaranteed issue basis—i.e., the insurer will issue up to some stipulated amount for each individual employee without evidence of the employee's insurability. Some insurers, in granting guaranteed issue underwriting, will do so only after screening the two or three individuals who are to be insured for the largest amounts of insurance, and may even require these individuals to complete a nonmedical form. Other insurers will offer guaranteed issue underwriting without such a screening process. The requirements for guaranteed issue underwriting also vary considerably from company to company. The following, however, will give some idea of the general practices followed by many insurers.

In most companies, the minimum number of lives required for guaranteed issue underwriting is ten, although a few insurers may go lower. If employees contribute, there will also be a minimum participation requirement, which ranges from about 75 percent for larger groups up to as much as 90 or even 100 percent for smaller groups.

Many insurers, particularly those who have not developed a special line of contracts for qualified plans, do not automatically use guaranteed issue when their requirements have been met but offer guaranteed issue underwriting only when requested. In these instances, there is usually a reduction in the agent's compensation as well as in dividends if guaranteed issue underwriting is utilized. A number of the insurers that have adopted special contracts for qualified plans reserve the right to determine whether or not guaranteed issue underwriting will be used, but tend to use this form of underwriting whenever possible. These insurers do not generally distinguish between regularly underwritten and guaranteed issue business insofar as dividends and the agent's compensation are concerned; however, a distinction might be made with respect to the gross premiums payable for such coverage.

A formula of some type usually is employed to determine the maximum amount of insurance that may be issued on any one life under a plan on a guaranteed issue basis. Typically, the formula will be one and one half or two times the average amount of insurance called for by the plan (after excluding amounts on lives over the maximum age for guaranteed issue coverage and any amounts in excess of some scheduled maximum). Frequently, some inside limit is also stipulated, so that regardless of the result the formula produces, the maximum amount cannot exceed this inside limit. A typical inside limit would be $1,000 or $1,500 multiplied by the number of employees covered under the plan. Another such limit might be an amount related to the total insurance to be written under the plan.

The amounts determined by such a formula are usually much lower than would be available under a typical group term life insurance program. One reason for this is that the insurer is in a position to adjust its yearly renewal rates and dividend or experience credits for group term life insurance in the event of adverse mortality experience. In individual policy plans, where the insurer accepts the risk on a long-term basis, a more conservative approach is indicated.

Once the guaranteed issue limit has been determined, the question arises as to what should be done with respect to the employee who is entitled to an initial amount of insurance which exceeds this limit by only a small amount—say, $1,000. Most insurers recognize this problem by allowing for a "spillover" which permits guaranteed issue underwriting for small amounts in excess of the stipulated limit. If an employee is initially entitled to an amount which exceeds the total of the guaranteed issue and the spillover limits, however, the coverage will be regularly underwritten for all amounts in excess of the guaranteed issue limit. The spillover, in other words, is for the convenience of the insurer, not for the employer or its employees.

One further question arises, as to how to handle increases in coverage that are written in subsequent years due to increases in salary. Usually, there is no problem in issuing these amounts on a guaranteed issue basis until the total amount of insurance in force on an employee's life has reached the guaranteed issue limit (plus the spillover, if applicable). After this point has been reached, the question is not as easy to resolve, and insurers differ widely in their treatment of this problem. Some insurers will reinstate the original guaranteed issue limit at the point where an individual is required to and does submit satisfactory evidence of his or her insurability. Other insurers will issue small amounts of insurance in subsequent years on a guaranteed issue basis up to some ultimate maximum limit. When this approach is followed, there will usually be some limit (such as $2,000 or $2,500) on the amount which the insurer will issue on a guaranteed issue basis at any one time after the employee's total insurance has reached the initial guaranteed issue limit. If an individual is entitled to an increase in benefit of less than this amount, it will be issued on a guaranteed issue basis, but if the amount of additional coverage exceeds this amount, the entire additional coverage will be subject to regular underwriting.

12

Plan Installation and Administration

The advantages that a qualified plan will provide for employers and employees have been amply noted in previous chapters. These advantages are most significant; and it is important, from the employer's viewpoint, that they be gained at minimum expense and with minimum administrative effort.

Many of the factors involved in the installation and administration of a qualified plan are interdependent, and the relative timing of certain events can be most significant. Moreover, several parties usually are involved in the installation and administration of the program, and very often these parties have differing interests. Efficient plan installation and administration requires that the efforts of these parties be coordinated and that there be complete and thorough communication between all concerned. The administrative complexities imposed by ERISA are such that great care must be taken by all concerned to assure that the plan is installed and operated in accordance with the law. The life underwriter or plan consultant plays an important role in this respect.

This chapter examines the steps involved in the installation of a qualified plan and discusses the various administrative aspects of such a program.[1] It is important to note, at the outset, that any person who has discretionary authority or control in the administration of a plan is a fiduciary under ERISA and must discharge all plan responsibilities as required under this law.

---

[1] The reporting requirements of ERISA are discussed separately in Chapter 13.

PLAN INSTALLATION

Preparation of Legal Documents

The first and most important step in the installation of any plan is the preparation of the necessary legal documents, such as the trust agreement or the plan instrument, authorizing resolutions, enrollment forms, and so on. The employer's attorney is responsible for preparing the trust agreement, the plan instrument, or both, as the case may be. If a group pension contract is involved, the insurance company prepares this document, but the employer's attorney should review the contract provisions.

Most insurers and corporate trustees have specimens of the various legal documents involved and will furnish them to the attorney who is working on a specific plan. It is particularly desirable for the attorney to have copies of these specimens (whether they are used or not), since they generally contain most of the requirements of the insurer or the trustee for the type of funding instrument involved. By giving the attorney this information, conflicts between the plan provisions and these requirements may be avoided or, at the least, these conflicts may be discussed before the instruments are finalized.

Plans Which Involve a Trust Agreement. It is possible to incorporate the plan provisions in the trust agreement, and this practice usually is followed in individual policy plans (particularly those that are fully insured) or where individuals are acting as trustees. It is also possible to have two separate documents—a plan instrument which establishes the details of the plan and a trust agreement which relates primarily to the duties, rights, and responsibilities of the trustee for the investment and accountability of the plan assets. This latter approach often is used if a corporate trustee is involved, since many employers prefer to limit the role of the corporate trustee in a pension or profit sharing plan to that of an investor of plan assets. Thus, they prefer that the documents clearly establish the fact that administrative duties and responsibilities are vested in the employer or in a committee appointed by the employer. Moreover, flexibility is obtained by having two instruments in that the trustee's consent is not necessary for any changes in the plan instrument alone.

If the plan is insured in any way, it is desirable to submit a draft of all documents to the insurer's home office for review prior to execution. As a matter of fact, this step is required by some insurers as a part of the underwriting process. It is a good practice for the parties involved to do this in order to avoid any possible conflicts between the plan provisions, the insurer's underwriting and adminstrative requirements, and the trustee's responsibilities. Similarly, if there is to be a corporate trustee, it is advisable to submit a draft of the documents to the bank or trust company for approval prior to execution.

If the employer is a corporation, its board of directors should pass a resolution or resolutions authorizing the plan and appointing the trustee. If applicable, a committee or committees also should be appointed. Also, if required by state law or the firm's charter or bylaws, it may be necessary that an authorizing resolution be passed by the firm's stockholders.

When all necessary papers have been prepared and are in acceptable form, the trust should be executed. At this time, the employer's first contribution usually is made to the trustee, although, if possible, some employers prefer not to make a contribution (or prefer to make only a token contribution) until an approval letter for the plan has been received from the Internal Revenue Service. However, if insurance is to be placed in force, a contribution of an amount necessary to pay the premiums will have to be made. Most insurers will agree to refund this premium, less a risk charge, to the trustee if the plan is disapproved by the Internal Revenue Service within one year.

In an insured plan, the trust agreement generally requires that the insurance or annuity contracts be applied for by the trustee and that the trustee pay the first premiums due on such contracts. Since the individual or corporation who is to be the trustee cannot act in this capacity until the trust is in effect, it is important to recognize that the creation of the trust is a necessary condition which must be met before the insurance may be placed in force.

If employees are to be enrolled, an enrollment form should be prepared. If the plan is contributory, this form should include an authorization for the employer to withhold any employee contributions. It is also desirable to prepare a refusal form should any employee elect not to participate. Such a refusal form, signed by the employee, would be a record that the employee had been informed of his or her rights but had declined plan participation.

Master and Prototype Arrangements. The concept of master or prototype plans (with or without a trust) was originally developed in conjunction with H.R. 10 plans. At that time, the Internal Revenue Service instituted administrative procedures under which a sponsoring institution such as an association, a bank, or an insurance company could obtain approval of a master or prototype plan. The Internal Revenue Service subsequently extended these same administrative procedures to corporate plans.

As is the case with master or prototype plans for self-employed individuals, the sponsoring organization submits the plan to the Internal Revenue Service for approval. Any corporation wishing to avail itself of an approved master or prototype plan simply executes a joinder or affiliation agreement. The master or prototype plan sets forth the general provisions for a qualified plan. The joinder or affiliation agreement permits the corporation to select various plan features such as the benefit formula, eligibility requirements, employee contribution levels, and vesting provisions.

Adoption of such an approved plan by a corporation does not mean that the corporation automatically has a qualified plan. It is still necessary that the plan be considered individually with particular reference to the individual circumstances involved.[2] The plan may be submitted to the Internal Revenue Service for individual consideration by utilizing appropriate Treasury Department forms.

Group Pension Plans. A trust agreement is not employed in most group pension plans. The provisions of the plan are contained either in a plan instrument or in the group contract itself. If a plan instrument is involved, the group contract is usually written by the insurer on a "reference" basis—i.e., the group contract, while not spelling out the plan provisions, refers to the actual plan instrument to determine items such as eligibility, retirement benefits, vesting, and so on. If a plan instrument is not involved, the group contract itself will contain these provisions. The employer's attorney will prepare any plan instrument involved and will review the terms of the group contract prepared by the insurer.

As in the case of a plan which employs a trust, it is necessary to have the board of directors (and, where appropriate, the stockholders) pass an appropriate resolution authorizing the plan.

When an employer has decided to establish a group pension program, the first step is usually for the employer to submit a letter of application to the insurer for the group contract. This letter of application, along with a premium deposit and all pertinent information relating to the plan (including the plan instrument, if applicable), is forwarded to the insurance company. If all preliminary underwriting requirements are met, the insurer will accept the application and will then prepare the actual group contract. In many situations, particularly if the contract incorporates the actual plan provisions, a draft of the contract will be sent for the employer's approval. Once the final contract has been prepared (incorporating any changes mutually agreed upon between the insurer and the employer), the insurer generally obtains approval to issue the contract from the appropriate state insurance department, if such approval is necessary.[3] After any necessary state insurance department approval has

[2] This is not the case if a self-employed individual adopts an approved master or prototype plan. In this event, the plan is deemed to meet the requirements of the Internal Revenue Code, and the Internal Revenue Service will no longer issue determination letters in such situations.

[3] This is the state where the contract will be delivered and is generally the state in which the employer's principal place of business is located if that state requires that group pension contracts be approved prior to issue. It should be noted that while insurers attempt to standardize the provisions of their group contracts as much as possible, many insurers, because of variations required in a particular case, will submit each contract to the appropriate state insurance department for approval to issue the contract on a "single-case" basis. Since, in this area, insurers do not have the advantage of working with preapproved contract or policy forms, a group contract may take longer to issue than individual contracts.

been received, the final contract will be sent for execution by the employer.

Announcing the Plan to Employees

It is necessary, with all qualified plans, that the plan be announced to employees.[4] This announcement may take the form of a letter (usually from the president of the firm), but it is often desirable to have a brochure or booklet printed for this purpose. If desired, most insurers will supply some form of printed announcement material for a group pension program and, prior to the actual printing of this material, usually will furnish copy to the employer for approval. The actual cost of preparing this material usually is charged to the employer through the insurer's divdend or experience rating formula. In the case of a trust fund plan or a plan funded with individual contracts, the cost of preparing announcement material is borne directly by the employer.

From the employer's viewpoint, the announcement material should be as attractive as possible, since it is the first as well as the major communication that employees will receive concerning the plan. A well-designed brochure or booklet will do a great deal in helping to obtain maximum employee awareness of the program and appreciation of its value. Many employers find that their communications program is enhanced if the preliminary announcement is followed by employee meetings and, at a later date, by more complete and permanent reference material.

The object of the announcement material is to explain the plan in clear and simple terms—but not at the price of accuracy. For this reason, it is important that this material be checked most carefully to make sure that it correctly describes the plan.

Enrollment of Employees

If the plan is contributory or if individual contracts are involved, an enrollment always is necessary. It sometimes is desirable to enroll employees under a noncontributory plan. The enrollment usually takes place at the time the plan is announced to employees or shortly thereafter. It normally involves the completion and signing of the enrollment form and, if the plan is contributory, the completion of the authorization for the employer to withhold the employee's contributions by payroll deduc-

---

[4] The announcement should state that a copy of the plan document is available for inspection and where and when such inspection may take place, and must communicate all other information required by ERISA. In addition, the employees must be notified of the plan's submission to the Internal Revenue Service along with a notification that employees have the right to comment on the submission or, under specified conditions, request the secretary of labor to make such comments. See the discussion of this requirement in Chapter 4.

tion. In a group program, the insurer usually will supply the enrollment and refusal cards that should be used. In trust fund plans, the corporate trustee will often be able to supply these forms, if desired.

In an individual policy plan, the application for the employee's insurance or annuity contract also will be completed at the time of enrollment and, if necessary, a medical examination will be arranged. Many medical examiners, when there are several lives to be examined, will agree to conduct these examinations at the employer's place of business. After the enrollment has been conducted, the insurance or annuity applications, appropriately signed by the trustee, should be submitted to the insurance company for underwriting approval. If the trust agreement is satisfactory to the insurer and if all of the insurer's underwriting requirements are met, both as to the plan and as to individual lives, contracts will be issued for delivery to the trustee.

Medical examinations are not generally required for group pension plans, although if group permanent insurance is involved, and if the plan requires amounts of insurance in excess of the nonmedical maximum, it is possible that a few employees will have to be examined.

Other Matters

Evidence of Participation. It usually is desirable that employees be given some evidence of their participation in the plan. Most insurers provide some form of certificate or statement of participation for both individual policy and group pension plans. In trust fund plans, the consultant will generally arrange to have this material prepared for the employer.

Signature Authority. If there is more than one trustee, the trust agreement usually states whether actions taken by the trustees must be unanimous or whether they may act by majority vote or by one of the trustees. The same generally is true for the committee of a plan with a corporate trustee. Where unanimous or majority action is required, the instruments may still permit the trustees or committe to delegate to any one of their number the authority to sign documents or to perform ministerial duties on behalf of all. When the instruments contain such a provision, most trustees and committees find it desirable that such a delegation be made for administrative convenience. The insurer or corporate trustee, or both, require that a copy of any such delegation be in their files if they are being asked to accept fewer than the full number of signatures otherwise required by the plan.

Checking Account. If individual trustees are involved, it also is desirable for the trustees to open a checking account, since they have the responsibility of maintaining adequate records of money received and disbursed. Canceled checks and the accompanying statements are generally accepted as proof of payment or receipt and, for this reason, the trustees' account is most important.

Administrative Records. In addition to the record furnished by the trustees' checking account, it is necessary that some or all of the administrative records described later in this chapter be established at the inception of the plan. Adequate administrative records, maintained from the very beginning, can prove to be a most valuable adjunct to the smooth administration of the entire program.

TAX ASPECTS OF INSTALLATION

To make sure that an employer receives a deduction for contributions made for the fiscal year in which the plan is established, it is important that all necessary requirements be met within the time allowed under federal tax law. Thus, if the plan involves a trust, the trust agreement should be executed by the close of the employer's fiscal year. The contribution need not be made until the due date for filing the employer's tax return (including extensions), so long as the liability to make the contribution is established by the close of the fiscal year involved.

If a group pension contract is involved (without a trust), it is not necessary that the group contract be executed by the close of the employer's fiscal year if the following steps have been taken by the end of such fiscal year:

1. The employer's board of directors has passed a resolution setting forth a definite plan for the purchase of retirement annuities under which a liability is created to provide the benefits.
2. An application has been made by the employer to the insurer for the group contract.
3. The insurer has accepted the application.
4. The group contract or an abstract has been prepared in sufficient detail to define the terms of the contract.
5. The plan has been communicated to employees.
6. An irrevocable part payment on account of the premiums due under the contract has been made.

If these steps have been taken, the actual execution and issuance of the final contract need not take place until the due date of the employer's tax return for the taxable year in which the plan is established (including extensions).

Obtaining an Advance Determination Letter

Regulations promulgated by the commissioner of internal revenue are very specific in listing the information that must be filed in order to obtain an advance determination letter as to the qualified status of the plan.[5] Although it is not absolutely necessary that such an advance determination letter be obtained, it will be necessary to submit detailed information along with the employer's tax return for the first year in which a deduction is claimed. As a practical matter, most employers will file for such an advance determination letter as soon as possible after the plan has been installed. One reason for doing this is the possibility that the Internal Revenue Service will find some feature of the plan to be unacceptable. The Internal Revenue Code permits a plan to be changed retroactively to its effective date if the change is made by the time the employer's tax return for the year is due, including extensions. If changes are necessary, the employer may make appropriate amendments to the plan within this period and thereby preserve the deductions to be claimed for the taxable year involved. On the other hand, if the employer does not file for an advance determination letter, the qualified status of the plan will be examined by the Service at the time the employer's tax return is audited. Any changes then required by the Service will, in all probability, be at a time which is beyond the period allowed for making a retroactive change. This could result in the employer's losing at least one year's deduction.

Substantiating the First-Year Deduction

At the end of the employer's fiscal year during which the plan was established, the employer is required to submit the same type of information that would be required for an advance determination letter, plus the financial and accounting information necessary to establish the deduction limit for contributions, the fact that actual contributions were made, and the amount of these contributions. This material should be submitted with the employer's tax return for the taxable year in question.

Taxpayer Identification Number

Each taxpayer is required to obtain an identifying number. Even though a qualified pension or profit sharing *trust* is tax-exempt, it, too, must obtain such a number. Treasury Department Form SS-4 is used by the trustee for this purpose.

PLAN ADMINISTRATION

As a generalization, it might be said that the administration of pension and profit sharing plans is divided into two broad areas—actions which

---

[5] This information is set forth in detail in Chapter 4.

relate to the plan as a whole (such as cost calculations, and tax aspects), and actions which relate to specific individuals (such as the processing of retirements and terminations of employment). Actions which relate to individuals may take place at any time during the plan year and often occur without any advance notice. Actions which relate to the plan as a whole generally take place once a year, usually around the anniversay date of the plan.

While group and individual policy pension and profit sharing plans are similar in many ways, they differ considerably in plan administration, particularly in the role played by the life underwriter. Generally speaking, most insurers utilize the same administrative practices for contracts issued for individual policy plans as they do for their ordinary life business as a whole. These systems are such that only infrequently will the home office of the insurer have direct contact with the employees or the employer. Thus, most contacts with the employer and employees will be at the field level. For this reason, the role played by the life underwriter and the agency office in the administration of individual policy plans is most important.

In contrast, most insurers will administer their group pension and profit sharing programs in a manner such that the home office is in direct contact with the employer—or the services of the local group field office will be utilized. The life underwriter and the agency office are generally involved only in important or unusual matters. To aid in this concept of direct administration between the employer and the home office, the insurer will usually furnish the employer with an administration manual or guide and a supply of administrative forms at the time the plan is installed. With this manual and supporting material, the employer is in a position to be in direct contact with the home office on most items of plan administration.

In trust fund plans, the plan administration is handled by the employer, frequently with the aid of the plan consultant, and the corporate trustee acts primarily as an investor of the plan assets and makes disbursements as directed by the employer or committee. Some larger employers even maintain a full-time staff to administer their employee benefit plans. Consultants are also frequently involved in insured plans, particularly those which employ some form of group pension contract. Here, much of the plan administration and record keeping normally performed by the insurer is handled by the employer or consultant, the insurer to a great extent acting within its contract terms as directed by the employer or consultant.

The following material discusses, very briefly, the major areas involved in plan administration. No attempt has been made to discuss specific administrative procedures, since these vary considerably among insurers, banks and trust companies, and consultants.

Cost and Actuarial Aspects

An important aspect of the administration of any pension plan is the determination of the annual contributions to be made under the plan. For a fully insured individual policy or group permanent plan, this is a relatively simple matter, since the annual contribution will be the sum of the premiums due on existing coverage plus the first premiums due on new coverage then being issued for new entrants or with respect to benefit increases, less any employer credits.

For a group deferred annuity contract, the annual contribution will be the premiums calculated by the insurer to purchase the future service benefits accruing during the year plus, if applicable, a premium toward the liquidation of any unfunded supplemental liability, less any employer credits.

The determination of annual contributions becomes a little more complicated for those plans which employ, in whole or in part, some form of unallocated funding instrument. Here, it is necessary that some form of actuarial valuation be made. For an individual policy or group permanent combination plan, a portion of the annual contribution will consist of premiums then due. The balance will consist of the deposit which must be made to the conversion fund, and this portion must be actuarially determined. Most insurers will perform the calculations necessary to determine the estimated deposits to this fund; in any event, the valuation must be performed by an enrolled actuary under ERISA. Certain data must be obtained each year to perform these calculations. These data include a revised employee census which indicates new entrants, changed benefits, terminations that have occurred during the prior year, and so on.

Most insurers will perform the actuarial valuations needed for unallocated group funding instruments, such as group deposit administration contracts, or will accept the actuarial valuations made for the plan by an actuarial consulting firm. In a trust fund plan, the actuarial valuations are performed by an actuarial firm. The actuary will need the employee information referred to above in order to perform these valuations. Usually, the consultant or the insurer will have given the employer detailed instructions as to when and how these data should be compiled. As noted above, the valuation must be made by an enrolled actuary.

Tax Aspects of Administration

Deductions. Form 5500 should be used for employers in claiming deductions for contributions made to a qualified plan.

Taxpayers need not make the actual contribution during a given taxable year and will be allowed a deduction for the contribution for such year if the actual contribution is made before the due date for filing the employer's tax return for such taxable year (including extensions) and if the contribution is designated as being on account of such taxable year.

Annual Information Returns—Forms 1099-R and W2-P. Treasurey Department Form 1099-R is an information return which the trustee must file for each beneficiary who receives a lump-sum payment or distribution from the trust of $600 or more in any calendar year.[6] Treasury Department Form W2-P is used when distribution is in the form of periodic payments. A copy must be given to the payee before January 31 of the year following the calendar year during which the payment was made. Returns on Form 1099-R are in the nature of unverified schedules showing the name and address of the payee, the kind and amount of income paid, and the name and address of the payor. The schedules are summarized on Treasury Department Form 1096, which is the actual "return" for the trust and which must be filed by the payor with the Internal Revenue Service by February 28 of the year following the calendar year in which the payments were made.

It should be noted that these forms must be filed even though the payment is made in part or in whole by the cash value of an insurance or an annuity contract which is being transferred out of the trust.

In a group pension plan without a trust, it is the responsibility of the insurance company to file these forms.

Withholding. A pensioner may elect to have federal income tax withheld from pension payments. This is accomplished by the pensioner's filing Treasury Department Form W-4P with the payor of the benefit (the trustee or the insurance company). The payor must begin withholding payments no later than the first payment due after three months following the date the withholding request was made. The withholding request may be revoked or changed by the pensioner. In either case, withholding must terminate or change no later than with the first payment due on or after the first status determination date (January 1, May 1, July 1, or October 1) occurring at least 30 days after the payor receives notice of revocation or change. The amount withheld should be a whole-dollar amount not less than $5 per month. Also, the amount withheld cannot reduce the monthly pension below $10.

If amounts are withheld, the payor must furnish the pensioner each year with a Treasury Department Form W2-P showing the gross amount of pension paid to the pensioner during the year along with any amount of tax withheld. This form must be given to the pensioner on or before January 31 following the calendar year of payment (or within 30 days after the last payment if payments are terminated during the year). A

---

[6] If the insurer makes the payment, it, too, must file this information, with the result that there is some duplication.

copy of Form W2-P must also be furnished by the payor to the Internal Revenue Service.

PS 58 Costs. A participant in a qualified plan who is protected by level premium life insurance is considered, under federal tax law, to be in constructive receipt of the value of the pure insurance protection of the life insurance contract.[7] The term cost of this pure insurance protection is, therefore, considered to be additional taxable income to the participant. This cost of insurance (often called the PS 58 cost because the original Treasury Department ruling on the subject was so numbered) in some cases is automatically furnished each year by the insurer or may be readily determined from tables supplied by the insurer.

It should be noted that the PS 58 costs are considered as a distribution from the trust and, if the amount involved (together with any other distributions) is $600 or more, the trustee must report this on Form 1099-R. In most situations the annual PS 58 cost will be less than this amount, with the result that the trustee will not be required to file Form 1099-R for actively employed paritcipants. This fact, however, does not relieve the employee of the obligation of including these amounts as taxable income each year. Failure to include these amounts as taxable income could result in the entire insurance proceeds being taxable as income to the employee's beneficiary. For this reason, many trustees report the PS 58 costs even though the amount involved is less than $600.

Records

A pension or a profit sharing plan can be expected to exist over a considerable length of time, and it is reasonable to expect that during its existence, several different individuals will be responsible for its administration. Thus, it is most important that adequate records be established at the outset of the plan and that these records be maintained in sufficient detail to permit orderly and consistent plan administration. This is particularly so since the advent of ERISA.

Records for the plan as a whole should include a list of the names, addresses, and telephone numbers of all individuals who are associated with the plan and its administration. This would include the trustees, any committee members, the life underwriter, the consultant, the attorney, the accountant, and so on. These plan records also should include a complete history of all plan receipts and disbursements. A digest of the major plan provisions would be most helpful to the plan administrator in avoiding repeated reference to the legal documents constituting

---

[7] If the plan is contributory and the plan so provides, employee contributions may be first applied to meet the cost of the insurance protection, thus eliminating or minimizing the employee's current tax liability for this benefit. Most plans are written in this manner.

the plan. A major portion of the permanent plan records generally includes appropriate memoranda, letters, or minutes which support decisions made in the interpretation of the legal documents or in the exercise of discretionary powers granted to the trustee or committee.

The record maintained for each employee should list such pertinent data as the employee's social security number, date of birth, the type of proof submitted to verify this birthdate, the date of birth of the employee's joint annuitant or spouse (if applicable), the effective date of participation in the plan, the employee's hours of service and the appropriate computation periods), the employee's scheduled normal retirement date, and current beneficiary designation (if applicable). This record should show, on a cumulative basis, the employee's earnings (if benefits are related to compensation), projected benefit under the plan, and current death benefit (if any). If the plan employs individual insurance or annuity contracts, the record should also include information relating to the employee's contract or contracts such as contract numbers, dates of issue, cash values, and rating action.

If employees contribute under the plan, the employee record should include a history of these contributions. Also, if PS 58 costs are involved, a record of these should be maintained, since such costs will be part of the employee's cost basis for any future distributions under the plan.

It also is desirable to maintain, with respect to each employee, a record of each calculation made to determine benefits. This could be most helpful in producing a consistent application of the plan's benefit formula.

Benefit Payments

Benefits generally are paid out under a pension plan only upon retirement, death, termination of employment, or disability. Benefits also may be paid out at other times under profit sharing and thrift and savings plans.

It is important to note that the trust or plan instrument often contains limitations as to what can or cannot be done in the way of benefit payments. Moreover, in an insured plan, the insurance company may impose certain limitations consistent with its underwriting and administrative systems. Any such limitations must be carefully observed in paying or providing benefits under any contingency.

Even though certain limitations may exist, the employee often will have a wide choice as to the manner in which benefits may be paid. The employee's options should be carefully and fully explained and, to the extent that the election or revocation of a spouse benefit is involved, ERISA requires that the employee be given reasonable notice of the terms and conditions of the benefit and the effect of not receiving benefits under this form of payment. It should also be remembered that tax consequences will frequently play an important role in reaching a decision as to how benefits should be received. In any situation where tax consequences could be of significance, the employee should seek the guidance of tax counsel before making a decision.[8]

Employee Communications

An important part of the administration of any plan is the manner in which employees are initially informed and then reminded of their plan benefits and the value of these benefits. Full disclosure, apart from being desirable from an employee relations viewpoint, is required by ERISA.

The employer's size often indicates the course of action best suited for communicating with employees. For example, if the employer is large enough to have some form of publication for employees, this is an ideal vehicle in which to periodically point out the benefits and value of the plan.

Many employers like to give each employee some type of annual report that shows the employee's accrued and projected plan benefits, as well as their value when this can be ascertained under the funding instrument or actuarial cost method involved. (ERISA, of course, gives each employee the right, once a year, to request a statement of accrued benefits and when such benefits are or will be vested.) It is also customary for this type of annual report to include information on the employer's other employee benefit plans such as group life insurance, disability income, and medical expense. This type of report can be most effective in giving an employee a better understanding of plan benefits as well as the total value of employment.

Other techniques for publicizing the plan are bulletin board announcements, payroll envelope stuffers, personal letters, contests, preretirement counseling, and so on. The important point to be kept in mind is that the plan should be repeatedly publicized by the method best suited for the particular employer, taking into account the employee relations pattern that has developed within the firm.

---

[8] Apart from the aspect of securing appropriate advice from tax counsel, there is the further consideration that any advice given to an employee should be full and complete. In *Gediman* v. *Anheuser Busch,* 299 F. 2d 537, the employer gave an employee advice concerning the various options available as to the distribution of his benefit. This advice did not make it sufficiently clear that if the employee elected one of the methods and died before receiving a distribution, his benefits would be considerably smaller than under the other methods. The court held the employer liable for negligence when the employee, in reliance on this advice, elected a method which caused his estate to lose benefits on his subsequent death. The court observed that: "[The employer,] having undertaken to advise, . . . was bound to advise clearly."

13

Disclosure

A major aspect of ERISA concerns the disclosure of information—to participants and their beneficiaries and to the government. While a limited amount of disclosure has been required in the past (under the Welfare and Pension Plans Disclosure Act and under several state laws), ERISA requires that more complete disclosure take place as a matter of course, and at prescribed times. In addition, ERISA applies to a greater variety of plans and covers a much larger number of employees than did the Welfare and Pension Plans Disclosure Act (WPPDA). The disclosure requirements of ERISA supersede those of the WPPDA, which has been repealed. ERISA also preempts state disclosure legislation.

Private employee pension and welfare plans maintained by most organizations whose employees are engaged in or affect interstate commerce are covered by ERISA. The most common plans affected are as follows:

1. Pension.
2. Profit sharing.
3. Thrift and savings.
4. Welfare.
   a. Life insurance.
   b. Hospital-surgical-medical insurance.
   c. Accident insurance.
   d. Disability income.
   e. Scholarship plans (which are funded).
   f. Supplemental unemployment.
   g. Prepaid legal services.

Regardless of the number of participants in pension, profit sharing or thrift and savings plans, such plans are subject to the disclosure requirements of ERISA. However, unfunded welfare plans—or those funded solely through insurance contracts—with fewer than 100 participants throughout a plan year are exempted from certain filing requirements as long as employee contributions are forwarded to the insurer within three months of receipt; any rebates are returned to contributing employees within three months; and contributors are informed when they join the plan about the allocation of rebates. A number of complete or partial exemptions are provided for many different plans, including a complete exemption for unfunded pension plans and unfunded or insured welfare plans provided for a "select group of management or highly compensated employees."[1]

Certain plans are excluded from coverage under ERISA. They are government plans, church plans, plans maintained outside the United States for the benefit of nonresident aliens, excess benefit plans, and plans established only to comply with workmen's compensation, unemployment compensation or disability laws.

For a plan which must comply with ERISA's disclosure requirements, the following items must be filed with the appropriate government agencies, at required times, as well as be made available to employees:

Summary plan description (the booklet, folder, binder, that is given to employees).

Plan description (Form EBS-1).

Plan amendment description (parts of Form EBS-1).

Annual report (Form 5500).

Annual report summary.

Plan termination reports.

ERISA requires the automatic distribution of the following items to plan participants under each plan and to beneficiaries receiving benefits under a pension plan:

Summary plan description.

Plan amendment summaries.

Summary of annual report (selected parts and attachments of the annual report filed with the secretary of labor).

Statement of benefits for all employees who terminate (as of the year they terminate).

Written explanation to any plan participant or beneficiary whose claim for benefits is denied.

---

[1] However, the Department of Labor must be notified of the existence of any such plan and the number of employees the plan covers.

TABLE 13–1

Document Summary of Disclosure Requirements

Item	To Plan Participants			To Government	
	Given Automatically	Given on Written Request*	Made Available for Review	Must Be Done . . .	To Be Filed With . . .	When . . .

Item	Given Automatically	Given on Written Request*	Made Available for Review	Must Be Done . . .	To Be Filed With . . .	When . . .
1. Summary plan description	X			For covered plans existing on 1/31/76: by 5/30/76, complete, up-to-date booklet or other format to be distributed to all participants and beneficiaries as of 3/2/76. After 3/2/76: within 90 days after employees become participants, or beneficiaries start receiving benefits. For plans established after 1/31/76: within 120 days after establishment. New complete summary at least every ten years (every five years if there have been changes).	Secretary of labor.	For covered plans existing on 1/31/76: complete, up-to-date booklet or other format by 5/30/76. For plans established after 1/31/76: within 120 days after establishment. New complete summary at least every 10 years (every 5 years if there have been changes).
2. Plan description (Form EBS–1)	X	X		By 5/30/76 for all covered plans existing on 1/31/76; as soon as form is filed with the secretary of labor for new plans.	Secretary of labor.	First 2 pages and signature page only by 8/31/75 for all covered plans; complete form by 5/30/76 for all covered plans existing on 1/31/76. For plans established after 1/31/76: within 120 days after establishment. Updated versions no more often than every 5 years if secretary of labor requires it.
3. Plan documents (any instrument under which the plan is operated)		X	X	By 1/1/75 for existing plans; as soon as possible after establishment of new plans.	Secretary of labor.	"Any documents relating to an employee benefit plan" at secretary of labor's request only.
4. Plan amendments (parts of Form EBS–1)		X	X	As soon as form is filed with secretary of labor.	Secretary of labor.	Beginning 5/30/76, within 60 days after amendment is made (unless filed with Summary Plan Description).

Document	To participants and beneficiaries	When furnished to participants	Filed with government	Filed with	When filed with government
5. Plan amendment summary description	X	Within 210 days after end of plan year in which amendment is made.			
6. Annual report (Form 5500)	X	As soon as report is filed with Secretary of Labor.	X	Secretary of labor.†	Within 210 days after close of plan year beginning after 12/31/74, i.e., by 7/28/76 for existing calendar-year plans; annually thereafter.††
7. Annual report summary (parts of Form EBS-2)	X	Within 210 days after close of plan year beginning after 12/31/74, i.e., by 7/28/76 for existing calendar-year plans; annually thereafter.	X	Filed as part of annual report.	
8. Benefits statement for terminating vested employees	X	For employees who terminate in plan years beginning after 12/31/75 within a period after termination to be set by the secretary of the treasury.	X		
9. Personal pension benefits statement	X (not more than once a year)	As of 1/1/75 for existing plans; as soon as possible after establishment of new plans.			
10. Written explanation of claims denial	X	As of 1/1/75, whenever a claim is denied, in whole or in part			
11. Plan termination report	X	After report is filed with Secretary of Labor.	X	Secretary of labor (at his discretion for welfare plans); Pension Benefit Guaranty Corporation (for pension plans only).	To secretary of labor at the same time the Annual Report is filed (within 210 days after close of plan year in which plan is terminated). To Pension Benefit Guaranty Corporation within 30 days after plan termination.

* Material must be supplied within 30 days of written request; a reasonable charge may be made for all requested material.

† Must also be filed with Treasury Department.

†† For Labor Department filing; Treasury Department filing of this form may be required at a different time.

Source: Towers, Perrin, Forster & Crosby, Inc.

Any item distributed automatically by mail must be sent by a class of mail that ensures delivery.

In addition, ERISA requires some items to be given to plan participants upon written request and/or to be made available for examination at the principal office of the plan administrator and at other locations convenient for participants. These items are as follows:

Plan description (Form EBS-1).

Supporting plan documents.

Plan amendment description.

Complete annual report (Form 5500).

Personal pension benefits statement (on written request only).

Plan termination report (should any pension plan "wind up its affairs").

The locations in which documents must be made available include any distinct physical location where business is performed and in which at least 50 participants work. Plan materials need not be kept at each location as long as they can be provided at the location within three working days after a request for disclosure. The employer may charge the actual cost of reproduction, up to 10 cents per page, for all materials requested (unless the material falls in a category where it must be furnished automatically).

For pension plans only, participants must be informed in writing of the terms and conditions of any joint and survivor annuity option and the effect of electing or revoking that option. This must be done within a reasonable period (at least 90 days before the annuity starting date, generally speaking) to give the employee enough time to make a well-informed choice.

Table 13–1 sets forth a summary of the information that must be disclosed to the government and to plan participants and beneficiaries. This table also indicates the dates by which such information must be disclosed and whether it must be automatically disclosed, given on written request, or made available for review. The balance of this chapter discusses these major areas in greater detail.

SUMMARY PLAN DESCRIPTION

The summary plan description is the employee booklet (or some other format) that describes the major features of each plan—positive or negative. It must do so in a "manner calculated to be understood by the average plan participant," with nothing in the format (including type size or style) that might mislead participants.

Starting March 2, 1976, the summary plan description must be given to new employees within 90 days after becoming participants and to beneficiaries within 90 days after they start receiving benefits. For plans that were in effect on January 31, 1976, the summary plan description had to be given to participants and beneficiaries by May 30, 1976, and for plans established after January 31, 1976, the initial summary plan description must be given to participants within 120 days after establishment of the plan. New, complete summaries must be distributed at least every ten years (every five years if there have been material changes). The summary plan description must also be filed with the secretary of labor within the same time limits.

The summary plan description must be in permanent form and must be up-to-date regarding all aspects of the plan and the information required by ERISA. The summary plan description must contain the following information:

Plan name and type of plan (e.g., for pension plans: defined contribution, defined benefit; for welfare plans: hospitalization, disability).

The type of administration of the plan (e.g., contract administration, joint board of trustees).

The name (or position title) and address of the person designated as agent for the service of legal process.

The name, business address, and business telephone number of the administrator.

The name and address of the employer.

The name and/or title, and business address of each trustee.

The employer identification number assigned by the Internal Revenue Service to the plan sponsor and the plan number assigned by the plan sponsor.

A list of relevant collective bargaining agreements specifying the pertinent sections of those agreements, the names of the parties to each agreement and the expiration date of each agreement (plans maintained under more than ten collective bargaining agreements need not list agreements and sections as long as they state the general topics of the relevant provisions and list all parties to the agreements).

Plan requirements respecting eligibility for participation and benefits (e.g., age, service, normal retirement age).

A description of the provisions for nonforfeitable pension benefits.

Information about forfeiture of pension benefits, credited service, breaks in service, etc.

A description of any joint and survivor benefits and any action necessary to elect or reject them.

Circumstances that may result in disqualification, ineligibility, or denial or loss of benefits.

A statement of the extent to which a pension plan is insured by the Pension Benefit Guaranty Corporation, where more information about this insurance is available (usually from the administrator), and the name and address of the PBGC. Also, a notification must appear prominently on the first page of text (for plans where applicable) stating, "Certain benefits under this plan are insured by the Pension Benefit Guaranty Corporation. Further information can be found on page . . . of this booklet."

The source of contributions to the plan, the method by which the amount of contributions is calculated, and the identity of any organation through which benefits are provided.

A description and explanation of plan benefits.

The date of the end of the plan year and whether the records of the plan are kept on a calendar, policy or fiscal year basis.

The procedures to be followed in presenting claims for benefits under the plan and the remedies available under the plan for the redress of claims that are denied in whole or in part.

When different classes of participants are covered with different benefits under the same plan, prominent notice must appear on the first page of the text listing the various classes for whom different summary plan descriptions have been prepared.

All this information must be "written in a manner calculated to be understood by the average plan participant" and should be "sufficiently accurate and comprehensive" to inform participants and beneficiaries of their rights and obligations under each plan. The explanations provided by legal plan texts and insurance contracts ordinarily will not meet these standards. The Regulations recommend the use of simple sentences, clarifying examples, clear cross-references and a table of contents in the summary plan description. The use of type is important. Varying sizes and styles of type may not be used when they may mislead participants.

If a plan covers 500 or more people who are literate only in a language other than English, or if 50 percent or more of the participants working at "a distinct physical place of business" are literate only in a non-English language, the summary plan description must have a special feature. The booklet may still be written in English, but it must include a prominent notice in the familiar language offering assistance in understanding the plan. The procedures necessary to obtain this assistance should be fully explained in the notice. The assistance must be provided in the familiar language, but need be oral only.

Retired and terminated vested plan participants come under ERISA's definition of "participants." They must be automatically furnished copies of summary plan descriptions relating only to the plans under which they are covered unless they already have been given an easily understood plan booklet (containing all of the previously listed information) and they are sent a notice saying that a copy of the summary plan description (for the current plan) is available free on request, that the booklet already in their possession provides all ERISA-required information, and that ERISA gives them certain specific rights to plan information. Irrelevant plan amendments need not be communicated to retirees or terminated vested employees, although they are entitled to copies free on request. Amendments which may affect them, however, must be provided.

PLAN DESCRIPTION (EBS-1)

The plan description is Department of Labor Form EBS-1. This form must be filed with the secretary of labor within 120 days of the date a plan becomes subject to the provisions of ERISA. (Plans in effect on January 1, 1976 were given until May 30, 1976 to file the initial EBS-1.) In addition, a copy of the completed EBS-1 must be given to any participant who requests it in writing, and it is to be made available for any participant or beneficiary to examine in the "principal office of the administrator" as well as other convenient locations. An updated version of the EBS-1 may be required by the secretary of labor no more often than every five years. Included in the information required by EBS-1 are these items:

Identification of the plan sponsor (usually the employer).

Identification of the plan administrator (may also be the employer).

Formal name of the plan (e.g., Retirement Plan for Salaried Employees of the ABC Corporation).

Plan identification number (the IRS-assigned nine-digit number followed by the three-digit number assigned by the plan sponsor).

Ending date of the plan's fiscal year.

Agent for service of legal process.

Type of plan (e.g., defined benefit plan, defined contribution plan).

ANNUAL REPORT (FORM 5500)

The annual report Form 5500 comprises a yearly financial report on each covered pension and welfare plan. This form must be filed with the secretary of labor within 210 days after the close of each plan year beginning after December 31, 1974.[2] At the time it is filed, the annual report is to be made available to plan participants and beneficiaries for inhouse examination or within 30 days of written request.

The annual report is designed to require a complete disclosure of all financial information relevant to the operation of the plan. Thus, for example, it includes items such as a statement of assets and liabilities presented by category and valued at current value, changes in assets and liabilities during the year, a statement of receipts and disbursements, details with respect to transactions with parties-in-interest, a schedule of loans and leases in default or uncollectable, and information on certain "reportable transactions" (e.g., transactions involving in excess of 3 percent of the current value of plan assets).

Certain financial statements in the annual report will have to be certified by an independent qualified public accountant. Any actuarial reports included for defined benefit plans will have to be certified by an enrolled actuary. In addition, insurance companies and banks are required, within 120 days after the end of each plan year (unless another date is permitted by regulations), to furnish any information necessary for the plan administrator to complete the annual report.

There are partial exemptions for unfunded or insured welfare and pension plans, regardless of the number of participants. These plans do not have to complete the financial information sections of the form, nor need they engage an accountant for an audit or include an accountant's opinion. Plans with fewer than 100 participants will file a simplified Form 5500–C.

ANNUAL REPORT SUMMARY

The annual report summary encompasses those parts of Form 5500, including attached schedules, "necessary to fairly summarize the latest annual report." Because the annual report summary is made up of extracts from the annual report, the Department of Labor receives it as a part of Form 5500. The real purpose of the annual report summary, however, is to make information about each plan's annual financial status readily available to plan participants and beneficiaries. Therefore, the summary is to be sent to them automatically. This must be done with respect to each annual report summary within 210 days after the close of the plan year to which it applies. (The first annual report summary under ERISA is due with respect to the plan year beginning on or after January 1, 1976.)

---

[2] It must also be filed with the Internal Revenue Service. The time for filing with the Internal Revenue Service was originally set to be the 15th day of the fifth month following the end of the employer's tax year; this may be changed to be consistent with the due date for filing Form 5500 with the Labor Department.

OTHER DISCLOSURE ITEMS

As noted earlier, there are a number of other items which must be disclosed to participants and their beneficiaries and to the government. The following material briefly summarizes the requirements applicable to such other items.

Plan Amendments

When there is a "material modification" to the plan, a form must be filed with the secretary of labor describing the change. Under ERISA, appropriate portions of Form EBS–1 are to be used for this filing. The plan amendment form must be filed with the secretary of labor within 60 days after the amendment is adopted or occurs (but not before the full EBS–1 has been filed). When amendments are included in a summary plan description that is filed within 60 days after the amendments are adopted, no separate form need be filed. Once appropriate parts of EBS–1 are filed, they must be made available within 30 days to participants and beneficiaries who request them in writing or who wish to review them in a convenient location.

A plan amendment summary description, written in clear language, must also be distributed to all plan participants and beneficiaries. The plan amendment summary description should be a reasonable and adequate summary of any material modification in the terms of a plan or in the information required in the summary plan description. This description must be furnished to participants and beneficiaries within 210 days after the end of the plan year in which the change was adopted.

Plan Documents

ERISA describes plan documents as "the bargaining agreement, trust agreement, contract or other instruments under which the plan is established or operated." Plan participants and beneficiaries who request any or all of these documents are entitled to receive them within 30 days of making written request. Also, plan documents must be made available for review in the employer's principal offices or plants. The secretary of labor may request these documents at any time.

Benefits Statements for Terminating Employees

Each plan participant who terminates service and who has a vested right in his or her accrued plan benefits should receive a clear statement of these accrued benefits and the percentage that is vested (i.e., nonforfeitable). The statement should include the nature, amount, and form of the deferred vested benefit. Any participant who has a break in service of one year (i.e., a 12-month period during which the employee has not completed more than 500 hours of service) is also automatically entitled to receive a benefits statement. Title II of ERISA (which does not directly deal with disclosure) also appears to require that a statement be given to employees who terminate or incur a one-year break in service without a vested interest, thus clearly communicating the fact that any such individual is not entitled to receive benefits under the plan. As of the time this material was prepared, the time limit for furnishing such benefits statements had not been established; practical considerations, however, suggest that the terminating employee be given a benefits statement by the earliest possible date.

Personal Benefits Statement

Each plan participant or beneficiary may request in writing to be given a statement of the individual's own benefits under a pension, deferred profit sharing or thrift and savings plan. This statement must be supplied within 30 days of the written request, but no participant or beneficiary is entitled to receive more than one such statement in any 12-month period.

The statement should include the total benefits accrued and the portion, if any, that is vested (i.e., nonforfeitable) or, if benefits are not vested, the earliest date on which they will become vested. If an employer furnishes annual statements to individual employees, and if such statements include the above information, it is expected that such a practice will satisfy this requirement of ERISA.

Written Explanation of Claims Denial

ERISA requires that every employee benefit plan "establish and maintain a reasonable claims procedure," which is to be set forth in the summary plan description and in EBS–1. Anyone denied a claim under any plan is entitled to a written statement giving the reasons for the denial. This explanation should be a clear, comprehensible statement of the specific reasons for the denial of the claim. The explanation also must include a description of any material or information necessary for the claimant to improve the claim and the reasons why this additional material is needed. Also in the explanation should be a full description of the plan's appeal procedure for denied claims. The claimant must be given at least 60 days thereafter to appeal the claim.

Plan Termination Report

A plan termination report is required to be filed for any pension, profit sharing, or thrift and savings plan that is winding up its affairs, no matter how many participants remain in the plan. Termination reports on welfare plans that are winding up their affairs may be required at the discretion of the secretary of labor. The secretary of labor receives the original of the termination report; a copy must also be filed with the Pension Benefit Guaranty Corporation. Employees must be given written notice as to the date notice was filed with the PBGC and the proposed date of plan termination. This notice may be transmitted by posting in locations normally used for posting employee notices or, if employees are unionized, by delivering notice to the union representative. Any plan participant or beneficiary is entitled to be sent a copy within 30 days of making written request. The plan termination report is to be filed with the annual report for the year in which the plan is terminated. Thus, it is due within 210 days after the close of such plan year.

ENFORCEMENT

ERISA provides for stronger enforcement than did the Welfare and Pension Plans Disclosure Act, with greater penalties for violation. Among the penalties are these:

If a plan administrator does not fill a participant's or beneficiary's written request within 30 days, the plan administrator may be personally liable to the individual who made the request for a fine of up to $100 per day.

Willful violation of any of the reporting and disclosure provisions may incur a criminal penalty of up to a $5,000 fine and/or one year in prison for an individual, and up to a $100,000 fine for a corporation.

Civil actions may be brought against a plan administrator by participants or beneficiaries to obtain information to which they are entitled under their plan, to enforce their rights under their plan, or to clarify their rights to future benefits under their plan.

Civil action may also be brought by the secretary of labor, by a participant, beneficiary, or by another fiduciary against an individual who breaches his or her fiduciary duty.

It is expected that random audits will be continually performed, and that a team of investigators will follow up on all discrepancies found and all complaints filed by plan participants or beneficiaries. Records are now required to be kept for a period of six years after the documents are due for filing, even for those plans that are exempt from filing.

14

Survivor Income Benefits

The majority of employers in the United States provide some form of death benefit for the surviving dependents of an employee.[1] Most commonly, this death benefit is provided by means of group term life insurance (sometimes supplemented by accidental death insurance) An employee also may be entitled to death benefits under his or her employer's retirement or profit sharing plan. Death benefits are sometimes provided in other forms, such as supplemental cash payments or the use of so-called split dollar insurance plans. Generally speaking, these death benefits are paid in a lump sum to the beneficiary designated by the employee. Although the option to have the proceeds payable in installments usually is available, it is seldom elected.

In recent years, interest has been growing in "survivor" death benefit plans. These plans are distinguishable from traditional employer-sponsored death benefit plans in that a benefit is payable only to certain specified dependents of the employee and only if these dependents survive the employee. Moreover, the benefit is payable in installments and, as a rule, only for the period that the dependency status continues to exist. A limited form of survivor benefit (to spouses only and under certain conditions) is now mandated by ERISA.

The purpose of this chapter is to review the factors that have led to the growth of these survivor benefit plans, their general features, and the ways in which they can be funded. The tax implications of these benefits also are discussed. Before doing so, however, it is desirable to

---

[1] The material in this chapter originally appeared as an article in *The Journal of Risk and Insurance,* vol. 37, no. 3, September 1970.

review the extent to which employer-provided death benefits are now provided in the United States.

EMPLOYER-PROVIDED DEATH BENEFITS

The major portion of these death benefits consists of benefits payable under group life insurance policies. At the end of 1974, group life insurance coverage in force in the United States amounted to $827.6 billion, the amount of new group life insurance written during 1974 having amounted to $114.7 billion. This group insurance was provided through 9.4 million group life certificates issued under 359,000 master policies. Not all of this insurance, of course, represents insurance issued with respect to employer-employee groups. Based upon a survey completed in 1973, however, it is reasonable to estimate that employer-employee groups accounted for approximately 89 percent of this total.[2]

Many factors have contributed to the growth of group life insurance since the early 1900s. It is, of course, low-cost death benefit protection. Employers have found this coverage to be an effective way of attracting and retaining employees. It also has proved a most effective way of compensating highly paid individuals. Group life insurance also enjoys certain tax advantages.[3] Another reason for the growth of group life insurance is that this form of benefit has been the subject of collective bargaining. Also, since a great deal of group life insurance in force is related to the earnings of covered employees, the inflationary trends experienced in recent years have brought about automatic increases in the amounts of group life insurance in force.

Although group life insurance is a low-cost form of protection for each individual, the aggregate cost involved in providing this benefit is sizable. An employer often finds that its contributions for group life insurance amount to 1 or 2 percent of annual payroll cost.

While a few group life insurance plans provide death benefits on the basis of a flat amount for each employee, or benefits whose amount is related to the employee's length of service, as was the practice in early years, the vast majority of these plans today provide benefits that are related to the employee's earnings or position. While the amount provided varies from employer to employer, group life insurance death benefits frequently range from one and a half to two times the employee's

---

[2] *Life Insurance Fact Book* (New York: Institute of Life Insurance, 1975).

[3] Generally speaking, employer contributions to these plans represent a tax deductible business expense, and unless the total amount of employer-provided insurance exceeds a stipulated amount, the employee does not have to report the employer's contribution as additional income. The stipulated amount of insurance is $50,000 or, if less, the maximum amount of group life insurance that can be issued for the employee under applicable state law. I.R.C. 79.

annual earnings. Plans providing as much as three or four times annual earnings are not uncommon.

The earnings-related schedule of benefits has been attractive because it accomplishes several things. From the employee's viewpoint, earnings are a reasonable way to measure his or her "human life value" and, presumably, the needs of his or her dependents. From the employer's viewpoint, the employee's worth to the organization can be measured by the employee's earnings rate; therefore, it is reasonable to measure the employer's obligation to the employee's dependents in the same fashion.

While in many cases the earnings-related approach to providing group life insurance benefits has worked out well, there has been growing recognition that plans of this type do not effectively meet either employer objectives or the needs of surviving dependents of employees. Criticisms of these plans include the following:

1. The death benefit, since it is related to earnings, will often fill a dependent's needs for only a limited period of time. In many cases too little coverage is provided.

2. The death benefit is provided regardless of the beneficiary's needs. For example, the beneficiary may not, in fact, be dependent upon the employee, or the beneficiary may be someone for whom the employer feels limited or no responsibility.

3. The availability of a large single sum of money may result in a surviving dependent living well beyond his or her means for a short period of time and, thereafter, having insufficient funds to continue to live in the manner to which he or she had become accustomed.

4. Normally, the maximum need to provide survivor's benefits exists between ages 30 and 60, the time when it is most likely there will be dependent children. However, earnings-related death benefits usually are low for younger employees and generally reach their maximum only when the employee is nearing retirement.

As a broad observation, it might be said that many group life insurance plans have been designed without serious consideration of the employer's philosophy and objectives in establishing and maintaining such a plan. Too often, the design of a plan follows patterns set in a particular industry or on a local basis. Generally, the objectives of a death benefit program, from an employer's viewpoint, are to provide cash for last illness and burial expenses, as well as some measure of replacement income for the employee's dependents.

Assuming the existence of an adequate medical expense program, a lump-sum death benefit of $2,000 to $5,000 usually is sufficient to cover last illness and burial expenses. Providing death benefits in much greater amounts than these for employees without surviving dependents could be considered unnecessary by some employers. For this reason, a program that provides a death benefit only to the extent that the employee leaves a surviving dependent (and only while that survivor remains in a dependency status) has proved to be of interest to many employers.

Another reason for the growing interest in survivor benefits is that union pressure for these benefits has increased considerably, particularly since the United Auto Workers succeeded in including these death benefits in the 1964 agreements with the auto industry and in liberalizing them in succeeding negotiations. Also, the increased internationalization of American business has made more business executives aware of survivor benefits provided under plans developed in foreign countries. For example, it is quite common for plans in West Germany, Belgium, the Netherlands, and Switzerland to provide widows' pensions of 60 to 65 percent of an employee's projected pension at retirement, plus supplemental orphan's benefits. A further reason for the developing interest in survivor income benefits is that these benefits exist under the Social Security Act and have been liberalized periodically; this has focused increased public attention on this area. Also, it seems logical to provide some income continuance for an employee's family upon death, since provision is often made for the employee's income continuance needs in the event of disability or old-age retirement. Finally, ERISA requires optional preretirement and mandatory postretirement benefits for spouses of deceased employees. Although ERISA permits the employee to be charged with the cost of such benefits, it is anticipated that many employers will assume the cost of at least the preretirement benefit, thus making this portion of the coverage automatic for all eligible employees.

FORM OF SURVIVOR BENEFITS

Survivor benefits, as presently provided in the United States, usually take one of the following forms:

1. Spouse or dependent spouse benefits payable under the employer's retirement plan.
2. "Bridge" group life insurance benefits (the UAW approach), which typically provide a monthly benefit to a spouse age 50 or older (at the time of the employee's death) until the spouse reaches age 60 or 62, with benefits not payable after remarriage or if the spouse is receiving social security benefits.

DESIGN CONSIDERATIONS

Employee Eligibility

Survivor income protection can be provided for active or retired employees, or for both groups. When provided before retirement, the coverage frequently has been limited to employees who satisfy an age (usually 50, 55, or 60) and a service (usually 10 or 15 years) requirement, but such requirements are not related to employee needs. This restricted eligibility most often is found when survivor benefits are provided under the employer's retirement plan and where eligibility for this benefit is related to the employee's eligibility for early retirement. ERISA requires that an employee who is eligible for early retirement (and is within ten years of normal retirement date), must have the option of electing a preretirement spouse benefit. ERISA also requires that the normal form for the payment of benefits to a married employee, unless otherwise elevated, be a spouse benefit.

Recently, however, there has been increasing recognition of the needs of younger employees and the comparatively low cost of coverage at these ages. As a result, there has been considerable liberalization of eligibility requirements for this benefit. Table 14–1 indicates the approximate

TABLE 14–1
Life Insurance Required to Purchase Widow's Life
Annuity

Age of Widow	Years' Pay Required to Purchase Annuity Equal to Percentages of Final Pay		
	25%	*35%*	*50%*
45	4.1	5.7	8.2
50	3.8	5.4	7.7
55	3.6	5.0	7.1
60	3.2	4.5	6.5
65	2.9	4.0	5.8
70	2.5	3.5	5.0

amount of insurance that would be needed to provide a widow with a life annuity equal to the amounts shown. As this table indicates, life insurance equal to 4.1 times the employee's annual pay would be needed to provide a widow, age 45, with a life annuity equal to 25 percent of the employee's pay. This amount decreases so that only 3.2 years' pay is needed to provide the same amount to a widow age 60.

Eligible Dependents

Eligible dependents may be classified as an employee's spouse, dependent spouse, dependent children, and sometimes dependent parents.[4] Ini-

---

[4] The dependent spouse classification includes both widows and widowers. A frequently used definition of dependent spouse is that the spouse's income in the year preceding the employee's death must have been less than 50 percent of their combined income for that year.

tially, many survivor income plans paid benefits solely to widows, but the Equal Employment Opportunity Commission has taken the position that such benefits constitute discrimination under Section VII of the Civil Rights Act. In view of this interpretation, most employers with plans providing widow's benefits have converted these to spouse or dependent spouse benefits.

Generally, the spouse benefit is not payable unless the employee was living with the spouse at the time of death and (in some cases) had been married for at least a short period of time such as one, two, or three years prior to death. The ERISA-required pre- and postretirement spouse benefits may be structured to require that the participant have been married for at least one year. Coverage for dependent children is still fairly uncommon, but is growing in popularity in the United States. Dependent parents are almost never covered in plans in the United States.

Amount of Income

The amount of income payable under survivor benefit plans may be determined in various ways.

Percentage of Pay. Survivor income protection for active employees may be equal to a percentage of the employee's pay (or average pay) immediately preceding death. The percentage of pay provided varies from a minimum of 10 to 15 percent to a maximum usually in the range of 40 to 50 percent. When provided, benefits for dependent children usually are in the 5 to 15 percent of pay range.

Percentage of Projected Pension. Survivor income coverage is sometimes based on the pension the employee would have received had he or she continued in employment at his or her current rate of pay until retirement.

Percentage of Accrued Pension. The most common pension benefit approach to the provision of survivor income bases such income on a percentage (e.g., 50 or 60 percent) of the employee's accrued pension to date of death. The percentage applies either to the employee's full accrued pension credit or to such credit adjusted by the appropriate early retirement factor for the employee's age at date of death. This, of course, results in low protection for younger employees. The minimum amount payable under an ERISA-required benefit, pre- or postretirement, is 50 percent of the participant's actuarially reduced pension.

Flat Dollar Benefit. The UAW approach to survivor income protection provides payment of a fixed dollar amount each month to the eligible survivor of any employee. Such fixed amounts provide a decreasing degree of relative protection as the employee's income increases.

Duration of Income

A survivor income plan may be designed to provide transition income to enable the survivors to adjust to the loss of the employee's income or to replace, at least in part, the income the employee would otherwise have earned had he or she remained alive. Transition income may be paid for comparatively short periods such as two, three, or four years, or for as long as 15 or 20 years. Lifetime benefits may be provided or income may be paid until age 65 or the survivor's eligibility for social security benefits. Payments often are discontinued if the survivor remarries. A variation of the remarriage provision is to continue payments for a minimum period (e.g., ten years) regardless of whether or not the spouse remarries, but to provide for payments beyond this period only if the spouse has not remarried and only for as long as the spouse does not remarry. Benefits for a dependent child typically are paid until the child reaches age 18 or 21 (sometimes until age 23 in the case of full-time students). A child's benefits may be discontinued upon marriage before reaching the stated age discontinuance date. ERISA-required benefits are payable for the lifetime of the surviving spouse and are not terminated if the spouse remarries.

To help control costs, when income is provided for a spouse's lifetime, the benefit payable frequently is reduced if the spouse is more than three to five years younger than the employee. For example, the monthly income benefit might be reduced by 3 percent for each year by which the spouse is more than five years younger than the employee. This type of reduction also is permitted in an ERISA-required benefit.

FUNDING CONSIDERATIONS

Current Disbursement and Advance Funding

An employer can provide survivor income benefits on a current disbursement basis or an advance-funded basis. The advantages and disadvantages of each approach are essentially the same as they are for the funding of retirement plans.

A major advantage of providing survivor income benefits on a current disbursement basis is the fact that initial outlays under this approach will be relatively low. This, in turn, means that more funds can be retained by the employer for the business. Also, the after-tax return on funds retained in the business might be greater than the net return that would be realized on funds held in reserve under an advance-funded survivor income plan. This is particularly so if the survivor income plan is funded under a group life insurance policy, since practically all of the reserves under such a policy, at this time, must be invested in fixed-income investments.[5]

Another advantage realized under the current disbursement approach is that the employer may be selective, not only in terms of who is covered under the plan, but in terms of the amount of benefit received. This is not generally the case under an advance-funded survivor income plan if it is funded under the employer's retirement plan, which must meet the nondiscriminatory requirements of the Internal Revenue Code, or under an insurance policy in which the insurance company will insist on at least some reasonable classifications that are designed to prevent antiselection. From the employee's viewpoint, the current disbursement approach has the possible advantage that since initial outlays are relatively low, more employers might be encouraged to establish these plans than would be the case if the plan were funded in advance.

The disadvantages of the current disbursement approach include the following:

1. Annual costs, although starting at a relatively low level, tend to increase rather sharply as more and more beneficiaries are added to the disbursement rolls.
2. The employer has no financial flexibility under this approach. Basically, the employer cannot suspend or discontinue contributions without suspending or discontinuing benefits to the same extent.
3. Since there are no reserves that can earn investment income, this method results in the largest outlay of contributions by the employer.
4. It is virtually impossible to require employee contributions under the current disbursement method.
5. From the employee's viewpoint, this method does not create any significant degree of benefit security.

The advantages and disadvantages of advance-funding survivor income benefits are implied in the previous discussion. Briefly, the advantages of advance funding are as follows: (1) This method ultimately requires the lowest employer contribution, since reserves will earn investment income which, in turn, will provide a portion of the plan benefit. (2) This method allows the employer to spread the cost of the benefit fairly evenly throughout the lifetime of the plan. (3) The relatively even distribution of outlays produces a more equitable charge against the employer's profits over the years. (4) Advance funding creates greater

---

[5] This would be the case if the income payable to the survivor is fixed in amount and, as a result, reserves for the benefit are part of the insurer's general portfolio. If a variable benefit could be provided under such a plan, reserves for the variable portion of the benefit would be invested in equities. The combination of variable benefits with survivor's income coverage would produce a program of real value to many employers and employees and is receiving consideration by the life insurance industry.

flexibility for the employer, since the accumulation of assets or reserves permits the suspension of contributions in periods of financial stress. (5) Employee contributions may be required in an advance-funded plan, thus reducing the overall employer cost of providing benefits. (6) A greater degree of benefit security for employees is achieved under advance funding.

A major disadvantage of advance funding is that the employer is required to make higher contributions during the early years of the plan than would be the case under the current disbursement approach. These funds will be withdrawn from the business, and the net return on invested assets under the survivor income plan might be lower than the after-tax income that the employer could realize on these funds if retained in the business. Also, advance funding frequently carries with it the requirement that the plan be reasonably nondiscriminatory in terms of who is covered and the levels of their benefits.

Funding Instruments

If survivor income benefits are advance-funded, the general approaches followed are to fund these benefits under the employer's retirement plan, under a special group life insurance contract, or under a combination of both.[6]

Several basic nontax arguments are advanced in favor of the retirement plan funding approach. First, the cost to provide survivor's income under a retirement plan should be less than under group life insurance, since investment earnings on funds held under qualified retirement plans tend to be higher due to more aggressive investment policies. Second, group life retention (insurer expense) charges are largely avoided. Third, it is easier to relate a survivor's benefit to an employee pension credit if both benefits are provided under a pension plan. Fourth, these plans are not subject to the myriad of state insurance laws which regulate group life insurance contracts.[7]

In recent years, a number of insurance companies have developed a variation of the so-called standard group term life insurance contract for the express purpose of providing survivor benefits. Frequently, however, this special coverage is available only as a rider to a basic group life insurance contract. This coverage is distinguished from standard group term life insurance in several ways. A significant difference is that,

---

[6] A Section 501(c)(9) trust also may be used to advance fund survivor income benefits. Such a trust is one that is exempt from tax under Section 501(c)(9) of the Internal Revenue Code, and may provide medical and disability income benefits, as well as death benefits.

[7] Most of these arguments also apply in favor of funding death benefits under a Section 501(c)(9) trust.

in keeping with the concept of survivor income coverage, a benefit is payable only if an eligible dependent survives the employee. A second difference is that the benefit is payable only in installments and only for so long as the dependency status exists within the terms of the contract. Thus, the benefit terminates with the death of the surviving dependent, and may terminate upon remarriage. Another difference is that the contract may not contain a conversion privilege with respect to the amount of survivor income coverage provided. Finally, a number of state insurance departments have taken the position that this coverage, since it is not group term life insurance in the accepted sense, is not subject to the statutory maximum limitation on the amount of group life insurance that can otherwise be provided. While these plans are still relatively new, it appears that when survivor income benefits are being provided under group life insurance, eligibility is more liberal than is the case for retirement plans. Younger employees generally are covered, and benefits frequently are provided for dependent children. While the benefit might be related to the employee's projected pension, more often it is related to current salary. It would appear, at this time, that lifetime benefits for surviving dependents are not frequently found when funded by means of group life insurance. Rather, the benefit tends to be payable for a fixed period of time, such as a stipulated number of years or until the beneficiary reaches some stated age. Sometimes the benefit is payable until the time the employee would have attained some stated age—e.g., age 65.

One of the basic nontax arguments advanced in favor of utilizing life insurance for providing survivor income benefits is that group life insurance is not subject to various limitations of the Internal Revenue Code which are imposed on qualified retirement plans, such as the prohibition against discrimination in favor of higher paid employees, rules for incidental benefits, and integration limits. Another argument is that in most situations it is simpler to require employee contributions for this coverage if it is provided under an insurance contract. Also, if a survivor's income is offset by the income value of a portion or all of the employee's regular group life insurance benefit, it is easier to provide both benefits under one integrated plan. Perhaps an even more significant consideration is that the risk involved in providing survivors' income is essentially the same as that for basic group life insurance; thus, it is argued that the benefits should be funded in the same way.

When group life insurance is utilized to provide this form of benefit, it is important to make sure that there are no problems in the state involved with respect to maximum limits. As indicated earlier, many insurance departments have taken the position that this form of coverage is not subject to the normal maximums that apply to group term life insurance. Since the value of survivor income coverage can be relatively substantial when related to annual earnings, it is most important that this particular aspect be clarified for any given situation.

There may be a similar problem in determining eligibility for this coverage. Most state insurance laws require that eligibility for group term life insurance be based solely on "conditions of employment." A program which bases eligibility on the existence of dependents will not meet this particular requirement if the state insurance department insists that survivor income coverage is a form of group term life insurance. However, this problem is alleviated when the survivor income coverage is added to a layer of basic group life insurance.

TAX CONSIDERATIONS

The preceding material has not taken into account the tax implications of survivor income benefits. These, of course, could influence an employer who is deciding between a retirement plan and life insurance as a means of providing this benefit. On balance, these tax considerations appear more favorable for the majority of employees when life insurance is utilized. The following is a brief summary of the major tax considerations involved.

Income Tax Liability of Employee While Alive

If survivor income benefits are provided under a qualified retirement plan, the employee will have no income tax liability with respect to this benefit while alive.[8] If the benefit is being provided under a group insurance contract, some part of the cost of this benefit might have to be included in the employee's taxable income. Here, the situation depends on whether the employee is actively employed or retired and whether or not the employee makes contributions. During active employment, the employee would be required to include, as taxable income each year, the cost of the insurance in excess of $50,000 or the applicable state limit, if less. If the employee contributes to the cost of this coverage, the foregoing would apply only to the coverage provided by the employer.

There appears to be some disagreement as to exactly how much the employee would have to include in gross income. The majority of insurance companies seem to feel that the rates set forth in Section 79 of the Internal Revenue Code would apply with respect to the value of insurance in excess of $50,000. Other viewpoints are that the actual premium rates must be used to determine the amount to be included as income, or that the PS 58 costs (the insurance costs used to determine taxable income under individual policy pension plans) would be applicable. During the period of actual retirement, no cost of insurance would

---

[8] The same result would also appear to apply to death benefits provided under a Section 501(c)(9) trust.

have to be included by the employee as taxable income. Overall, it would appear that even though some additional tax liability might result for an employee if insurance is used, the result is not burdensome.

Taxation of Payments to Survivor

Generally speaking, payments made to a survivor under a qualified retirement plan that are attributable to employer contributions are considered as taxable income. These payments are taxed under the annuity rules, and the survivor is permitted to consider up to $5,000 as an investment in the contract to the extent that the employee's rights to this amount were forfeitable.[9]

Investment in the contract also would include any employee contributions. The normal rule is to determine the ratio of this investment in the contract to the survivor's expected return (depending upon the survivor's life expectancy and the expected total payments). This establishes the portion of each payment that would be recovered free of income tax; the balance would be taxable. However, if the survivor would receive more than the investment in the contract during the first three years, all payments would be excluded until this amount had been recovered; thereafter, all payments would be taxable.[10] The net result is that a significant portion of the payments to a survivor under a qualified retirement plan will be taxable as income.

The annuity rule treatment also would apply to benefits payable under a group insurance contract. However, the survivor's investment in the contract would be considered as the present value of the expected payments. Thus, the ratio of this present value to the total of the expected payments would be applied to each payment to determine the amount received income tax-free. While the balance of each payment would be taxable as income, the survivor should be entitled to a $1,000-a-year exemption (if the survivor is a spouse), since the proceeds would appear to qualify as insurance proceeds. Under this approach, therefore, most of the income payments should escape income taxation.[11]

Estate Tax Considerations

The value of a survivor benefit, if provided under a retirement plan, is free of federal estate tax to the extent that it is attributable to employer

---

[9] I.R.C. 72; 101(b).

[10] I.R.C. 72(d).

[11] Just how the benefit payable to the survivor under a Section 501(c)(9) trust would be taxed is not clear. Some authorities claim that the benefit should be treated as though it were life insurance; others feel that the benefit should be taxable as income to the survivor. The Internal Revenue Service has not yet taken a public and official position on this issue, thus rendering the use of a Section 501(c)(9) trust, of and by itself, somewhat questionable for a death benefit plan.

contributions. The situation is not completely clear where the benefit is provided by a group insurance coverage. If the plan is noncontributory, it could be argued the employee has no rights of ownership in this coverage (i.e., no right to terminate the coverage or change the beneficiary). Accordingly, it would seem logical that in this situation, the proceeds should not be included in the employee's estate.[12] If the employee is considered to have any rights of ownership (e.g., the right to terminate coverage by ceasing to make contributions under a contributory plan), it would seem that an effective assignment of his or her rights could result in the proceeds being excluded from the employee's estate.

THE FUTURE

It is reasonable to assume that survivor income plans, which provide more coverage in the aggregate than typical group life insurance plans, will involve annual costs averaging 2 to 3 percent of payroll. Such cost levels might tend to slow the growth of these plans. Nevertheless, survivor income plans may become more prevalent in the future, as employers seek to provide an adequate and logical program of death benefits for their employees. Accepting the fact that providing some form of death benefit is a desirable goal for most employers, the survivor income plan is a method through which the employer can utilize corporate funds in a highly efficient manner in providing benefits where they are needed most. The fact that ERISA requires both optional and mandatory protection of an employee's spouse could create a major impetus for this type of benefit.

Of course, some potential problems are associated with survivor income plans. One of these is that in states where this form of insurance is not considered to be group life insurance, employees might not be protected by a conversion privilege when they terminate employment.

Another potential problem of survivor benefit coverage is that the total value of the benefit to an employee can be quite substantial. The employee who places great reliance on this benefit may be faced with a major disruption in his or her own estate plan when changing jobs and going to work for an employer with less liberal benefits.

Overall, however, survivor benefits are likely to become a major development in employee benefit planning, and they will likely produce substantial increases in income protection via private plans.

---

[12] *Estate of James H. Lumpkin, Jr., Deceased, Christine T. Hamilton, Executrix* v. *Commissioner of Internal Revenue,* 56 TCxx, No. 63, Dkt. No. 1715–68, July 19, 1971.

15

Profit Sharing Plans

Profit sharing plans constitute an important component in the overall structure of fringe benefit programs in the United States. ERISA's requirements as to vesting, minimum funding and employer liabilities for plan terminations suggest that there may be growing interest in the money-purchase or individual account types of retirement programs in the future. If this proves to be the case, profit sharing and thrift plans would have considerable appeal, since they embody the individual account concept without imposing on employers any fixed commitment to provide any specific level of benefits. Thus, one might expect to see greater use of profit sharing plans in lieu of pension plans, or of a basic pension benefit plus a supplemental savings or profit sharing program.

The purpose of this chapter is to discuss the basic features of qualified profit sharing plans. Consideration also will be given to the way in which profit sharing funds might be invested in insurance contracts.

DEFINITION OF PROFIT SHARING

Many definitions of profit sharing have been suggested.[1] One expert in this area defines profit sharing as a plan in which the company's contributions are based upon business profits, regardless of whether the benefit payments are made in cash, are deferred, or are a combination of the two.[2] This definition suggests three basic types of profit sharing plans, which may be defined as follows:[3] (1) current (cash)—profits are paid

---

[1] For a discussion of these definitions, see B. L. Metzger, *Profit Sharing in Perspective* (Evanston, Ill.: Profit Sharing Research Foundation, 1964), p. 1.

[2] Ibid.

[3] Ibid., p. 2.

directly to employees in cash, check, or stock as soon as profits are determined (for example, monthly, quarterly, semiannually, or annually); (2) deferred—profits are credited to employee accounts to be paid at retirement or other stated dates or circumstances (for example, disability, death, severance, or under withdrawal provisions); and (3) combination—part of the profit is paid out currently in cash and part is deferred; this can take place under one plan with both current and deferred features, or under two separate plans, one cash and the other deferred, covering, by and large, the same employee groups.[4]

Since this chapter is concerned with qualified plans, let us now turn to a consideration of the definition of a profit sharing plan as set forth in federal income tax regulations:

> A profit sharing plan is a plan established and maintained by an employer to provide for the participation in his profits by his employees or their beneficiaries. The plan must provide a definite predetermined formula for allocating the contributions made to the plan among the participants and for distributing the funds accumulated under the plan after a fixed number of years, the attainment of a stated age, or upon the prior occurrence of some event such as layoff, illness, disability, retirement, death, or severance of employment.[5]

Qualification of profit sharing plans for tax exemption under Section 401 of the Internal Revenue Code, then, is restricted to deferred or combination type plans. Current or cash profit sharing plans, therefore, are not treated in this chapter.

QUALIFICATION REQUIREMENTS

The qualification requirements for profit sharing plans are, for the most part, identical to those applicable to pension plans, a detailed discussion of which can be found in Chapter 4. However, it is appropriate in this chapter to discuss these requirements in terms of their application specifically to profit sharing plans.

Coverage Requirements

To qualify, a profit sharing plan must be for the exclusive benefit of employees or their beneficiaries. Therefore, a plan will not qualify if

---

[4] If any plan adopted after June 27, 1974 permits an employee to *elect* to receive part of his or her compensation in alternate forms, one of which is currently taxable, the employee will be in constructive receipt of the amount of compensation involved. Plans of this type that were in effect on June 27, 1974 will not be affected by this provision of ERISA prior to January 1, 1977. At that time, the Internal Revenue Service will have the authority to issue regulations that will treat all plans in the same fashion.

[5] Reg. 1.40–1(b) (1) (ii).

the coverage requirements result in discrimination in favor of officers, stockholders, or highly compensated employees. Restriction of coverage by type of employment (for example, salaried employees, hourly employees, sales representatives) is permitted, provided that such coverage requirements do not result in the prohibited discrimination.

Most profit sharing plans exclude seasonal and part-time employees. Relatively few plans impose a minimum age requirement, but practically all profit sharing plans specify a service requirement as a condition for participation in the plan. ERISA permits the use of a minimum age of up to 25 and a service requirement of up to one year (three years if the plan provides for full and immediate vesting). Maximum age requirements, often found in pension plans, cannot be employed under profit sharing plans. Lastly, minimum compensation requirements as a condition for participation are seldom found in profit sharing plans.

Apart from the requirements of ERISA, eligibility requirements under profit sharing plans generally tend to be less restrictive than those usually found under pension plans. There are several possible explanations for this fact. First of all, profit sharing plans often are established to provide a direct incentive for employees to increase output and reduce operating costs. If this is the primary objective of the plan, it is only logical that few restrictions on participation be imposed. Second, if the employer is establishing the plan primarily for personal tax reasons, liberal eligibility requirements may produce relatively favorable results for the owners of the business. Since the nonvested accumulations of terminating employees are reallocated among remaining participants, the employer may be less concerned about the scope of coverage under the plan. Third, the cost problem of funding a defined benefit for an older entrant under a pension plan is nonexistent in the case of a profit sharing plan. Since a participant under a profit sharing plan is never entitled to any more than the accumulations credited to his or her account, there is no need to impose a maximum age requirement. Lastly, as will be seen, few profit sharing plans are integrated with social security benefits because of limitations imposed on this type of plan under federal tax law.

Contribution Requirements

The Internal Revenue Code does not require, as a condition for qualification, that a profit sharing plan include a definite predetermined contribution formula. However, the regulations require that "substantial and recurring" contributions must be made out of profits if the requirement of plan permanency is to be met.

Contributions under a profit sharing plan, then, may be made on a discretionary basis (for example, as determined annually by the board of directors of the company) or in accordance with a definite predetermined formula. The discretionary approach offers the advantage of contribution flexibility. The board of directors can adjust contributions in view of the firm's current financial position and capital needs. Also, the discretionary basis precludes the possibility that contribution payments will exceed the maximum amount currently deductible for federal income tax purposes (to be discussed later in this chapter). If the amount of contribution is discretionary, the plan often imposes certain minimums and maximums. For example, the plan may provide that "contributions cannot exceed 15 percent of profits, but it is discretionary up to that limit" or "10 to 30 percent of profits—percentage to be determined by board of directors" or "discretionary, but approximately 25 percent of profits before taxes."[6]

There are advantages in using a definite predetermined formula. A definite formula promotes increased employee morale and feelings of security. Without a definite formula, employees may feel that they cannot count on a share of what they have helped to produce. Also, the Wage-Hour Division of the Department of Labor requires a definite formula if a company wants to exclude its contributions from regular pay rates in computing overtime. In other words, failure to use a definite formula may result in the payment of extra overtime.[7]

Whether a definite formula or a discretionary contribution approach is to be used, management must still determine the extent to which employees are to share in the firm's profits. In arriving at this decision, management must take into account such factors as the objectives of the plan, the nature of the firm's business, the pattern of profits, and the age and sex composition of the employee group. Obviously, a good deal more thought must be given to this matter if a definite contribution formula is used.

The contribution commitment under definite formula plans generally is expressed as a fixed percentage or a sliding scale of percentages of profits. The specified percentages usually are applied to profits before taxes, although the base of after-tax profits also is permitted. The sliding scale formulas provide for higher percentage contributions for higher levels of profits. A percentage of compensation formula also can be used, if the plan imposes conditions pertaining to levels of profits. Without this condition, a percentage of compensation plan would probably be classified as a defined contribution (money-purchase) pension plan rather than a profit sharing plan.

---

[6] Metzer, *Profit Sharing in Perspective,* p. 47.

[7] The absence of a definite formula will not automatically produce this result as, for example, in a plan that allocates the employer's contribution on a basis that takes overtime into account or in a plan that provides full and immediate vesting. In these situations, the company may exclude its contributions when calculating overtime rates even though a definite formula is not used.

Whether a definite formula or discretionary basis is used, the plan usually specifies some limitation on the amount of annual contribution payable. One reason for this is to assure stockholders of a minimum rate of return on capital. Limitations on contribution payments can be expressed in several different ways. For example, the plan may provide that no contribution will be made in years in which dividend payments are less than a specified amount, or unless aggregate profits exceed a stated amount, or if profits are less than a given percentage of the firm's capital funds. Many plans also impose the limitation that contributions in any one year cannot exceed the maximum amount deductible for federal income tax purposes.

Employee Contributions

It is conceptually illogical to require employee contributions under profit sharing plans. Furthermore, in those plans that require employee contributions, the employer's contribution is based on the amount of the employee's contribution, subject to the requirement that there must be profits. For these reasons, contributory plans are generally referred to as thrift or savings plans to distinguish them from the traditional profit sharing plans. For a complete discussion of thrift plans, see Chapter 16.

Contribution Allocation Formula

It was noted above that the Internal Revenue Service does not require that the plan include a definite *contribution* formula as a condition for qualification. However, it is necessary that the plan include a definite *allocation* formula to become qualified. Since contributions to the plan generally are based on profits, a method or formula is needed to determine the amount to be credited to each participant's account.

The employer must decide the basis upon which the contributions to the plan are to be divided among the various participants. The allocation of contributions to the account of each participant usually is made on the basis of compensation, or a combination of compensation and service. If compensation is used, then allocations are made on the basis of the proportion of each participant's compensation to the total compensation of all participants. For example, if employee A earns $10,000 a year and the total annual compensation for all participants is $200,000, A will be credited with 5 percent of the employer's total annual contributions. Under a formula which reflects both compensation and service, a unit of credit might, for example, be given for each year of service and an additional unit for each $100 of compensation. With 20 years of service, employee A would have 20 units for service and 100 units for compensation of $10,000 a year. Employee A's share of contributions will be determined, therefore, by the fraction of 120 over the total number of units similarly calculated for all participants.

The Internal Revenue Service requires a definite allocation formula in qualified plans so that it may determine whether contributions are shared in a nondiscriminatory manner. In general, allocations based on compensation meet the test of nondiscrimination. However, introduction of years of service into the formula may produce discrimination, in view of the fact that employees included in the prohibited group often have long periods of service with the firm. If application of the allocation formula indicates that discrimination might result, the Internal Revenue Service may require modification of the formula before issuing an approval letter. The most popular allocation formulas are those based on compensation, although many plans use a combination of compensation and years of service.

Lest there be any confusion, the allocation formula is used to determine the employee's share of contributions for accounting or record-keeping purposes. The contribution dollars are not segregated on behalf of each participant. Contributions are received, administered, and invested by the trustee as one common fund. The balance in each participant's account represents the participant's share at that moment of the assets of the fund. Whether the participant is currently entitled to all or a part of the money credited to his or her account depends upon the provisions of the plan. An exception is the case where the trust permits each participant's account to be invested in "earmarked" investments, such as an insurance contract.

Finally, it should be noted that the allocation of employer contributions is subject to the 25 percent/$25,000 annual contribution limit and the 140 percent combined limit imposed by ERISA. These limits are described in Chapter 2.

Integration with Social Security

As mentioned earlier, profit sharing plans are seldom integrated with social security benefits. However, these plans can be integrated with social security benefits, subject to the requirements imposed by the Internal Revenue Service. For example, it is permissible to establish a plan in which only employees earning in excess of the social security maximum taxable wage base are eligible for participation. In that case, however, the maximum deductible amount that can be allocated to each participant's account in any one year is limited to 7 percent of the participant's annual compensation in excess of the current maximum taxable wage base. It should be noted that the maximum of 7 percent pertains to the aggregate of employer contributions and forfeitures during the year of nonvested accumulations. In nonintegrated profit sharing plans, the maximum deductible annual contribution is 15 percent of compensation. Furthermore, if the plan is not integrated, forfeitures may be reallocated among remaining participants without reducing the 15 percent maximum. In an excess integrated profit sharing plan, employer contributions *plus* forfeitures allocated to any participant in any year must not exceed 7 percent of the participant's annual compensation in excess of the current taxable wage base. Also, nonintegrated plans have a credit carryover feature (to be discussed later in this chapter) which permits, under certain circumstances, annual contributions to exceed the basic 15 percent of compensation limit. The 7 percent limitation under an excess integrated plan is applied without the benefit of any carry-over provision. Lastly, if an employer has integrated both its pension and profit sharing plans covering any of the same employees, the integration under both plans cannot exceed 100 percent of the integration capability of a single plan. The objective of this requirement is to avoid the discrimination in favor of higher salaried employees that would otherwise result.

In addition to the excess formula, stepped-up integration formulas can also be used with profit sharing plans. Under a stepped-up formula, eligibility for participation would not be based on compensation. Furthermore, the contribution percentage applicable to earnings in excess of the social security taxable wage base can be increased by the amount of contribution applied to earnings below the taxable wage base.

Provision for Distributions

As indicated earlier, the definition of profit sharing in the regulations permits distributions "after a fixed number of years, the attainment of a stated age, or upon the prior occurrence of some event such as layoff, illness, disability, retirement, death, or severance of employment."

The primary objective of many deferred profit sharing plans is to permit the employee to build up an equity in the fund to enhance his or her economic security after retirement. The law requires that the accumulations credited to the employee's account vest in full at retirement date. Most plans also fully vest the amounts credited to the employee upon death, while a lesser but still significant number of plans provide full and immediate vesting upon the occurrence of disability.

Whether an employee is entitled to a distribution from the fund upon voluntary termination of employment or upon being laid off depends upon the vesting provisions of the plan. Of course, if the plan is contributory, the employee is always entitled, as a minimum, to a return of the benefit attributable to his or her contributions upon death, disability, or severance of employment.

The value of employer-provided contributions under a deferred profit sharing plan also must vest upon severance of employment in accordance with the requirements of ERISA. Thus, the plan must satisfy the 10-year rule, the 5 to 15 rule, or the rule of 45.[8] It also is quite possible that the Internal Revenue Service might exercise its authority to require more stringent vesting because of the potential for discrimination in favor of highly paid employees. The reason for this lies in the fact that under profit sharing plans, the nonvested accumulations of terminating employees are reallocated among the remaining participants. Since employees in the prohibited group tend to be long-service employees, the forfeitures of terminating employees would substantially increase the shares of the employees in the former group. Over a long period of time, a very substantial proportion of all employer contributions would effectively accrue to the benefit of stockholders and other high-salaried employees. Thus, the absence of a vesting provision in the plan for separating employees could be viewed by the Internal Revenue Service as being discriminatory. It will be recalled that employer credits attributable to the nonvested portion of benefits under pension plans are applied toward a reduction of future employer contributions. In the case of a profit sharing plan, the employer is entitled to the full maximum annual contribution without reduction for the amount forfeited by terminating employees. (An exception is the case of an integrated profit sharing plan in which the maximum annual contribution is reduced by forfeitures reallocated during the year.) The possibility for discrimination under a profit sharing plan due to an absence of a vesting provision should, therefore, be clear. It should be observed, however, that the Congressional Committee Report, in commenting on the authority of the Service to impose more stringent vesting standards, directs that the Service not require a vesting schedule more stringent than 40 percent vesting after four years of employment with 5 percent additional vesting for each of the next two years, and 10 percent vesting for each of the following five years.

Therefore, under most profit sharing plans, there will still be some forfeited amounts to be reallocated among remaining participants. The reallocations generally are based on the compensation of each remaining participant in relation to the total compensation of remaining participants. The Internal Revenue Service will not permit reallocations on the basis of the account balance of each of the remaining participants if such a procedure would produce discrimination. Furthermore, if this allocation approach is used, the employer must resubmit for a new determination letter each year. However, it should be noted that the investment income of a qualified profit sharing trust may be allocated on the basis of the account balances of participants. Thus, it is possible to have

---

[8] See Chapter 2 for a full discussion of ERISA's vesting requirements.

different allocation formulas for contributions, forfeitures, and investment income.

Some plans also permit participants to withdraw a portion of their vested benefits in the plan prior to separation of employment. The regulations permit distributions from a qualified profit sharing plan "after a fixed number of years." The Internal Revenue Service has interpreted this to mean that accumulations cannot be distributed in less than two years. In other words, if contributions have been credited to an employee's account for three years, he or she can withdraw an amount equal to the first year's contribution and the investment income credited in that year (assuming that the plan permits such withdrawals). Withdrawal provisions are more prevalent in thrift plans. The right to withdraw may be restricted to employee contributions, or it may apply to the vested portion of accumulations attributable to employer contributions. Of course, the participant must report the withdrawn amount as taxable income in the year in which it is received, and such amount will be taxable as ordinary income. The question also arises as to whether the right to withdraw constitutes constructive receipt of allocated annual contributions and investment income, with the possible result that such amounts will be taxable as income whether or not they are actually withdrawn. In general, it is necessary to assess some form of substantial penalty to avoid application of the doctrine of constructive receipt to the annual allocations not withdrawn; at the same time, the penalty imposed cannot violate the nonforfeitability requirements of ERISA—i.e., once fully vested, benefits cannot be forfeited for any reason except death. Although a withdrawal provision may be desirable in a plan, care should be exercised, since a provision that is too liberal could result in defeating the long-term savings objective of the plan.

Loan provisions also are found in a number of deferred profit sharing plans. Under a loan provision, a participant generally is entitled to borrow up to a specified percentage (75 percent, for example) of the vested portion of his or her account (including any employee contributions). The loan must be repaid in accordance with a specified repayment schedule and must bear a reasonable rate of interest. The loan provision has an advantage over a withdrawal provision in that repayment of the loan will permit achievement of the objective of a long-term program geared toward retirement. However, some employers may prefer the withdrawal provision, since such a provision might help in avoiding possible employee dissatisfaction that could result from the feeling that they must pay interest on the use of their "own" money. The loan provision is also advantageous in that the sums borrowed are not subject to federal income tax. The deductibility of interest payments enhances the attractiveness of this provision. However, there is a trend on the part of the Internal Revenue Service to be more restrictive in connection with loans to members, and it has requested in some cases that loan durations be limited to two years.[9] Also, ERISA requires that loans be available to all participants on a reasonably equivalent basis and that a loan not be made available to highly compensated employees, officers, and stockholders in an amount greater than the amount made available to other employees.

Other Requirements

Qualified profit sharing plans, like qualified pension plans, must meet the requirements of the Internal Revenue Code. Thus, they must be in writing, permanent, communicated to employees, and must preclude diversion or recapture by the employer of contributions to the plan. In the case of profit sharing plans, the regulations require that "substantial and recurring" contributions be made out of profits as evidence of the permanency of the plan. Also, the requirement that a qualified pension plan provide definitely determinable benefits obviously does not apply in the case of qualified profit sharing plans.

Qualified profit sharing plans also must meet most of the requirements of ERISA. Thus, in addition to the items already mentioned in this chapter, a qualified profit sharing plan must treat service as required by ERISA, must permit employees to "buy back" their benefits under stated conditions, and must include a number of other features such as a prohibition against assignments, the protection of an employee's benefits in the event of plan merger or consolidation, and the payment of benefits by prescribed times. (Certain provisions of ERISA, however, are not applicable to qualified profit sharing plans—e.g., the minimum funding standards and the plan termination insurance requirements.)

LIMITS ON DEDUCTIBILITY OF EMPLOYER CONTRIBUTIONS

The limits on the deductibility of employer contributions to a profit sharing plan are set forth in the provision of Section 404(a)(3) of the Internal Revenue Code.

The basic principle of these limits is that employer contributions to a qualified profit sharing plan cannot exceed an average of 15 percent of the annual compensation of participants. To permit achievement of the maximum deduction over a period of years, the Code provides for certain carry-over features. Since contributions are based on profits, it is hardly likely that annual contributions always will equal 15 percent of covered compensation. Therefore, with the availability of carry-over

---

[9] Samuel J. Savitz, "Guidelines for Decision—Where a Pension Plan Serves Best," *Trust and Estates Magazine,* January 1966, p. 29, footnote 10.

provisions, the employer is able, over a period of time, to secure the maximum deduction (assuming, of course, that the employer seeks to contribute the maximum amount).

There are two carry-over provisions: (a) a credit carry-over, and (2) a contribution carry-over. A credit carry-over is created whenever the contribution formula calls for an annual contribution that is less than the maximum allowable deduction (i.e., 15 percent of covered compensation). This unused credit is carried forward and may be applied in any subsequent year in which contributions exceed 15 percent of the then current annual compensation of participants. Therefore, deductions for contributions made in a given year can exceed 15 percent of annual compensation if a credit carry-over is available. However, there is a limit, in that the credit carry-over cannot exceed 15 percent of the current covered annual compensation. Also, there is an overall annual limitation when a credit carry-over is involved. This overall limit is 25 percent of current covered payroll.

A contribution carry-over is created whenever annual contributions exceed the maximum allowable deduction. The excess of contributions over the deductable limit is not lost forever. Contribution carry-overs can be deducted in subsequent years in which contribution payments are less than the maximum allowable deduction. However, the deduction in any one year, inclusive of contribution carry-overs, cannot exceed 15 percent of the current covered annual compensation.

If the employer maintains both a qualified pension plan and a qualified profit sharing plan covering the same group of employees, the maximum allowable deduction in any one year for both plans is generally 25 percent of covered compensation. It should be noted that the limit for profit sharing plans still applies—i.e., if the contribution to the pension plan is only 5 percent of compensation, this does not mean that the resulting limit for contributions to the profit sharing plan can be 20 percent of compensation; the 15 percent limit will still apply. However, in a situation where both a pension and a profit sharing plan are in effect, the contribution carry-over provision could result in a total maximum deductible amount (for both plans) of 25 percent of current compensation.

Table 15–1 illustrates the application of the carry-over provisions for a hypothetical profit sharing plan. For simplicity, it has been assumed that the compensation of covered employees will remain constant at $500,000 a year throughout the period indicated. It has also been assumed that the plan specifies a contribution formula of 10 percent of net profits before federal income tax. Therefore, contributions of $100,000 to the plan in 1969 exceed the maximum allowable deduction (15 percent of compensation) by $25,000, thus creating a contribution carry-over of this amount. In 1970, profits dropped sharply, producing

TABLE 15–1
Annual Deduction under a Profit Sharing Plan
(in thousands)

	Profit before Tax	Contri- butions	Compen- sation	Deduc- tion	Carry-Over Contri- bution	Credit
1969	$1,000	$100	$ 500	$ 75	$25	0
1970	600	60	500	75	10	0
1971	500	50	500	60	0	15
1972	800	80	500	80	0	10
1973	900	90	500	85	5	0
1974	500	50	500	55	0	20
1975	850	85	500	85	0	10
	$5,150	$515	$3,500	$515	0	$10

a contribution of $60,000, which is $15,000 less than the maximum amount deductible. Thus, $15,000 of the excess contributions made in 1969 can be deducted in 1970, leaving $10,000 of contributions to be carried forward to future years. A contribution carry-over, then, can be deducted in subsequent years as long as the aggregate deduction does not exceed 15 percent of payroll. In 1971, profits dropped further, resulting in a contribution of $50,000, which is $25,000 less than the maximum deduction. The remaining $10,000 of contribution carry-over, then, can be deducted in 1971, producing a total deduction of $60,000, which is $15,000 less than the maximum allowable deduction. Therefore, a credit carry-over of $15,000 exists as of 1971. In 1972, contributions exceed the maximum deduction by $5,000, but the total contribution is deductible because the credit carry-over exceeds this amount by $10,000. The reader should now be able to explain the results for the remaining three years. Reviewing the cumulative results for the seven-year period, we find that net profits before tax amounted to $5,150,000, of which 10 percent or $515,000 was contributed to the plan. The maximum deductible amount is 15 percent of the total compensation of $3,500,000, or $525,000. Since total contributions were $515,000, all contributions were deductible, and a credit carry-over of $10,000 is outstanding as of the end of 1975.

Thus, the carry-over provisions permit considerable flexibility in meeting contribution limitations under the law. Furthermore, the contribution formula can specify that contributions in any one year cannot exceed the maximum amount deductible for federal income tax purposes, if such a result is desired. Also, the reader will recall that the limitations on deductions are different for profit-sharing plans that are integrated with social security benefits.

TAXATION OF DISTRIBUTIONS

The taxation of distributions from a qualified profit sharing plan is identical to the tax treatment of distributions from a qualified pension plan, which is discussed in detail in Chapter 5. However, the tax treatment of distributions of securities of the employer should be mentioned here because the practice of investing a portion of trust assets in the securities of the employer seems to be more prevalent under profit sharing plans than under pension plans. Securities of the employer include stock, bonds, and debentures issued by the employer's parent or subsidiary corporations. If a total distribution of the employee's equity is made under conditions qualifying for favorable tax treatment, the value of the securities of the employer for the purpose of determining the employee's gain is the cost to the trust and not the fair market value of the securities. In other words, the employee is not taxed at the time of distribution on the unrealized appreciation. This value then becomes the employee's cost basis should the securities be sold at a later date. However, if the employee should die before disposing of the securities, the appreciation in value never will be subject to federal income tax. If the securities of the employer are included in a partial distribution not subject to favorable tax treatment, only the portion of the securities attributable to employee contributions can be valued on the basis of cost to the trust.

TERMINATION OF PLAN

Although a qualified profit sharing plan must be permanent, the Internal Revenue Service does permit inclusion of a provision giving the employer the right to amend or terminate the plan. However, if the vesting schedule is changed, any participant with at least five years of service must be given the election to remain under the preamendment vesting schedule. If the plan is terminated for reasons other than "business necessity" with a few years from its inception, this action will be considered by the Service as evidence that the plan, from its inception, was not a bona fide program for the exclusive benefit of employees in general. If business necessity exists, the employer may terminate the plan without adverse tax consequences. However, it generally will be more difficult to prove "business necessity" in the case of a profit sharing plan than with a pension plan, since contributions are not required under profit sharing plans during periods of financial difficulties.

If a plan is terminated, all assets in the fund are immediately vested in plan participants. Since all plan assets are allocated to specific participants, there is no problem regarding any order of priorities in the distribution of the fund. Each participant is entitled to the balance in his or her account.

Upon termination of the plan, the trustees will determine, in accordance with plan provisions, a method of distributing the plan assets. The participants' shares may be distributed in a lump sum, distributed in installments over a period of years, or used to purchase immediate or deferred annuities (either fixed or variable), or the assets may be distributed in kind.

USES OF INSURANCE

The trust agreement of a qualified profit sharing plan can be written to permit the investment of part of the trust funds in life and health insurance contracts. Also, all or a portion of trust funds can be used to purchase annuities for participants. Profit sharing funds may be used to purchase insurance on the lives of participants or key personnel.

Insurance on Participants

The Internal Revenue Service has ruled that trust funds not otherwise available for distribution may be used to purchase ordinary life insurance for participants, provided that the premium payments for such insurance coverage are "incidental." The Internal Revenue Service has defined "incidental" as follows:

1. If only ordinary life insurance contracts are purchased, the aggregate premiums in the case of each participant must be less than one half of the total contributions and forfeitures allocated to his or her account.

2. If only accident and health insurance contracts (including hospitalization, major medical, or similar types of insurance) are purchased, the payments for premiums may not exceed 25 percent of the funds allocated to the employee's account.

3. If both ordinary life and accident or health insurance contracts are purchased, the amount spent for the accident and health insurance premiums plus one half of the amount spent for the ordinary life insurance premiums may not, together, exceed 25 percent of the funds allocated to the employee's account.

The reason for the requirement that insurance benefits under a profit sharing plan be incidental is obvious. Since the plan is qualified under tax rules pertaining to profit sharing plans, it is inappropriate for the plan to be essentially a life and health insurance plan.

In addition to the above test, the purchase of ordinary life insurance contracts by the trust will be incidental only if the plan requires the trustee to convert the entire value of the life insurance contract at or before retirement into cash, or to provide periodic income so that no portion of such value may be used to continue life insurance protection beyond retirement, or to distribute the contract to the participant.

It should be noted, however, that these restrictions apply only when the trustee is using funds that have accumulated for less than two years and when the form of insurance purchased is ordinary life (or health insurance). If the trustee is using funds which have accumulated for more than two years, or if the life insurance purchased is of an endowment or retirement income variety, these restrictions are not applicable.

Profit sharing trust funds are seldom used to purchase health insurance coverage for participants, since there are no particular advantages in providing such insurance through the trust. The full premiums for health insurance contracts are viewed as current distributions from the trust and therefore constitute taxable income to participants as these premiums are paid. Furthermore, benefit payments under health insurance contracts owned by the trust offer no special tax advantages. Therefore, the purchase of these coverages out of personal income or through the use of a group health insurance contract outside the trust generally is preferred.

On the other hand, there are many reasons why life insurance for participants under a profit sharing plan might prove advantageous. Life insurance is a convenient method of providing substantial death benefits for participants during their early years under the plan. Over a long period of time, the accumulations in the employee's account available upon death may indeed amount to a very substantial sum. However, during the early years of participation, the accumulations will be rather modest. Also, the young employee with a limited period of participation under the plan usually is the person with substantial life insurance needs. Therefore, life insurance offers considerable flexibility in achieving an objective of substantial immediate and long-term death benefits under the plan. Also, death benefits paid to a named personal beneficiary under a qualified profit sharing plan are accorded favorable federal estate tax treatment. This advantage may be particularly appealing to key employees and stockholder employees. It should be noted at this point that insurance coverages need not be purchased for all participants to preserve the qualified status of the trust. The trust agreement should specifically grant each participant the right to direct the trustee as to the purchase of specific investments for the account of each participant. If the trust agreement authorizes the trustee to purchase investments earmarked for the accounts of participants (and all participants have the right to so direct the trustee), then any participant can instruct the trustee to purchase life insurance without disqualifying the plan.

Still another advantage in the use of whole life insurance coverage is the guaranteed annuity option available under such contracts. Furthermore, most insurance companies permit the participant to supplement the cash value at retirement with additional sums and convert the total amount to an annuity at the guaranteed rates. (For example, the insurer might guarantee to accept whatever amount is necessary to provide a monthly income at the rate of $30 for each $1,000 of face amount.) Thus, immediately prior to retirement, the participant can direct the trustee to use part or all of the remainder of his or her share to supplement the annuity benefit that can be provided by the cash value of the contract. Lastly, investments in life insurance contracts can be viewed as the fixed-income portion of the profit sharing portfolio. The high degree of security of life insurance investments could permit the trustee to assume a more speculative attitude in the investment of the remainder of trust assets.

In practice, the amount used as premiums for ordinary life insurance generally does not exceed 25 to 33⅓ percent of expected average annual contributions. The reason for this practice should be apparent. If premiums approach the legal limit, the annual premium may exceed the limit if contributions fall off in future years. For the same reason, it often is preferable that insurance contracts not be purchased until the plan has been in existence for a period of time. The accumulations in the participant's account will provide a cushion if contributions should drop off in future years.

The participant has a current tax liability when life insurance contracts are purchased under a qualified profit sharing plan. The premium for the pure insurance protection (i.e., face amount less the cash value) is viewed as a current distribution from the trust and therefore currently taxable as income to the employee. The amount of reportable income, then, is calculated by multiplying the pure protection portion of the contract by the term insurance premium rate at the participant's attained age.

Any type of life insurance policy can be purchased by a profit sharing trust. A group contract can be issued, with its attendant cost advantage and absence of insurability requirements. However, group contracts seldom are used. The principal problems of using a group contract are the requirements of minimum participation and possible limitations on the maximum amount of insurance on any one life. Of the individual policies, ordinary life, life paid up at 65, or policies maturing for a fixed amount (such as $400 per $1,000 of face amount) generally are used. Of course, retirement annuity contracts also can be used. Since there is no pure insurance protection under these contracts, there is no limit on the portion of contributions that can be applied to the purchase of these contracts. However, once again, since life insurance normally is desired if investments are made in insurance company contracts, retirement annuities seldom are purchased by a profit sharing fund except possibly at a participant's retirement date. With the favorable single-premium immediate annuity rates offered in recent years by many insurers, retiring participants may become more interested in purchasing such annuities.

The insurance contracts purchased on the lives of participants are owned by the trust. The premiums for these contracts are charged directly to the accounts of the particular participants. Likewise, upon the death of a participant, the insurance proceeds are credited in full to the account of the deceased participant or, as generally is the case, the proceeds are paid by the insurer directly to the deceased participant's beneficiary.

Upon retirement, the trustee can surrender the contract and pay the cash value sum to the participant; if the participant desires, the cash value can be converted into an annuity; and, lastly, the trustee can distribute the policy to the participant. If the insurance contract is distributed, the employee can keep the contract in force by continuing to pay the premiums required under the contract. If the contract is kept in force, the cash value as of the date of distribution is taxable income to the employee. Favorable tax treatment applies if the necessary conditions are met, particularly for the balance of the participant's account.

The disposition of the contract upon severance of employment before retirement depends on the vesting provisions of the plan. If the participant's vested equity exceeds the cash value of the contract, the trustee can distribute the insurance contract, which can be kept in force if the participant so desires. If the vested value is less than the cash value: (1) the participant can acquire the contract by paying the trustee the nonvested portion of the cash value; (2) the trustee can make a loan from the insurer to the extent of the nonvested portion of the cash value and assign the contract, subject to the loan, to the participant[10]; or (3) the trustee can surrender the contract for its cash value and pay the participant's vested interest in cash. The right to keep the insurance contract in force is, of course, quite important for employees who are in poor health.

Life Insurance on Key Personnel

A profit sharing trust has an insurable interest in the lives of officers, stockholder employees, and key employees of the corporation. Contributions to the plan are dependent on the continued profitability of the business. The future profitability of a business firm may well depend, particularly in the case of small and medium-sized corporations, on the performance of a few key employees. Therefore, a profit sharing trust may wish to protect itself, through the purchase of insurance, against reductions of future levels of contributions attributable to the death of such key employees. It would seem necessary, under most state laws, that the trust agreement give the trustee the necessary authority to make such a purchase.

Insurance contracts are purchased and owned by the trust. The trust also is named as the beneficiary under such contracts. The premiums

---

[10] Presumably, such a loan will not be considered to be a prohibited transaction under ERISA.

for insurance are paid by the trustee out of trust assets. Upon the death of the insured, the insurance proceeds are paid to the trust and usually are allocated among participants on the basis of the account balances of each participant.

The purchase of insurance on key employees creates no current tax liability for participants. Likewise, the tests regarding the incidental nature of insurance are not applicable in the case of such insurance purchases. Since the purchase is for the benefit of the trust, the percentage limitation on contributions applied as premiums will not be applicable. As a practical matter, the trust is not likely to invest the bulk of contributions in such insurance contracts. Furthermore, there may be a fiduciary issue under ERISA as to whether the application of a substantial portion of the contributions to the plan for such insurance is truly in the best interests of all participants.

PENSION VERSUS PROFIT SHARING PLANS

Qualified pension and profit sharing plans are two extremely effective methods of providing deferred compensation and economic security for employees during their retirement years. Although the broader objectives of both plans may be somewhat similar, the basic characteristics of each method are different in several important respects. Therefore, the employer must evaluate carefully the advantages of each plan in deciding on the program that best suits its needs. Thus, it might be of value to review briefly the characteristics of both plans in the context of the more important factors that an employer considers in choosing one over the other. Since these features have been discussed at length in other parts of the text, the following discussion avoids detailed consideration of these features.

Objective of Plan

The employer must first decide on the primary objective that it hopes to achieve with the establishment of the plan. If the employer is interested primarily in a plan that offers employees an incentive to perform more efficiently and productively, a profit sharing plan might be the better choice. It is true that a pension plan also should enhance the productivity of employees. However, under a profit sharing plan, the employees are likely to recognize a closer connection between their productivity and their financial rewards under the plan.

On the other hand, if the employer believes that its interests would be better served by a plan that provides a known level of retirement security for employees, then a pension plan might be best.

Also, the employer may desire a plan that permits the maximum tax advantages to accrue to key employees. In that case, the tax aspects of both plans should be reviewed with this objective in mind.

Adequacy of Retirement Benefits

The accumulations under a profit sharing plan can grow to a substantial level over a long period of years. However, for short periods of participation, the accumulations, of necessity, must be rather modest. Therefore, employees entering the plan at advanced ages cannot expect much in the way of a retirement benefit. This may be an important factor for stockholder-employees, who generally are advanced in years at the inception of the plan. Although past service may be recognized in the contribution allocation formula under a profit sharing plan, this factor alone would not offset the adverse effect of a short participation period on the size of the accumulation.

Pension benefit formulas, however, can be designed to provide substantial benefits without reference to the participant's length of participation in the plan. For example, an employee aged 60 at the inception of the plan may be able to retire with a lifetime benefit of, say, 40 percent of compensation. As a result of this, older employees at the inception of the plan (often the stockholder employees) will receive a greater portion of the employer's total contribution under a pension plan than they would under an equivalent contribution made to a profit sharing plan. The appeal of the pension plan for these employees, therefore, is obvious.

Also, the Internal Revenue Service permits integration with social security benefits under both pension and profit sharing plans. However, the integration rules are much more favorable under pension plans than under profit sharing plans. Thus, the higher salaried employees generally fare much better under an integrated pension plan.

Death Benefits

A qualified pension plan can provide a death benefit of up to 100 times the monthly pension benefit (or the reserve under an insurance contract, if higher). Thus, a pension plan can provide a substantial amount of death benefit and, in view of the estate tax advantages, this benefit may be quite appealing to stockholders and high-salaried employees.

Life insurance also can be used in conjunction with profit sharing plans. However, the premium for life insurance must be less than 50 percent of the total accumulations credited to a participant's account. For older employees, this limitation is likely to produce a lower level of death benefit (total of insurance proceeds and remainder of account balance) under profit sharing plans.

Timing of Distributions

Pension plans provide a retirement benefit and, in addition, may provide death and disability benefits. Profit sharing plans may permit distributions upon the occurrence of any of the above contingencies and, in addition, may permit withdrawals or loans of part of a participant's account balance while continuing to participate in the plan. Profit sharing plans, then, offer slightly greater flexibility in benefit distributions. The right to withdraw or the right to borrow to meet emergency situations or to build a home may enhance employee awareness and immediate appreciation of the true value of the plan.

The rate of vesting under profit sharing has been and may continue to be more rapid than under pension plans. The rapid vesting under profit sharing plans is an important benefit for participants. However, from the employer's viewpoint, the attitude of the Internal Revenue Service on vesting may encourage the employer to establish a pension plan.

Contribution Flexibility

An important advantage generally offered in favor of a profit sharing plan is the fact that the employer is not committed to a relatively fixed cost under the plan. Contribution formulas can be amended or contributions to the plan can be made on a discretionary basis. However, the Internal Revenue Service does require as evidence of the permanency of the plan that substantial and recurring contributions be made.

Pension plans generally promise a definite benefit, and therefore the funding must be adequate to provide these benefits. ERISA does permit some flexibility in the timing of contribution payments, but this flexibility clearly is not as great as that available under a profit sharing plan.

However, there are two sides to the coin of contribution flexibility. There is also the question of the maximum limitation on the deductibility of employer contributions under these plans. Under profit sharing plans, the employer cannot deduct aggregate contributions in excess of 15 percent of aggregate compensation of participants. Under a pension plan, there are no percentage maximums on the deductibility of employer contributions. Therefore, if an employer is interested in contributing as much as possible to a plan, a pension plan might be more desirable.

Appreciation of Participant's Equity

A participant's share in a profit sharing plan is increased by allocations of contributions, investment earnings and appreciation, and reallocation of the forfeitures of nonvested accumulations of terminating employees. The assets of a profit sharing plan can be invested in a wide range of securities, a substantial proportion of which are generally equity investments. Investment gains and losses are reflected in the account balances of participants. In the case of a pension plan, the impact of investment gains and losses are enjoyed or borne primarily by the employer (ignoring the question of possible insurer guarantees) rather than by participants. Also, forfeitures under profit sharing plans may accrue to the benefit of the remaining participants, whereas forfeitures under pension plans are applied to the reduction of the employer's future contributions. However, to the extent that more rapid vesting is required under profit sharing plans, the above advantage attributable to forfeitures is somewhat reduced. Nevertheless, it must be recognized that since profit sharing plans usually provide more rapid vesting, and since favorable investment experience is passed on to participants, the cost to the employer per dollar of retirement benefit generally is higher under profit sharing plans than under pension plans.

PENSION AND PROFIT SHARING PLANS

The above discussion assumes the viewpoint that the employer is faced with the decision of establishing one or the other type of plan. This may well be the typical situation in the small and medium-sized corporation. However, it is quite possible that an employer may wish to establish both types of plans covering essentially the same group of employees. A number of corporations (usually larger firms) actually have established both types of plans. The profit sharing plans in these cases usually are viewed as a supplement to the pension plan. There is no question that the advantages of both plans can be combined to offer an enviable package of deferred compensation for employees. It must be recognized, however, that ERISA imposes a 140 percent combined limitation on contributions and benefits when an employer provides both a pension and a profit sharing plan.

EMPLOYEE STOCK OWNERSHIP PLANS

In a broad sense, an employee stock ownership plan (ESOP) could be defined as any type of qualified employee benefit plan (including profit-sharing and thrift) that invests some or all of its assets in employer securities. The definition of an ESOP contained in ERISA, however, is much narrower in scope. Specifically, ERISA defines an ESOP as a qualified stock bonus plan or a combination qualified stock bonus plan and defined contribution (money purchase) plan designed to invest primarily in employer securities. Regulations of the Internal Revenue Service, in turn, define a stock bonus plan as a "plan established and maintained by an employer to provide benefits similar to those of a profit-sharing plan, except that the contributions by the employer are not necessarily dependent upon profits and the benefits are distributable in the stock of the employer company."

As the above definition suggests, the plan design aspects of ESOPs closely resemble those of a typical deferred profit sharing plan. Participation and vesting provisions must meet the requirements of ERISA and, while the contribution formula may be based on profits, it generally requires a contribution that is a specified percentage of compensation. ESOPs are also subject to the same provisions of the Code as to the deductibility of contributions and the limitation on benefits and contributions for individuals as are qualified pension and profit sharing plans.

Contributions to an ESOP may be made in cash or by transferring employer securities to the trust. While such securities could include marketable obligations of the employer, the typical employer security used is stock. The number of shares of stock that would be contributed would be a function of the application of the contribution formula and the fair market value of the stock. For example, if the formula required a contribution of $150,000, the number of shares contributed would be determined by dividing $150,000 by the fair market value of the stock. If the stock is regularly traded on a stock exchange, determination of fair market value should present no difficulty. If the stock of the corporation is closely held or not publicly traded, then a procedure must be developed for appraising and determining fair market value of the stock.

One type of ESOP introduces debt and, as a result, leveraging, into an ESOP, and it is this type of ESOP that is discussed in the remaining material of this chapter. Under this variation, the trustee of the trust created under the plan arranges for a loan from a lending institution and uses the loan to purchase employer stock—usually newly issued. The employer stock so obtained is held by the trustee and gradually allocated to participants as contributions are made on their behalf under the plan. The stock is pledged as collateral for the loan. Because the trust cannot generate income on its own, the corporation usually is required to guarantee the loan. The loan (including interest) is repaid by the trustee from the contributions of the employer. This type of loan under an ESOP is exempted from the prohibited transactions provisions of ERISA provided the loan is made primarily for the benefit of participants in the plan and the interest is not in excess of a reasonable rate. The Congressional Conference Committee Report notes that these loans "will be subject to special scrutiny by the Department of Labor and the Internal Revenue Service to ensure that they are primarily for the benefit of plan participants and beneficiaries." Advocates of the ESOP claim that since the employer's contributions are tax-deductible, the debt created in conjunction with the ESOP is retired with pre-tax dollars and that as a result, the ESOP is a tax-efficient way in which to raise capital (as contrasted with conventional debt and equity financing).

This claim, at best, is an oversimplification. Technically the trust, not the employer, incurs the debt, with the employer having contingent liability as the guarantor of the loan. The debt is retired by the trust with contributions made by the employer. However, the employer is entitled to the deduction only because its contributions are being made to a qualified employee benefit plan. Thus, while the debt is indirectly retired with pre-tax dollars, it must be clearly understood that the way in which it is being done is a charge to earnings. A careful financial analysis will indicate that all other things being equal, the employer contributions to an ESOP will result in lower net income and lower earnings per share. Cash flow under an ESOP would be less favorable than under equity financing. The comparison of cash flow under debt financing is somewhat more complicated but initially, the ESOP should have a more positive cash flow; however, this advantage is offset by dividends paid on the increase in outstanding shares and the opportunity cost of the increase in market value of the shares sold to the trust. Also, it must be remembered that employer contributions (and resulting expense) should be expected to continue under the ESOP long after this debt has been retired.

Such a financial analysis leads to the conclusion that any claim that an ESOP is a tax-efficient way to raise capital must be questioned. An ESOP, of course, can be considered for other very good reasons. First and foremost, it can be a very effective employee benefit plan that is capable of satisfying several important employer objectives. It can also be an effective device for converting a public company to a private organization, for disposing of a division of the corporation (the selling corporation would establish a new corporation which, in turn, would establish an ESOP for the purpose of raising capital and purchasing the division), and for providing estate liquidity to a major shareholder.

In any event, if an organization is considering the adoption of an ESOP, there are several legal and tax issues that must be given careful consideration:

— The first of these concerns the fiduciary provisions of ERISA. ESOPS are exempted from the diversity requirements of this law; however, they are not exempted from the prudency requirements nor are they exempted from the requirement that fiduciaries must act solely for the exclusive benefit of employees and their beneficiaries.

— If an employee becomes entitled to a distribution before the debt has been retired (and while some portion of the vested shares credited to his or her account are still subject to collateral assignment by the trustee for the purpose of securing the loan), he or she will only receive those shares that have been released from the assignment, with the remaining number of vested shares being distributed at a later date when they are free from assignment. This raises a question whether the initial distribution to the particicpant will qualify for favorable tax treatment since there has not been a distribution of the entire amount standing to the participant's account.

— Another problem involves the possible application of "unrelated business income" concepts to an ESOP. Some authorities have voiced the opinion that increases in the value of unallocated employer stock may be considered as unrelated business income and, thus, subject to tax.

— In the case of a public corporation, there are further issues relative to SEC requirements regarding registration, resale restrictions and insider trading. Further, Federal Reserve Board borrowing limits may apply when margined stock is held by the lender as collateral.

An ESOP presents advantages and disadvantages, both to the employer and to its employees. On the one hand, the employer gains the advantage of avoiding some of the expenses and complexity of selling stock to the public and/or existing shareholders. Also, the plan creates a proprietary interest on the part of employees and can supplement existing compensation and benefit plans. From the employee's viewpoint, the plan is similar to profit-sharing, but with greater assurance of employer contributions. On the other hand, there is the disadvantage that no portion of the stock held in the unallocated trust account can revert to the employer if the trust is terminated prematurely. Also, from the employer's viewpoint, there may be some risk of disqualification because of failure to meet the "exclusive benefit" requirements of the law. Another potential drawback to the employer is that an ESOP could be an inefficient compensation tool if the stock appreciates in value because the company foregoes a tax deduction for capital appreciation on shares that under a typical nonleveraged plan would have been made in future years. A disadvantage to employees of an ESOP is that their security may be too closely tied to the fortunes of the employer.

Like any other employee benefit plan, careful consideration should be given to the employer's objectives and the plan's relative advantages and disadvantages before it is adopted. If all such considerations are favorable, an ESOP can be a very attractive employee benefit plan that can also serve other employer objectives.

16

Thrift and Savings Plans

Thrift and savings plans have become an increasingly popular form of employee benefit. Having started with the large petroleum companies, they have spread gradually to many corporations in a number of other industries. Many of the major companies in manufacturing and service industries now have such plans for their employees.

Unlike other employee benefit plans, which usually are designed with a specific purpose or objective in mind, savings plans generally meet a number of objectives and provide for the payment of benefits under several different contingencies. From an employer's viewpoint, they offer most of the advantages of profit sharing plans, but at a considerably lower cost. As a result, many employers have instituted savings plans to provide relatively low-cost supplemental benefits in the event of the retirement, death, or disability of an employee, as well as to provide meaningful benefits during active employment. It generally is recognized, however, that because of relatively lower contribution levels, savings plans do not have the same incentive value for employees as do profit sharing plans.

Under federal tax law, a savings plan may achieve a qualified status and, as a result, the employer and employees may obtain the favorable tax benefits that flow from having such a plan. For this purpose, savings plans are considered to be profit sharing plans and must meet the qualification requirements applicable to profit sharing plans. Thus, with the exception of employee and employer contribution patterns, savings plans possess most of the general characteristics of deferred profit sharing plans. The significant characteristics of savings plans are as follows:

1.   Employee participation in the plan is voluntary and, to participate, an employee must agree to make contributions.

2.   An employee usually has the option of determining the level of his or her contributions—i.e., the employee may choose to make contributions at the minimum or maximum level set by the plan or at permitted intermediate levels.

3.   Employer contributions usually are made in an amount equal to some fraction of the contributions made by employees. (Employer contributions sometimes are made in full or in part by means of a profit sharing formula or on a discretionary basis; however, in most savings plans the employer contributes a fixed percentage of employee contributions.)

4.   Both employer and employee contributions are made to a trust fund.

5.   Assets of the trust usually are invested in one or more investment funds, with the employee frequently having the option of choosing how his or her own contributions (and sometimes the employer contributions on the employee's behalf) will be invested. In some plans, employer contributions are invested automatically in securities of the employer, with the employee having an investment option only for his or her own contributions.

6.   An employee's account generally is paid to the employee (or on behalf of the employee) in the event of retirement, death, disability, or termination of employment. Benefits on termination of employment are, of course, limited to the employee's vested interest. However, savings plans usually have relatively liberal vesting provisions.

7.   Most savings plans permit an employee, during active employment, to withdraw the value of employee contributions as well as all or part of the employee's vested interest in employer contributions. Such withdrawals, however, usually are subject to some form of penalty (such as a period of suspended participation) unless they are limited to withdrawals made for specific financial needs such as those associated with illness, the purchase of a home, college education, and the like.

The balance of this chapter discusses the various objectives that may be met with savings plans, as well as their basic features.

SAVINGS PLAN OBJECTIVES

As noted earlier, a savings plan may serve a number of different objectives. It is important, when designing such a plan, to establish those objectives which are of paramount importance to the employer. This is necessary since the design of the plan will be influenced by the objectives it is to serve. For example, if a major objective of a particular plan is to provide supplemental retirement income, it is quite likely that withdrawal privileges, if provided for at all, will be relatively restricted; otherwise, an employee could defeat the employer's basic objective by making substantial withdrawals from his or her account prior to retirement.

Savings plans usually serve one or more of the following objectives:

1. To attract and retain employees.
2. To provide deferred compensation on an advantageous tax basis.
3. To encourage employee thrift and savings.
4. To provide benefits to supplement other employee benefit plans in the event of illness, disability, death, retirement, or termination of employment.
5. To accumulate funds for other purposes.
6. To foster a greater sense of company identification through the purchase of company securities.

Each of these objectives and its influence on plan design is discussed below.

Attracting and Retaining Employees

Generally speaking, most employee benefit plans serve the broad purpose of attracting and retaining employees. In that sense, then, savings plans are the same as other benefit programs. However, savings plans (and profit sharing plans) have a somewhat greater appeal to younger employees, since they offer immediate and tangible benefits during the early years of employment. For this reason, savings plans can be particularly effective in attracting new employees.

Where this is a primary objective of a savings plan, it would generally indicate that the plan be designed with minimum eligibility requirements, a definite formula for determining employer contributions, relatively generous benefits, and liberal vesting requirements.

Deferred Compensation

As noted earlier, a savings plan, if it meets the necessary requirements, may be considered a qualified plan under federal tax law. While an employee's contributions under such a plan are not tax deductible, the employer contributions made on behalf of the employee are not currently taxable (even though the employee has a vested right to such contributions) until they are distributed or made available to him or her. Moreover, investment income earned on both employer and employee contributions qualifies for the same deferred tax treatment. Distributions to an employee, when they are made, frequently qualify for favorable tax treatment. For these reasons, a significant objective of many savings plans is to provide tax-deferred compensation.

Where deferred compensation is a key objective, the plan generally is designed to permit maximum employer and employee contributions.

Employee Thrift and Savings

Despite the fact that they are called thrift and savings plans, the specific objective of encouraging employees to be thrifty and to save is not always a primary consideration in the establishment of such a plan. Nevertheless, many employers do feel it important that employees should plan on meeting at least part of their own economic security needs without relying fully on government and employer-provided benefits. A savings plan is a most efficient vehicle in meeting such an objective.

A savings plan to further such an objective generally is designed with liberal eligibility requirements and with maximum flexibility in terms of the levels at which an employee may contribute. The plan also may permit employees to contribute additional amounts (without a matching employer contribution) up to the maximum permitted by federal tax law. Also, to overcome any reluctance on the part of an employee to tie up savings until some future event such as retirement, death, or termination of employment, the plan probably should permit withdrawals during active employment—at least to the extent of the employee's own contributions.

Supplemental Benefits

The vested portion of an employee's account under a savings plan is paid to the employee (or on behalf of the employee) in the event of retirement, death, disability, or termination of employment. As a result, a savings plan can provide meaningful benefits to supplement an employer's other benefit plans that deal with these contingencies. As a matter of fact, it is not uncommon for an employer to adopt a savings plan for the specific purpose of supplementing another such plan, rather than making direct improvements in the plan itself. For example, an employer might feel that the level of benefits provided under its pension plan is not adequate. Rather than improving the benefit formula under its retirement plan, the employer might seek to remedy the inadequacy of the retirement plan by instituting a savings plan. The two plans together could meet the employer's objectives in terms of total retirement income and, at the same time, create the additional advantages that could accrue from the savings plan itself.

If supplementing other employee benefit plans is an important objective of a savings plan, this will have a material influence on the design of the plan as it relates to employer contributions. Also, this objective generally suggests that employees be given limited, if any, withdrawal privileges during active employment, since to do otherwise could defeat a major plan objective.

Accumulation of Funds

In many situations, a savings plan is adopted for no other purpose than savings in general and to serve as a vehicle for the accumulation of capital funds. If a plan is adopted with this general purpose in mind, it is common to find the plan designed with utmost flexibility in almost all major plan provisions.

Company Identification

It is quite possible, in the case of a publicly held corporation, that a major objective of instituting a savings plan might be to promote a greater sense of company identification by having employees become corporate shareholders. While this also may be accomplished with other plans, a savings plan under which part of the assets is invested in employer securities can assist in achieving this employer objective. On occasion, the assets of a savings plan of a privately held firm are invested in the same fashion; however, this is relatively uncommon.

If assets are to be invested in employer securities, a common plan provision is to require that all employer contributions be invested in this manner while employees have the option of having their own contributions invested in fixed income or equity investments. Employees sometimes are given the option of having their own contributions invested in employer securities. Some plans, rather than mandating that employer contributions be invested in employer securities, give the employee complete investment options for both employer and employee contributions.

BASIC FEATURES

The preceding discussion has touched generally upon the basic features of savings plans. The balance of this chapter discusses each of the following major plan provisions in greater detail: eligibility requirements, employee contributions, employer contributions, allocation to employee accounts, investment of funds, vesting, withdrawals and loans, and the distribution of benefits.

Eligibility Requirements

As is the case with pension and profit sharing plans, savings plans generally limit eligibility for participation to regular, full-time employees.

Thus, part-time and seasonal employees usually are excluded from coverage. Beyond this, an employee also must satisfy any other eligibility requirements imposed by the plan before becoming eligible to participate. Typically, an employee will be required to meet some minimum service requirement and to have attained some minimum age before being given the opportunity to join the plan. Under ERISA, the service requirement cannot exceed one year (three years if the plan provides for full and immediate vesting), and the minimum age cannot be higher than 25. A maximum age is not permissible under a savings plan.

It is also possible to use other eligibility requirements such as a minimum compensation level or employment classification. Such requirements, however, are relatively rare in savings plans.

As a final observation, it should be noted that if a savings plan is to be considered a qualified plan under federal tax law, it must not discriminate in favor of the prohibited group of employees—officers, stockholders, and highly paid employees. Thus, the eligibility requirements chosen must not result in discrimination in favor of the prohibited group.

Employee Contributions

As noted earlier, most savings plans are contributory. Thus, an eligible employee must agree to make contributions to participate. While it is possible to have a single employee contribution rate, it is customary to permit an employee to elect to contribute at any one of several different levels. Thus, for example, the plan may permit an employee to contribute 1, 2, or 3 percent of compensation. Another common provision is to permit the employee contribution rate to be any whole percentage of from 1 to 6 percent. Employee contributions also can be established as flat dollar amounts or by the use of earnings brackets. In order to prevent discrimination, the Internal Revenue Service generally takes the position that 6 percent is the maximum employee contribution rate for which there can be a corresponding employer contribution. The reasoning behind this position is that very few lower paid employees could afford to make higher contributions and take advantage of the resulting additional employer contributions that would be made. Higher paid employees, on the other hand, could afford to contribute at a rate in excess of 6 percent and receive these additional employer contributions. In such circumstances, the plan would tend to operate in favor of the prohibited group of employees.

This position of the Service does not prevent the plan from providing for employee contributions at a rate in excess of 6 percent as long as no corresponding employer contributions are made for such excess contributions. The Service has stated that such additional employee contributions may be made up to a rate of 10 percent of compensation. Because of this attitude of the Service and because of their very nature, many savings plans permit additional employee contributions to be made. Any such contributions would become part of the employee's account and, until distributed or made available to him or her, investment income on such contributions would not be subject to federal income tax. However, any such additional employee contributions, to the extent they exceed 6 percent of pay, will be considered as part of the maximum annual addition that may be made on behalf of an employee under ERISA.

Permitting an employee to elect the level at which he or she wishes to participate generally is desirable, since each employee can select the pattern that is best fitted to individual needs. This flexibility is generally continued by permitting the employee to change contribution rates from time to time after becoming a participant. Thus, for example, an employee who initially contributed at a rate of 3 percent might, after participating for a year or so and finding that personal circumstances have changed, reduce the contribution rate to 2 percent or increase it to 6 percent, assuming that these rates are permitted by the plan. By the same token, the employee usually is granted the privilege of suspending contributions for some period of time.

The right to change contribution rates or to suspend contributions usually may be exercised, after reasonable notice, at various times during the plan year. Some plans restrict these rights so that they may be exercised only at the beginning of each quarter; others are more flexible and permit change at the beginning of any pay period following the required notice. For administrative reasons, most plans do impose some form of limitation on the number of times such changes might be made. For example, the right to change or suspend contributions might be limited so that the right can be exercised only once in any 12-month period. Also, for administrative reasons, most plans require that if an employee suspends contributions this must be done for a minimum period, such as six months or one year.

Consistent with the above, most savings plans do not impose any penalty on employees who do not elect to participate when first eligible. Any such employee usually is permitted to join the plan on any subsequent entry date.

Employer Contributions

Under federal tax law, savings plans are considered to be profit sharing plans. Accordingly, employer contributions may be made only from current or accumulated profits. As a practical matter, however, most such plans contemplate that employer contributions will be made on a fixed basis that is related to employee contributions, even though the plan contains a nominal provision that conforms to the concept that it is a profit sharing plan.[1]

The basic approach used by most savings plans is to provide for an employer contribution equal to some percentage of the employee's contribution. Typical employer contribution schedules would call for an employer contribution of 25 or 50 percent of the employee's contribution.[2] One variation of this basic approach is to increase the employer's contribution as the employee's length of participation increases. The plan, for example, could provide for an employer contribution rate of 50 percent during the first 10 years of the employee's participation, 75 percent during the next 10 years, and 100 percent for participation in excess of 20 years. This approach generally is acceptable to the Internal Revenue Service. However, it is probable that most employees in the prohibited group will have long service and will tend to benefit from such an increasing contribution schedule. Accordingly, the Internal Revenue Service will examine such a plan, perhaps annually, to establish that the contribution pattern does not provide for a disproportionate share of the employer's contribution to be allocated among the prohibited group.

Another variation in determining employer contribution levels is to provide for a basic contribution related to employee contributions, such as that described, plus a supplemental contribution that is related to current profits. Such a supplemental contribution might be made in accordance with a predetermined formula or it could be made on a discretionary basis. It also is possible to design a plan so that the entire employer contribution is determined on a current profit basis; such a provision, however, is relatively uncommon in savings plans.

As is the case with profit sharing plans, forfeitures that arise when participating employees terminate without full vesting may be reallocated among employees or may be used to reduce employer contributions. While the majority of profit sharing plans reallocate such forfeitures among employees, the common provision in savings plans is to use them to reduce employer contributions.

---

[1] The Internal Revenue Code does not recognize savings plans as a separate category of deferred compensation plans. Since savings plans possess many of the characteristics of profit sharing plans, they have been considered in that category. However, the rules for profit sharing plans clearly require that contributions be made only out of current or accumulated profits. If a savings plan requires that employer contributions be made regardless of profits it would become, in effect, a defined contribution pension plan. As such, it could not include features available in profit sharing plans such as withdrawals during active employment.

[2] This would apply only for the employee's basic contribution. A corresponding employer contribution is not made with respect to supplemental employee contributions.

Allocations to Employee Accounts

An individual account is maintained for each participating employee under a savings plan. An employee's account is credited with the employee's own contributions, including any supplemental contributions, along with employer contributions made on the employee's behalf. The employee's account also is credited with its proportionate share of the investment income (or loss) of the trust fund. In this regard, the employee's account might be subdivided to reflect the different investment funds available under the plan and the different investment results that these funds might have achieved.

If the plan so provides, the employee's account also is credited with the employee's share of any forfeitures that might arise. When this is the case, forfeitures usually are allocated among employees based on the compensation of each participating employee in relation to the total compensation of all participating employees. While it is possible to reallocate forfeitures on the basis of account balances, this practice could produce discrimination in favor of the prohibited group of employees. To insure that the prohibited discrimination will not occur, the Internal Revenue Service will not approve the account balance method of reallocation for more than one year at a time.

Investment of Funds

Although individual accounts are maintained for each participating employee for record-keeping purposes, contributions and actual trust funds are not segregated on behalf of each individual participant. Such contributions are turned over to a trustee (or trustees) who invests these contributions for the benefit of the participating employees.

Many savings plans are structured so that all contributions are held and invested as a single investment fund. This is particularly so when the size of the fund is relatively small. Under such an arrangement, the employee has no choice as to how the value of his or her account will be invested.

A growing number of savings plans provide for two or more investment funds and give the employee a choice as to the investment of account values.[3] For example, the plan might provide for two funds, one consisting primarily of fixed-income securities and the other consisting of equity-type investments. The employee would then be permitted to

---

[3] It is expected that because of the fiduciary requirements of ERISA, many plans will be changed to permit such a choice by employees. By doing this, employees will have had some voice in the investment of their funds, thus reducing some of the criticism that might otherwise be addressed to the plan fiduciaries in the event of poor investment performance of one or more of the funds held under the plan.

have all of his or her account values invested in either fund or to have part of such values invested in each fund.

Other investment variations are, of course, possible. Some savings plans also give employees the opportunity of investing in more than one equity-type fund, each having a varying degree of potential risk and return. Also, if employer securities are to be involved, a separate fund usually is established for this purpose.[4] A further investment variation is to give an employee the opportunity to direct that a portion of his or her account be invested in life insurance.

A number of plans give an employee an additional investment opportunity, as the employee approaches retirement age, by permitting the employee to transfer all or part of his or her account to a savings account. Such a provision enables an employee to exercise some degree of control over the timing of the liquidation of account values and protects the employee from being forced to accept the market conditions that might exist at the time of retirement.

Regardless of the number of investment funds involved, there remains the further question of the investment powers of the trustee. Under some plans, the trustee is granted full authority for the investment of the fund; under others, the trustee is subject to control that ranges from broad directives to the approval of each investment. In some situations, the employer might retain investment counsel to be responsible for the investment of plan assets, with the trustee acting primarily as a custodian. In making investments, the trustee might maintain an individually managed portfolio or might utilize one or more common trust funds.[5]

If an employee is given investment options, usually some restrictions are imposed upon the employee's right to make and change investment elections. Generally speaking, if more than one fund is available, the employee will be limited in terms of the percentages of the account that can be so invested. For example, the plan may permit the employee to invest 100 percent of account values in either of two available funds, 50 percent in each fund, or 25 percent in one fund and 75 percent in the other. Another similar restriction would be that the employee can exercise investment options only in multiples of 10 percent.

An employee generally is permitted to change investment election only

---

[4] If the employee has the option of having any portion of his or her account invested in employer securities, it may be necessary to register the plan with the Securities and Exchange Commission; it is then necessary that requirements of the SEC be observed, with particular reference to any descriptive or enrollment material given to employees. Also, it will be necessary that employees be given a prospectus. However, it may be possible to apply for and receive exemption from registration under Regulation A, depending on the aggregate amount that is available, at the election of employees, for investment in employer securities.

[5] The manner in which investment responsibilities are handled can have a significant affect on the fiduciary responsibilities of the parties involved. These fiduciary responsibilities are discussed in Chapter 21.

as of a date that the funds are being valued. Some savings plans are valued quarterly, with the result that there are only four times a year that an employee could make such a change. Still other plans are valued only once a year. Even if a plan is valued more frequently than quarterly, the employee's right to make changes might still be restricted to a limited number of valuation dates during the year. Again, for administrative reasons, it is customary to limit the employee's rights so that such a change cannot be made more than once in any 12-month period.

A further aspect of changing investment elections relates to the question of whether the change will apply only to prospective contributions to be added to the employee's account, to the value of prior contributions, or to both. It would seem reasonable that the right to change investment direction should apply both to prior and future contributions. A number of plans, however, grant this privilege only for future contributions or grant only limited rights of change for the value of prior contributions.

Vesting

All savings plans provide that 100 percent of the value of an employee's account is paid to the employee (or on behalf of the employee) in the event of retirement, disability, or death. For this purpose, retirement is usually defined as retirement in accordance with the employer's retirement plan. The definition of disability is more varied, but frequently is the same as that applicable to the employer's disability income plan.

A few savings plans also provide for 100 percent vesting in the event of severance of employment. However, most plans require that the employee must have completed some period of service before being entitled to full vesting of the value of employer contributions.[6] While plans vary considerably as to the degree of service or participation required for vesting, the general pattern is that full vesting is achieved after a relatively short time. As a matter of fact, savings plans frequently develop vesting provisions which are even more liberal than those found in profit sharing plans. A typical vesting provision might provide that an employee will be vested at the rate of 20 percent for each year of service, so that full vesting is achieved after five years of employment. Another plan might provide for vesting at the rate of 10 percent a year with full vesting achieved after ten years, or might provide for no vesting during the first three years, at which time the employee would achieve a 30 percent vested status with an additional 10 percent vesting being granted for each subsequent year of service. In any event, a savings plan must meet the requirements of ERISA and satisfy the 10-year rule, the 5 to 15 rule, the rule of 45, or such other requirements as the Internal Revenue

---

[6] The value attributable to the employee's own contributions is, of course, always vested.

Service might impose, unless class year vesting is employed. Under this latter approach, vesting is applied to each year's contribution. Typically, a year's contribution is fully vested in an employee after some period of time has expired. The period of service most frequently used for this purpose is three years, and the maximum permitted by ERISA is five plan years. Thus, at any given time, the employee is never fully vested (except for retirement, disability, or death) and regardless of the total length of service or participation, will always stand to forfeit contributions made during the last few years. The major argument advanced in favor of class vesting is that it assists in reducing turnover, since a terminating employee always stands to lose some part of the value of his or her account. As a practical matter, however, the amount forfeited is relatively small and probably does not act as a major deterrent to an employee who is thinking of leaving for other reasons.

Withdrawals and Loans

A most valuable aspect of a savings plan is the fact that it can be designed to permit the distribution of benefits during active employment. Such a distribution may be made by permitting employees either to make withdrawals or to make loans.

Withdrawal Provisions.   Since a savings plan is considered to be a profit sharing plan under federal tax law, it is possible to make distributions to employees after a "fixed number of years." This provision has been interpreted by the Internal Revenue Service to be a period of at least two years. Thus, it is possible to permit the withdrawal of funds that have been held in the fund for at least two years. While a withdrawal provision will not prevent the plan from achieving a qualified status, the right to withdraw must not be so broad as to result in the employee's being considered in constructive receipt of the amount that is otherwise available for this purpose. In other words, if an employee has an unrestricted right to withdraw, the Internal Revenue Service takes the position that the employee is in constructive receipt of the value available for withdrawal and will require the employee to include this amount as currently taxable income. Accordingly, the right to withdraw is usually subject to some form of penalty or restriction to prevent application of the doctrine of constructive receipt.

Withdrawal provisions vary widely and very much reflect the desires and objectives of individual employers. For example, some plans permit withdrawal rights only for the value of employee contributions. Others permit withdrawal of the value of vested employer contributions, but only after the value of employee contributions has been withdrawn. It is not uncommon to limit the right of withdrawal so that only 50 or 100 percent of the value of the employee's contributions may be withdrawn and, if a right to withdraw employer contributions also is granted, a similar percentage restriction also might apply.

Withdrawals usually are permitted only on a date that the fund is otherwise being valued (often at the end of each quarter). Also, despite other provisions, there usually is a requirement that the minimum amount withdrawn be at least some dollar amount, such as $200 or $250. Further, once a withdrawal has been made, the employee usually is not permitted to make a second withdrawal until some period of time has expired. A typical provision would be to restrict withdrawals to not more than one in any 12-month period.

There are other approaches to establishing the withdrawal rights of an employee. Some plans, for example, might grant a withdrawal privilege for the contribution made each year at some stated time at least two years after the contribution was made. For example, an employee might be given the right, each year, to withdraw the value of the employer contribution that was made the third year preceding the year of the withdrawal. If the employee fails to make a withdrawal of a particular year's contribution within the time designated, the value of this contribution will remain in the employee's account to be distributed at some future event such as retirement, death, or severance of employment.

As noted earlier, it is important to design the withdrawal provisions so that the employee is not considered in constructive receipt of amounts that are otherwise available for withdrawal. At the same time, any penalty established cannot, under ERISA, require the forfeiture of employer contributions after the employee has achieved at least a 50 percent vested interest. One approach would be to suspend an employee's participation in a plan for a period of time following withdrawal. The suspension operates as a penalty, since it automatically results in the employee's forgoing some amount of future employer contributions. When the suspension approach is used, it is important to establish a period that will constitute a sufficient penalty in this regard. Also, it is important to establish an increasingly greater suspension period if various levels of withdrawal are permitted. For example, if an employee is entitled to withdraw both 50 and 100 percent of the value of employer contributions, the suspension period for withdrawing 100 percent should be greater than the suspension period for withdrawing only 50 percent. Otherwise the employee, once having incurred the penalty of a suspension period for the partial withdrawal, would incur no further penalty if a full withdrawal were made. If that were the case, the Internal Revenue Service would take the position that the employee is in constructive receipt of the total value of the account—since it is available without further restriction—even though only part is withdrawn.

Another approach is to permit withdrawals only with committee consent and only upon proven financial need in the event of contingencies such as the education of children, the purchase of a home, and severe illness. Under such a withdrawal provision, a penalty need not be established.

Loans.   A less popular but still common provision to permit an employee to utilize the value of his or her account during active employment is the loan provision. Under a loan provision, an employee is usually allowed to borrow up to a specified percentage (such as 75 percent) of the vested portion of the employee's account. The employee generally repays the loan in accordance with a specified repayment schedule. Under ERISA, the loan provision must be available to all participants on a reasonably equivalent basis and must not be made available to officers, shareholders or highly compensated employees in an amount greater than the amount made available to other employees. ERISA also requires that this loan bear a reasonable rate of interest and be adequately secured.

Distribution of Benefits

Most savings plans provide that the value of an employee's account be distributed in the form of a cash payment. Usually, there also is a provision that allows an employee to elect to have distribution in the form of installments over a period of time or to have all or part of the account applied to the purchase of an annuity contract. If the possibility exists that the benefit could be paid out in the form of a life annuity, ERISA requirements with respect to joint and survival annuities for married employees will apply. Thus, the normal form of payment under such a plan for a married employee must be a 50% joint and survivor annuity.

Where any part of the employee's account is invested in employer securities, it also is customary to provide that this portion will be distributed in the form of securities rather than in cash. This could produce a tax advantage to an employee who receives such a distribution upon severance of employment and under circumstances where the entire value of his account is distributed within one year. Under such circumstances, the value of the securities is their cost to the trust and not their fair market value. Thus, the employee would not be taxed, at the time of distribution, on any unrealized appreciation that has taken place since the time the securities were acquired by the trust. If the employee should subsequently sell the securities, the gain would then be taxable.

17

Plans for the Self-Employed

For many years, employed corporate stockholders have been able to enjoy the tax benefits of qualified pension and profit sharing plans. Self-employed individuals, on the other hand, were denied these tax benefits, even though they were permitted to establish such plans for their employees. For approximately 11 years, Congress considered a number of different bills in an effort to remove this tax inequity; the culmination of these efforts occurred in 1962 with the passage of the "Self-Employed Individuals Tax Retirement Act," more popularly known as H.R. 10 or Keogh.

This law permits a self-employed individual to establish a qualified pension or profit sharing plan, but with certain restrictions and limitations when compared with the choices and benefits available to an employed corporate stockholder. Briefly, a self-employed individual may establish such a plan if all full-time employees who have been employed for at least three years are also covered. The amount the self-employed individual can contribute for his or her own benefit is limited to 15 percent of earned income, but, in any event, this contribution cannot exceed $7,500 a year. However, only the first $100,000 of earned income is to be considered in applying this limitation. The result is that a self-employed individual with earned income in excess of $100,000 must establish a 7½ percent contribution rate to deduct the maximum of $7,500. A self-employed retirement plan also may be set up on a defined benefit basis as will be discussed shortly. Also a minimum annual deduction provision for a self-employed person permits a deduction for any year up to the lesser of $750 or 100 percent of earned income, regardless of the 15 percent of earned income limit.[1]

Benefits under the plan may be distributed only under certain circumstances if penalties are to be avoided. Under ERISA, lump-sum distributions to self-employed individuals now qualify for long-term capital gains treatment and ten-year averaging, but any death benefit paid on behalf of a self-employed individual still will be included in his or her gross estate for federal estate tax purposes, even though paid to a named personal beneficiary.

Effective January 1, 1976, ERISA permits the deductible contributions of an H.R. 10 plan to be established on the basis of defined benefit accruals. Under such a defined benefit plan, in some instances, the amount deductible may exceed or be less than the amount that otherwise would be deductible under the 15 percent/$7,500 limits. The defined benefit limits are set in terms of the cost of the amount of pension that may be accrued in each year. Thus, such a program operates as a modified form of career pay plan. Each year, the self-employed individual is permitted to accrue a pension benefit equal to a percentage of earned income, up to $50,000, for such year. The allowable percentage of earned income is determined by the self-employed's age when participation in the plan started and is not decreased with increasing age. These percentages are discussed in greater detail later in this chapter.

A comparison of the provisions of H.R. 10, as described in this brief summary, with the provisions of the federal tax law relating to qualified corporate plans indicates that H.R. 10 plans fall short of providing self-employed individuals with the same tax benefits available to employed corporate stockholders, though the plans are coming closer together since ERISA.

The purpose of this chapter is to review the major provisions of this law with specific reference to its requirements and limitations in the area of plan provisions, the deductibility of contributions, and the taxation of distributions. The chapter also includes a brief discussion of the different funding instruments commonly being used for H.R. 10 plans and the manner in which Internal Revenue Service approval is obtained.

PLAN PROVISIONS

Before discussing H.R. 10 as it relates to actual plan provisions, it is important to recognize that the law distinguishes between *self-employed individuals* and *owner-employees*. All owner-employees are self-employed

---

[1] A recent interpretation by the Internal Revenue Service raises questions about the original intent of this provision. The interpretation said that the minimum deduction was subject to the 25 percent, $25,000 limitation. Under this ruling if an individual earned $500 in self-employment income the maximum that could be deducted would be $125 whereas it appears the intent of the law was clearly to allow the full $500 deduction.

individuals, but not all self-employed individuals are owner-employees. The key to the distinction is the amount of proprietary interest held by the individual. An owner-employee is a self-employed individual who owns the entire interest in an unincorporated business (i.e., a sole proprietor) or, if a partner, owns more than 10 percent of the capital or profit interest of the partnership. Thus, a partner owning 10 percent or less of the capital or profit interest of the partnership is not an owner-employee, even though he or she is a self-employed individual. This distinction is important, since some provisions of the law are more restrictive for self-employed individuals who also are owner-employees.

One further point to be noted is that if a self-employed individual establishes a plan for his or her employees but does not cover himself or herself or any other self-employed individual, the rules for qualification and the tax treatment of contributions and benefits are the same as those applicable to plans established by corporate employers. The requirements and limitations of H.R. 10 apply when a self-employed individual is included in the plan.

Coverage Requirements

If an owner-employee wishes to establish and participate in an H.R. 10 plan, he or she must cover all full-time employees who have completed at least three years of service. The employer may, of course, cover them as soon as they are employed or after they have completed any period of service up to three years, provided that any service requirement imposed does not discriminate in favor of supervisory or highly paid personnel. Thus, the owner-employee may not establish other eligibility requirements, such as a minimum or maximum age, nor may a minimum earnings requirement be used. Moreover, if the plan is contributory, an employee cannot be excluded because of refusal or failure to make contributions.

The law does not require the inclusion of part-time or seasonal employees. Keogh plans also are subject to the same rules as govern corporate plans.

The above limitations do not apply to a plan that covers only self-employed individuals who are not owner-employees, as would be the case in a large partnership where no partner owns more than 10 percent of the capital or profit interest of the partnership. In this situation, regular eligibility requirements may be used, provided that they do not produce discrimination in favor of supervisory and highly paid personnel.

Limitation on Contributions

The contribution made each year on behalf of an owner-employee is limited to 15 percent of his or her *earned income* for such year. Moreover, there is a further limitation in that the annual contribution for an owner-employee cannot exceed $7,500. As noted, only the first $100,000 of earned income can be considered.

When a defined benefit plan covering a self-employed individual is used, the 15 percent $7,500 limit is not applicable. Instead, the limit is established as the cost of providing a benefit equal to a percentage of annual earned income for each year of plan participation. Only the first $50,000 of earned income can be considered, and the corporate limits on benefits (100 percent/$75,000) and deductions will then apply. Table 17–1 shows the allowable percentages.

TABLE 17–1

Age When Participation Began	Applicable Percentage
30 or less	6.5
35	5.4
40	4.4
45	3.6
50	3.0
55	2.5
60 or over	2.0

Several important points should be noted about the defined benefit plan for self-employed individuals. The allowable percentages are available only for a benefit payable on a pure life annuity basis at age 65; reductions in these percentages are required for plans that provide ancillary benefits. If a self-employed individual establishes a plan that utilizes less than the allowable percentage or applies the percentage to only part of earned income, any change that increases the percentage or earned income base constitutes a new period of participation for the increase and is subject to the percentage limitations applicable for the individual's then attained age. After December 31, 1977, the allowable percentages may be changed by the Internal Revenue Service to reflect prevailing interest and mortality rates occurring after 1973. Finally, a defined benefit plan for self-employed individuals under these provisions of ERISA may not be integrated with social security benefits. These limitations do not apply to a self-employed individual who is not an owner-employee.

If the plan covers individuals other than owner-employees, and if the plan permits voluntary additional employee contributions, the owner-employee may make a further annual contribution, as an employee, of up to 10 percent of his or her earned income or $2,500, whichever is smaller; however, the rate at which these additional contributions are made cannot be at a rate greater than that permitted for other employees. ERISA now permits an owner-employee to withdraw voluntary contributions.

The contributions made on behalf of other employees under the plan must be made on a basis which does not produce discrimination in favor of the self-employed individuals or in favor of supervisory and highly paid personnel. This does not mean that contributions for employees must be at identically the same rate as those made for self-employed individuals, just so long as the net effect does not result in the prohibited discrimination. Thus, if a plan employs a defined benefit formula in which the benefits are not discriminatory, the fact that the contributions made for the self-employed individuals are at a higher rate than that for the other employees would not make the plan objectionable.

Determination of Earned Income

Earned income may be defined as net earnings from self-employment in the trade or business for which the plan is established to the extent such income is received as compensation for personal services actually rendered, or to the extent such income is received from a proprietorship or partnership where capital and personal services are both income-producing factors. Thus, the self-employed individual must be rendering personal services if any part of his or her net profit is to be considered as earned income for the purpose of H.R. 10.

A self-employed's earned income will be reduced by whatever contributions he or she is making to the plan for individuals who are not self-employed. For example, if a doctor's earned income otherwise is $40,000 and he is making a $2,000 contribution to the plan for his nurses, his earned income is reduced to $38,000. However, it is not necessary to reduce his earned income by the amount of the contributions he is making under the plan on his own behalf.

One further limitation on the determination of earned income may be involved if regular employees are covered under the plan. If the contribution for regular employees is related only to their basic compensation (i.e., excluding overtime, bonuses, and other forms of additional compensation), the self-employed's earned income must be reduced. This is done by taking a percentage of the self-employed's earned income. This percentage is determined by dividing the total compensation paid to all regular employees into the total basic compensation of all such employees. This limitation will not apply if the contribution made for these regular employees is related to their total compensation.

Integration with Social Security

The extent to which plan benefits may be coordinated with social security benefits has been considerably modified in the case of H.R. 10 plans. For corporate plans, the limitations for formulas integrated with social security relate to benefits or contribution differentials based on compensation levels of participants.[2] For H.R. 10 plans, however, the integration rules take into account the social security taxes paid by the owner-employee. Basically, an owner-employee may offset the contribution which would otherwise have been made for an employee by the amount of the social security taxes the owner-employee pays for the employee, the contribution for the owner-employee being similarly reduced by the owner-employee's own social security taxes. If owner-employees participate in a defined contribution H.R. 10 plan, integration is permitted on the basis of social security taxes if owner employees do not receive more than 33⅓ percent of total plan contributions. The IRS will issue rules for the application of the $100,000 earned income limit to integrated defined contribution plans. Defined benefit plans are prohibited from being integrated with social security when an owner-employee is covered.

If the plan does not cover any owner-employees (i.e., it covers self-employed individuals who are not owner-employees and regular employees), the regular rules relating to integration of benefits under a corporate plan will apply.

Excess Contributions

The excess contribution limitations of H.R. 10 do not apply to self-employed individuals who are not owner-employees. However, a contribution for an owner-employee will be considered excessive if it is greater than 15 percent of earned income or if it exceeds $7,500. As previously indicated, voluntary additional contributions may be made by an owner-employee if regular employees are included in the plan and have the same opportunity to make additional contributions. These additional contributions cannot exceed the smaller of 10 percent of earned income or $2,500.

When the contribution is used to purchase insurance policies, that portion of the premium allocable to the cost of life, accident, health, or other insurance is not taken into account. In a typical insured plan, this means that the cost of insurance (the PS 58 cost) is not considered as a part of the contribution. While this would ostensibly permit the establishment of a fully insured plan where the total premium exceeds the allowable contribution by the cost of insurance, such a plan would ultimately involve an excess contribution because of the constantly reducing cost of insurance element of a retirement income contract. For example, if an owner-employee were permitted to make the maximum contribution of $7,500 and purchased a retirement income contract with

---

[2] See Chapter 2.

a premium of $7,550, there would not be the problem of having made an excess contribution so long as the annual cost of insurance under the contract was more than $50. However, the continued payment of $7,550 will ultimately lead to an excess contribution, since the annual cost of insurance will at some point reduce to less than $50.

A special provision in the law permits an owner-employee to purchase level premium life insurance, endowment, or annuity contracts without fear of making an excess contribution in a year when the otherwise allowable contribution would be below the premium required under the contract. To take advantage of this provision, the contribution for the owner-employee must be limited to the average maximum amount that could have been contributed based upon the owner-employee's earned income for the three taxable years preceding issuance of the last contract under the plan.[3] In addition, the premium, including all contract extras such as waiver of premium, cannot exceed $7,500. (If the three-year averaging approach is not used and if the basic premium is $7,500 or less, there will not be an excess contribution if these contract extras bring the total annual premium to an amount in excess of $7,500.)

When excess contributions have been made, ERISA established a nondeductible 6 percent excise tax on excess contributions (but not to exceed 6 percent of the assets of the account) made by owner-employees for their accounts. Under the rules established by ERISA, an excess contribution can be reduced in subsequent years by repayment or where less than the maximum permitted contribution is made. Until corrected, the 6 percent excise tax will be levied each year on a cumulative basis.

Nonforfeitability of Benefits

The contributions made for employees of an owner-employee must be nonforfeitable at the time they are made. This means that no condition can be established in the plan which would deprive such an employee of benefits even if discharged for cause. Thus, the plan must provide for full and immediate vesting; however, payment of a terminating employee's interest may be postponed until his or her normal retirement date or, if earlier, death. It should be noted that if the plan does not cover any owner-employees (i.e., it covers only self-employed individuals who are not owner-employees and regular employees), this requirement does not apply, and the vesting provisions of the plan may be as desired,

---

[3] I.R.C. 401(e)(3); Reg. 1.401–13(c). If the owner-employee has not had earned income from the trade or business for at least three taxable years when the plan is established, the average may be based on the actual taxable years that earned income was received. Also, even though the owner-employee may make contributions that might otherwise be considered excessive under this provision, the allowable deduction will still be based upon actual earned income for the year in question.

subject to ERISA requirements, so long as they do not produce discrimination in favor of supervisory or highly paid personnel.

Limitations on Distributions

Distributions may not be made to an owner-employee before attaining 59½ years of age except in the event of death or total and permanent disability. This limitation does not apply to regular employees or to a self-employed individual who is not an owner-employee.

If a distribution is made to an owner-employee before he or she attains age 59½ (other than by reason of death or disability), it is considered a premature distribution; a penalty tax of 10 percent of the amount of the taxable distribution is imposed. This tax is in addition to any other income tax payable on the distribution. The owner-employee is also barred from participation in the plan for five years.

It should be noted that an owner-employee who makes a loan against an annuity or life insurance contract or who assigns any portion of the trust funds before age 59½ is considered to have received a premature distribution.

The law also requires that distributions to an owner-employee must begin before the end of the taxable year in which he or she attains the age of 70½, even though he or she has not actually retired. As long as the owner-employee is working, however, he or she can continue to make contributions to the plan, despite the fact that benefits are being drawn. For other employees, including self-employed individuals who are not owner-employees, distribution need not commence until actual retirement, even though retirement is later than age 70½.

There also is a limitation as to the period over which the distribution may be made. This limitation applies to all employees, whether or not they are self-employed. Thus, payment of an individual's interest must be made over a period not exceeding one of the following:

1. The life of the employee.
2. The lives of the employee and his or her spouse.
3. A period certain not longer than the life expectancy of the employee.
4. A period certain not longer than the joint life and last survivor expectancy of the employee and his or her spouse.

If an owner-employee's full interest has not been distributed at death, the remainder must be distributed within five years or used within five years to purchase an immediate annuity for the owner-employee's beneficiary, payable for life or over a period certain no longer than the beneficiary's life expectancy. Such a distribution within five years is not required if the owner-employee had commenced to receive payments and the distribution was for a term certain over a period which did not exceed the joint life and last survivor expectancy of the owner-employee and his or her spouse, determined when the distribution began to the owner-employee. This limitation does not apply to regular employees or to self-employed individuals who are not owner-employees.

Other Provisions

Controlled Business. The plan may not cover any owner-employee or group of owner-employees who control either individually or collectively another trade or business unless a plan is established for the employees of such other trade or business. Control means the full ownership of a business by an owner-employee or ownership of more than 50 percent of the capital or profit interest of a partnership or corporation. If the plan provides contributions or benefits for an owner-employee or group of owner-employees who individually or collectively control the trade or business for which the plan is established, the plans established for all such trades or businesses will be taken together and viewed as a single plan for the purposes of plan qualification, minimum participation standards, minimum vesting, funding standards and limitation of benefits. If the owner-employee or group of owner-employees do not control the trade or business with respect to which the plan is established, the plan which they are required to provide for the employees of the trade or business which they control must provide contributions and benefits which are not less favorable than the contributions and benefits provided for the owner-employee or owner-employees under any plan in which they are participating as owner-employees. The following examples will help to clarify this requirement.

1. Jones owns a 15 percent interest in the Parker and Jones partnership and also owns a 51 percent interest in the Jones and Smith partnership. Before she can participate in a plan established by Parker and Jones, she must establish a comparable plan for the employees of Jones and Smith, which she controls. If Jones had only a 50 percent or less interest in Jones and Smith, she would not have to establish such a plan, since it would not be a controlled business. Likewise, had she owned 10 percent or less of Parker and Jones she would not be required to establish a plan in Jones and Smith (even though she had a controlling interest in Jones and Smith), since she would not be an owner-employee in Parker and Jones.

2. Williams and Ward each own 15 percent of the Williams and Ward partnership. Each also owns a 26 percent interest in Baldwin and Associates, a partnership. They would have to establish a comparable plan in the Baldwin firm, which they collectively control, before they could participate in the Williams and Ward plan.

If a controlled partnership owns an interest in another firm, the partners will be considered to own the same interest in the second. For example, if the controlled partnership had more than a 50 percent interest in the second firm, the owner-employees controlling the first would also control the second firm.

Owner-Employee's Consent Required.   The plan must provide that no owner-employee may be covered without his or her consent. Note, however, that an owner-employee who is a partner does not have the unilateral right to establish a plan for himself or herself. The plan must be established by the partnership, and each individual partner who is an owner-employee may determine whether or not he or she wishes to join the plan.

Profit Sharing Plans.   H.R. 10 permits the establishment of profit-sharing plans as well as pension plans. There must, however, be a definite formula for determining the contribution for employees other than owner-employees. Moreover, this formula may not be changed except for a valid business reason.

The regulations state that if the employer's contribution for regular employees is related to the earned income of the self-employed individual, the plan will be a profit sharing plan. This would permit a plan which provides for a contribution for the self-employed individual of 15 percent of earned income, with a maximum annual contribution of $7,500, but only the first $100,000 of earned income can be counted. The contribution for each other employee which is a percentage of his or her salary determined by dividing the contribution for the self-employed individual by the earned income of the self-employed individual. To illustrate, if the self-employed individual's earned income is $60,000 in one year and the maximum contribution of $7,500 is made for the self-employed individual, the contribution for each regular employee in that year will be 12½ percent of the employee's salary ($7,500 divided by $60,000).

DEDUCTIBILITY OF CONTRIBUTIONS

A self-employed individual may deduct the full contribution made to the plan for regular employees. And, as previously noted, the amount of these contributions must be deducted from the self-employed's earned income when determining the allowable contribution that may be made on his or her own behalf.

The allowable annual contribution made on behalf of the self-employed individual (regardless of whether or not an owner-employee) is deductible up to a maximum of $7,500 a year.[4] That portion of the contribution used to provide life, accident, and health insurance is subtracted from

---

[4] I.R.C. 404(a)(10); I.R.C. 404(e); Reg. 1.404(e)-1(c). It should be noted that if contributions are being made under the three-year averaging approach, the self-employed's deduction will be based on actual earned income for the year in question. Thus, the deduction limit for any year will be 15 percent of the self-employed's earned income for such year, with an overall annual deduction limit of $7,500.

the contribution before determining the amount which is deductible. For example, if the contribution on behalf of a self-employed individual is $7,500, and if the value of insurance protection is $1,000, the net contribution of $6,500 is deductible.

Although a self-employed individual who is not an owner-employee may make a contribution in excess of $7,500 without such contribution being considered excessive, the $7,500 deduction limit will apply. To illustrate this point, if a self-employed individual who is not an owner-employee receives earned income of $55,000, and if the plan calls for a 15 percent contribution, the amount that may be contributed is $8,250. However, his or her deduction would be limited to $7,500. Similarly, if a self-employed individual makes permissible voluntary additional contributions, these will not be deductible.

Accrual and cash basis taxpayers may make contributions up to the time for filing their income tax return plus extensions for plan years beginning after September 2, 1974.

The deduction limit for the contributions made on behalf of self-employed individuals is determined on a year-to-year basis, so that no carry-over of unused deductions is permissible. However, a self-employed individual may take advantage of the carry-over provisions for contributions made for regular employees.

One further point is that deductions for contributions on behalf of a self-employed individual may not be used to create or increase a net operating loss.

TAXATION OF DISTRIBUTIONS

As far as regular employees are concerned, distributions will be taxed in exactly the same fashion as distributions made from a qualified plan established by a corporate employer.[5] Lump-sum distributions to self-employed individuals, since ERISA, are treated in the same manner as regular employees, that is, lump-sum distributions now may qualify for long-term capital gains treatment and the ten-year averaging rule can be used. Death benefits will still be included in the self-employed's gross estate for federal estate tax purposes even though paid to a named personal beneficiary.

Retirement and Severance Benefits

Generally speaking, distributions in the form of periodic payments will be taxed as ordinary income in accordance with the annuity rules of Section 72 of the Internal Revenue Code. The self-employed's cost basis for this purpose will be the sum of the amounts which he or she

---

[5] For a complete discussion of this subject, see Chapter 5.

was not able to deduct. In the case of a self-employed individual who is also an owner-employee, however, his or her cost basis will not include that portion of the nondeductible contribution applicable to the cost of life, accident, or health insurance.

As previously mentioned, if a self-employed individual receives a benefit in the form of a lump-sum payment, the tax treatment applicable to qualified corporate plan distributions (including the possibility of having some part of the distribution treated as a long-term capital gain) is available.

Death Benefits

If a life insurance benefit is provided by the plan, the beneficiary of a self-employed individual may consider the pure insurance portion of the benefit (i.e., the excess of the face amount over the cash value of the contract) as income tax-free life insurance proceeds. The cash value of the contract, however, as well as any other form of cash distribution under the plan, is considered taxable income to the beneficiary. The beneficiary's cost basis is the same as the self-employed individual's cost basis at the time of his or her death, and the tax treatment of the distribution is the same as that described for distributions to the self-employed. The $5,000 employee death benefit exclusion provided under Section 101(b) of the Code (and available with respect to distributions under qualified corporate plans) is not available to the beneficiary of a self-employed individual. Also, as previously noted, the full amount of the death benefit is considered part of the self-employed individual's gross estate for federal estate tax purposes even though paid to a named personal beneficiary.

Other Tax Considerations

The gift tax exemption generally available for qualified corporate plans is not available to self-employed individuals, nor is the sick pay exclusion for disability benefits.

FUNDING INSTRUMENTS

Basically, the funding instruments available for corporate plans also may be used in conjunction with H.R. 10 plans. As a practical matter, however, some of these funding instruments (for example, group pension contracts) will be feasible only when the H.R. 10 program is being adopted by an association or a large firm and the total number of individuals participating warrants the use of the funding instrument.

In addition to these funding instruments, the law authorizes the use of custodial accounts, face-amount certificates, a special series of U.S. government bonds, and the issuance of certain insurance and annuity contracts without the intervention of a trust. These funding instruments also are available to corporate plans.

Trusteed Plans

If the plan involves a trust agreement, the law requires that the trustee be a bank or a trust company or "other qualified persons or organizations" that demonstrate to the satisfaction of the Internal Revenue Service that the H.R. 10 plan will be administered in accordance with the law, unless all funds are invested in typical retirement income or annuity contracts and all proceeds are payable directly to the employee or his or her beneficiary.[6] Under these circumstances, an individual or several individuals may be named to act as trustee. In plans which require a bank or trust company to act as trustee, the self-employed individual may still reserve the right to direct investments or to disapprove of proposed investments.

Custodial Accounts

Instead of having a trust, a self-employed individual may use a custodial account if the following conditions are met:

1. The custodian is a bank or a trust company or "other qualified persons."
2. The funds are invested solely in the stock of a regulated investment company issuing only redeemable stock (for example, a mutual fund) or solely in annuity, endowment, or life insurance contracts.

For all purposes under the Code, a qualified custodial account is considered to be a qualified trust.

It should be noted that even though an actual trust agreement is not involved, there is still the need for a complete and detailed plan instrument setting forth such items as eligibility requirements and the benefit formula.

Nontransferable Annuity Contracts

As previously indicated, it is possible for a self-employed individual to establish a trust and have the trustee invest in annuity contracts (in-

---

[6] The regulations specify among other things that a nonbank trustee must demonstrate fiduciary ability (continuity of performance, diversity in ownership, etc.), have an established location, possess fiduciary experience or expertise, show fiduciary experience and responsibility, and demonstrate the capacity to account along with the fitness to handle funds.

cluding variable annuity contracts). It is also possible for a self-employed individual to purchase such a contract directly from the insurance company, provided the contract is suitably endorsed as "nontransferable" and provided there is an adequate plan instrument setting forth all required plan provisions. A typical retirement income contract is considered an annuity contract within this provision of the law, since the insurance protection afforded is considered incidental to the primary purpose of providing retirement benefits.

Face-Amount Certificates

A face-amount certificate is an investment contract between the purchaser and the company issuing the certificate under which the purchaser, in return for a lump-sum payment or payments over a specified period of time, receives the certificate's face amount at maturity. Such certificates are considered annuities under the law, and for this reason may be purchased either by the trustee or directly by the self-employed individual if the certificate is suitably endorsed as nontransferable. Again, it is still necessary that the plan provisions be spelled out in an appropriate document.

U.S. Government Bond Purchase Plan

A totally new funding instrument for qualified plans, both for corporations and for self-employed individuals, was introduced with the passage of H.R. 10. This is a new series of U.S. government bonds which are sold at par in denominations of $50, $100, $500, and $1,000. The investment yield on these bonds is compounded semiannually, but interest will be paid only upon redemption. The bonds may not be redeemed until the individual is 59½ years of age, dies, or becomes disabled. They are issued in the name of the individual on whose behalf they are bought and are nontransferable.

OBTAINING AN ADVANCE DETERMINATION LETTER

A self-employed individual may wish to "tailor-make" the plan. If this is done, and if it is desired to obtain an advance determination letter, the same procedures that are followed for obtaining such a letter for a corporate plan will apply.

The Internal Revenue Service, however, has established procedures under which a sponsoring organization such as an association, a bank, or an insurance company may obtain approval of a master or prototype plan. A master plan is defined as a standardized form of plan, with or without a trust, administered by the sponsoring organization for the purpose of providing plan benefits on a standardized basis. An example of a master plan would be a plan established by some professional association for its members. A prototype plan refers to a standardized form of plan, with or without a related form of trust, which is made available by the sponsoring organization for use without charge by employers who wish to adopt such a plan. The sponsoring organization does not, however, administer the plan. The plans offered by most insurance companies are prototype plans.

In either case, the sponsoring organization submits the plan to the Internal Revenue Service for approval. Once the master or prototype plan has been approved, a serial number is issued. The Internal Revenue Service no longer issues determination letters on plans of self-employed individuals who have adopted an approved master or prototype plan. If such an approved master or prototype plan is adopted by a self-employed individual, the plan provisions are deemed to meet the requirements of the Internal Revenue Code.

18

Individual Retirement Savings

Despite the rapid growth of the private pension system, more than 40 million American workers were not covered by qualified pension or profit sharing plans at the beginning of 1974. Congress, in recognition of this fact, included provisions in ERISA that would enable such individuals to establish their own retirement plans on a tax-deferred basis beginning in 1975. An eligible individual may make tax deductible contributions (up to prescribed limits) under such a plan, and the investment income earned on such contributions generally will be free from income tax. Such contributions and investment income will be taxed as ordinary income as they are received or made available.

It is also expected that many employers (both incorporated and unincorporated) will utilize or sponsor individual retirement savings plans in lieu of the traditional qualified plans. Such employer-sponsored plans will be considered to be plans that are subject to ERISA.

The material in this chapter discusses eligibility to participate in an individual retirement savings plan, the deductible contribution limits, and how such plans may be funded. Also discussed are the requirements relative to distributions from such a plan, the taxation of such distributions, and rollover provisions.

ELIGIBILITY AND AMOUNT OF DEDUCTIBLE CONTRIBUTION

Eligibility

A key requirement that must be met before an individual is eligible to participate in an individual retirement savings plan is that such individual must have earned income from personal services—investment in-

340

come will not qualify for such a plan. However, receipt of retirement benefits will not preclude the establishment of a plan if the individual is in concurrent receipt of earned income that is the basis for the contribution to the individual retirement savings plan.

Any individual who has earned income is eligible to establish an individual retirement savings plan if he or she is not participating in a qualified pension, profit sharing, stock bonus, annuity or bond purchase plan of an employer. By the same token, if an individual is participating in an H.R. 10 plan, is covered by a tax-deferred annuity contract, or is covered under a retirement plan established by the government of the United States, a state or local government or by an agency or instrumentality of any such branch of government, he or she will not be eligible to establish an individual retirement savings plan. In this regard, an individual retirement savings plan differs from an H.R. 10 plan. An individual can be covered under a qualified plan and also may establish an H.R. 10 plan for self-employment income—such cannot be done with an individual retirement savings plan. It should also be noted that a self-employed individual may elect to use either an individual retirement savings plan or an H.R. 10 plan. Election to use the former will generally produce lower deductible limits but will not require the inclusion of employees; election of an H.R. 10 plan, of course, will require the inclusion of otherwise eligible employees but could produce higher deductible limits for the self-employed individual. The H.R. 10 plan also provides the opportunity for more favorable tax treatment of qualifying lump sum distributions.

If an individual is eligible to participate in a qualified retirement plan and elects not to do so, he or she may establish and contribute to an individual retirement savings plan. If, however, the individual later elects to participate in the qualified plan, the status of the individual retirement savings plan will depend upon the way in which prior service is recognized under the employer's plan. If the individual receives a benefit accrual under such plan for all prior years, the individual retirement savings plan could be disqualified retroactively. If prior service is recognized only for vesting purposes, the qualified status of the individual retirement savings plan will not be affected.

If an individual and his or her spouse both have compensation or self-employment income during a taxable year (and are otherwise eligible), each spouse may establish an individual retirement savings plan. Community property laws do not apply to such plans. The amount of deductible contributions will be established separately for each spouse, even though they file a joint return.

In any event, an individual will cease to be eligible to make contributions to an individual retirement savings plan on and after the taxable year in which the individual attains age 70½.

Amount of Deductible Contribution

An individual who establishes an individual retirement savings plan may make a deductible contribution each taxable year in an amount equal to 15 percent of earned income in that year up to a maximum contribution of $1,500. Since this deduction is against gross income, it may be taken even though the individual does not itemize deductions. If the individual's employer makes the contribution directly to the plan on behalf of the individual, it must still be reported and taken as a deduction against gross income. This contribution will be subject to FICA and FUTA but not to withholding taxes.

The contribution must be made in cash before the end of the taxable year in which the deduction is claimed. Thus, the contribution of existing property (e.g., an insurance policy) will not be permitted.

Any contribution which is in excess of the deductible limits is considered to be an excess contribution and is subject to a nondeductible 6 percent excise tax. The amount of the tax, however, cannot in any tax year exceed 6 percent of the value of the assets held in the plan. If the distribution to the individual is made after the due date for the tax return, the entire distribution is subject to the 6 percent excise tax; also, if the individual is not disabled or has not attained age 59½ at the time of such distribution, it also will be subject to a 10 percent additional tax as it will be considered a premature distribution.

Any excess contributions not taken as a distribution may be eliminated in later years by contributing less than the maximum allowable deduction in such years. For example, if an individual contributed $1,600 in one year, the situation can be remedied by contributing only $1,400 the following year. If excess contributions are not eliminated through these steps, the excess amounts will be subject to a cumulative 6 percent excise tax each year until they are eliminated.

FUNDING

An individual may establish an individual retirement savings plan by making contributions to one or more of the following:

1. An *individual retirement account.*
2. An *individual retirement annuity.*
3. A *U.S. retirement bond.*

The following material discusses each of these approaches in greater detail, as well as the restrictions of the Internal Revenue Code for prohibited transactions and unrelated business income.

INDIVIDUAL RETIREMENT ACCOUNT

This type of plan entails the establishment of a trust or a custodial account. The trustee or custodian may be a bank, another person or an organization that demonstrates to the satisfaction of the Internal Revenue Service that the individual retirement account (IRA) will be administered in accordance with the law.

The only restriction on investments in such an IRA is that the assets cannot be invested in life insurance contracts. It is expected that most such IRAs will be invested in assets such as bank pooled funds, saving accounts, certificates of deposits, savings and loan association accounts, mutual fund shares, face-amount certificates, and insured credit union accounts.

The key requirements of an individual retirement account are as follows:

1. The annual contribution must be made in cash and cannot exceed $1,500.
2. The entire value of the account must be nonforfeitable.
3. No part of the funds may be invested in life insurance contracts.
4. The assets in the account cannot be commingled with any other property (except the assets of other qualified trusts).
5. Distributions must be made in accordance with the restrictions imposed by the law.[1]

The Internal Revenue Service has issued prototype trust and custodial agreements (Forms 5305 and 5305A). If these prototypes are used, the plan is considered as automatically approved by the Internal Revenue Service. If the trustee or custodian wishes to utilize its own agreement, it may do this and submit the agreement to the Internal Revenue Service for approval on Form 5306. An individual who utilizes such approved plans does not need to submit his or her individual plan for Internal Revenue Service approval.

Individual Retirement Annuity

Under this type of plan, the individual's contribution is invested through the device of purchasing an individual retirement annuity (IRA) from a legally licensed life insurance company. Endowment contracts and retirement income contracts are considered to be annuity contracts under the Internal Revenue Code for purposes of funding an IRA, but any part of the premium that is attributable to life insurance will not be deductible. (However, the difference between the allowable amount of the contribution under the insurance contract and the maxi-

---

[1] These restrictions are discussed on pp. 346–48.

mum contribution otherwise permitted may be contributed and deducted under a separate individual retirement savings plan.)

The annuity contract may involve level or flexible premiums and may be participating or nonparticipating. Also, the annuity may be fixed or variable. The key requirements of an individual retirement annuity plan are as follows:

1.   The annual premium cannot exceed $1,500 (including the cost of additional features such as waiver of premium or substandard ratings).
2.   The contract must be nontransferable.
3.   The individual's interest in the contract must be nonforfeitable.
4.   Dividends must be used before the end of the next year to purchase additional benefits or to reduce future premiums.
5.   Distributions must be made in accordance with the restrictions imposed by law.[2]

An insurance company may utilize a prototype plan or, as will most likely be the case, develop special editions of their standard contracts that contain the specific requirements of the law. By using Internal Revenue Service Form 5306, the insurance company may secure Internal Revenue Service approval of its prototype plan or modified contracts. Any individual who uses such an approved arrangement need not submit his or her individual plan for Internal Revenue Service approval.

U.S. Retirement Bond

The U.S. government has issued a special series of retirement bonds under the Second Liberty Bond Act. These special bonds include all the requirements of the Internal Revenue Code for individual retirement savings plans and do not require the use of a separate plan, trust, or custodial agreement. These bonds contain the following provisions:

1.   All interest is accumulated and is paid only upon redemption.
2.   The bonds may be redeemed at any time.
3.   No interest is payable if a bond is redeemed within 12 months.
4.   No interest is paid after the earlier of age 70½ or five years after the registered owner's death.
5.   The maximum amount of bonds that can be purchased each year is $1,500.
6.   The bonds are nontransferable.
7.   The bonds cannot be pledged as collateral for a loan.

These bonds are sold in denominations of $50, $100, and $500 and bear interest of 6 percent, compounded semiannually. They may be pur-

---

[2] These restrictions are discussed on pp. 346–48.

chased over the counter or by mail from Federal Reserve banks and branches and the Bureau of Public Debt.

When a bond is redeemed, the proceeds will be considered as taxable income in the year of redemption (unless rolled over into an individual retirement account or annuity). In the year in which the individual attains age 70½, the total value of any bonds not previously redeemed must be included in taxable income for such year even though not actually redeemed. However, the proceeds may be transferred to an individual retirement account or annuity. If this is done, no tax will be due on the amount transferred, but distribution must commence under the new individual account or annuity.

Selection of Funding Arrangement

There are no restrictions on the number of individual retirement savings plans that an individual may establish; however, the aggregate contributions made to all plans in a given year cannot exceed the allowable contribution limits. Also, as a practical matter, the combination of the maximum permissible contribution and the minimum contribution requirements of the institutions offering such plans effectively limits the number of plans which can be operated at the same time.

Selection of the appropriate funding arrangement involves many of the same considerations taken into account in the selection of a funding instrument for a qualified pension plan. Thus, the individual must give consideration to potential investment return as well as investment risk. The expenses associated with the particular funding arrangement also must be taken into account, as must benefit security and services provided.

Prohibited Transactions

Individual retirement savings plans are subject to the prohibited transactions provisions of ERISA. If the individual engages in a prohibited transaction, the plan will be disqualified as of the first day of the taxable year in which the transaction occurred. The individual must then include the fair market value of the assets of the plan (determined as of the first day of such year) in ordinary income. In addition, if the individual has not attained age 59½ (or is not disabled), an additional 10 percent tax will be levied since this is treated as a premature distribution.

The prohibited transactions provisions of ERISA are discussed in Chapter 21. Generally speaking, fiduciaries and parties-in-interest are prohibited from engaging in the following:

1. The sale, exchange, or leasing of property.
2. Lending money or extending credit.

3. Furnishing goods, services, or facilities.
4. Transfer to or use of plan assets.

There are, of course, exceptions to the prohibited transaction rules. One of the more significant exceptions permits a financial institution to provide ancillary services where this is done without interference with the interests of the participants and beneficiaries, where not more than reasonable compensation is charged, and where adequate internal safeguards exist to prevent providing services in an excessive or unreasonable manner.

Except for the individual (and his or her beneficiary), a party-in-interest who engages in a prohibited transaction will be subject to an excise tax of 5 percent of the amount involved. If the situation is not corrected within the time allowed (90 days unless extended by the Internal Revenue Service), a further excise tax of 100 percent of the amount involved will be levied.

Unrelated Business Income

An individual retirement savings plan is subject to federal income tax on any unrelated business income that arises from the conduct of any trade or business which is not substantially related to the exempt purpose of the plan. If a plan develops such unrelated business income, the plan will not be disqualified; however, such income will be subject to tax.

DISTRIBUTIONS

ERISA contains very specific provisions that relate to distributions from individual retirement savings plans. In general, these provisions are designed to support the basic purpose of such plans—that they should provide retirement income. Thus, premature and lump-sum distributions are discouraged. On the other hand, the individual is expected to begin receiving payments by age 70½ and is encouraged to draw down benefits over his or her remaining lifetime (or the joint lifetimes of the individual and his or her spouse).

The following material discusses ERISA's basic limitations on payments, the taxation of distributions, and the treatment of premature distributions.

Limitation on Distributions

Except in the event of the individual's death or disability, distribution from an individual retirement savings plan may not be made prior to age 59½ without incurring additional tax liability. For purposes of

ERISA, an individual is considered to be disabled "if he is unable to engage in any substantial gainful activity by reason of any medically determinable physical or mental impairment which can be expected to result in death or to be of long-continued and indefinite character."

In any case, distribution must commence prior to the end of the year in which the individual attains age 70½. These distributions may be in the form of a lump sum, or in periodic payments not to exceed the life expectancy of the individual or the joint life expectancy of the individual and his or her spouse. If an individual or surviving spouse entitled to benefits dies before the entire interest is distributed, the remaining amounts must be used within five years to make a lump-sum distribution or to buy an immediate life annuity for the beneficiary. The term of the annuity cannot exceed the life expectancy of the beneficiary.

If plan assets are not distributed at least as rapidly as described above, an excise tax will be levied. This excise tax will be 50 percent of the "excess accumulation." The excess accumulation is the difference between the amount that was distributed during the year and the amount that should have been distributed under the rules described above.

Taxation of Distributions

Distributions from an individual retirement savings plan (whether to the individual or his or her beneficiary) are taxed as ordinary income to the recipient in the year of payment. Lump-sum distributions do not qualify for long-term capital gains treatment, nor do they qualify for the special ten-year averaging treatment made available to qualified pension and profit sharing plans; however, the regular five-year backward averaging provisions of the Code will be applicable to any distributions from an individual retirement savings plan.

The federal estate and gift tax exclusions applicable to qualified pension and profit sharing plans do not apply to distributions and elections made under individual retirement savings plans.

Premature Distributions

If an individual is not disabled and receives a distribution from an individual retirement savings plan before attaining age 59½, this will be considered to be a premature distribution. The amount of the premature distribution will have to be included in the individual's gross income in the year of receipt. There also will be an additional tax of 10 percent of the amount of the premature distribution.

If an individual has an individual retirement *annuity* and borrows any money under or by use of that annuity contract, the annuity will lose its tax-exempt status as of the first day of the taxable year in which the transaction occurred. The fair market value of such annuity (as of the first day of such taxable year) will have to be included in the individual's gross income for such year. If the individual has not attained age 59½ or is not disabled at such time, this also will be considered to be a premature distribution and the additional tax of 10 percent of the amount involved will be levied.

If an individual has an individual retirement *account* and uses all or any portion of the account as security for a loan, the portion so used will be treated and taxed as a distribution. Again, if the individual has not attained age 59½ or is not disabled, the 10 percent additional tax also will be levied.

ROLLOVERS

The rollover provisions of the law permit the transfer of assets from one individual retirement savings plan to another, and permit an employee who receives a lump-sum distribution from a qualified pension or profit sharing plan to transfer the distribution so received into an individual retirement savings plan. The following first discusses rollovers that occur between individual plans and then rollovers that involve qualified plans.

Individual Plan Rollovers

In general, an individual may withdraw all or part of the assets from one individual retirement savings plan and transfer the amount so withdrawn to another individual retirement savings plan without the imposition of any taxes. (The amount so transferred, of course, will not represent a currently deductible contribution.) To qualify as a tax-free rollover, the following conditions must be met:

1. The full amount of the distribution (which may be cash or property) must be transferred to the new plan within 60 days after the distribution is made.
2. The new individual retirement savings plan must contain no assets other than those received from the distributing plan.
3. After such a rollover is made, no additional rollovers between individual retirement savings plans may be made for three years.
4. If property was received as part of the distribution, the same property must be reinvested in the new plan.

Transfers from an individual retirement account to a qualified endowment contract will be treated as a rollover contribution. However, the amount of the assets that are used to purchase life insurance protection are considered to be amounts distributed and must be included in the individual's gross income. This amount will not be considered a premature distribution and, thus, will not attract the 10 percent additional tax.

No limitations are imposed on the amounts that may be transferred and the transfer may be made prior to age 59½ without being considered a premature distribution. A rollover also may be made at a time when the individual is not otherwise eligible to make a tax deductible contribution to an individual retirement savings plan (e.g., because of participation during that year in a qualified pension or profit sharing plan or because of the absence of earned income). Rollovers also may occur after age 70½, although in this event the rollover may not be made to a U.S. government retirement bond and the new plan must provide for distributions in accordance with the rules previously described.

Qualified Plan Rollovers

An individual who receives a lump-sum distribution from a qualified pension or profit sharing plan may transfer the amount of such distribution to an individual retirement savings plan. If such transfer is made in accordance with the following requirements, the individual will not have to pay any income tax on the amount so transferred until such time as a distribution is made from the individual retirement savings plan. The requirements that must be met are as follows:

1. The distribution from the qualified plan must be such that it is considered a lump-sum distribution that qualifies for the special ten-year averaging tax treatment. Thus, the distribution must represent the full amount standing to the individual's account and must be made within one taxable year of the recipient. Moreover, it would appear that the individual must have participated in the qualified plan for at least five years and, unless he or she has attained age 59½, the distribution must have been made on account of retirement, death, disability, or other severance of employment. (Distributions on account of plan termination—unless after age 59½ or coincident with severance of employment—may not be transferred to an individual retirement savings plan.)
2. The full amount of the lump-sum distribution must be transferred to the individual retirement savings plan within 60 days after the distribution is made.
3. The individual retirement savings plan must contain no assets other than those received in the lump-sum distribution.
4. If property was received as part of the lump-sum distribution, the same property must be reinvested in the individual retirement savings plan.

As is the case for rollovers between individual retirement savings plans, many of the restrictions that otherwise apply to individual retirement savings plans do not apply to rollovers from qualified plans. Thus, there is no restriction on the amount that may be transferred and this rollover is available even though the individual is a participant in a qualified plan or has no earned income. Further, the minimum and maximum age restrictions are not applicable. The provision that restricts rollovers to one every three years does not apply to transfers that are rolled over from a qualified plan.

If employee contributions represent any part of the lump-sum distribution from the qualified plan, they are not transferable to an individual retirement savings plan. The individual's cost basis in the individual plan always is zero; thus, if employee contributions from the prior qualified plan were permitted to be included in the individual retirement savings plan, they would ultimately be taxed twice.

Amounts that have been transferred from a qualified pension or profit sharing plan to an individual retirement savings plan may later be transferred back to a qualified pension or profit sharing plan if the new qualified plan permits such a transfer. Any such transfer from an individual retirement savings plan to a qualified pension or profit sharing plan must be made within 60 days after the distribution is made from the individual retirement savings plan. The entire amount of the assets in the individual retirement savings plan must be distributed and transferred to the new qualified plan.

Distributions from H.R. 10 plans may be transferred to individual retirement savings plans, but, in the case of self-employed individuals, such amounts may not be subsequently transferred to a qualified pension or profit sharing plan.

While the possibility of using an individual retirement savings plan appears to be an attractive way of deferring tax liability when an individual receives a lump-sum distribution from a qualified pension or profit sharing plan, it must be remembered that other alternatives are available and, in many circumstances, might be preferable. For example, the distribution could be made in the form of a nontransferable annuity contract. Such an arrangement also would avoid any current income tax at the time of distribution and would preserve the estate and gift tax exclusions that apply to qualified plans. In addition, should the individual decide to surrender the annuity contract prior to attaining age 59½, it will not be considered a premature distribution that results in a 10 percent additional tax. In any event, it seems clear that all relevant features and options should be considered before utilizing an individual retirement savings plan as a means of deferring tax liability when a lump-sum distribution is received from a qualified pension or profit sharing plan.

19

Nonqualified Deferred
Compensation

Our discussion has been confined, for the most part, to qualified plans of deferred compensation. In the broadest sense, however, the term deferred compensation embraces all arrangements by which the payment to employees of compensation for past or current services is postponed to some future date. In this chapter, however, our discussion is limited primarily to those plans that only are subject to the reporting and disclosure requirements of ERISA which are maintained primarily to provide deferred compensation to a select group of management or highly compensated employees and are unfunded.[1] If there is an unfunded plan that extends beyond the select group, ERISA requires that the plan be funded. Also, any funded plan must comply with ERISA. It should also be pointed out that unfunded "excess benefit" plans (to provide for benefits in excess of ERISA's limits) are not within the scope of the plans covered by this chapter.

Such arrangements may be motivated by the need of employees for income after they retire or by the employer's need for the goodwill and continued satisfaction of its employees. Tax considerations may be an important motivating factor also. Indeed, an employee may prefer to defer current compensation primarily because he or she expects to retain more dollars, after taxes, by virtue of the deferral.

---

[1] Under a proposed regulation in 1975, "unfunded" nonqualified deferred compensation for employees who are members of a select group of management or who are highly compensated is not subject to any of the reporting and disclosure requirements of ERISA except for the filing with the secretary of labor of a simple "statement" declaring the existence of the plan.

Definition

A nonqualified deferred compensation plan implies nothing more than an agreement whereby one person (or legal entity) promises to compensate another for services rendered currently with actual payment for those services delayed until sometime in the future. Such agreements are almost invariably reduced to writing, and are mutually supported by the employer's promise to pay deferred benefits and the employee's promise to render services in exchange therefor.

Distinguishing between Funded and Unfunded Plans

When an agreement and nothing more exists, we speak of an *unfunded* deferred compensation plan. When the employer sets aside a fund to meet future liabilites under such an agreement, with the understanding that any such fund remains the sole property of the employer, we speak of an informally funded plan. The distinction between the two is of no legal significance, since in either case the employee acquires no interest in any specific assets but merely has a right to enforce performance by the employer.

On the other hand, a *funded* deferred compensation arrangement refers to a plan to which the employer makes contributions for the benefit of an employee. Amounts set aside by the employer are placed beyond the control of the employer and will not be available to the general creditors of the employer. It is distinguishable from an informally funded arrangement in that the employee has a beneficial interest in specific funds or property, as contrasted with a mere contractual right. Because nonqualified funded plans ordinarily will not achieve the tax objectives of the parties (without introducing substantial tax risks), they are not commonly used.[2] If the plan is funded, even if it only covers highly compensated employees, it is subject to all the requirements of ERISA. In turn, among other requirements, the funded plan will have to meet the minimum participation standards of ERISA.

THE USE OF NONQUALIFIED DEFERRED COMPENSATION

Few employees whose spendable income is inadequate to meet their present needs will have any interest in deferring income they might otherwise receive currently. It is only when current income substantially exceeds current expenses that a deferral of income appears desirable.

Deferred compensation has greatest appeal to employees in fairly high income tax brackets and who anticipate that they will continue to be

---

[2] This chapter will be confined, primarily, to unfunded and informally funded plans (terms frequently employed interchangeably); some discussion of funded plans is necessary for an understanding of the tax consequences of security devices.

in a high bracket for some time.[3] Yet, even if their bracket is likely to remain high (or to increase), deferral of income may still be unprofitable. Income should be deferred voluntarily only when one can reasonably anticipate that the tax bracket will be lower at the time of receipt and that the advantages of potentially lower taxes at a later date is greater than the loss of use of funds currently even though they are taxed.

Finally, the employee must be reasonably certain that the deferred payments will in fact be paid. The employee must have confidence in the employer and its continued solvency before being enthusiastic about accepting the employer's unsecured (and frequently conditional) promise to pay benefits in the future.[4] The employer, on the other hand, must have a high regard for the employee in order to be willing to enter into an arrangement that may extend for many years beyond the latter's period of employment. Good draftsmanship—though important—will not, by itself, avoid future controversy. Although the parties would not knowingly contract for a future lawsuit, many agreements (particularly those of long duration) are ultimately construed in court. Good faith, then, may be equal in importance to a carefully drafted instrument.

GENERAL CONSIDERATIONS IN PLAN DESIGN

To a limited extent, deferred compensation plans follow certain general patterns. Yet, the design of any particular deferred compensation contract will vary from case to case. Many plan provisions emerge as the result of arm's-length bargaining between employer and employee. Frequently, tax considerations determine the basic outlines of the plan, as well as the nature of its specific provisions.

Relative Bargaining Positions

An employer may decide to provide an employee or the employee's beneficiary with a specific or determinable benefit upon the happening

---

[3] Highly paid employees are not unaware of the limitations of current compensation as a means of building future financial security. Our graduated income tax structure exacts a costly toll from the salaried executive. Consider, for example, the impact of current taxation on additional compensation. For a married taxpayer filing a joint return, the amounts of additional before-tax compensation needed to provide $2,000 of after-tax income at the taxable income level shown at left are:

$24,000	$3,125
28,000	3,279
32,000	3,448
36,000	3,636
40,000	3,846

The Tax Reform Act of 1969 (P.L. 91–172) offers taxpayers some meaningful relief by limiting the amount of tax payable on earned income (see *I.R.C.* 1348). However, these new limits do not apply to deferred compensation payments.

[4] Secured commitments may involve serious tax risks. See section on "Security Devices."

of certain events. Such a *benefit-oriented* plan is likely to arise as the employer's own idea. The employer may feel the need to do something to retain the employee, or may feel a moral obligation to do more for the employee than is available for employees generally under the firm's established employee benefit plans. Benefits paid under such an arrangement will generally be considered as income that is subject to FICA taxes and that could also operate to disqualify the individual from receiving social security benefits.

On the other hand, the primary consideration may merely be to defer compensation to some future date rather than to pay it currently. Such a *deferment-oriented* plan may be suggested by employees who seek employer cooperation in reducing their income tax liabilities, or it may be an integral part of an employer's executive compensation system. It may involve the foregoing of an increase in salary or a bonus, or even a request for a reduction in salary. In such instances, employees may be more concerned with a deferral of income than with the specific benefits to be provided. It is not surprising, therefore, that such plans frequently are of the defined contribution (money-purchase) type.[5] When income is deferred, it is nevertheless considered as income for FICA purposes in the year earned. Thus, no FICA taxes would be due in the year of payment, nor would receipt of this income disqualify the individual from receiving social security benefits. Assuming that the individual was earning in excess of the social security wage base in the year of deferral, no FICA taxes would be payable with respect to the amount so deferred.

In the final analysis, the motivation of the parties and their relative bargaining power will influence heavily the major provisions of the agreement, such as the level and kind of benefits, the time and rate of vesting, whether vested benefits are to be received in cash on termination of employment, and the like.

Tax Considerations in Plan Design

Tax objectives (and the relative willingness to take tax risks) determine many of the plan provisions. Thus, for example, provisions setting forth conditions under which a forfeiture of benefits may occur may

---

[5] As long as the plan is limited to a select group of management or highly compensated employees, this approach should be acceptable under ERISA. However, if the covered group is broader in scope there could be difficulties encountered under the "salary reduction" provisions of ERISA. These provisions state that for any plan adopted after June 27, 1974 that permits an employee to elect to receive part of his or her compensation in alternate forms, one of which is currently taxable, the employee will be in constructive receipt of the amount of compensation involved. Plans of this type that were in effect on June 27, 1974 will not be affected by this provision of ERISA prior to January 1, 1977. At that time, the Internal Revenue Service will have the authority to issue regulations that will treat all plans in the same fashion.

be included principally for tax reasons. Again, for tax reasons, a plan may deny the employee the right to assign his or her interest or the right to have a lump-sum cash benefit at retirement, death, or other termination of employment.

Vesting

The decision relating to vesting is a critical one. The ultimate cost of the plan to the employer and the real value of the benefits to the employee depends in large measure on the benefits, if any, that are payable if employment terminates prior to a specified retirement date.

When a current reduction in salary (or foregoing an increase) is involved, the employee is likely to insist on full and immediate vesting. At the other extreme, where an employer undertakes to establish a plan without being under any pressure to do so, there may be little or no vesting (except, perhaps, for death benefits). Most cases fall somewhere between these extremes.

Whether or not there is a current reduction in salary or a forgoing of future increases, a deferred compensation agreement becomes part of the consideration for the future performance of services by the employee. The employee will not, without careful thought, agree to a loss of accrued benefits. An acceptable compromise is to provide that there will be no vesting if the employee voluntarily terminates employment before retirement, but, in general, to provide for vesting under other circumstances.

Cost Considerations

The employer's cost of providing benefits under a nonqualified plan will depend directly upon: (1) the level of benefits provided; (2) the extent to which benefits are vested; (3) the investment results of any reserve or fund established to meet the employer's future liability under the plan; and (4) the administrative costs, if any, involved. It also may depend upon the time of the employee's death or upon the commencement and duration of any disability, if any benefits arise or terminate upon the happening of either such event.

And, indirectly, the employer's cost depends upon any tax consequences to it as a result of undertaking the agreement. Such consequences may include: (1) the loss of any current tax deduction that would have been available had cash compensation been paid instead, (2) the tax on any investment gains or income on any reserve fund established, and (3) any deduction available to the employer after payment of benefits commences.

Where benefits (or costs) are determined by anticipating their tax consequences, one may speak of *after-tax funding*. Thus, a plan may be designed under which the level of benefits, or the net cost of providing them, takes into account future marginal tax brackets of both the employer and the employee. The impossibility of precise cost prediction is obvious. No one can know what the tax brackets of the employee will be during the payout years—or, for that matter, during the years of active employment.

Relating Benefits to Costs in Insured Plans

If a plan is benefit-oriented, costs can be determined with a reasonable degree of accuracy. But they cannot be precisely determined. Conversely, if a plan is deferment-oriented, its cost will be fixed.

But there are many instances where neither orientation dominates. The employer may want assurance that costs will be fixed. On the other hand, the employee may be in a position to demand guaranteed benefits without regard for future cost variables. Indeed, it is in such instances that the parties may be most likely to look to life insurance as an acceptable solution.

Suppose, for example, that an employer is willing to assume an obligation to pay specified premiums on a life insurance policy of a given size and on a particular plan (irrespective of current tax brackets in the premium payment years), and to obligate itself to pay benefits equal to the amount that can be provided by the insurance policy. Thus, using a retirement income policy in the face amount of $100,000, the employer might obligate itself to pay a death benefit of $100,000 in case of death before retirement or to pay retirement benefits of $1,000 per month. The amount of such benefits can, of course, be specified directly in the agreement.

However, if the agreement provides for any vesting prior to the designated retirement age, provision should be made for such reduced benefits as would be provided by the value of the insurance policy at the time employment is terminated. Hence, it would appear necessary to: (1) incorporate the values of the insurance policy in the deferred compensation agreement by specific reference, (2) reproduce the values of the insurance policy in the deferred compensation contract itself, or (3) include in the agreement a scale of benefits to be paid in the event of termination, expressed either in dollars or as a percentage of the benefits otherwise payable at retirement.

These are by no means the only choices available. In fact, any provision for benefits which the employer and employee can agree upon and which is sufficiently definite or determinable to be reduced to writing would be entirely proper. One might have an agreement with benefits measured in terms of policy values in turn to be multiplied by an appropriate factor determined by the employer's marginal tax bracket in pay-out years. Or, the employee's contribution to policy values might itself be a function of his or her tax bracket in premium-paying years.[6]

Drafting the Deferred Compensation Agreement

Once the employer and the employee have agreed on the general nature of the deferred compensation arrangement, the substance of their agreement must then be reduced to writing. The instrument should contain recitals of the purposes of the agreement and the mutual consideration being given by the parties.

In addition, the instrument should describe as precisely as possible the amount, time, and manner of payment of all deferred benefits. Ideally, the well-drafted instrument will also cover virtually any contingency that might arise, and should not overlook possible changes in the relationship between the parties and the circumstances under which the agreement may be modified or terminated.

The responsibility for drafting the agreement rests, of course, with the parties' attorneys. In theory, if not always in practice, the agreement should be reviewed by both the employer's and the employee's attorneys. Unfortunately, separate counsel are not always retained, a practice that may lead to unnecessary future controversy and, possibly, litigation.

DEFERRAL OF EMPLOYEE'S INCOME TAX LIABILITY

For federal tax purposes, the term "income" is not confined to money or property actually received but includes amounts which for all practical purposes are currently receivable, as well as the value of economic benefits received by the taxpayer. Thus, without actual receipt of income, a tax may be imposed under either the doctrine of constructive receipt or the economic benefit theory.

Constructive Receipt

Federal tax regulations contain the following provision with respect to constructive receipt:

> Income although not actually reduced to a taxpayer's possession is constructively received by him in the taxable year during which it

---

[6] This device introduces the problem of paying level premiums on an insurance policy out of variable employer contributions. A similar problem is encountered in deferment-oriented plans which defer a percentage of income (for example, plans for successful commission sales representatives). Various solutions to this problem can be suggested: (*a*) use of an auxiliary investment fund for some part of the contribution, (*b*) a flexible premium rider, (*c*) employing an automatic premium loan provision.

is credited to his account or set apart for him so that he may draw upon it at any time. . . . However, income is not constructively received if the taxpayer's control of its receipt is subject to substantial limitations or restrictions. . . .[7]

Thus, income will be constructively received if it is available upon demand, i.e., without substantial restrictions or limitations on the right to its receipt. In essence, constructive receipt involves the turning of one's back on available income for no significant purpose other than the hoped-for deferral of tax liability.

Economic Benefit

The economic benefit (or cash equivalent) theory of income taxation has been applied by the courts to impose current tax liability on taxpayers who, although not in constructive receipt of income, nevertheless receive an economic benefit (for example, something other than cash but of measurable value) or receive a cash equivalent (for example, something readily convertible into cash). It would appear that the cash equivalent theory is merely a special case of the economic benefit theory.

In one case, an executive received, in lieu of cash, deferred compensation in the form of a single-premium deferred retirement annuity contract. The executive was the owner of the contract, but it was nonassignable and had no cash surrender value. The court held that although the doctrine of constructive receipt did not apply, the executive was currently subject to taxation on the value of the annuity because he received unconditionally the economic benefit of the annuity contract.[8]

Concepts as broad as constructive receipt and economic benefit of necessity left much room for uncertainty on the part of cautious tax practitioners. However, much of the uncertainty was eliminated in 1960 when the Internal Revenue Service published Revenue Ruling 60–31.[9]

It appears from the ruling that a deferred compensation arrangement will not result in constructive receipt of income by the employee (or by a beneficiary of the employee) even though the employee's rights may be nonforfeitable, provided the arrangement is not formally funded and provided the employee has no current right to receive the compensation in question. However, a reserve may be established on the employer's books, credited with earnings allocable to it, and earmarked (in an accounting sense) for future performance of the employer's obligation. But no property should be so segregated or set aside as to require that it

---

[7] Reg. 1.451–2(a).

[8] *Renton K. Brodie,* 1 TC 275 (1942); Rev. Rul. 55–691, 1955 CB 21.

[9] Rev. Rul. 60–31, 1960 CB 174. Although not necessarily discussed in this ruling, the economic benefit doctrine would probably not have had any effect on the various deferred compensation arrangements described.

be devoted to fulfilling the agreement. Any insurance policy or other property acquired by the employer pursuant to the arrangement must remain an unrestricted general asset of the employer. Under such an informally funded plan, the employee can safely be given nonforfeitable, unconditional, vested rights by the employer, provided there is nothing supporting these rights except the unsecured promise of the employer.

Moreover, there seems to be no reason why an employee cannot take a reduction in future cash compensation concurrently with entering into an agreement for deferred payments.[10] Obviously, however, the employee could no more forego salary already due for past services than the employee could repay salary actually received. The promise of deferred payments need not be made only to an employee in the common-law sense of that term. The employee may be an independent contractor, provided only that the agreement to defer applies to compensation not yet earned.

Statutory Considerations

While both the constructive receipt and economic benefit doctrines are a product of administrative and judicial decisions rather than statute, there is statutory authority for the economic benefit doctrine as applied to contributions to a funded, nonqualified plan established for the benefit of an employee. Section 402(b) of the Internal Revenue Code provides that:

> Contributions to an employee's trust made by an employer . . . for which the trust is not exempt from tax under section 501(a) shall be included in the gross income of the employee in accordance with section 83. . . .[11]

This would appear to represent a basic change in the law. Before the Tax Reform Act of 1969, if the employee's rights were forfeitable at the time of the employer's contribution, such contribution did not represent reportable income to the employee even if the employee's rights to such contribution became nonforfeitable at a later date. Under such circumstances, prior employer contributions were reportable only when the employee actually received payment. Under present law, however, contributions to a trust are not exempt from tax under Section 501(a) and would represent income to the employee at the moment the employee's rights were no longer subject to a substantial risk of forfeiture.

While statutory provisions are expressly applicable only to trusts and annuities, in any case where an employee acquires a nonforfeitable interest in a contribution of the employer or in property acquired by such

---

[10] See footnote 5.

[11] Tax Reform Act of 1969, Section 321(b)(1), I.R.C. 402(b).

contribution, a finding of currently taxable income is likely. It may be determined that the employee's equitable interest in the contribution amounts to an interest in trust. Alternatively, it may be held that the application of the economic benefit doctrine will result in currently taxable income without reference to the statute.[12]

Summary of Income Tax Deferral

It is evident that with an unfunded or informally funded plan, the employee's income tax on the benefits will be successfully deferred so long as the doctrines of constructive receipt or economic benefit do not apply. Particular care should be exercised to make certain, moreover, that neither doctrine becomes applicable at the time benefit payments commence.[13]

TAX CONSIDERATIONS AFTER EMPLOYEE'S DEATH

Many deferred compensation arrangements provide that upon the employee's death, deferred payments will be made to the employee's estate or to designated beneficiaries. An agreement may provide that such payments are to be made in the event of death before or after retirement, or both. Indeed, some agreements—frequently referred to as salary continuation agreements—provide for death benefits exclusively, and usually only if death occurs before retirement of the employee.

Estate Tax

So long as the employee had an enforceable contract at the time of death, the employee's gross estate, as determined for federal estate tax purposes, will include the value of the promised benefits. The value of such benefits is their commuted value at the date of death. However, under circumstances where the promisor's financial condition is such as to cast serious doubt on the ability to perform as agreed, a reasonable case may be made for a lower value. Conditions of the agreement which might lead to forfeiture during the employee's life but which become inoperative at death have no effect on valuation.

Income Tax

Death benefits are taxable as ordinary income to the recipient (estate or beneficiaries) in the year received. However, an exclusion of up to

---

[12] See Rev. Rul. 60–31, Example (4).

[13] Constructive receipt may occur at termination of employment if the employee possesses the option to receive benefits in a lump sum. On the other hand, the doctrine of economic benefit may be applied if the employee's benefit payments are guaranteed by an insurance company. See footnote 8.

$5,000 is allowed if the employee did not have a nonforfeitable right to receive the benefits while living.

The impact of both estate and income taxes being imposed is, to a limited extent, mitigated by a deduction allowable against the income received. Payments received on account of the employee's death represent "income in respect of a decedent." Thus, the payee will receive an income tax deduction for the portion of the estate tax actually paid that is deemed to be attributable to each income payment. It is important to note that this is a deduction against gross income, not a credit against the income tax.

THE EMPLOYER'S DEDUCTION

In computing its income tax liability, an employer is entitled to a deduction for all ordinary and necessary business expenses. Compensation and fringe benefits paid to (or with respect to) an employee (or former employee) are deductible as ordinary and necessary business expenses to the extent that such payments (and their cost) represent reasonable overall compensation for services rendered.

Reasonableness of Compensation

While the courts and the commissioner are not unduly harsh in applying the test of reasonableness, they are by no means reluctant to disallow a deduction in an extreme situation. There are numerous decisions in which the courts have been fairly liberal in allowing deductions for substantial amounts of deferred compensation payments. But the fact that those cases reached the courts is ample evidence that the Internal Revenue Service and employers do not always see eye to eye on the question of reasonableness.

The Service is inclined to give much closer scrutiny to compensation or fringe benefits provided for substantial stockholders. Thus, what may be thought of by the parties as current or deferred compensation may be viewed by the Service as the payment of current or deferred dividends, as the case may be. Nor will the language of an agreement be of much help where the substance of the agreement clearly indicates that the employee was being paid benefits that, were he or she not a substantial stockholder, most likely would not have been furnished.

This point is well illustrated in *Willmark* which sustained the commissioner's disallowance of a deduction for payments made to a deceased employee-stockholder's widow pursuant to a deferred compensation contract.[14] The decedent had owned 50 percent of the corporation's stock. His brother, for whom there was an identical deferred compensation agreement, owned the remaining 50 percent. The court held that the

---

[14] *Willmark Service System, Inc.,* 368 F. 2d 359 (CA-2, 1966).

employer had the burden of proving not only that the payments were made pursuant to a plan deferring the receipt of compensation for past services but also that the amounts to be paid under the plan constituted reasonable compensation for such services. It held that the employer had failed to establish either.

Funded Plans

Section 404(a)(5) of the Internal Revenue Code as amended by the Tax Reform Act of 1969 provides in part as follows:

> . . . if compensation is paid or accrued on account of any employee under a plan deferring the receipt of such compensation, such contributions . . . shall be deductible under this section . . . if the plan is not . . . [a qualified plan] in the taxable year in which an amount attributable to the contribution is includible in the gross income of employees participating in the plan. . . .

But Section 1.404(a)–12 of the regulations imposes a harsh, and surprising, limitation on the foregoing, as follows:

> If an amount is paid during the taxable year to a trust or under a plan and the employee's rights to such amounts are *forfeitable* at the time the amount is paid, *no deduction is allowable for such amount for any taxable year*." [Emphasis added.]

The Service may have considered such harsh limitations necessary in view of its interpretation of former Sections 402(b) and 403(c) of the Code. In light of the changes in the foregoing sections made by the Tax Reform Act of 1969, it appears that Reg. 1.404(a)–12 is inconsistent with the present statutory scheme.

It is certainly an open question whether Reg. 1.404(a)–12 represented a reasonable interpretation of the statute. In two cases decided by the U.S. Court of Claims, the court held the regulation to be invalid and allowed the employer deductions as payments were actually made under the plans. Yet in another situation, the Service went back to the original interpretation.[15]

THE ROLE OF LIFE INSURANCE

Whether life insurance is an essential ingredient of or merely a desirable adjunct to a deferred compensation plan depends on the purposes and provisions of the plan.

---

[15] *Russell Mfg. Co.* v. *U.S.*, 175 F. Supp. 159 (Ct. Cl., 1959) and *Mississippi River Fuel Corp.* v. *U.S.*, 314 F. 2d 953 (Ct. Cl. 1963). Rev. Rul. 59–383, 1959–2 CB 456 (in which the Service states that it will not follow Russell Mfg. Co.). Many employers will be reluctant to take the risk of never obtaining a deduction, and may wish to proceed cautiously until Reg. 1.404(a)–12 is revised.

Clearly, if the plan contemplates the payment of substantial death benefits, life insurance is essential. So, also, if the employer agrees to pay the employee a deferred income for life, the employer may wish to shift the mortality risk to an insurance company. Where neither of these elements is present, a life insurance policy may nevertheless serve as a convenient medium for building a reserve against the employer's deferred liabilities. And, unlike many other investment vehicles, it does offer a tax shelter to the earnings on the reserve.

Ownership of the Policy

Any insurance policy carried in conjunction with the plan should be paid for by, owned by, and payable solely to the employer. Ordinarily, the deferred compensation contract should be drawn so as to establish the rights and liabilities of the parties without regard to any such insurance policy or the values created thereby.

Indeed, some writers have cautioned against any reference to the insurance policy being made in the deferred compensation agreement.[16] But such extreme caution no longer seems warranted.[17] However, the agreement should specify that the policy is, and shall remain, a general, unpledged, unrestricted asset of the employer.

Tax Consequences to the Employer

When an employer informally funds a deferred compensation agreement by maintaining an investment account (whether using life insurance or some other medium), the tax consequences are unchanged. Where a life insurance contract is used, any death proceeds received by the corporation are excluded from its gross income. No deduction is allowed the employer for premiums paid. If the policy matures or is surrendered for cash during the insured's lifetime, any excess of maturity proceeds or surrender value received over the aggregate net premiums paid for the policy is taxable to the employer as ordinary income. However, if the amount received on maturity or surrender is less than the aggregate premiums paid, no deductible loss is allowed.

If installment or annuity payments are made out of the maturity or surrender proceeds during the lifetime of the insured, an exclusion ratio is determined in order to arrive at the portion of each payment that

---

[16]See, for example, Arthur E. Schmauder, "Keyman Insurance in Deferred Compensation Arrangements," *Insurance Law Journal,* June 1959, p. 365.

[17]This would appear to be a necessary implication of *Casale* v. *Comm'r.,* 247 F. 2d 440, and of Rev. Rul. 60-31 (Note 8). See also Rev. Rul. 68-99, 1968-1, CB 193. For a case involving an unusual—and unwise—insurance arrangement, see *Frost* v. *Comm'r.,* 52 TC 9 (1969).

is excluded from the employer's gross income as a return of capital; the balance of each payment will be taxable to the employer as ordinary income.

Use of Settlement Options

In order to provide a payout over a period of years while attempting to protect the employee from possible future insolvency of the employer, it is sometimes suggested that the employee be designated as direct beneficiary of an employer-owned insurance policy.

However, a reasonable tax analysis of such an arrangement would require treating the guarantee of payments by the insurance company as though the policy had been distributed to the employee. The employee's tax liability would accrue all in one year, thus defeating a principal tax objectives of the plan. Therefore, it would seem necessary that the employer be designated as beneficiary for all payments under the contract, receive all such payments, and itself make all distributions to the employee (or the employee's beneficiary) until the payout is completed.

As each periodic installment payment is received by the employer, the employer should draw its own check (or endorse the insurance company's check) to the employee. Or, it may be administratively more convenient for the employer to give the insurance company a revocable instruction to make installment payments directly to the employee until further notice.[18] So long as the employer reserves the right to redirect all future payments to itself, income tax consequences (to both employer and employee) are the same as if each installment payment were actually received by the employer and distributed by it to the employee.

Improper Accumulation of Surplus

Does a corporation run afoul of the accumulated earnings tax by establishing a reserve against deferred compensation liabilities through an insurance policy on an employee's life with premiums paid from profits?[19] If the deferred compensation agreement is truly compensatory, as in the case of an agreement with an employee who is not a substantial stockholder of the corporation, there is no problem in this regard. However, in the case of an employee who owns a substantial amount of stock, such an agreement might be viewed not as compensatory but as an ar-

---

[18] Some caution must be expressed here, as the practices of insurance companies vary with respect to the availability of settlement options on business life insurance.

[19] See I.R.C. 531–537. The tax is not imposed on earnings retained for a reasonable business purpose and, in any case, a corporation is allowed to accumulate at least $150,000 of earnings.

rangement for deferring dividends. Each case—and the conclusion reached—will depend, of course, upon its facts.

If it is feared that the agreement might be construed as a device to defer dividends, careful consideration should be given to justifying the insurance from a business purpose viewpoint. In the case of a substantial stockholder for whom deferred compensation may not be justifiable, the carrying of insurance may, nevertheless, be justified solely for key personnel purposes. However, to attempt to characterize the insurance as key personnel coverage merely by avoiding any reference to it in the deferred compensation agreement may be a little unrealistic.

Considerable attention should be given, also, to the plan of insurance selected. A retirement income or other endowment plan, for example, can probably be justified only on the basis of a deferred compensation obligation of the employer. Thus, before deciding on such a plan of insurance, the employer (and its advisers) should be satisfied that the deferred compensation agreement can be justified as, in fact, compensatory. Regardless of the type of policy used, however, justification for the retention of earnings is only as good as the reality of the key employee need or the reality of the deferred compensation arrangement contemplated.

CHARITABLE CORPORATIONS

The tax treatment of certain charitable organizations and their employees is sufficiently different to warrant special consideration. The principal differences are: (1) such employers are exempt from tax; (2) their employees enjoy a unique opportunity to defer tax liability, using employer-purchased annuities;[20] and (3) under nonqualified annuity plans, employees are taxable if their rights are not subject to a substantial risk of forfeiture.[21]

None of the foregoing considerations would inhibit establishing a plan of the type discussed in this chapter. In general, the tax, design, and other considerations that have been discussed would still apply. But for charitable employers, the tax differences are such that more can be done to protect the employee without adverse tax consequences to employer or employee.

SECURITY DEVICES

One important limitation of nonqualified deferred compensation arrangements has been previously alluded to in this chapter: What assur-

---

[20] I.R.C. 403(b). For a discussion of tax-deferred annuities, see Chapter 20.

[21] Except to the extent that benefits are not subject to a substantial risk of forfeiture.

ance does an employee have that the employer will be financially able to perform its contractual obligations when the date for performance arrives? In general, the answer is—little.

One of the risks that the employee takes when entering an unfunded deferred compensation plan is the employer's possible future insolvency. Indeed, it is the potential of future insolvency that offers assurance that neither the doctrine of constructive receipt nor the doctrine of economic benefit will apply. Generally, such risk is minimal if the employer is large and financially sound.

Employer's Tax Risk

If the employer is willing to give the employee security and is willing to take a tax risk in the bargain, tax safety for the employee can be achieved by including in the deferred compensation contract one or more bona fide conditions under which a forfeiture of the employee's benefits will occur. While the employee should thus have little or no risk of current taxation or of loss of benefits arising out of employer insolvency, the employee does take on a risk of loss of benefits if a forfeiture should occur.

But if the employee's rights are forfeitable, the employer may be denied a tax deduction for any amount paid at any time. Whether the courts will support such a disallowance is uncertain, but the employer may have some chance in view of the *Russell Mfg. Co.* and *Mississippi River Fuel* cases.[22]

Employee's Tax Risk

The tax risk to the employee is, of course, that any secured contractual promise will be construed as establishing a funded plan and covered under ERISA. In this event, if the employee's rights are nonforfeitable, the employee will be subject to income tax liability each year in which contributions are made. If, on the other hand, the employee's rights are subject to a substantial risk of forfeiture, current tax will be avoided.

Evaluation of Secured Agreements

Secured, unfunded deferred compensation arrangements should be viewed with particular caution until such time as court decisions or further regulations clarify whether or not an employer forever loses its deduction in the case of plans involving forfeitable rights which later become nonforfeitable.

---

[22] See footnote 15.

SUMMARY

Qualified retirement plans prohibit discrimination in favor of selected key executives. For this reason, employers often will seek ways to provide adequate benefits—and incentives—for key members of management. Nonqualified deferred compensation arrangements are one way to reward executives and other key employees without regard to the nondiscrimination requirements of qualified plans.

20

Tax-Deferred Annuities

In some respects, the "tax-deferred annuity" resembles the deferred compensation plans discussed in Chapter 19. The motive of income tax deferral is, of course, the same. And, while the applicability of tax-deferred annuities is considerably more limited, where they do apply they offer some significant advantages. In other respects, tax-deferred annuities resemble qualified pension plans. But they by no means offer all of the tax advantages of a qualified plan.

STATUTORY ASPECTS

Background

Ever since 1942, the Internal Revenue Code has contained a provision which permitted certain tax-exempt charitable employers to purchase annuity contracts for their employees without current income tax liability to the employees. ERISA, for the first time authorized funds to be placed in a custodial account for the purchase of shares of a regulated investment company (mutual funds). Eligible employers are those that qualified under Section 101(6) of the 1939 Code, or Section 501(c)(3) of the 1954 Code. Under the original statutory provision: ". . . if an annuity contract is purchased for an employee by an employer exempt under Section 101(6), the employee shall include in his income the amounts received under such contract for the year received. . . ." In the absence of such a statutory provision, taxable income would arise as premiums are paid.

As the public became aware of this provision in the Code, some individuals began to avail themselves of this tax advantage to a far greater extent than the commissioner of internal revenue felt proper. Thus, the commissioner attempted to limit the circumstances under which, and the extent to which, the statutory provision would be deemed applicable.

The Internal Revenue Code of 1954 made no modification in the statutory provisions. However, by the Technical Amendments Act of 1958, a considerably more detailed provision, Section 403(b), was enacted which established the concept of a 20 percent exclusion allowance. Then, by the Revenue Act of 1961, Section 403(b) was amended to extend tax deferral for such annuity purchases to employees of public school systems. And, finally, after a number of years, regulations were promulgated interpreting the new provision. ERISA also made certain changes affecting tax-deferred annuity plans. These changes will be discussed where appropriate in the following sections.

The Present Statute

Section 403(b) of the Code, as amended, now provides in part that:

> If an annuity contract is purchased for an employee by an employer described in section 501(c)(3) . . . or for an employee . . . who performs services for an educational institution (as defined in section 151(e)(4), by an employer which is a State, a political subdivision of a State, or an agency or instrumentality of any one or more of the foregoing . . . and the employee's rights under the contract are nonforfeitable, except for failure to pay future premiums, then amounts contributed by such employer for such annuity contract . . . shall be excluded from the gross income of the employee for the taxable year to the extent that the aggregate of such amounts does not exceed the *exclusion allowance*[1] for such taxable year.

ERISA amended Section 403(b) of the Code to add Section 403(b)(7) which states in part:

> For purposes of this title, amounts paid by an employer . . . to a custodial account . . . shall be treated as amounts contributed to an annuity contract for the employee if the amounts . . . are to be invested in regulated investment company stock to be held in the custodial account.

Thus, the essential requirements to achieve the desired tax shelter are as follows:

1. The participant must be employed by a duly qualified charitable organization or by a public school system.

---

[1] Emphasis added. The exclusion allowance will be examined in great detail subsequently.

2. The participant must be a bona fide employee.
3. The annuity contract must be purchased by such employer or the employer must make a deposit to a custodial account which will purchase mutual fund shares.
4. The participant's rights under the contract must be nonforfeitable.
5. The amount paid in any year should not exceed the exclusion allowance for the year in question (and will be currently taxable to the extent that it does exceed such allowance).

While these are the essential ingredients of a tax-deferred annuity, each of these requirements calls for examination in considerable detail.

REQUIREMENTS OF A TAX-DEFERRED ANNUITY

Qualified Employers

If the employee is to qualify for tax-deferred annuity treatment his employer must be either:

a. A charitable organization qualified under Section 501(c)(3) of the Internal Revenue Code (for example, a tax-exempt hospital, church, school, or other such organization or foundation).
b. A public school system (for example, one operated by the state, or by a county, city, town, school district, or other political subdivision or agency of a state).

Note that not every tax-exempt organization is a qualified employer, but only those which qualify under Section 501(c)(3).

Note also that not all types of publicly operated facilities can qualify, but only public school systems. Certain other publicly operated facilites (hospitals or other charities, for example) may or may not qualify. For the qualification of such organizations, a ruling should be obtained from the Internal Revenue Service.[2]

Eligible Employees

To be eligible for the tax shelter, the individual must be an employee of a qualified charitable organization or of a public school system. The individual may be the top executive or the lowest paid clerk. He or she may be a seasonal, part-time, or full-time employee. But he or she

---

[2] If the activity of the facility is such that if it were not publicly operated it could qualify under Section 501(c)(3), and if it has sufficient independence from the state, and so on, it may be able to obtain a ruling that it is a counterpart of a Section 501(c)(3) organization.

must be an employee—not an independent contractor. This point requires particular attention in connection with certain professional people (such as radiologists, pathologists, and anesthesiologists) who may or may not, in a given set of circumstances, in fact be employees.[3] Clerical, administrative, supervisory, and custodial employees of public school systems qualify, as well as teachers.[4]

Annuity Contract Purchased by an Employer

In speaking of "an annuity contract . . . purchased . . . by an employer," the statute gives no indication of what constitutes an annuity contract or a purchase by an employer. Presumably, an annuity contract refers to a contract to pay annuity benefits issued by an insurance company regularly engaged in the business of issuing such contracts.[5] It would appear to make no difference whether such a contract is a single-premium or annual-premium contract or whether it provides for fixed or variable annuity payments, immediate or deferred, with or without a refund provision.

For many years the Internal Revenue Service took the position that a contract which provided a life insurance benefit would not qualify as a tax-deferred annuity. But the regulations now provide that "an individual contract issued after December 31, 1962, or a group contract which provides incidental life insurance protection may be purchased as an annuity contract" to which Section 403(b) applies. The expression incidental life insurance protection presumably has the same meaning as it has with respect to insurance purchased under qualified trusts.[6]

Also, after December 31, 1962 the term annuity includes a so-called face-amount certificate but does not include a contract or certificate

---

[3] Some professionals in the service of tax-exempt organizations may be barred by ethical or legal considerations from meeting the tests for the required employer-employee relationship. See Rev. Rul. 66–274, 1966–2 CB 446 for an outline of criteria for determining the relationship between a physician and a hospital. Also, see *Ravel v. Comm'r.*, 26 TCM 885 (1967) and *Azad v. U.S.*, 388 F. 2d 74 (1968).

[4] In addition, the regulations provide that one who is elected or appointed to certain public offices may qualify if there is a requirement that to hold the office such person must be trained or experienced in the field of education. For example, a regent or trustee of a state university or a member of a board of education is not eligible. But a commissioner or superintendent of education will generally be eligible. Reg. 1.403(b)–1(b)(5).

[5] Including fraternal benefit associations. It seems doubtful that the term would include a contract issued by the charitable employer itself, even though such an employer may upon occasion enter into an annuity contract for other purposes. Annuity guarantees of a funded state system, existing as a separate entity, satisfy the statutory requirement. Rev. Rul. 67–387, IRB 1967–45.

[6] For a discussion of the meaning of incidental life insurance under qualified plans, see Chapter 2.

issued after that date which is transferable.[7] The regulations spell out
in some detail what is meant by the term nontransferable, and their
language has been used as a guide by insurers in appropriately endorsing
their contracts.

Thus, any annuity contract, individual or group, ordinarily issued by
an insurance company may be used to provide a tax-deferred annuity,
provided it contains an appropriate restriction respecting transferability.

In recent years, new contracts have been developed by many insurers
to accommodate the needs of the tax-deferred annuity market. One can
now find contracts with premiums payable for only nine or ten consecutive months during a year, in order to meet the needs of payroll schedules
of educational institutions. Contracts also are available which permit
variations in the amount of premiums paid each year and therefore are
readily adaptable to varying incomes (hence, varying annual exclusion
allowances).

It would appear that payment of premiums will satisfy the "purchase"
requirement of the statute. Thus, a qualified employer may assume the
payment of premiums on an individual annuity contract already owned
by one of its employees and will be considered as having purchased a
tax-deferred annuity for the employee in each year that premiums are
so paid, to the extent of the available exclusion allowance and provided
that the contract contains the requisite restriction as to transferability.

As was mentioned previously, ERISA substantially expands the range
of permissible investments and terminates the heretofore statutorily sanc-
tioned insurance company monopoly in the field of tax-deferred annuities. Amounts paid by an employer can be placed in a custodial account
on behalf of an eligible employee for the purpose of purchasing shares
of a regulated investment company (mutual fund).[8]

Employee's Rights Nonforfeitable

Attempted definitions of nonforfeitability are elusive. Without a trust,
the employee's rights under the contract would appear to be nonforfeitable if ownership of the contract is vested solely in him. The same would
appear to be true if there is some form of joint ownership of the contract,
together with an agreement between employer and employee whereby
the employee could not be deprived of benefits provided by annuity pre-

---

[7] I.R.C. 401(g), which reads in its entirety as follows: "For purposes of this section
and sections 402, 403, and 404, the term 'annuity' includes a face-amount certificate,
as defined in section 2(a)(15) of the Investment Company Act of 1940 (15 U.S.C.
sec. 80a–2); but does not include any contract or certificate issued after December
31, 1962, which is transferable, if any person other than the trustee of a trust described in section 401(a) which is exempt from tax under section 501(a) is the
owner of such contract or certificate."

[8] Act, p. 1022(e) adding I.R.C. p. 403(b)(7).

miums previously paid, even though the employer could exercise control over the time of enjoyment of those benefits.

As a practical matter, it would appear that ownership ordinarily is vested solely in the employee, thus leaving him or her free of any restrictions or problems that might arise by virtue of insolvency or change of management of the employer. As sole owner of the contract, the employee is free to exercise any of his or her contractual rights, subject, of course, to restrictions on transferability. Thus, where an insurance company product is involved, the employee may be free to elect a reduced paid-up annuity, to change the contract for a reduced annuity with an earlier maturity date, to surrender the contract, or to borrow against its cash value from the insurer.

Exclusion Allowance

The exclusion allowance for an employee for the taxable year is defined as:

> an amount equal to the excess, if any, of—
> (A) the amount determined by multiplying (i) 20 percent of his includible compensation, by (ii) the number of years of service over
> (B) the aggregate of the amounts contributed by the employer for annuity contracts and excludable from the gross income of the employee for any prior taxable year.

Thus, in general, the measure of the amount that an employer may pay for an employee—without current income tax to the employee—is determined in the following manner. First, 20 percent of the current year's includible compensation is multiplied by the total period of employment (expressed in years).[9] From the product are deducted the sum of prior amounts so expended and certain other similar employer expenditures.

ERISA has established that a Section 403(b) tax-deferred annuity is a defined contribution plan and therefore the annual contribution is subject to a limitation of the lesser of $25,000 or 25 percent of the participant's annual compensation. However, the act does not repeal the exclusion allowance limitations under prior law. The excess difference is the permitted tax-deferred amount for the current year, of course, subject to the 25 percent, $25,000 limitation imposed by ERISA.

If the maximum exclusion allowance as so determined is utilized fully in the current year (for example, by purchase of a single-premium annu-

---

[9] This employment is only employment with the current employer. Prior employment with another qualified employer may not be taken into account. Rev. Rul. 69–629, IRB 1969–51. Also, includible compensation does not include any cost of life insurance under a typical retirement income contract, even though such amount is otherwise reportable as taxable income. Rev. Rul. 68–304, IRB 1968–24.

ity), the exclusion allowance available for future years ordinarily will be merely 20 percent of the then current compensation.

Any contributions of the employer to any other tax-deferred annuity; qualified pension, profit sharing, or annuity plan; qualified bond purchase plan; and so on would be charged against the current year's exclusion allowance—if the employee has previously not been taxed thereon for any reason. Thus, for example, if contributions are being made by the same employer to a qualified plan, the amounts so contributed would reduce the 20 percent available under Section 403(b).

If the employer has never made any prior tax-deferred payments for a particular employee (whether by payment of annuity premiums, by contributions to a qualified plan, or otherwise), the amount described in (B) above will be zero. If this is the employee's first year of employment, the exclusion allowance will be merely 20 percent of his or her includible compensation for the current year.

The computation of the exclusion allowance can be an exceedingly easy or an exceedingly difficult matter, depending upon the complexity of the facts involved. Complicating factors may be introduced by part-time employment, salary reduction agreements, or other benefit plans being currently funded by the same employer which provide tax-deferred compensation. Such complicating factors will be considered subsequently in this chapter.[10]

The initial application of the exclusion allowance formula for an employee with past service may produce a very large exclusion allowance.[11] Ordinarily, a single-premium annuity intended to fully utilize this allowance immediately is not feasible. If less than the full allowance is used, the unused portion will increase the allowance available in future years over what it would have been had the entire past service allowance been fully used, of course, subject to the limits of ERISA.[12]

As practical matter, it is frequently desirable to purchase an annual-premium annuity, so selecting the amount of gross annual premium that: (1) by the normal retirement date, full benefit will have been taken

---

[10] See the section on "Arithmetic of the Exclusion Allowance."

[11] For example, with $10,000 of current includable compensation and 10 years of past service, the exclusion allowance is $0.20 \times \$10,000 \times 10 = \$20,000$.

[12] No reference to "past service allowance" is made in either Section 403(b) or in the regulations. However, use of such an expression will be helpful in examining the operation of the exclusion allowance. It refers to the exclusion allowance that would be available to an employee as a consequence of past service with the same employer which has not otherwise been utilized.

If the full $20,000 exclusion allowance was used after the 10th year of employment, the 11th year exclusion allowance (assuming includible compensation continues at $10,000) is $(0.20 \times \$10,000 \times 11) - \$20,000 = \$22,000 - \$20,000 = \$2,000$. However, if only $15,000 of the initial exclusion allowance had been used, then the 11th year exclusion allowance would be $(0.20 \times \$10,000 \times 11) - \$15,000 = \$22,000 - \$15,000 = \$7,000$. However, ERISA would limit this contribution to $2,500, i.e., 25% of the individual's $10,000 compensation.

of the past service allowance, and (2) in each year the available exclusion allowance will be equal to or greater than the premium payable. In other words, we wish to determine the maximum level amount that may be paid by the employer each year that will take full advantage of the past service allowance over the remaining years of employment.

To do so, first determine the total number of years that will have elapsed between the employee's date of employment and his or her projected retirement date and assume that this present rate of annual includible compensation will continue until retirement.[13] The maximum annual premium will then be 20 percent of includible compensation times total years of service (past and future) divided by future years of premium payments. This may be expressed algebraically as:

$$P = \frac{0.20 \times S \times T}{F}$$

where P is the maximum annual premium, S represents salary, T total years of service (both past and future), and F future years of premium payments.[14] This may be simplified to:

$$P = \frac{S \times T}{5F} \tag{1}$$

If premiums are paid other than annually, the sum of the periodic premiums should not exceed the level premium so determined.[15] If the years of service are actually less than one, the number of years of service should be taken as one.

Special consideration was given in ERISA to certain categories of employees (educational institutions, hospitals, and home health service agencies) to allow those employees who have made little or no contributions in their early careers to make larger catch-up contributions. The three alternatives allowed are as follows:

1. The $25,000 maximum rule. Under this approach, an employee terminating employment can, on a onetime only basis, make up the contributions that could have been made, but were not, during the ten-year period ending on the date of separation. (This amount is 20 percent of the employee's includible compensation multiplied by the number of

---

[13] This assumption will prove to have been too conservative if compensation is subsequently increased. Conversely, it will have been too liberal if compensation decreases. See the section "Caveat about Future Salary Reductions" below.

[14] Thus, in effect, we are finding the employee's total working lifetime exclusion allowance and prorating it over his or her remaining working years.

[15] It is the sum of the periodic premiums actually paid by the employer during a year that should be kept within the limits of the year's exclusion allowance. So if premiums are to be paid, for example, monthly, the size of the annuity or insurance contract will be slightly smaller than if premiums were paid annually.

years of service for the employer not exceeding ten, minus employer contributions already made during the relevant period.) Although no percentage limitation applies, this "one shot catch-up" contribution is limited to a maximum of $25,000.

2. The $15,000 maximum rule. Under this alternative, annual contributions can be made, at any time, equal to the lesser of 25 percent of includible compensation plus $4,000 or the exclusion allowance normally allowed under Internal Revenue Code Section 403(b). The maximum annual deduction allowable under this approach is $15,000.

3. The 25 percent/$25,000 rule. This rule allows the employee to ignore the limitations of the exclusion allowance of 403(b)(2)(A) and use the general limits of ERISA. In this approach, the maximum contribution is limited to the lesser of $25,000 or 25% of compensation. However, the tax deferred annuity contribution must be aggregated with other qualified plan contributions to meet this test. Where the employee is covered by a defined benefit plan and wishes to make a contribution under this rule, the aggregation rules for all plans apply and a defined benefit fraction, as explained in Section 415, IRC, must be determined.

Any election made under one of these special rules will be irrevocable. This is understood to mean that an employee electing to contribute under a special rule must continue to use the same rule in future years.

INCOME TAXATION OF BENEFITS

Income Tax Consequences during Lifetime

During his or her lifetime, and prior to actual receipt of any benefits under the contract, the employee will incur no income tax liability if: (1) the annuity contract contains no element of insurance protection, and (2) all premiums paid by the employer in each year are within the exclusion allowance available for the particular year.

Where the contract provides an incidental insurance benefit, the employee will be taxable in each year on the value of such incidental benefit.[16] Also, any premiums will be currently taxable to the employee to the extent that they exceed the exclusion allowance for the particular year.[17]

---

[16] I.R.C. 72(m)(3)(B); Reg. 1.403(b)–1(c)(3), and 1.72–16(b). The so-called PS 58 (term) costs of the amount at risk under the contract (expected proceeds minus cash value) will be the appropriate measure of the employee's currently taxable benefit. Rev. Rul. 68–304, IRB 1968–24.

[17] If a maximum tax-deferred annuity using a contract providing an incidental insurance benefit is desired, the premium may exceed the exclusion allowance by the (PS 58) cost of the insurance benefit for the year in question. Rev. Rul. 68–304, IRB 1968–24.

Where a Section 403(b) program permits contributions to a custodial account for the purpose of purchasing mutual fund shares, a 6 percent tax is imposed on excess contributions. For the purposes of the imposition of this tax, "excess contributions" means the sum of: (1) the contributions made for a taxable year to the extent that they exceed the lesser of the amount excludable under Section 403(b) or under Section 415, and (2) the amount determined under the same provision for the preceding taxable year, reduced by certain allowable but unused deductions and the sum of the distributions out of the account that have been included in gross income under Section 72(e) of the Internal Revenue Code.

When the employee actually commences receiving benefits, the amounts received are taxable to him or her under Section 72 of the Internal Revenue Code. However, neither capital gains treatment nor the ten-year averaging rule is available with respect to any lump-sum payments. If the employee contributed nothing to the cost of the contract, and if all contributions of the employer were within the limits of the exclusion allowance in each year so that the employee was previously subject to no income tax on such contributions, everything received by the employee will be includible in his or her gross income as received.

If the employee made any contributions (or is deemed to have made contributions), he or she will be entitled to a tax-free recovery of such contributions. The employee will have made, or will be deemed to have made, contributions to the extent that: (1) he or she actually made such contributions out of after-tax money, (2) employer contributions were taxable to the employee by virtue of having exceeded the exclusion allowance for one or more years, or (3) incidental insurance costs were taxable to the employee.

If the benefits are received in one sum, the employee will have ordinary income to the extent of the excess of the amount received over the aggregate contributions. If the employee receives installment payments, an exclusion ratio will be determined, and a portion of each payment proportional to the employee's contributions will be excludable from gross income. The balance of each payment is includible in gross income as received.

But if the employee's aggregate contributions are small enough so that the total guaranteed payments receivable by him or her during the first three years of such payments will exceed the aggregate contributions, the so-called accelerated recovery-of-cost rule is used in lieu of the exclusion ratio (as in the case of retirement benefits under a qualified plan). Thus, under such circumstances, the employee excludes all payments from gross income until he or she has received a tax-free return of the cost (any dividends being fully taxable). Thereafter, all amounts received are taxable to the employee as ordinary income.

Income Tax Consequences after Death

In the case of a true annuity contract, taxation of benefits paid after the employee's death depends upon whether the employee had actually commenced to receive annuity payments prior to death. If such payments had not already begun, the beneficiary would be taxed as if he or she were the employee in the manner described above.

If the employee had already begun to receive payments, taxation of the beneficiary depends on the particular mode of payment applicable at the employee's death. If the only amounts payable after death are in the nature of refund payments, such amounts will be taxable as ordinary income, but only after the amounts so received by the beneficiary (together with all amounts received tax free by the employee during his or her lifetime) exceed the aggregate contributions of the employee. On the other hand, if the amounts payable to the beneficiary are a continuation of installment certain payments (without life contingency), or are payments to a surviving annuitant under a joint and survivor annuity, the beneficiary continues to exclude a portion of payments received each year in accordance with the exclusion ratio determined for the employee.

Beneficiaries under contracts which provide an incidental insurance benefit are taxed in virtually the same manner as beneficiaries of a deceased insured under a qualified pension plan; but capital gains treatment and the ten-year averaging rule are not available for lump-sum payments. The death benefit is composed of Section 101 and Section 72 proceeds, the former being the amount at risk under the insurance contract as of the date of death and the latter being the cash value of the contract determined as of that date.

The Section 101 proceeds will be treated the same as regular personal life insurance: income tax free if received in one sum; or, if received in installments, taxable to the extent that installment payments in any year exceed a pro rata portion of the one-sum proceeds, with the spouse's $1,000 exclusion applicable.

The Section 72 proceeds (i.e., the cash value as of the date of death) will be taxable in the same manner and to the same extent as if the employee had received such proceeds during his or her lifetime, with the single exception that the $5,000 employee death benefit exclusion of Section 101(b) will be applicable under certain circumstances. To the extent applicable, the $5,000 death benefit is deemed to increase the employee's contributions for purposes of determining the beneficiary's taxable income.

The $5,000 death benefit exclusion applies to tax-deferred annuities only under the same circumstances that it would be available with respect to deceased participants of qualified plans. The benefit must be paid, by reason of the employee's death within one taxable year of the distributee. But this tax-free death benefit is not available for employees of public school systems. Nor is it available for employees of every Section 501(c)(3) organization, but only to a certain subclass.[18] If the individual was employed by an organization of the latter type, the choice of how death benefits best may be received will involve a balancing of factors.[19]

ESTATE AND GIFT TAXES

Estate Tax

Unless the employee is employed by an organization which is a member of the previously mentioned subclass of Section 501(c)(3) organizations, the value of all amounts payable after death will be includible in the employee's gross estate for federal estate tax purposes, whether payable to his or her estate or to a named beneficiary.[20] Where, however, the employer is a member of this subclass, the estate tax benefits available for qualified plans will be available for any death benefit under a true annuity contract. Thus, if such payments are to or for the benefit of the estate, they will be included in the gross estate.

On the other hand, if payments are to a named beneficiary, at least some portion of them will be excluded. If the employee made no contributions to the cost of the annuity (and none were attributed to the employee), nothing will be includible in the gross estate upon his or her death. Where contributions were made by (or attributed to) the employee, there will be included in his or her gross estate only such fractional part of the value of the death benefit payable to the beneficiary as corresponds to the ratio of the employee's contributions to the total cost of the annuity.

The favorable estate tax treatment just described in inapplicable to employees of public school systems.

---

[18] That subclass consists of those Section 501(c)(3) organizations exempt from tax under Section 501(a) which are referred to in Section 503(b)(1), (2) or (3): namely, schools (not publicly operated) having a student body in attendance; churches, or conventions or associations of churches; or organizations receiving a substantial part of their support from the general public or from some governmental body.

[19] If proceeds are not taken in one sum, any otherwise available $5,000 exclusion will generally be lost, but the tax liability of the beneficiary is spread out over the years of payment. If proceeds are taken in one sum (provided the employer was a member of the subclass), tax liability will all arise in one year, but an amount of up to $5,000 may entirely escape taxation.

[20] There is no possibility of an employee escaping estate tax liability by transferring his or her rights to another, as any such transfer is barred by the restrictions on transferability required by Section 401(g).

Gift Tax

Where an employee who is employed by a member of the subclass previously mentioned designates a beneficiary to receive refund payments under a tax-deferred annuity or elects a joint and survivor annuity, such designation or election will not constitute a transfer within the meaning of the gift tax laws.[21]

SALARY REDUCTIONS

Current Salary Reductions

At one time the commissioner of internal revenue took the position that the postponing of tax liability would apply only where the annuity is "merely a supplement to past or current compensation," and that, therefore, there would be no postponing of tax liability if the annuity premiums were paid in lieu of existing salary, or even "in lieu of an increase in current compensation" if this were done at the employee's request.

Under the regulations, this position still stands for amounts paid by an employer during taxable years beginning before January 1, 1958. But for taxable years beginning thereafter, a salary reduction in the amount of the payment permitted, and the funds paid out of what would otherwise have been paid as salary will not be constructively received, provided only that:

1. There is an agreement between employer and employee for the latter "to take a reduction in salary, or to forgo an increase in salary, but only to the extent that amounts are earned by the employee after the agreement becomes effective." Such an agreement must be legally binding and irrevocable with respect to amounts earned while the agreement is in effect.
2. The employee must not be permitted to make more than one such agreement with the same employer during any taxable year of the employee.[22]
3. "There may be no substitution of annuity premium or mutual fund contribution for salary already earned."

---

[21] I.R.C. 2517 (which also applies to a participant in a qualified plan). Note that such a designation is not a "transfer" prohibited by the restrictive endorsement required by Section 401(g). Also, this favorable gift tax treatment does not apply to employees of public school systems. Rev. Rul. 68–294, IRB 1968–24.

[22] The reduction may be expressed as a percentage of compensation rather than as a fixed dollar amount. Thus, while the percentage cannot be changed for the balance of the taxable year, the dollar amount actually contributed may change due to changes in compensation. Rev. Rul. 68–58, IRB 1968–6. Also, a change in insurers during a year will not constitute a new agreement. Rev. Rul. 68–179, IRB 1968–16.

Also, it is now clear that the arrangement may be instigated at the request of the employee.

Salary Reduction Agreement

While, from the tax viewpoint, the employee may instigate a salary reduction, there must be a real reduction in his or her compensation. For the employee to merely request that the employer deduct a specified amount from his or her compensation to be applied to a tax-deferred annuity will not suffice. The distinction between a reduction and a deduction cannot be overemphasized. The former will produce the desired tax deferral. The latter will not.

Thus, the employer must enter into a written agreement with the employee for the salary reduction, such agreement to be applicable to compensation for services thereafter rendered until such time as the agreement shall have been terminated by either party.

Caveat about Future Salary Reductions

In the normal course of events, it is unlikely that an employee's compensation will continue without change until retirement, although such an assumption might be made for purposes of determining the maximum annual amount that may be paid without exceeding the employee's projected exclusion allowances. No difficulty will be encountered (with respect to the adequacy of exclusion allowances for future years to cover fully level annual premiums) if the employee receives periodic increases in compensation.[23]

In the remote event, however, that an employee should, in the future, find it necessary to take a cut in compensation, the situation will require a careful review in the first year such a reduction occurs to ascertain the effect upon the current year's (and, perhaps, subsequent years') exclusion allowance.

When and if the reduced compensation problem arises, there would appear to be three possible alternatives: (1) the employee may take a reduced paid-up annuity; (2) the employee may have the employer continue to pay the annuity premium or mutual fund payment, recognizing that the amount paid will currently be taxable to the employee (but only to the extent that it exceeds the exclusion allowance for the year in question); or (3) the employee may pay the premium. The possibility that the reduced compensation problem will arise is not serious. And, if it does arise, satisfactory solutions are available. It would, therefore,

---

[23] As a matter of fact, it may be well to review the picture from time to time to see whether the increase in compensation is sufficient to warrant the purchase of an additional annuity.

seem that this possibility should never discourage one from taking advantage of this provision of the law. However, the possibility should be recognized.

ARITHMETIC OF THE EXCLUSION ALLOWANCE

We have previously considered the problem of determining the maximum amount, P, that may be safely paid by the employer each year to take full advantage of the past service allowance over the remaining years of employment. We noted that:

$$P = \frac{S \times T}{5F} \tag{1}$$

where S represents salary, T total years of service (past and future), and F future years of payments.

But we have made two major assumptions that may not be valid in a given situation, namely: (1) that the annual amount is paid from the employer's own funds without reduction in the employee's current compensation, and (2) that no other tax-deferred contribution (for example, to a qualified pension plan) currently is being made by the employer for the employee. Now, let us consider the situation when one or both of these factors is present.

Maximum Amount—Negotiated Salary Reduction

One important caution must be observed where there is to be a salary reduction while attempting to take advantage of the maximum exclusion allowance. The exclusion allowed is based on 20 percent of the employee's includible compensation, i.e., his or her compensation exclusive of amounts received tax free. Therefore (ignoring past service for the moment), one cannot take a 20 percent reduction in salary and have the reduction applied to tax-deferred payments, since this would produce a consideration equal to 25 percent of the remaining includible compensation. If, however, the salary reduction is limited to one sixth of that paid prior to reduction, then that one sixth of salary will give the maximum excludable annual amount for a future service annuity.[24]

Suppose that an employee (with independent income sources) wishes to take the maximum reduction in salary that would be possible to have the largest possible future annual amount that would utilize his or her exclusion allowance, based on both past and future service, up to the limit.

Assume that there are no prior contributions to be deducted (or future

[24] Since one sixth of salary before reduction is equal to 20 percent of the five sixths of salary which remain after the reduction.

contributions to any other tax-deferred plan or trust for the employee's benefit) and that the salary prior to any reduction, S, would (except for the negotiated reduction) remain constant throughout his or her remaining years of employment. Then the maximum annual amount, P, that can be paid and still be excludable can be expressed as:

$$P = \frac{0.20 \times (S - P) \times T}{F}$$

(noting that $(S - P)$ represents includible compensation after S has been reduced by P). This may be simplified to:[25]

$$P = \frac{S \times T}{5F + T} \tag{2}$$

Maximum Amounts—Other Tax-Deferred Contributions

Where the amount is paid solely from the employer's own funds, i.e., no salary reduction is involved but other tax-deferred contributions are involved (for example, pension contributions), the maximum annual amount, P, is determined by subtracting the aggregate amount of such tax-deferred contributions, C, from 20 percent of includible compensation times total years of service, and dividing the difference so determined by future years of payments.[26] Thus,

$$P = \frac{0.20 \times S \times T - C}{F}$$

This may be simplified to:

$$P = \frac{S \times T - 5C}{5F} \tag{3}$$

Suppose that the ratio of the employer's pension contributions to the employee's salary prior to reduction is known, as in the case of a defined

---

[25] To illustrate the application of the formula, assume a 55-year-old employee with a present salary of $15,000. Suppose that he has 10 years of future service and 30 years of past service. Thus, $S = \$15,000$, $T = 30 + 10 = 40$, and $F = 10$. Therefore, the maximum amount again, of course, subject to ERISA limits (and hence, the maximum salary reduction) would be:

$$P = \frac{S \times T}{5F + T} = \frac{\$15,000 \times 40}{(5 \times 10) + 40} = \$6,666.66.$$

ERISA, however, would impose the 25%/$25,000 limitation so that the maximum amount in this case would be 25% of the employee's salary after the reduction.

[26] Thus, in effect, we are finding the employee's total working lifetime exclusion allowance by first subtracting the total of other tax-deferred contributions and then prorating it over the remaining working years.

contribution (money-purchase) pension plan. Designate this ratio as Q. Then if $C = Q \times S \times T$ (i.e., if the aggregate of pension contributions during the working years equals a constant percentage of S times total years of service), Formula (3) may be expressed in the form:

$$P = \frac{S \times T - 5(Q \times S \times T)}{5F}$$

that is,

$$P = \frac{(1 - 5Q)ST}{5F} \tag{4}$$

Salary Reduction and Other Tax-Deferred Contributions

It will be recalled that in cases where there is to be a salary reduction (and ignoring past service), the employee's current cash compensation should be reduced by not more than one sixth if the amount paid via the salary reduction is not to exceed 20 percent of includible compensation after salary reduction.

Suppose that the employer is making current pension contributions for the employee (but has not previously done so). If the ratio of the employer's pension contribution to the employee's salary prior to reduction is Q, then the maximum permissible salary reduction, P, to be devoted to the tax-deferred annuity must be such that:

$$P + Q \times S = 0.20(S - P)$$

i.e., the sum of tax-deferred contributions equals 20 percent of includible compensation (after salary reduction). Solving for P, this may be reduced algebraically to the formula[27]:

$$P = \frac{(1 - 5Q)S}{6} \tag{5}$$

In Formula (5), no past service was taken into account. In Formula (4), no salary reduction is involved. Where both such factors must be considered,

$$P = \frac{0.20(S - P)T - Q \times S \times T}{F}$$

---

[27] It will be observed that if $Q = 0$ (i.e., if there is no employer contribution to a qualified plan with respect to the employee), we would have

$$P = \frac{(1 - 0)S}{6} = \frac{S}{6}$$

In other words, we arrive at the familiar salary reduction of one sixth.

that is,[28]

$$P = \frac{(1 - 5Q)ST}{5F + T} \qquad (6)$$

Employer Pension Contributions Unknown

Frequently, the actual amount previously contributed by the employer to provide pension benefits for a specified employee are not known. The plan may expressly describe the retirement benefits to be furnished, leaving the amount necessary to fund the plan to be actuarially determined, without allocation of actual contributions among individual employees. For such situations, the regulations provide explicit rules for the computation of the excludable amounts to be charged against the employee's annual exclusion allowance.

Part-Time Employees

If an employee is a part-time employee or is a full-time employee for only part of a year, he or she is allowed only an appropriate fraction of a year in computing the number of years of service. The fraction to be used is the ratio of the time spent by the employee in the employer's service during that year to the time that would be spent on a similar job for the same employer by a full-time employee.

For example, a full-time instructor at a college with the usual nine-month year is a full-time employee; but a librarian employed by an organization whose employees normally work the year round (and get no vacation) is a three-quarter-time employee if he or she works for the organization for only nine months during the year. If the normal teaching load at a college is 12 hours per week, a part-time instructor carrying a 9-hour load for the nine-month academic year would be a three-quarter-time employee. If the instructor carries a nine-hour load for only four and one half months during the year, he or she is a three eighths-time employee.

These fractional years of service are then aggregated to find the number of years of service.[29] This is then multiplied by 20 percent of annualized includible compensation to arrive at the exclusion allowance. But if the employee's part-time work is constant—for example, if he or she works one quarter of a year every year, and his or her salary in that one

---

[28] The mathematically astute reader will note that Formula (6) is a generalized form of Formulas (2) and (5), all involving salary reductions. Also, Formula (3) is a generalized form of Formulas (1) and (4), neither of which involves salary reductions.

[29] But if the number of years of service thus computed for a part-time employee is less than one whole year, the number of years of service should be taken as one.

quarter of a year is the same for at least the previous four years, or as many years as are necessary to aggregate one full year of employment, we can completely ignore the part-time status and treat the employee for purposes of the formulas as though he or she were a full-time employee.

SOME FURTHER TAX CONSIDERATIONS

Social Security Taxes and Benefits

In 1953, the Revenue Service ruled that the payment of a premium by the employer on a tax-deferred annuity for an employee does not constitute "wages" as defined under the Federal Insurance Contributions Act and, therefore, that such payment was "not subject to withholding for federal employment or income tax purposes." This ruling also held that the employer was not required to file an information return Form 1099 for such payment.

A 1965 ruling, while reaffirming the prior ruling generally, distinguished it, insofar as FICA considerations are concerned, where voluntary salary reduction agreements are involved. Amounts used by the employer pursuant to a salary reduction agreement to purchase an annuity for the employee are now considered as "wages" for purposes of the FICA, even though such amounts are excludable from gross income. The prior ruling still applies to a situation where the employer uses its own funds, rather than one where the employee takes a voluntary salary reduction to provide the necessary funds. Thus, for FICA purposes, a salary reduction to purchase a tax-deferred annuity is treated as though the annuity premium was received currently as wages by the employee.

Wage Withholding

Any amount excludable from gross income under Section 403(b) is not subject to withholding of income tax (whether or not a voluntary salary reduction agreement is involved). If the contract includes life insurance, however, the PS 58 cost of insurance is subject to withholding.

Measure of Pension Benefits

An employer who maintains a qualified pension plan may define compensation covered by the plan to include premiums on tax-deferred annuities, as well as cash compensation paid. Even though a salary reduction is effected to provide for the purchase of a tax-deferred annuity, other retirement benefits provided by the employer may be measured by the amount of unreduced salary.

CONSIDERATIONS OF LOCAL LAW

Employees of Public School Systems

When the use of public funds is involved in the proposed purchase of a tax-deferred annuity, many questions of state law arise. May such funds be used to purchase a tax-deferred annuity? If so, is an incidental insurance benefit permitted or prohibited? Is a voluntary salary reduction agreement allowed? Unfortunately, these questions have not been answered in all states.

Where a voluntary salary reduction agreement is permitted, does such a reduction also require a reduction in the teacher's benefits under the state retirement system? In most states, no such reduction is required. The rulings that have dealt with this issue, expressly or by implication, were concerned with a voluntary salary reduction agreement. It may be inferred that state law may not permit the use of public funds to purchase tax-deferred annuities except on a voluntary salary reduction basis. Otherwise, there may be a violation of salary scales established by law.

State Income Taxes

No uniform pattern has as yet developed as to the tax status of tax-deferred annuities for state income tax purposes, whether they be purchased for employees of Section 501(c)(3) organizations or public school systems. Some states have ruled that the annuity premiums would be excludable from gross income under the state income tax law to the extent excludable under the federal income tax laws; other states have taken a contrary position.

State Premium Taxes

A significant portion of the total tax burden imposed on life insurance companies arises out of the premium taxes imposed by the states. However, only about one half of the states impose such a tax on annuity premiums. Where such taxes are imposed, the current rates range from 1 to 2.5 percent. While the majority of states which impose a tax on annuity premiums give no special relief to tax-deferred annuity premiums, some states do give them preferential treatment.

21

Employee Retirement Income Security Act of 1974

The Employee Retirement Income Security Act of 1974 (ERISA) became law on September 2, 1974. The act applied immediately for new employee benefit plans; for most existing plans, the effective date of many of the act's significant provisions was established as the first day of the plan year beginning after December 31, 1975—for calendar year plans, an effective date of January 1, 1976.

Although thought of primarily as a law that relates to pension plans, ERISA is quite broad in scope. The definition of "pension plan," for example, includes most deferred compensation plans—whether or not qualified under federal tax law. Thus, this term includes qualified pension, profit sharing, thrift and savings and stock bonus plans, as well as most nonqualified plans of deferred compensation and special pension arrangements that frequently have been established on a nonqualified current disbursement basis (e.g., special early retirement subsidies, cost of living increases provided for retired employees, and so on).[1] Employee welfare plans (e.g., life insurance, medical benefits, disability income, and so forth) also are covered by ERISA, but only to the extent of its disclosure and fiduciary provisions.

Certain plans are excluded from coverage. The excluded plans include government plans, church plans (unless they elect coverage), plans main-

---

[1] Nonqualified deferred compensation plans maintained for a select group of management or highly paid employees are subject only to the disclosure provisions of ERISA; however, the secretary of labor currently has exempted these plans from ERISA's disclosure requirements, and only requires that the Department of Labor be notified of the existence of any such plan and the number of employees covered by the plan.

tained outside the United States primarily for aliens employed abroad, plans maintained solely to provide statutory workmen's compensation, unemployment compensation or disability benefits, and plans to provide contributions or benefits in excess of the limits set for qualified plans. Plans maintained by an employer who is engaged only in intrastate commerce are not subject to the act.

ERISA establishes a number of different standards and requirements for "pension plans." The major areas where ERISA has set standards or has legislated change are as follows:

A. Plan provisions.
    1. Definition of service.
    2. Eligibility for participation.
    3. Vesting (including accrual of benefits).
    4. Spouse benefits.
    5. Limits on benefits and contributions.
    6. Termination of plan.
B. Funding.
    1. Minimum funding.
    2. Tax deduction limits.
C. Plan administration.
    1. Disclosure.
    2. Fiduciary responsibility.
    3. Taxation of lump-sum distributions.
D. Plan termination insurance.
E. Individual retirement savings (IRAs).
F. Plans for the self-employed.

The purpose of this chapter is to provide an overview of these major features of ERISA as they apply to pension plans and to indicate the significant changes from prior law. Of necessity, this overview presupposes a basic knowledge of pension and profit sharing plans. Those features of ERISA which are discussed in the previous chapters of this text (e.g., plan design, funding) are treated only in summary form. It is recognized that this approach creates a certain amount of redundancy; however, at this early stage of compliance with ERISA such redundancy seems both unavoidable and desirable. Those features that are not discussed elsewhere in this text (e.g., fiduciary responsibilities, plan termination insurance) are treated in greater detail in the discussion that follows. They are treated here, rather than in the balance of the text, since, except in a broad sense, they had no counterpart in prior law and practice with specific reference to pension planning. It should be observed, however, that any definitive analysis of ERISA will have to await further rules and regulations, court decisions and, possibly, corrective legislation.

PLAN PROVISIONS

Prior to the passage of ERISA, employers had a great deal of flexibility in choosing various plan provisions. As indicated earlier, however, minimum standards now must be met for matters such as the way in which service is determined and the criteria set for eligibility requirements and for vesting.[2] The following material discusses the major requirements of ERISA that deal with plan provisions.

Definition of Service

To the extent that service is taken into account in determining eligibility for participation or for vesting, it must meet the explicit minimum requirements set forth in ERISA. Generally speaking, a plan must give an employee credit for a year of service for any computation period during which the employee works 1,000 hours. (The computation period is a 12-month period and may be established as a plan year, calendar year, or an employment year; however, in the case of service used for eligibility purposes, the initial 12-month computation period must begin with date of employment.) The minimum requirement with respect to the crediting of hours of service is that the employee must receive credit for each hour for which services were performed and for which the employee is entitled to direct or indirect compensation. With the exceptions noted below, service must be taken into account to the extent that it occurs after age 22, even though rendered while the employee is not a participant in the plan. Also, service must include periods of employment with any corporation that is a member of a controlled group of corporations (i.e., where there is 80 percent control). Similar principles apply for service in an unincorporated business under common control. Service with a predecessor employer also must be taken into account if the employer maintains the plan of the predecessor; if the employer maintains a plan which is not the plan of the predecessor, service with the predecessor will have to be considered to the extent prescribed in regulations.

The following periods of service may be disregarded:

1. Service prior to age 22 (unless the plan's vesting provisions are based upon the rule of 45, in which event, service prior to age 22 must be taken into account if it is rendered while the employee is a participant in the plan).
2. Any period during which the employee did not elect to contribute under a plan requiring employee contributions.
3. Years of service prior to the establishment of the plan (or predecessor plan).

---

[2] It is, of course, permissible to utilize plan provisions that are more liberal than those required by ERISA.

4. Employment prior to January 1, 1971 but only if the employee has not had three years of service after December 31, 1970.

In the case of seasonal industries where the customary period of employment is less than 1,000 hours during a calendar year, the term "year of service" will be determined by regulation. In the maritime industry, 125 days of service will be treated as the equivalent of 1,000 hours of service.

One of the many significant provisions in ERISA is the "break in service" rule. In the past, it was unusual for plans to aggregate service for an employee with several different periods of employment. Under ERISA, however, broken service must be aggregated under certain conditions. A "break in service" is defined to be a 12-month computation period (the computation period used for determining vested rights) during which the employee has worked 500 hours or less. In determining the employee's hours of service for purposes of applying the break in service rule, all hours for which the employee is entitled to compensation must be counted even though no services were performed (e.g., sickpay). (If an employee terminates employment and returns within a year and under conditions that there was no break in service for plan purposes, the employee will be treated as though no termination had occurred.) If an employee returns to work for at least one year after a break in service, prior service will have to be taken into account if: (1) the employee was vested (even though only partially) when the break in service occurred; or (2) the period of absence was less than the employee's period of pre-break service. In recognition of the practical problems of reconstructing prior employment records, the break-in-service rule applies on a prospective basis only; current plan provisions will be permitted to apply to periods of broken service that occurred prior to the time the plan must comply with the terms of ERISA. In the case of a defined contribution plan or in the case of a fully insured pension plan, it is not required that years of service after a break in service be taken into account for the purposes of determining the employee's vested interest for employer contributions made prior to the break in service.

Eligibility for Participation

The primary changes legislated by ERISA in the area of eligibility for participation concern the use of years of service and minimum and maximum ages. In brief, if a plan bases eligibility on minimum age or service, eligibility cannot be delayed beyond the time an employee reaches age 25 and completes one year of service—i.e., the maximum service period that can be used is one year and the highest minimum age that can be used is age 25. The only exception to the one-year service requirement occurs when a plan provides for full and immediate vesting. Here, the plan may require up to three years of service in addition to the permissible minimum age requirement of 25.

In addition, the use of entry dates cannot delay the participation of an employee more than six months once he has met the eligibility requirements. Thus, if it is desired to use a service requirement of one year or a minimum age of 25, the plan should provide for at least semiannual entry dates. (Alternately, a six-month service and a 24½ year minimum age requirement could be combined with an annual entry date.)

A defined contribution plan (pension, profit sharing, or thrift and savings) may no longer use a maximum age for participation. A defined benefit plan (including a target benefit plan), however, may exclude employees who are hired less than five years before the plan's normal retirement date. If a defined benefit plan uses a normal retirement schedule of age 65 or the completion of ten years of service, whichever occurs last, a maximum age provision is not possible.

Besides the above changes, ERISA permits a plan to exclude employees covered by a collective bargaining agreement if there is evidence of good faith bargaining on pensions. Also, aliens employed abroad by a U.S. employer may be excluded even though U.S. citizens at the location are included in the plan.

ERISA continues to permit the use of other nondiscriminatory classifications in determining eligibility for participation. Thus, for example, it continues to be possible to exclude part-time employees, hourly employees, or employees earning less than some minimum compensation level.

Vesting

A major objective of ERISA was to require vesting of an employee's accrued benefits after some reasonable period of service. Accordingly, the vesting provisions of ERISA are of particular significance.

If the plan involves employee contributions, then the employee's right to that portion of the accrued benefit that is attributable to his or her own contributions must be fully vested at all times.[3] The vesting of accrued benefits attributable to employer contributions must be in accordance with one of the three following rules:

1. *The ten-year rule.* No vesting is required prior to the completion of ten years of service; thereafter, the employee must be 100 percent vested.
2. *The 5 to 15 rule.* Graduated vesting is provided, beginning with

---

[3] Note that this does not necessarily require a minimum benefit equal to the amount the employee contributed. In a defined contribution plan, for example, there may have been investment losses that result in value of the employee's contributions being less than the amounts actually contributed by the employee.

25 percent after 5 years of service, increasing 5 percent a year for the next 5 years and 10 percent for the next 5 years, thus producing a 50 percent vested interest after 10 years of service, and a 100 percent vested interest after 15 years of service.

3. *The rule of 45.* The employee achieves a 50 percent interest after the earlier of ten years of service or when the combination of years of service (minimum of five years) and the employee's age total 45; thereafter, the employee's vested interest increases 10 percent per year for the next five years.

The Internal Revenue Service is given the authority to impose more stringent vesting requirements if such action is necessary, in the opinion of the Service, to prevent discrimination. The Congressional Committee Report, however, directs the Internal Revenue Service not to require a vesting schedule more stringent than 40 percent vesting after four years of employment with 5 percent additional vesting for each of the next two years, and 10 percent vesting for each of the following five years. It is quite possible that the Service will impose stricter standards on profit sharing and thrift and savings plans, as has been the case in the past, in order to avoid problems of discrimination.

Class-year vesting (where each year's employer contribution vests after a specified period of time) continues to be permissible provided that not more than five years elapse between the contribution year and the year when full vesting of that contribution is achieved.[4]

ERISA also stipulates minimum standards that must be followed in determining an employee's accrued benefit for purposes of applying one of the above vesting schedules. Again, the plan will be acceptable if it meets any one of three rules:

1. *The 3 percent method.* The employee's accrued benefit must be at least equal to 3 percent of the projected normal retirement benefit for each year of *participation,* to a maximum of 100 percent after $33\frac{1}{3}$ years of participation.
2. *The $133\frac{1}{3}$ percent rule.* The accrued benefit may be the employee's actual benefit earned to date under the plan, provided that any future annual rate of benefit accrual is not more than $133\frac{1}{3}$ percent of the current annual benefit accrual rate.
3. *The fractional rule.* The employee's accrued benefit is not less than the projected normal retirement benefit prorated for years of plan participation.

It is expected that a number of plans will not be able to meet the 3 percent method since this test generally cannot be satisfied in any plan that gives credit for service in excess of $33\frac{1}{3}$ years. However, most plans are

---

[4] Class-year vesting is typically found in thrift and savings plans.

expected to be able to satisfy either or both the 133⅓ percent rule and the fractional rule. A fully insured plan (under which premiums have been paid to date and where there are no loans outstanding) satisfies the accrued benefit requirements. In the case of a defined contribution plan, the employee's accrued benefit will be his or her current account balance.

An employee's accrued benefit does not have to include any ancillary benefits such as death or disability benefits, or benefits designed to make up for anticipated social security benefits.

ERISA also establishes a number of other requirements with respect to the vesting and payment of an employee's benefits.

1. If an employee is less than 50 percent vested and withdraws his or her mandatory contributions, any benefits attributable to employer contributions may be canceled, but any such employee must be permitted to "buy back" the forfeited benefits upon repayment of the withdrawn contributions plus compound interest (currently set at 5 percent). If the employee's vested interest is 50 percent or more, withdrawal of employee contributions cannot result in a cancellation of benefits attributable to employer contributions. (In the case of a defined contribution plan, such a buy back is required only before the employee has incurred a one-year break in service, and interest need not be paid.)

2. Except as provided above, an employee's vested benefit cannot be forfeited under any circumstances (other than death), even if termination of employment is due to dishonesty.

3. The automatic cash-out of an employee's entire interest is permitted upon termination of employment where the value attributable to employer contributions does not exceed $1,750. Under such circumstances and for purposes of determining the employee's accrued benefit, the plan may disregard service for which the employee has received such a payment. If the amount exceeds $1,750 the same will hold true but only if the employee agreed to the cash payment. In any event, if the plan wishes to disregard such service, a terminating employee who has received a cash-out must be permitted to "buy back" the accrued benefit by repaying the cash payment with compound interest (currently set at 5 percent). (In the case of a defined contribution plan, such a buy back is required only before the employee has incurred a one-year break in service, and interest need not be paid.)

4. Any employee who terminates employment must be given written notification of his or her rights, the amount of his or her accrued benefits, the portion (if any) that is vested, and the applicable payment provisions.

5. A terminated employee's vested benefit or a retiree's benefit cannot

be decreased by reason of increases in social security benefits that take place after the date of termination of employment or retirement.

6. If the plan allows an active employee to elect early retirement after attaining a stated age and completing a specified period of service, a terminated employee who has completed the service requirement must have the right to receive vested benefits after reaching the early retirement age specified. However, the benefit for the terminated employee can be reduced actuarially even though the active employee might have the advantage of subsidized early retirement benefits.

7. Any plan amendment cannot decrease an employee's accrued benefit. Also, if the vesting schedule is changed, any participant with at least five years of service must be given the election to remain under the pre-amendment vesting schedule (for both pre- and postamendment benefit accruals).

Spouse Benefits

ERISA requires that if an employee has been married for at least one year prior to his death (or was married on his retirement date), the normal form for the payment of his or her retirement benefit must be at least a 50 percent joint and survivor annuity—i.e., at least 50 percent of the amount of the retirement benefit being paid to the employee during the joint lifetimes of the employee and his or her spouse must be continued to the surviving spouse for the lifetime of such survivor. The employee must be given the right to elect another form of annuity and must be given reasonable notice concerning the terms and conditions of the joint and survivor annuity and the effect of an election not to receive benefits under this form of payment. To prevent anti-selection, the plan is permitted to require that any revocation will become effective only after a time period of up to two years; however, if the employee dies as a result of an accident after retiring and within the revocation period set by the plan (up to the two-year limit), the revocation will be rescinded and the surviving spouse will be entitled to receive benefits.

The provisions applicable to an active employee are different. Here, an employee must have the *option* of electing a preretirement spouse benefit. (ERISA permits the plan to require that the employee and spouse must have been married at least one year at the time of the employee's death.) This option must be given to an employee who is eligible for early retirement (but need not be made available, in any event, until the employee is within ten years of normal retirement). The benefit payable to a surviving spouse under this option must be at least 50 percent of the actuarially reduced amount the employee would be entitled to receive upon early retirement. Again, a two-year preelection period may be required. This preretirement option need not be made available to terminated employees who have a vested interest.

In both cases—the mandatory postretirement and optional preretirement benefit—it will be permissible to charge the employee for the cost of the benefit. Typically, this will be done by reducing the amount of the benefit payable. Thus, while the initial amount of the employee's pension under the plan may be calculated on some other annuity form (e.g., a life annuity or a life annuity with ten years certain), the actual amount of pension payable can be reduced to make payment on the 50 percent joint and survivor annuity basis. The cost of the preretirement spouse benefit also may be charged to the employee by reducing the amount of pension payable to the employee after retirement (or to the surviving spouse if the employee dies before retirement).

Limits on Benefits and Contributions

The annual employer-provided benefit for an employee under a defined benefit plan cannot exceed $75,000 (adjusted for future increases in the Consumer Price Index) or, if lesser, 100 percent of the employee's average annual pay for the three consecutive years of highest pay.[5] These limits do not apply to employee-provided benefits and need not be adjusted for preretirement ancillary benefits such as death or disability benefits. If early retirement cannot occur before age 55, no adjustment need be made even for subsidized early retirement benefits; however, if retirement can occur prior to age 55, the $75,000 limit must be actuarially reduced. The limits are reduced proportionately if the employee completes less than ten years of service before retirement. The limits also must be reduced for the value of any pension-related, postretirement death benefits (e.g., a ten-year certain and continuous benefit); however, a reduction will not be required if payments are made on a joint and survivor basis (even if the percentage continued is 100 percent) and the joint annuitant is the employee's spouse.

If the plan was in existence on October 2, 1973, these limits are subject to a special provision. In essence, this provision permits the payment of a pension in an amount calculated in accordance with the plan provisions in effect on October 2, 1973 and ignoring any pay increases after that date. While this amount may exceed $75,000, it will not be permitted to exceed 100 percent of the employee's annual rate of pay on October 2, 1973.

In the case of a defined contribution plan, the limitation is expressed

---

[5] If an employee has never been covered by a defined contribution plan of the employer, an annual pension of up to $10,000 can be paid even if it exceeds 100 percent of pay; however, this limit will be reduced proportionately if the employee has less than ten years of service.

in terms of the maximum annual addition that may be made to the employee's account.[6] This maximum annual addition is limited to the lesser of 25 percent of annual pay or $25,000 (adjusted for future increases in the Consumer Price Index).[7] The annual addition is defined to include employer contributions and reallocated forfeitures and, in some situations, part of the employee's own contributions. If the employee's contributions are 6 percent of pay or less, such contributions will not be considered as part of the annual addition. If the employee's contributions (including both mandatory and voluntary contributions) exceed 6 percent of pay, the lesser of the employee's contributions that exceed 6 percent of pay or 50 percent of the total employee contributions will be considered as part of the annual addition.

If an employer maintains both a defined benefit and a defined contribution plan, there will be a combined limit of 140 percent of the limits considered individually. The combined limit is applied on a cumulative basis that reflects the maximum allowable amounts for years of prior service.

Where any limit is applicable, the employer may establish an excess benefit plan to restore the benefits or contributions lost by reason of the application of the limit. Such a plan is not subject to the provisions of ERISA, but may not be qualified or prefunded on a tax deductible basis.

If an employee is participating in the plans of another incorporated or unincorporated business under common control (only a 50 percent interest is necessary for this purpose), the plans of all such businesses must be aggregated for purposes of applying the limitations on benefits and contributions.

Termination of Plan

ERISA prescribes the order in which plan assets are to be allocated in the event of plan termination. This order is as follows:

1. Voluntary employee contributions.
2. Mandatory employee contributions.
3. Benefits for employees who have been retired for at least three years or who were eligible to retire at least three years prior to the plan termination date (but based upon the provisions of the plan in effect five years prior to the plan termination date).
4. All other benefits which are guaranteed by the Pension Benefit Guaranty Corporation.

---

[6] Target benefit plans are considered to be defined contribution plans for the purpose of applying these limits.

[7] Note that this is a limit that is separate and apart from the average annual deductible contribution limit of 15 percent of payroll that applies to profit sharing plans.

5. All other vested benefits.
6. All other accrued benefits.

If assets are insufficient to accommodate the benefits in any one of the first four and the sixth classes, the assets will be prorated within that class. For the fifth class, assets also are to be allocated on a pro rata basis in the event they are insufficient to provide full benefits, but the allocation will recognize any plan amendments made during the preceding five years. Thus, the allocation will be made as of the most recent amendment which permits a full allocation (if at all), and the prorating will apply only to any excess assets on the basis of the next following amendment, and so forth.

It should be noted that these provisions of ERISA became effective on July 1, 1974 for single-employer plans. The effective date for negotiated multiemployer plans is January 1, 1978.

Other Plan Provisions

Several other areas of plan design also are affected by ERISA. The most significant of these areas are as follows:

1. *Cash/Deferred Profit Sharing Plans; Salary Reduction Plans.* If any new plan (one adopted after June 27, 1974) permits an employee to elect to receive part of his or her compensation in one or more alternative forms, the employee will be considered in constructive receipt of the amount of compensation involved. Thus, even though the employee elects to defer such amount, it will have to be reported as currently taxable income. The major impact of this change will be felt in the profit sharing field where cash/deferred profit sharing plans have allowed employees to elect to receive current contributions in cash or to have them deferred and placed in trust, and in salary reduction plans where employees agree to take a reduction in compensation in order to participate in a deferred benefit plan. Plans of this type that were in effect on June 27, 1974 will not be affected prior to January 1, 1977. At that time, the Internal Revenue Service will have the authority to issue regulations that could treat existing and new plans in the same fashion.
2. *Assignments.* The plan must prohibit the assignment or alienation of benefits; however, the plan may be written to permit an employee to assign up to 10 percent of any benefit payment.
3. *Loans.* An employee may use his or her vested interest as collateral for a loan from the plan (if such loan is not a prohibited transaction) without violating the prohibition against assignments.
4. *Mergers and Consolidations.* A plan also must provide that the

value of an employee's benefit cannot be diminished in any way by any merger or consolidation with, or transfer of assets or liabilities to, any other plan.

5. *Payment of Benefits.* Benefit payments must commence, unless otherwise elected by the employee, no later than the 60th day after the *latest* of the close of the plan year in which the employee:

   a. Attains the earlier of age 65 or the normal retirement age specified in the plan,

   b. Completes ten years of participation, or

   c. Terminates employment.

6. *Increases in Social Security.* If social security benefits increase after an employee retires or after termination of employment with a vested interest, such increases cannot operate to reduce the employee's plan benefits.

FUNDING

The major provisions of ERISA that impact on funding are those that establish minimum funding requirements and those that affect tax deductible limits.

Minimum Funding Standards

For plans adopted after January 1, 1974, the minimum funding standards apply for plan years beginning after September 2, 1974. For plans in effect on January 1, 1974, the requirements generally become effective with the first plan year beginning after December 31, 1975; for existing collectively bargained plans, however, they become effective for the earlier of plan years beginning after the termination date of the last bargaining agreement (not before December 31, 1975), or December 31, 1980. These minimum funding requirements apply to all pension plans, whether qualified or not, except for deferred compensation plans maintained for a select group of management or highly paid employees. Fully insured plans are not subject to the minimum funding standards if all premiums have been paid to date and if there are no outstanding loans or obligations.

Until fully funded, the minimum funding requirement is equal, on a cumulative basis, to the sum of the plan's normal cost plus the amortization of unfunded liabilities over stipulated periods of time. The amortization periods for different liabilities and for different plans are shown in Table 21–1.

The actuarial methods and assumptions used to determine minimum funding requirements must be reasonable, in the aggregate, and must offer the actuary's best estimate of anticipated experience under the plan.

TABLE 21–1
Amortization Requirements

Sources of Unfunded Liability	Single-Employer Plan	Negotiated Multi-employer Plan
Plans in existence on 1/1/74.	40 years	40 years
New plans	30 years	40 years
Amendments (increased liability)	30 years	40 years
Actuarial gains or losses, net.	15 years	20 years
Change in actuarial assumptions	30 years	30 years

Also, the value of plan assets must be determined on a basis which takes fair market value into account.[8]

An alternate minimum funding standard is available. This alternative method utilizes the unit credit cost method and requires that assets be reflected at full fair market value.

An excise tax may be imposed in any plan year in which there is a funding deficiency. The initial tax will be 5 percent of the funding deficiency; if the deficiency is not corrected after notice from the Internal Revenue Service and within the time limit allowed (90 days unless extended by the Service), a further tax of 100 percent of the funding deficiency will be imposed.

Tax Deductible Limits

ERISA made four changes in tax deductible limits for qualified pension plans:

1. The 5 percent of pay deduction limit was discontinued.
2. The maximum tax deductible limit was increased from the normal cost of the plan plus 10 percent of the actuarial liability to normal cost of the plan plus an amount necessary to amortize the actuarial liability over ten years.
3. The maximum tax deductible limit was in any event increased to whatever amount is necessary to satisfy ERISA's minimum funding requirements, but not in excess of the full funding limit.
4. The former possible 30 percent of pay limit for contributions plus contribution carryovers to pension and deferred profit sharing plans was reduced to 25 percent.

---

[8] This does not require that exact market value be reflected; however, some part of market value should be recognized under any acceptable technique (e.g., using an adjusted market value or a time-weighted average of market values).

PLAN ADMINISTRATION

The administrative burden imposed upon employers by ERISA is quite substantial. In addition to the obvious administrative aspects of all of the matters discussed in this chapter, there are three separate items of plan administration that deserve specific attention. These items are: (1) disclosure requirements; (2) fiduciary responisbilities; and (3) taxation of lump-sum distributions.

Disclosure

The disclosure requirements of ERISA are discussed at length in Chapter 13. Accordingly, only the major aspects are summarized in the following material.

These disclosure requirements apply (unless exemptions are granted) to all plans, regardless of size. In addition, some organizations that were previously exempt from disclosure (e.g., Section 501(c)(3) organizations) must now comply with these disclosure requirements.

The following items must be filed with appropriate government agencies, at prescribed times, as well as be made available to employees:

1. Summary plan description (the booklet or other communication that is given to employees).
2. Plan description (Form EBS–1).
3. Plan amendments (parts of Form EBS–1).
4. Annual report (Form 5500).
5. Annual report summary.
6. Plan termination reports.

Plans participants (and beneficiaries receiving benefits under pension plans) must receive the following:

1. Summary plan description.
2. Plan amendment summaries.
3. Summary of annual report.
4. Statement of benefits (for employees who have terminated employment).
5. Written explanation to any participant or beneficiary whose claim for benefits is denied.
6. Notification of rights to elect or revoke options providing for the payment of spouse benefits, including information as to the effect of making or not making any such election or revocation.

In addition to the above, certain items must be given to plan participants upon written request and/or made available for examination at the principal office of the plan administrator and at other convenient locations. These items are as follows: (1) the plan description (EBS–1);

(2) supporting plan documents; (3) a complete annual report (Form 5500); (4) a personal pension benefits statement; (4) termination reports (should any pension plan wind up its affairs); and (6) plan amendment description.

Fiduciary Responsibilities

The fiduciary provisions of ERISA were generally effective on January 1, 1975. The prohibited transactions provisions, however, will not become effective until June 30 1984 in the case of investments where, on July 1, 1974, the plan was not in violation of the then applicable law and where the situation continues to be at least as favorable as an arm's-length transaction with an unrelated party. Likewise, the effective date for the prohibited services provisions will be June 30, 1977 if such services were ordinarily and customarily offered on June 30, 1974. Provision was also made to extend the effective date until January 1, 1976 with respect to specific plans where the secretary of labor determines that the delay is necessary and that it will not adversely affect plan participants.

A person (or corporation) will be considered a fiduciary under ERISA if that person exercises any discretionary authority or control over the management of the plan, any authority or control over assets held under the plan or the disposition of plan assets, renders investment advice for direct or indirect compensation (or has any authority or responsibility to do so), or has any discretionary authority or responsibility in the administration of the plan.

Fiduciary Duties.   A fiduciary is required to discharge all duties solely in the interest of participants and beneficiaries and for the exclusive purpose of providing plan benefits and defraying reasonable administrative expenses. In addition, a fiduciary is charged with using the care, skill, prudence, and diligence that a prudent person who is familiar with such matters would use under the circumstances then prevailing—a standard that has come to be called the "prudent expert" rule. A fiduciary also is responsible for diversifying investments so as to minimize the risk of large losses unless it is clearly prudent not to diversify. Finally, the fiduciary must conform with the documents governing the plan and must invest only in assets subject to the jurisdiction of the U.S. courts.

Liability of a Fiduciary.   Under the labor provisions of ERISA, a fiduciary will be personally liable for any breach or violation of responsibilities, and will be liable to restore any profits made through the use of plan assets. Under the tax provisions, a fiduciary also may be subject to excise taxes for violation of the prohibited transaction provisions.

A fiduciary also may be liable for the violations of a co-fiduciary if the fiduciary knowingly participates in or conceals a violation, has knowledge of a violation, or by the fiduciary's own violation enables the co-fiduciary to commit a violation. However, if a plan uses separate trusts, a trustee of one trust is not responsible as a co-trustee of the other trust. Also, a fiduciary will not be responsible for the acts of a duly appointed investment manager (except to the extent that the fiduciary did not act prudently in selecting or continuing the use of the investment manager). A trustee also is not responsible for following the direction of named fiduciaries in making investment decisions (if the plan so provides).

Noninvestment activities can be delegated by a fiduciary if the plan so permits and the procedure for doing so is clearly spelled out; however, fiduciaries remain responsible, under the prudent "expert" rule, for persons delegated those responsibilities. Similarly, they remain responsible for the acts of their agents in performing ministerial duties.

Plan provisions that purport to relieve a fiduciary of responsibilities under ERISA are void and of no effect. However, a plan, employer, union, or fiduciary may purchase insurance to cover the fiduciary's liability, but if the plan purchases this insurance the insurer must have subrogation rights against the fiduciary. An employer or union may also agree to indemnify a fiduciary against personal liability.

Prohibited Transactions.   Both the labor and tax provisions of ERISA prohibit certain transactions between the plan and parties in interest. A party in interest is broadly defined and includes, for example, any fiduciary, a person providing services to the plan, any employer or employee organization whose employees or members are covered by the plan, a direct or indirect owner of 50 percent or more of the business interest, a relative of any of the above, and an employee, officer, director or a person having 10 percent or more of the ownership interest in any of the above.

The following are prohibited transactions between the plan and a party of interest:

1. The sale, exchange or leasing of property.
2. Lending money or extending credit (including the funding of the plan by contribution of debt securities).
3. Furnishing goods, services or facilities.
4. Transfer to or use of plan assets.
5. Acquisition of qualifying employer securities and real property in excess of allowable limits.

Additionally, a fiduciary cannot deal with assets in his or her own interest or for his or her own account, act in any capacity involving the plan on behalf of anyone having an adverse interest, or receive any consideration for the fiduciary's own personal account from any party dealing with the plan.

A number of exemptions to the prohibited transaction rules are specifically provided for in ERISA, and there also is a provision for applying for additional exemptions. Among the specific exemptions granted are loans to participants (if available in a nondiscriminatory fashion to all participants, if adequately secured, and if the loan bears a reasonable rate of interest), the furnishing of office space and services for reasonable compensation, the providing of ancillary banking services where this is done without interference with the interests of the plan and the plan participants and, in the case of banks and insurance companies, the utilization of their own facilities to fund their own plans.

If a qualified plan engages in a prohibited transaction, it will no longer disqualify the plan. However, an excise tax of 5 percent of the amount involved will be levied. If the situation is not corrected within the time allowed (90 days unless extended by the Internal Revenue Service), a further excise tax of 100 percent of the amount involved will be levied upon the fiduciary who participated in the prohibited transaction.

Investment in Employer Securities and Real Property. Qualifying employer securities include stock. Qualifying employer securities also include marketable obligations under specified rules relating to the source of the purchase, the establishment of the price, and the percentage of the issue held by the plan and other persons. Qualifying employer real property is real property which is dispersed geographically, is suitable for more than one use, and has been leased to the employer.

Profit sharing, stock bonus, and thrift and savings plans that specifically so provide may invest without limit in qualifying employer securities or real property.[9] If the plan does not specifically provide for the amount of employer securities or real property to be held, the 10 percent limit described below will be applicable.

A pension plan may not acquire (by any means) employer securities and real property if the immediate effect of this would cause more than 10 percent of the fair market value of plan assets to be so held. If a plan held more than 10 percent of its assets in employer securities and real property on January 1, 1975, it will have until December 31, 1984 to conform to the 10 percent rule; 50 percent compliance must be achieved by December 31, 1979.

Prohibition against Holding Office. If convicted of certain specified crimes, a person cannot serve as a plan administrator, fiduciary, officer, trustee, custodian, counsel, agent, employee, or consultant for five years after conviction (or the end of imprisonment, if later). This prohibition will not apply if citizenship rights have been restored or if approved by the United States Board of Parole.

---

[9] This also applies to defined contribution pension plans that so provided on September 2, 1974. Other defined contribution pension plans are subject to the 10 percent limit.

Bonding. The bonding provisions of the Welfare and Pension Plans Disclosure Act have been transferred to the fiduciary provisions of ERISA. All fiduciaries and persons who handle plan funds or other plan assets are to be bonded for 10 percent of the aggregate amount handled, with a minimum bond of $1,000 and a maximum bond of $500,000. The secretary of labor may raise the $500,000 maximum. Bonding generally is not required of corporate trustees or insurance companies with combined capital and surplus of at least $1 million, if the only assets from which benefits are paid are the general assets of the employer or a union, or if the secretary of labor finds that other bonding arrangements or the overall financial condition of the plan is adequate to protect participants.

Establishment of Plan and Trust. A pension plan must be established and maintained pursuant to a written instrument that specifically provides for one or more named fiduciaries. Each plan must provide a procedure for establishing and carrying out a funding policy and method to achieve plan objectives, and must describe any procedure for allocating operational and administrative responsibilities. There also must be a provision which sets forth the amendment procedure and identifies the persons who have authority to amend. The plan also must specify the basis on which payments are made to and from the plan.

Refunds to Employers. Plan assets cannot revert to the employer except in certain specified situations. If a contribution was made in error, it can be returned to the employer within one year from the date the contribution was made to the plan. Also, a contribution may be conditioned upon a favorable ruling from the Internal Revenue Service as to the qualified status of the plan, or upon being allowed as a deduction. If a favorable ruling is not received or if the deduction is disallowed (but only to the extent of the disallowance), the contribution may be returned within one year from the date of denial of tax qualification or tax deduction.

Excess contributions under H.R. 10 plans and individual retirement accounts also may be returned. And, as in the past, if a plan is terminated and there are surplus assets (due to "actuarial error"), these surplus assets may be returned.

Taxation of Lump-Sum Distributions

The Tax Reform Act of 1969 created many problems in its effort to change the taxation of lump-sum distributions from qualified plans. ERISA changes in this area were designed to resolve these difficulties and to create more favorable tax treatment. These changes legislated by ERISA were effective as of January 1, 1974.

In general, a lump-sum distribution is defined as the full payment, within one taxable year of the distributee, of the entire value standing to the account of the employee upon death, disability, termination of employment (not applicable to self-employed individuals under H.R. 10 plans), or after attaining age 59½. For this purpose, all trusts under a single type of plan (e.g., defined benefit or defined contribution) and all plans within a given category (pension, profit sharing, or stock bonus) are aggregated and treated as a single plan.

An employee who did not participate in the plan prior to 1974 and who has been a participant for at least five years may elect to treat such a lump-sum distribution under a ten-year averaging rule. Under this rule, the tax is determined by taking one tenth of the distribution and calculating the ordinary income tax on this portion using single tax-payer rates and assuming no exemptions, deductions or other income. The actual tax is then determined by multiplying this amount by ten. There is a minimum distribution allowance equal to the lesser of $10,000 or 50 percent of the total taxable amount, reduced by 20 percent of the amount by which the total taxable amount exceeds $20,000. If available, the minimum distribution allowance is subtracted from the total taxable distribution before calculating the tax.

If the employee participated prior to 1974, a portion of the lump-sum distribution will be treated as a long-term capital gain. Essentially, this will be determined by dividing the employee's total years of participation into the employee's years of participation prior to 1974, and applying the resulting percentage to the total lump-sum distribution. The result so obtained will be the portion of the distribution that qualifies for long-term capital gains treatment. The balance of the distribution will be treated as ordinary income under the ten-year averaging rule.

To determine the amount of tax under the ten-year averaging rule for such an employee, it will be first necessary to calculate the tax that would be applicable to the total distribution as if the entire amount were being taxed under that rule. The actual amount of the tax will be determined by dividing the employee's total years of participation into the employee's years of participation after 1973 and applying the resulting percentage to the tax first determined as though the total distribution were being taxed under the ten-year rule. Years of participation will be measured in years and months, except that any partial year of participation prior to 1974 will be considered a full year.

Several important points should be noted about the taxation of lump-sum distributions:

1. Employee contributions are returnable tax free.
2. Community property laws are disregarded.
3. Regular income-averaging rules continue to be available.

4. The option to elect ten-year averaging is available only once after age 59½.
5. A special five-year look back rule will be applied to aggregate distributions and to calculate the marginal tax rate when the recipient has received more than one lump-sum distribution in the six years ending with the year in which the current lump-sum distribution is being made.
6. If employer securities are included in a lump-sum distribution, prior tax treatment continues to apply and the unrealized appreciation of these securities will not be currently taxable.
7. The value of any annuity contract distributed (including contracts distributed during the preceding five years), even though this amount is not currently taxable, must be taken into account in determining the marginal tax rate on the amount of the distribution that is being taxed under the ten-year averaging rule.
8. The new tax treatment of lump-sum distributions also applies to self-employed individuals who receive lump-sum distributions from H.R. 10 plans at death, disability or after age 59½; moreover, this treatment will apply to assets created under the H.R. 10 plan prior to the passage of ERISA.

PLAN TERMINATION INSURANCE

One of the most significant provisions of ERISA is the guarantee that certain pension benefits will be paid should a pension plan terminate with insufficient assets. To accomplish this, a Pension Benefit Guaranty Corporation (PBGC) was formed. The board of directors of the PBGC consists of the secretaries of the treasury, labor, and commerce. The board will be assisted by a seven-member committee of nongovernment experts appointed by the president. Two members of the advisory committee will represent labor, two will represent employers, and three will represent the general public.

ERISA's plan termination insurance provisions apply to plans that are covered by the vesting and funding provisions of the law. For the most part, coverage is extended only to qualified or qualifiable defined benefit plans. Defined contribution plans are not covered, along with target benefit plans, plans maintained by professional service employers with less than 26 participants, and plans maintained exclusively for substantial owners (i.e., individuals with greater than 10 percent ownership of the business).

Plans that have been in effect for at least five years were fully covered by the plan termination insurance provisions as of July 1, 1974—except to the extent of increased benefits attributable to plan amendments dur-

ing the immediately preceding five years, and except in the case of negotiated multiemployer plans where coverage generally will not take effect
until January 1, 1978.

The following material describes the benefits that are insured by the
PBGC, the premium structure for the coverage provided, the additional
liability that employers might have in the event of plan termination and
the right of the PBGC to recapture certain payments. Also discussed
are the events that must be reported to the PBGC.

Benefits Insured

Only vested pension benefits are insured. The amount insured is
limited to the lesser of: (1) 100 percent of average monthly pay for
the five consecutive years of highest pay or actual years, if less than
five; and (2) $750 increased by the ratio that the social security tax
base in the year of plan termination bears to $13,200 (the social security
tax base in 1974).[10] The benefit guaranteed is on the basis of a life annuity
only, payable at age 65. Ancillary benefits are not guaranteed although
the PBGC may provide optional insurance for such benefits at some
future time.

For a new plan, coverage takes effect at the rate of 20 percent a
year. Thus, for example, if such a plan had been in effect for five years,
full coverage would be available; if it had been in effect for only three
years, the initial level of coverage would be 60 percent.

The five-year concept also applies to increases in benefits due to plan
amendments. Such increases in benefits will be insured only at the rate
of 20 percent for each year that the amendment has been in effect. Thus,
it is possible for a plan to have been in effect for more than five years
but, because of recent amendments, to be insured for less than the full
amount otherwise provided.

In any plan where substantial owners are covered (individuals with
more than a 10 percent ownership interest) the 5-year concept is replaced
by a 30-year phase-in of coverage. Here, the increase in coverage is based
upon the ratio of the owner's years of participation to 30.

Premiums

The initial premium for plan termination insurance was set at an
annual rate of $1 per participant ($0.50 per participant in the case
of negotiated multiemployer plans) and was collected, on a pro rata
basis, for the period from September 2, 1974 through the balance of
the plan's then current plan year. This same premium was collected
for the first and second full plan years that next followed. For subse-

---

[10] In 1976, with a taxable wage base of $15,300, this $750 became $869.

quent full plan years, the plan administrator has the choice of paying 50 percent of this premium or an alternate premium based on the sum of 0.1 percent (0.025 percent in the case of negotiated multiemployer plans) of the unfunded liability for insured benefits, plus a rate to be determined by the PBGC that will apply to the total liability for insured benefits.

Employer Liability

If a plan is terminated, the employer has a potential liability to the PBGC for any insured benefits provided for plan participants. This potential liability is limited to the unfunded liability for the benefits insured by the PBGC, up to a maximum of 30 percent of the employer's net worth determined as of a date within 120 days prior to the plan termination date.

The PBGC expects to provide contingent employer liability insurance to cover this potential liability. However, it will be some years before this coverage can be fully effective—by 1975 such insurance had not been developed and, after it is developed, it will take five years before full coverage is provided.

It should be observed that this liability may be incurred by an employer with respect to the plans of organizations acquired by the employer. Also, special provisions apply to the withdrawal of an employer from a negotiated multiemployer plan.

Recapture of Payments

If a plan is terminated, the PBGC may recover payments made to participants who retired or terminated within the three years preceding the plan termination. The amount that may be recaptured from any such participant is the amount by which his or her benefit payments in each of the three years exceeded $10,000. The right of recapture does not apply to payments made on account of disability or death.

Reportable Events

An employer is required to make special reports to the PBGC. The events that must be reported include the following:

1. The disqualification of the plan by the Internal Revenue Service or receipt of a noncompliance determination from the secretary of labor.
2. A decrease in plan benefits due to a plan amendment.
3. A decrease in the number of plan participants to fewer than 80 percent of the number at the beginning of the plan year or 75 percent of the number at the beginning of the preceding plan year.

4. The determination by the Internal Revenue Service that there has been a complete or partial termination of the plan.
5. Failure to meet the minimum funding standards of ERISA.
6. Inability to pay plan benefits when due.
7. A distribution of more than $10,000 paid to a substantial owner while the plan has an unfunded liability for vested benefits. (This does not apply to benefits paid on account of the death of a substantial owner.)
8. The merger or consolidation of plans or the transfer of plan assets.
9. Any other event indicating a need for plan termination.

The PBGC has the right to terminate the plan if the minimum funding standards have not been met, if the plan is unable to pay benefits when due, if a distribution of more than $10,000 has been made to a substantial owner, or if the PBGC believes that failure to terminate the plan will result in an unreasonable increase in its possible long-run losses.

INDIVIDUAL RETIREMENT SAVINGS

ERISA introduced an important new concept in U.S. pension planning by creating the ability for individuals not covered under qualified plans to save for their own retirement on a tax-deferred basis. Since individual retirement savings plans were discussed in detail in Chapter 18, the following material contains only a very brief summary of the major portions of ERISA that cover these plans.

The individual retirement savings provisions of ERISA generally became effective on January 1, 1975. These provisions allow any individual who is not covered by a qualified plan (including tax-deferred annuities and government plans) to make tax deductible contributions to a qualified individual retirement savings plan. The maximum annual contribution, which must be made in cash by the close of the year, is limited to the lesser of 15 percent of compensation for such year or $1,500. The amount of the contribution will actually be reported by the individual as gross income and will be taken as a deduction against gross income. This contribution will be subject to FICA and FUTA but not to withholding taxes. The allowance for taking such a deduction terminates with the year in which the individual attains age 70½.

A self-employed individual may utilize an individual retirement savings plan, rather than an H.R. 10 plan (in which event, employees need not be included). The right to establish an individual retirement savings plan also extends to employees who are eligible but do not elect to participate under a contributory qualified plan maintained by an employer. Husbands and wives, if they both receive compensation, can qualify for separate contributions and deductions.

An individual retirement savings plan can be established by utilizing an individual retirement account (a trust or custodial account), an individual retirement annuity, or special government retirement bonds. If a trust or a custodial account, investment in life insurance will not be permitted. If an individual retirement annuity (which includes an endowment contract) is used, it must be nontransferable, dividends cannot be paid in cash, and the premium must be limited to $1,500. If life insurance is involved, the cost of the life insurance (presumably PS 58 costs) will not be deductible. Both approaches require that distributions be made only as prescribed by the law. The special government retirement bonds will be issued under the Second Liberty Bond Act and will pay interest only at redemption. Interest will not be payable under these bonds after age 70½ or for more than five years following death. The bond will fully mature at age 70½ and the proceeds then will be taxable unless transferred to a qualified individual retirement account or annuity. The bond will be nontransferable.

Income earned on funds held under a qualified individual retirement savings plan will be income tax free until distributed; however, any unrelated business income will be taxable.

Distributions may be made at death, disability, or after the individual attains age 59½. The distribution must be made over a period that does not exceed the life expectancy of the individual or the joint life expectancy of the individual and his or her spouse. The distribution must commence not later than the year in which the individual attains age 70½. If the amount distributed in any year is less than the minimum required, an excise tax will be levied. This excise tax will be 50 percent of the amount by which the minimum requirement exceeds the actual payment. If a premature distribution is made, a 10 percent penalty tax must be paid. If the individual borrows against an individual retirement annuity, the entire value of the annuity will be treated as a distribution. If the individual uses any part of an individual retirement account as security for a loan, the portion so used will be considered to be a distribution.

Distributions are taxable as ordinary income. A lump-sum distribution will not qualify as a long-term capital gain and ten-year averaging tax treatment will not be available; however, the individual may take advantage of the regular five-year income averaging provisions of the Internal Revenue Code. Any amount payable from an individual retirement savings plan upon death will be includable in the individual's gross estate.[11] Also, the gift tax exclusion available to qualified plans is not available to individual retirement savings plans.

Tax-free rollovers are permitted. Under this provision, distributions of employer contributions from qualified plans may be placed in an

---

[11] The potential estate tax liability cannot be avoided by assignment since the individual's rights are nontransferable.

individual retirement savings plan without incurring any current income tax liability. Such amounts may be transferred back from the individual retirement savings plan to another qualified plan. These rollover provisions thus create limited portability.

If an individual makes an excess contribution to an individual retirement savings plan, a 6 percent excise tax may be levied each year until the situation is corrected. Individual retirement savings plans are also subject to prohibited transaction restrictions.

PLANS FOR THE SELF-EMPLOYED

ERISA made a number of changes, almost all of them positive, with respect to plans for the self-employed (H.R. 10 plans). Generally, these changes became effective as of January 1, 1974.

Perhaps the most significant improvement legislated for H.R. 10 plans was the increase in the maximum allowable annual tax deductible contribution. Prior to ERISA, the maximum tax deductible contribution was 10 percent of earned income or $2,500, whichever was smaller. The new maximum is 15 percent of earned income (up to $100,000) or $7,500, whichever is smaller. These new maximums also apply to the shareholders of a Subchapter S corporation. The voluntary contribution limits remain unchanged.

ERISA also established a minimum contribution for H.R. 10 plans. This minimum is 100 percent of earned income up to $750.[12]

Beginning on January 1, 1976, the tax deductible limits for H.R. 10 plans may be set on the basis of defined benefit accruals. Under such a defined benefit plan, the amount deductible may, in some situations, exceed the amount that would otherwise be permitted under the 15 percent/$7,500 limits; it may also be less. The defined benefit limits are set in terms of the cost of the amount of pension that may be accrued in each year. Essentially, the program will operate as a modified form of career pay plan. Each year, the self-employed individual will be permitted to accrue a pension benefit equal to a percentage of earned income (up to $50,000) for such year. The allowable percentage will be determined by the self-employed's age when participation in the plan commenced and will not be decreased with increasing age. Several important points should be noted about these defined benefit plans for self-employed individuals:

1. The allowable percentages are permissible only for a benefit payable on a pure life annuity basis at age 65; reductions in these percentages will be required for plans that provide ancillary benefits.

---

[12] In 1975, the Internal Revenue Service had taken the tentative position that this 100 percent minimum contribution provision was in conflict with the 25 percent maximum contribution limits also imposed by ERISA.

2. If a self-employed individual has established a plan that utilizes less than the allowable percentage or applies the percentage to only part of earned income, any change that increases the percentage or earned income base will constitute a new period of participation with respect to the increase and will be subject to the percentage limitations applicable for the individual's then attained age.
3. Beginning after December 31, 1977, the allowable percentages may be changed by the Internal Revenue Service to reflect prevailing interest and mortality rates occurring after 1973.
4. A defined benefit plan covering owner-employees under these provisions of ERISA may not be integrated with social security benefits.

A major improvement for H.R. 10 plans, already noted, is that favorable tax treatment (long-term capital gains and ten-year averaging) has been extended to lump-sum distributions to self-employed individuals.

The treatment of excess contributions under H.R. 10 plans has been changed. Under ERISA, an excess contribution will attract an annual excise tax of 6 percent until the situation has been corrected. The treatment of premature distributions was also changed to require the payment of a penalty tax equal to 10 percent of the distribution. Other changes that affect H.R. 10 plans are: (1) voluntary contributions may now be withdrawn; (2) contributions may be made up to the time the self-employed individual's tax return is due (including extensions) ; (3) corporate limits on benefits and contributions will apply to H.R. 10 plans; (4) corporate trustees are no longer required; and (5) rules applicable to corporate plans for determining service and the exclusion of bargaining employees will apply; and (6) the controlled business provisions apply to incorporated as well as unincorporated businesses.

Index

This book has been set in 11 and 10 point Baskerville, leaded 1 point. Chapter numbers are 30 point Helvetica and chapter titles are 24 point (small) Helvetica. The size of the type page is 27 x 45½ picas.